Saint Augustine
Man, Pastor, Mystic

D1153755

Saint Augustine

Man, Pastor, Mystic

By

Agostino Trapè, O.S.A.

Illustrated

CATHOLIC BOOK PUBLISHING CO.
NEW YORK

NIHIL OBSTAT: Daniel V. Flynn, J.C.D.
Censor Librorum

IMPRIMATUR: ✠ Joseph T. O'Keefe, D.D.
Vicar General, Archdiocese of New York

SPIRITUALITY FOR TODAY SERIES
*A new series designed to make available
spiritual books of lasting value*

Volume IV

GENERAL EDITOR
John E. Rotelle, O.S.A.

Vol. I: *Give What You Command*
Vol. II: *Christians in the World*
Vol. III: *Council Digest*

This book was originally published in Italian under the title *S. Agostino: L'Uomo, II Pastore, Il Mistico* by Editrice Esperienze. The English translation was made by Matthew J. O'Connell.

(T-172)

Preface

SAINT *Augustine, Man, Pastor, Mystic* is a monumental work on Saint Augustine of Hippo, a masterful yet very readable study of various facets of Augustine's thought and personality. Those who read this book will come to a greater appreciation of the person of Augustine, a better understanding of Augustine's theology, and a deeper knowledge of the times in which Augustine lived. They will also realize Augustine's contribution to spirituality.

The author, Father Agostino Trapè of the Order of Saint Augustine, needs no introduction in international circles, but he is not yet well known on the national scene.

Father Trapè was born in Montegiorgio (Ascoli Piceno), Italy, on 9 January 1915. He moved to Rome in 1933 and has lived there since then. He was ordained a priest in Rome on 15 July 1937 and obtained his doctorate in theology from Gregorian University in 1938.

From 1939 he has been teaching in the Order's international college, Santa Monica. He was also regent of this international college for 15 years. From 1960 to 1983 he was a professor at Lateran University. He also taught at Gregorian University (1964-1965). Since 1981 he has been teaching at the Augustinianum. Father Trapè is the founder of the Patristic Institute "Augustinianum," which opened its doors in 1970. He is currently president of the Patristic Institute and continues to teach about Augustine at this Institute. Father Trapè has also been president and professor at the "Center for Theology for the Laity" of the diocese of Rome since 1966.

This formidable Augustinian scholar has published many articles and books on Augustine. He has lectured in many parts of the world and has promoted the writings of Augustine in many ways. He is founder and director of "Nuova Biblioteca Agostiniana," which is now publishing all the works of Augustine in a bilingual edition (Latin and Italian). The series to date numbers 22 volumes. He also founded the Augustinian Historical Institute and the series "Corpus Scriptorum Augustinianorum," which seeks to publish unedited works of famous Augustinian writers.

Concerning the Augustinian Order, Father Trapè was Assistant General of the Order from 1953 to 1959. He was a member of the theological preparatory commission of the Second Vatican Council, then was named peritus to the Council, and finally as Prior General, was a member of the Council.

From 1965 to 1971 Father Trapè served as Prior General of the Order of Saint Augustine. During that time he guided the renewal of the Order in the post-conciliar period and under his term the new Constitutions of the Order were developed and promulgated.

Father Trapè's years of teaching, lecturing, and writing on Augustine are reflected in this publication, which is the culminating point of his writing career and the fruit of his love for Augustine. The book, first published in Italian, is presented here for the first time in English translation. The Italian edition is now in its 7th printing. It is my pleasure to introduce the English translation of this brilliant work by my former teacher, and confrère, Agostino Trapè, who did so much to instill within me a great love of Augustine.

It is my hope that these pages will educate the reader in knowledge of Augustine, inspire the reader to maintain in some way the particular thought of Augustine, and produce a love for the man who saw everything in relation to the glory of God.

John E. Rotelle, O.S.A.

28 August 1986

Introduction

HAVING written a book, I am obliged to explain its intention and method. The indulgent reader will be quickly satisfied on this score.

My aim has been to give an uncluttered picture of Augustine as man, pastor, and mystic. These are the three main facets of his rich personality. He was a magnanimous and single-hearted man who proudly challenged the Catholic faith and then rediscovered that faith after long interior travail; having rediscovered it, he determined, at the cost of difficult renunciations, to be among those who abandon all earthly hopes for love of the Wisdom that is Christ. He was a bishop who shrank from the pastoral ministry and accepted it only against his wishes, but who then exercised it with total dedication. He was a mystic who joined to ascetical practices the ascents of contemplation and to ardent love his luminious intuitions of truth.

Other aspects of Augustine's personality have been left aside in whole or in part. Of Augustine the thinker and writer I have said only what is or seems necessary to explain his pastoral action and interior life. No comparison is made between his teaching and that of the Fathers before him or between his teaching and later currents of thought; at most, there is an occasional reference. I trust nonetheless that my presentation of the Saint, though thus limited for obvious reasons of space, will not be without its usefulness. It will at least show how the complex and admirable person of the Bishop of Hippo can or ought to be viewed now that scholars have made so many advances in their study of him.

Augustine has exercised a deep and continuing influence on the western world. Not surprisingly, he has been variously interpreted from century to century in light of the problems and interests of the time. Scholasticism, the Reformation, Jansenism, the Enlightenment, Modernism: all have had their own Augustine.

Today too there are varying interpretations, not all of them favorable. I offer the one that many years' study of Augustine's own works and of works on Augustine (more of the former than the latter) have convinced me is the only true one or at least the most probable one. In it I discuss three areas. The first is Augustine's interior development; here I endeavor to bring out the essential elements, often obscured by criticism that is not entirely dispassionate. The second is the many lengthy controversies in which Augustine was engaged; I indicate the subject of each dispute and the solution which he gave; in not a few cases the solution was not what later generations often took it to be. The third area is the Saint's mystical ascents, which are one of the most important but least heeded facets of Augustine the writer and pastor.

I regret not having been able to discuss the opinions of other scholars and to give fuller evidence for my own. For the former I have had to limit myself to a few typical references; for the latter I send the reader to the sources. I have focused my attention on these and cited them rather abundantly. Augustine wrote many works and I have tried not to neglect any of them. In my view, the most serious mistake that can be made in dealing with an author as complex as Augustine, an author who advanced as far as he did in the science of faith, is to dwell on certain texts while neglecting others or, in other words, to abandon the task of harmonizing, as far as possible (and it is almost always possible), passages that are in seeming contradiction.

This writer is convinced that the "real" Augustine (often so different from the Augustine of fashionable "Augustinianisms") can help us still, and in no small measure, to know ourselves and God, to understand our problems, which are not so different from his, and to clarify and solve them. Augustine provides Christian believers with the joy of contemplating the depth, continuity, and efficacy of their faith from the lofty vantage point of his magnificent synthesis. To those who do not have this faith he speaks words that can reveal them to themselves and make them aware of their natural dignity, their aspirations, their hopes. If Augustine is to speak to them in this way he must, of course, be presented as he really was, with his areas of light and shadow, without distorting superstructures, without onesided or arbitrary interpretations, and without unnecessary mystification.

Agostino Trapè, O.S.A.

Contents

Part I

The Man

Part II

The Pastor

Part III

The Mystic

Part IV

The Last Years

Part I

The Man

1

Roman in Culture and Language

LTHOUGH Augustine was born in Africa and, according to all indications, was an African by descent,[1] he was a Roman in culture and language. Tagaste, his birthplace, was one of the many towns which the Romans had scattered around North Africa. As everyone knows, after conquering Carthage the Romans undertook a monumental transformation of these vast regions by laying down an extensive network of roads, building cities, erecting country houses, encouraging agriculture, and bringing culture, trade and prosperity to every corner of the land.[2]

Tagaste

Tagaste was not a large city; it is called *civitas parva*, "a small town," by the anonymous author of the Latin version of the *Life of St. Melania the younger*.[3] In fact it offered only the first stage of public education, the schools taught by the *primus magister* ("instructor in the rudiments) or, in modern parlance, elementary schools. The town had no special importance except that it was a place where many of the roads of the Mediterranean hinterland met: one of the three roads from Hippo to Carthage passed through it, as did the road from Carthage to Cirta, Sitifis, and distant Caesarea in Mauritania, and the road from Hippo southward to Theveste (Tebessa). The mansion or inn of Tagaste was therefore a well-known one and allowed the citizens of this little town to come in contact with the commercial and cultural doings of a large area of Roman Africa.[4]

The town was situated in a pleasant location on the broad and fertile altiplano of Numidia, 2,200 feet above sea level. It was surrounded by fragrant woods[5] in which Augustine went on long excursions hunting birds[6] and by vines[7] and olive groves[8]; it was rich in grains, fruits, and pasturage.[9]

To the east stretched the broad valley of the Medjerda (the Bagradas of the ancients), river which descended a distance of 155 miles to Carthage. To the south the vast altiplano ran to the

15

Aures Mountains, beyond which, almost on the verge of the
Sahara, a chain of fortresses protected—not always effectively[10]—the frontiers and territory of the *pax romana*. To the
west the altiplano of Cirta (the modern Constantine) stretched as
far as the two Mauretanians. To the north, beyond the hills, lay
the valley of the Seybouse (the Ubus of the Romans), which
emptied into the sea near Hippo Regius, about 60 miles away.

Roman Tagaste lies buried under the white houses of the
modern Souk-Ahras (Algeria) or under the green of the olive
groves on some of the nearby hills. But the excavations which
have brought to light the splendid ruins of other cities of ancient
Numidia[11] allow us to form an idea of its life, its houses and its
public places (forum, baths, theater, circus[12]) and also enable us
to understand and partially to excuse the pompous title of "Most
Illustrious" with which the municipal council adorned it.

When Augustine was born there on November 13,[13] 354,[14]
Tagaste had already been in existence for 300 years, and the
splendor of its historic places, even if not utterly gone, was certainly in decline. On the other hand, its true history, which is completely bound up with that of Augustine and his mother Monica,
was only beginning.

At Tagaste, as in the other cities, of Roman Africa for that
matter, people of the most varied social condition met and often
came in conflict: immigrants and natives, bosses and servants,
those who enjoyed unbridled luxury and those who lived in
squalid wretchedness. Luxury prevailed in the cities, wretchedness in the rural areas where the sumptuous countryhouses of the
great landowners were the focal point for a swarm of tenant-
farmers who worked the soil with difficulty while envying the
bosses.[15] The language and culture were Latin, but many people
in the rural areas and the hills spoke and understood only Punic.[16]

Family

Between these opposed extremes a middle class had formed
which was for the most part African in origin but Roman by education and mentality and which by now was fully absorbed into
the organization of the empire. This was the class of the small

landowners who took part in the running of civic affairs and wanted their sons to pass through all the levels of instruction in order that they might become magistrates, rhetoricians, or lawyers. It was to this class that Augustine's family belonged.

By comparison with other families of Tagaste, that of Alypius, for example, which was one of the leading families of the town[17] or that of Romanianus which was very wealthy,[18] Augustine's could be called poor. That is in fact how Augustine himself thought of it. He says that his father was "a poor freedman from Tagaste,"[19] and speaks of himself as having been "born of poor parents."[20]

The reader should not take these words to mean what they would mean nowadays. "Poverty" at that time did not exclude a certain degree of comfort. As a matter of fact, Augustine's parents had domestic servants[21] and owned some land[22]; they could afford to send their son to school at Madauros, 20 miles away, and conceive the ambitious plan of sending him to Carthage to complete his studies.

But comfort did not mean wealth. The ambitious plan would probably have never been carried out, despite the sacrifices made by the family, unless a fellow citizen, Romanianus, a relative of Alypius[23] and one of those who were and were called rich, had come to Augustine's aid.

Augustine was to recall with admiration both the generosity of this patron[24] and the determination and sacrifices of the father who spent on his son more than he could really afford. "Who did not then highly commend my father for laying out in my behalf, even beyond the strength of his means, what was necessary for carrying on my studies at that great distance from home! Many citizens, far wealthier than he, did no such thing for their children."[25]

Augustine's patrimony did not amount to more than one twentieth of the property of the Church of Hippo, and Hippo was not a wealthy Church.[26] His patrimony was therefore a quite modest one, although once he became bishop he helped his relatives, as he helped the other poor, that "they might not suffer want or at least suffer less from it."[27]

It does not appear that Augustine's brother Navigius and his sister, whose name we do not know, had the good fortune of attending the classes of the "master of grammar" at Madauros. Certainly his cousins Lastidianus and Rusticus did not have it.[28]

Augustine's family, then, was not wealthy, but it was certainly distinguished and respected. His father, Patricius, was a member of the municipal council[29]; his mother, the devout Monica, won admiration for her noble character and outstanding virtues.[30]

Language

The family was probably of African origin but had become Romanized. In Patricius' house all, including the servants, spoke Latin and only Latin.[31] This should not surprise us. We know that not everyone in Hippo knew Punic[32] and that even among the clergy few were able to make use of it.[33] In any case, before learning Latin in school Augustine had already learned it at home, "by observing others, without being frightened into it or forced by the rod, amid the flatterings of my nurses, and the jests of such as smiled upon me, and the mirth of those who played with me." He learned it because he felt a desire and need to express his own thoughts.[34]

As a matter of fact, Latin was the first language in which Augustine expressed himself and the only one that he mastered fully.

As for Punic, a term which I use here in the (to us) rather vague sense in which Augustine used it,[35] he would later on as bishop cite a few proverbs from that language and indicate the Punic words corresponding to a few Latin terms,[36] but when he had to make himself understood by the peasants of his diocese he used an interpreter,[37] as did the Donatist bishop Macrobius.[38]

In like manner, when Augustine refers to Punic literature in which "many wise things have been handed down," he draws not on personal experience but on the authority of the more learned: "as is attested by very learned men."[39] We must conclude, therefore, that he had but a limited and general knowledge of it that did not allow him to make use of it.

His knowledge of Greek was another matter again. He learned it in school at Madauros, but learned it unwillingly, either because his own natural inclination was more to poetry than to drier studies that elicited no feelings in him (and the study of a dictionary was one of these), or because the current methods of instruction were based on "painful forms of punishment."[40] He never became really at home with Greek. It was not that he did not know it, for he did know enough of it to serve various purposes. He could consult the Greek text of the Bible and use it, if need be, to correct the Latin version (as he habitually did[41]). He could judge the accuracy of a translation, even one of Jerome's[42] He could himself make an accurate translation of a passage from the Fathers[43] or Plotinus.[44] He could go directly to the original Greek of a work.[45] But he did not know it well enough to be able to read the works of the Fathers with the fluency that he would have liked to possess and that he would have needed if he were to make good use of the few "drops" of time available to him.[46]

His culture, then, unlike that of many of his contemporaries (Jerome, for example, or Ambrose), was essentially Latin or, more accurately, was obtained through the medium of Latin.

Rhetoric

When it came to Latin, however, Augustine was master of all its riches of content and form, all its secrets, all its resources. He spoke it indeed with a typically African accent that caused the Italians to make fun of him,[47] and he displayed stylistic peculiarities proper to a writer of the late imperial age who was both an African and a pastor of souls. But he was also a consummate artist in language, with the ability to make it express every nuance of thought and every variety of style. To realize this, the reader need only compare the *Confessions* with the *City of God* or the *Letters* or the *Sermons*.[48]

He studied the rudiments of Latin in Tagaste, grammar in Madauros, and rhetoric in Carthage. When he had completed his studies, he opened a grammar school in Tagaste,[49] and then, after a year or two, a school of rhetoric first in Carthage, then in Rome. Finally, he taught rhetoric at the imperial court in Milan.

In Carthage he entered a poetry competition and was
crowned poet by Vindicianus the proconsul.[50] At Rome Symmachus the prefect tested his abilities as a speaker and sent him
to Milan as professor of elocution; this first success would lead to
even greater successes.[51] In his capacity as professor at Milan he
delivered the panegyric for the consulate of Bauto and, a few
months later, the official encomium on the emperor, who was at
that time, as we know, the fourteen-year-old Valentinian II.[52]
Twelve years of teaching and intense study,[53] added to the years
already spent in school, gave him the opportunity to gain a deeper
knowledge of the liberal arts and to fulfill the great ambition of
many in that age[54] by becoming a "most learned and eloquent"
man.

The vast learning he had acquired made it possible for him,
even as a new convert, to conceive the grandiose scheme of writing a series on the *Disciplines,* a kind of encyclopedia on the liberal arts. In it he would show how to pass, as by a series of sure
steps, from corporeal things to spiritual, and from these in turn to
God. He did write a volume on grammar, now lost, and began the
treatise on music; this he finished in Africa, having written six
books on the element of rhythm in music. For the other five liberal arts—dialectic, rhetoric, geometry, arithmetic and philosophy—he made only sketches, but even these have been lost.[55]

Even as a bishop, Augustine always retained a deep sense of
admiration, gratitude, and even, we may say, affection for the authors from whom he had gained his own literary formation. He
felt this way especially toward Virgil, over whose pages he had
shed so many tears[56]; toward Cicero, who had awakened him
from a deadly slumber and given him a love of wisdom[57]; and
toward Varro, the most erudite of the Romans,[58] whose works
were of great use to him in writing the *City of God.*

These sentiments manifest themselves in, for example, the
following letter, which dates from 415 when Augustine had already entered his sixties and been bishop for about twenty years.
Evodius, a friend and fellow townsman, has asked him the meaning of St. Peter's words about the descent of Christ into hell and
the liberation of those confined there (1 Pet 3:18; Acts 2:24). Augustine answers:

If we say that on that occasion all who were there were set free without distinction, who could fail to be pleased (if we could prove it), especially in regard to those whose writings have made them familiar to us and whose genius we admire? I am not referring only to the poets and other orators who have heaped scorn and ridicule on their own false pagan gods and at times have even acknowledged the only true God, while admittedly sharing with all their contemporaries in a superstitious form of worship. I am also referring to those who asserted the same truths not in poems or discourses but in works of philosophy. I am speaking even of the many learned persons whose works have not reached us but whose praiseworthy lives (praiseworthy at least from one point of view) are known to us from the writings of others.

All these individuals did not worship God but erred by adoring false gods as ordered by the laws of the state and by serving creatures rather than the Creator. But in the rest of the conduct of their lives they are rightly proposed as models for imitation by reason of their frugality, continence, chastity, sobriety, scorn of the death they faced in order to save their country, fidelity to the word they had given not only to compatriots but even to enemies. . . . Because of our natural inclination we would be greatly pleased if persons so endowed with virtues were, singly and together with everyone else, freed from the torments of hell.[59]

This passage, with its contrast between natural inclination and the teaching of the Christian faith, shows better than any other the profound humanity of Augustine and the extent to which he belonged to the Greco-Roman world. He was a Roman not only in language and culture, but also in feelings and heart.

2

Christian by Education

AUGUSTINE was, however, above all a Christian. He always remained one, at least in intention, even when he abandoned the Catholic faith. We must keep this in mind if we are to understand his interior growth and one aspect, perhaps the most extraordinary, of his personality.

Milieu

The atmosphere in which Augustine passed his childhood was Christian, but not completely so. Although paganism was in irreversible decline it was still alive; here and there it was even vigorous and militant. This was the case at Madauros where Augustine was a student from his eleventh to his fifteenth year.

In this city that had been the birthplace of Apuleius pagans were still in the majority.[1] They were even a proud majority who honored their gods with wild and unbridled bacchanalia[2] and had only scorn for Christians.[3] They were certainly included among those Augustine refers to in a sermon to the people: "Wherever they find Christians, their custom is to insult and harass them, to deride them and treat them as fools and idiots, as people without feelings, as good-for-nothings."[4]

Carthage was no less pagan; in fact, being a great metropolis it was even more pagan. When Augustine went there at the age of seventeen he was able to attend, and did attend, the tawdry spectacle in which obscene honors were paid to the goddess Caelestis, protectress of the city, as her image was carried down to the sea for the ritual of purification.[5] When the emperors ordered her temple closed, the pagans rioted.[6]

Tagaste was not a Madauros, much less a Carthage, yet even here paganism made its presence felt. Pagans, now a minority, had passed from an attitude of hostility to one of indifference. Augustine had an example of this in his own home, for his father, unlike the other members of the family, was a pagan.[7] He was nonetheless a good man, open and affectionate, though easily

22

angered and sometimes profligate in his ways. He had married a very devout Christian woman and he lived in peace, that is, without profound or lasting strife (though the credit for this belonged more to his virtuous wife than to him), in a family of solid Christian faith. Nor did he oppose the Christian education of his children. He was nonetheless a pagan and retained certain pagan attitudes and judgments.[8] He did not enroll in the catechumenate until about 370 and was baptized only shortly before his death.[9]

But the submissive attitude of many pagans, like those (it seems) of Tagaste, did not mean that paganism had ceased to exert an influence. As late as Augustine's childhood years there was an anti-Christian revival instigated by Emperor Julian. Moreover, the yielding attitude, at least among intellectuals, often concealed a no less dangerous snare: the insidious attitude of those who in the name of an equivocal pluralism regarded Christianity and paganism as two equally valid ways of honoring the divinity.

We find this conviction expressed in Ammianus Marcellinus, Symmachus, and some of Augustine's pagan correspondents, as, for example, Nectarius of Calama and Maximus of Madauros.[10]

In any case, even if paganism no longer spoke from its temples,[11] it still spoke from monuments, books, and the theaters. To take but one example, in the forum of Madauros Augustine came upon "two statues of Mars (one showing him unarmed, the other in his armor) and, opposite them, a statue of a man with three fingers thrust out in order to hinder the power of Mars, which is calamitous for the city."[12]

The textbooks used were the classical writers, and these were filled with myths that, as Cicero put it, transferred "human attributes to the gods"[13] or, in Augustine's amended version, "attributed divinity to wicked men, that such crimes might not be considered as crimes, and that whosoever committed them might not seem to have imitated wicked men, but heavenly deities."[14] The bishop of Hippo lamented bitterly that words, those "choice and precious vessels," should be filled with such empty and immoral contents; he gave as an example a scene from a comedy by his fellow countryman Terence.[15]

Then there were "the varied obsenities of the theaters, the madness of the circus, and the cruelty of the amphitheater," so many places where the pagan ideal took flesh and was translated into the plots of comedies, gladiatorial fights, races, and gambling. Bets, which led to disputes and deadly brawls, were laid on "pernicious fellows such as mimes, actors, pantomimists, charioteers and hunters."[16] This was the judgment of Augustine as a bishop, but as a young man he himself had been a victim of that environment.

Yet despite such a milieu and environment Augustine's Christian formation was sincere and thorough, and it left an ineradicable mark on him. For the mother who instructed him was a wise pedagogue.

Monica

Monica was an exceptional woman, endowed by nature with a fine mind, strong character, and profound sensibilities. She was born at Tagaste in 331[17] into a family that had long been Christian, and was taught by an elderly servant of the house to honor God, love her fellows, respect authority, and rise above her natural feelings and inclinations. The educational goal of this austere and wise servant woman to whose special care Monica's parents had entrusted her was a very noble one: to let nothing dishonorable seem pleasing.[18] In this she succeeded. It was this proud sense of honor that enabled Monica, after an unjust and offensive reprimand from another servant, to break the habit she had developed of taking sips of wine without her parents knowing it.[19]

We do not know when Monica married. We do know, however, that she was twenty-three when Augustine was born, and he seems to have been her first child.[20] She was an ideal wife. Her husband, who "was hot-tempered," "respected, loved, and admired her" for her goodness, patience, and sweet temper; she put up with him and won him to the faith.[21] Within the family she maintained the peace, overcoming the suspicions of her mother-in-law and the tale-bearing of the servants.[22]

Her main concern as a mother was to raise her children as Christians. "I had heard, even as a boy, of life eternal promised to us by the humility of your Son, the Lord our God, descending to cure our pride. I was already signed with the sign of his cross, and was seasoned with his salt, even from the womb of my mother who had much hope in you."[23] These words of Augustine take us back to the beginning of Monica's formative action. It was an action that struck deep roots in Augustine's soul because it was backed by the example of a life of faith, dedication, and piety. He later described his mother as

> so chaste and prudent a widow, giving frequent alms, ever-ready and dutiful to your saints, never omitting one day to attend the sacrifice at your altar; twice a day, morning and evening, coming to your church without failing, not for vain gossiping and idle talk, but that she might hear you in your words, and you hear her in her prayers.[24]

Monica's life before her husband's death must have been of the same kind. She was faithful to the practice of fasting, so much so that at Milan she inquired of Ambrose whether in her fast she should follow the custom of Tagaste or that of the Church of Milan. She displayed moderation and great love in observing the custom, in use at Tagaste and widespread throughout Africa, of bringing food to the tombs of the martyrs.[25] She was diligent in prayer[26] and accepted unreservedly the authority of the bishop. At Milan, somewhat to the astonishment of her son, she readily accepted Ambrose's judgment about fasting[27] and his prohibition against celebrating banquets on the tombs of the martyrs.[28]

In his *Confessions* and the *Dialogues* of Cassiciacum Augustine has left us a much admired biography of his mother. He finds only two faults to mention: she had deferred his baptism, and she had failed to steer the adolescent with his erupting passions into the safe harbor of marriage in good time.

He looks for some explanation of these failures and sees as a reason for the deferral of baptism Monica's fear of the "waves of temptation" that lay threateningly in wait for the boy after his childhood had ended. "She chose rather to expose to them *the clay,* from which I was afterward to be *molded,* than the image already formed."[29] Augustine the bishop would subsequently find this explanation unsatisfactory. We may add that Monica's fears were certainly intensified by the presence and example of Patricius, who was still a pagan. In addition, the custom of deferring baptism to adulthood must not infrequently have been followed at Tagaste.[30]

Augustine thinks that Monica's second failure was explained by her desire, in which she was in full agreement with his father, to have him finish his studies before marrying. She was convinced—and in this she manifests a not unimportant aspect of her personality—that a solid cultural formation would not only not harm her son but would even help bring him closer to God. She was therefore unwilling to have his course of studies interrupted by an early marriage.[31]

The Church of Tagaste

Monica's action in forming Augustine as a Christian was supplemented by that of the Church of Tagaste, a vital and fervent ecclesial community with the bishop as its center. We have a great deal of information about Christian Tagaste, but only from the time when Augustine returned there as a convert and settled down with his friends in order to try a new life-style. We know little about Tagaste before that date.

Augustine's return brought the spread of monastic life. In 394 Paulinus of Nola sent greetings to the brethren who were devoting themselves there to prayer, asceticism, and study.[32] In 410 Melania the Younger took up residence and remained for seven years under the spiritual direction of Alypius; she also founded two monasteries, one for religious women and another for religious men, with 130 and 80 members respectively.[33] Within a few years Tagaste had given four of its sons to the African episcopate, to the great benefit of both the local Churches and the universal Church. The four were: Alypius at Tagaste itself, Augustine at Hippo, Evodius at Uzalis, and Severus at Milevis. In the space of a few decades four saints venerated by the Catholic Church prayed with the faithful in the basilica of Tagaste: Monica, Augustine, Alypius, and Melania the Younger.

As I said above, information about Augustine's native city prior to his return to it is very limited. One detail, however, that we do have is very valuable. The Church of Tagaste had at one time gone over completely to Donatism; later, as a result of imperial legislation, it returned to Catholic unity and became hence-forth a bulwark of Catholicism. In fact, it had such a detestation of the Donatist schism that "it seemed never to have belonged to that sect."[34] By 411 this Catholic unity of the town was already "of long standing," and at the conference of Carthage in that year Bishop Alypius could speak of it as an example and protection for others.[35] Donatists were rarely to be met at Tagaste. The Catholic bishop had no rivals, and the faithful enjoyed the peace that flows from Catholic unity and communion.

The Maurists date the return of the town to Catholic unity in about 346,[36] that is, a few years before Augustine's birth, on occasion of the edict which Constantius II issued when Macarius was commissioner. Augustine, the great apostle of unity, was therefore received as a child into an ecclesial community that was united in faith and love, free of divisions and conflicts.

This state of affairs cannot fail to have exerted a positive influence on Augustine's soul, since it confirmed and extended the action of his mother. This child, whose tongue was loosed in prayer,[37] prayed with the praying Church and believed with the believing Church. He did not experience in those days the sad division among Christians that he would later expend so much time and energy in healing. In fact, so deeply rooted in him was his Christian faith that it determined the direction and development of his entire life.

The fruits of a Christian education

Not only did Augustine always believe in God and providence[38] and in a future life and divine judgments.[39] He also always had in his heart the name of Jesus, which he drank in (he says) with his mother's milk.[40]

On the tortuous road that he traveled from the age of nineteen to the age of thirty-three we may distinguish four key points: his reading of the *Hortensius*, his acceptance of Manichaeism, his disillusionment with this sect, and his discovery of the Neoplatonists. At each of these moments we find the name of Jesus present, not as something to be discussed or rejected, but as a criterion for accepting or rejecting other solutions.

The reading of the *Hortensius* effected a radical change in his interior attitude. Yet these pages did not win him over completely, because "they did not mention the name of Christ." He explains: "Whatever was without this name, no matter how learned or polished or truthful it might be, could not win me wholly."[41]

He then joined the Manichees, but the main reason for his doing so was that they called themselves followers of Christ and even claimed that, unlike the Catholics, theirs was a pure and spiritual Christianity. "I fell among men who were raving with pride, exceedingly carnal, and great talkers, in whose mouths were the snares of Satan and a bird-lime made up of a mixture of the syllables of your name, and of that of our Lord Jesus Christ, and of the Paraclete, the Holy Spirit, our Comforter. All these names were always in their mouths."[42] As we shall see, this was not his only reason, but it was the decisive one. Without it the others would not have effectively moved him.

If the name of Christ had been the bait by which the Manichaeans captured him, it was also the bit that checked him from following the philosophers. Once he discovered the inadequacy of Manichaeism he asked himself what path he should now take. He saw adherence to a philosophical school as one possible way. He had already read many of the philosophers and remembered them well,[43] but they did not speak the name of Christ. "I resolved, once for all to leave the Manichaeans, thinking that I ought not even for that time of my doubt to remain any longer in that sect to which I already preferred some of the philosophers. Nevertheless, I refused absolutely to commit the cure of my sick soul to these philosophers because they were without the saving name of Christ."[44]

He then set out on the wearisome road back, and it was here that he discovered the teaching of the Neoplatonists. The discovery filled him with immense enthusiasm. Once again, however, the enthusiasm was followed by disillusionment. And once again he needed only have recourse to Christ in order to overcome his disappointment. "I seized eagerly on the venerable writings inspired by your Holy Spirit, especially those of St. Paul."[45] Here the *Confessions* are in agreement with the *Dialogues:*

"In my perplexity, enthusiasm, and uncertainty I began to read Paul the Apostle. . . . I read him with great attention and interest."

Just before these last words Augustine refers to his conversion and writes: "I turned . . . to the religion which had been instilled in me as a child and which had entered into the very marrow of my being."[46] He is here simply recalling the lasting effects of the education he had received. Again, when he draws up a program for himself for acquiring wisdom, he says that he wishes never to withdraw himself from the authority of Christ: "I determined never under any circumstances to depart from the authority of Christ, for I know of none that is stronger."[47] In saying this, he is simply repeating the truth that had been the source of light in his life and would be until his death.

The profound crisis that occurred when Augustine was nineteen and that I shall describe in a moment, was one of ecclesiology, not of christology. Augustine consciously withdrew from the Catholic Church, but he never thought even for a moment of distancing himself from Christ.[48]

But before speaking of this serious crisis I must discuss some points in which the reader will certainly be interested: Augustine's natural physical constitution, his talents, and, above all, his experience of sin.

3

Child of Great Expectations

IT is natural that we should want to know everything about great men and women, even their external appearance. Unfortunately, we do not know what Augustine looked like,[1] but we do know quite a bit about his bodily constitution, which was sound but delicate and subject to frequent illnesses.

As a boy he suddenly fell into a fever one day due to a stomach disorder and almost died.[2] At the age of 29 he was struck down in Rome by an unspecified but serious illness that carried him to the threshold of the grave.[3] At the age of 33, while in Milan, he developed a weakness of the lungs that caused him a good deal of chest pain, made breathing difficult, and prevented him from speaking clearly and at length.[4] Not long afterward, at Cassiciacum, he suffered an agonizing toothache that kept him from speaking at all.[5] When he was about 56 living in Hippo, an illness forced him into a period of convalescence outside the town, during which he had a relapse and new attacks of fever.[6] When he was about 73, Count Boniface came to visit him at Hippo and found him so weak that he could hardly speak.[7]

In addition to these instances of severe illness, such as often attack even the most robust, Augustine was rather sickly. Recently returned from Italy, he wrote to his friend Nebridius that bodily weakness was keeping him from doing what he had planned, unless, he says jokingly, "I stop wishing to do what I cannot."[8] Many years later, almost at the end of his life, he would tell the people that while he was now old in years, he had already been old for a long time because of bodily illness: *per infirmitatem corporis olim sum senex.*[9]

And in fact it was not "any indisposition of mind" but "weak health" that kept him from the journeys on and across the sea which his brother bishops undertook for the sake of their ministry.[10] He could not stand the cold[11]; he was tortured by "the pain and swelling of hermorrhoids" that often kept him abed[12]; his voice was so weak that he could not be heard unless there was complete silence[13]; more than once while speaking he confessed to weakness and a failing voice.[14]

Despite all this, it must be said that Augustine had a great deal of physical stamina. Otherwise there is no explaining the prodigious amount of work he did, the many long and uncomfortable journeys he undertook on land, and the longevity that brought him to "a good old age."[15] His extraordinary strength of mind and soul explains a good deal, but not everything.

Temperament

Nature gave Augustine a delicate physique and a vivacious spirit; it gave him as well a mind that was kind, affectionate, and refined, but also strong and decisive. There was something of his mother about him. He loved order, quiet, and friendship; above all he loved truth. He was easily touched, but evil evoked his indignation and, when the occasion required, he could not be moved from his purposes.

In the *Confessions* he writes of himself as a child:

> For even then I was, I lived, I felt. I had a care for the maintenance of this my being, an imprint of that mysterious Unity from which I derived my origin. I watched over the integrity of my senses with an interior sense. Even in little things, and in the thoughts about the little things, I was delighted with truth. I was unwilling to be deceived; I had a powerful memory, facility of speech, found charm in friendship. I fled from pain, meanness, and ignorance. What was there in such a living being that was not wonderful and praiseworthy? But all these things are the gifts of my God. It was not I who gave them to myself; and they are good, and they are myself.[16]

All of Augustine is here in germ: the Augustine that the years would reveal and that others would esteem. From his very first contacts with literature he showed his gifts as poet and speaker; at the age of nineteen he revealed himself to be a philosopher as well. The unhappy fate of Dido moved him to tears,[17] and when he had to repeat in prose what Virgil has said in verse (one of the most important exercises in the teaching methods of his day), he put so much ardor and warmth into it that he won the applause of his fellow students.[18]

At Carthage he was "a leader in the school of rhetoric."[19] At about the age of twenty he read and understood without help a work of Aristotle, the *Categories*, which was regarded as so difficult that "my teacher at Carthage and others who were regarded as learned spoke of it with cheeks almost bursting with pride."[20] He also read and understood on his own all the treatises in the "liberal arts" that he could put his hands on. "Whatever was taught concerning the art of speaking and of reasoning, concerning the dimensions of figures, and of music, and of numbers, I understood with no great difficulty, without any teacher. You know it, O Lord my God; for both quickness of apprehension and sharpness of wit for learning are your gifts."[21]

Expansive mind and rich imagination

In addition, Augustine had an expansive mind and rich imagination. It did not bother him that he had to study under the threat of the teacher's cane.[22] He liked to play games,[23] make a lot of noise in public places,[24] attend the shows and imitate the actors,[25] and go bird-hunting in the woods.[26] Yet toward his own family he was very respectful. When dying, his mother would be unable to recall ever hearing a harsh or abusive word from his mouth, and would tell him for his consolation that he had been a good son to her.[27] Never a harsh word to his mother! Not even, therefore, when, proudly and disdainfully, she refused to allow him into the house because he had become a Manichean.[28] Not even when in Carthage she insisted "with all her strength" that he not go to Rome.

As we know, on this last occasion Augustine resorted to a trick that allowed him to do as he wished without having to use strong words or act uncivilly toward his mother. Nonetheless, he had bitter memories of this incident for the rest of his life. "I told a lie to my mother—and to such a mother!"[29]

Another element in Augustine's naturally good disposition was his deep aversion to the uproar caused by the *eversores* ("Subverters"). This was a band of restless mischief-makers among the students. They pestered the more naive among their fellows with insolent words, "annoying them and making sport of them without cause, only to gratify their own malicious mirth."[30] Boldly entering classrooms "with an attitude approaching madness," they disturbed good order. "They commit many outrages with strange blindness that would be punishable by law."[31]

In Carthage Augustine found himself among these fellows. He even enjoyed their company at times, but he always felt abhorrence at their doings and never took part in them. A fellow student from that time, a man who had subsequently become the Donatist bishop of Cartenna (in Mauritania Caesariensis), wrote to Augustine: "I've known you well ever since the days when you were far from the Christian faith and devoting yourself to literary studies. You were a lover of peace and decency."[32]

What he neither did nor approved as a student, he also refused to allow as a professor. The "most important reason, and almost the only one," why he left Carthage for Rome was the assurance that over there "the behavior of young students was quieter. Discipline was stricter." A decree of Emperors Valentinian, Valens, and Gratian in 370 had prescribed stern measures for dealing with the students of Rome[33] and it had had positive results. In Carthage, on the other hand, the students enjoyed "a shameful and intolerable liberty."[34]

Cult of friendship

When he himself was among them as a fellow student, he wanted to give everyone the impression that he was a man of the world.[35] The young man not only desired but in fact did cut a fine figure. Yet there is another side of him that must be emphasized if we are not to have an inadequate idea of his personality: I am referring to his feeling for friendship, and even, I might say, his cult of friendship. He experienced friendship in all its forms: the "unfriendly" friendship that leads to evildoing; the purely human friendship that despairs when faced with the scandal of death; the Christian friendship that is deeper and more serene and lasts, in hope, into eternity.

At every moment he felt within himself the truth of the words he wrote one day to a devout Roman matron: "Nothing human is attractive to the person who has no friend."[36]

He experienced "unfriendly" friendship at the age of sixteen when he found himself among companions who were ashamed of not being shameless. It was this friendship that persuaded him to commit the theft of the pears, for on his own he would never have done it. "O fiendish friendship! O seduction of the mind . . . ! O desire for another's loss without any gain to myself or passion for revenge! Someone cries, "Let's go, let's do it,' and we are ashamed of not being shameless."[37]

He experienced purely human friendship when he was twenty-one and living at Tagaste during his first stint as a teacher. There he found a contemporary who had been his schoolmate and playmate, and he bound himself to this man with tender affection. "There was sweetness in our friendship, mellowed by the eager pursuit of similar studies. . . . A friendship that was sweeter to me beyond all the sweetness of that life of mine."[38]

Suddenly, however, the friend died, and his death caused Augustine to despair:

> Great was the grief with which my heart was darkened, and whatever I looked upon was death to me. My own country became a torture to me, and my father's house a strange unhappiness; and whatever I had shared with him was turned into a frightful torment to me, now that I was without him. My eyes longed for him everywhere, but nowhere was he given to me; and I hated all things, because they had him not, nor could they now tell me, "Behold, he will come," as before in his lifetime when he was absent. And I became a great riddle to myself. . . .
>
> I wondered that the rest of mortals could live, because he was dead whom I had loved, as if he were never to die. I wondered still more that I myself, who was a second self to him, could live when he was gone. Well did one say of his friend that he was one half of his soul in two bodies: and hence, I loathed life, unwilling to live by halves; and, therefore, perhaps I was afraid to die, lest he whom I had loved so much should die completely. . . .
>
> I carried about with me a soul all wounded and bleeding, impatient to be any longer borne by me, and where to lay it down to rest I did not find. It could take no delight in pleasant groves, not in plays and music, nor in fragrant odors nor in elegant banquets, nor in the pleasures of the chamber and the bed, nor in fine books and poems. All things looked ghastly. even the very light, and whatever was not he, was loathsome and hateful to me, except sighs and tears, for in these alone I found a little rest.[39]

This astonishing passage from the *Confessions* lays bare the inmost recesses of Augustine's soul and shows us his rich humanity, his capacity for affection, his nobility. And yet in his own eyes that friendship had not been a true friendship. "That friendship only is true, by which such as adhere to you are fastened together by you, by *Charity which is poured forth in our hearts by the Holy Spirit who has been given to us.*"[40]

This Christian friendship does not exclude but rather supposes and renders perfect that other, human friendship. When Augustine had been converted he experienced the attraction, saw the ideal, and interpreted the requirements of this higher friendship. He saw it as characterized by a love unto tenderness, a trust that is not disturbed by the friend's possible infidelity, a communion marked by generous giving and joyous receiving, and a disinterestedness that requires of the friend only that he or she advance in wisdom, union with God, and love of Christ.

Above all, he experienced and emphasized the consolation friendship brings. "Where can we find consolation in this human tangle of error and toil except in the fidelity and mutual affection of true and virtuous friends?"[41] We think immediately of Alypius, "the brother of my heart,"[42] of Nebridius, "my very dear friend,"[43] of Severus, "my dear fellow townsman,"[44] of Profuturus, "my other self,"[45] and of so many others to whom he gave much and from whom he received much.[46]

In addition to his capacity for friendship, there is another essential aspect of Augustine's personality that must be emphasized: his love of wisdom. Of that I shall speak later on. For the moment we must pause a little and consider his sad experience of sin as a young man.

4

Sinner

A GREAT deal has been written on this subject, but it is not always to the point. Some writers exaggerate, others play down.

The various appraisals offered take their cue from the tone of Augustine's story, which is filled with intense sorrow, repentance, bitter regret at sins committed, and ardent gratitude to God for the liberation he had granted Augustine.

Some have interpreted these accents as a sign that Augustine's sins were objectively serious. Others see them as distorting the facts. The latter emphasize the apologetic purpose of the *Confessions* and claim that because of it Augustine unwittingly falsified the facts in order to exalt the grace of God. Augustine was not really the sinner he would have us believe.

The controversy, which is part of a broader dispute over the historical reliability of the *Confessions* generally and the relation of the *Confessions* to the *Dialogues* of Cassiciacum, has had a long history. A great deal of study has been devoted to these problems but the results achieved have not been very great.[1] The controversy may now be said to have ended. On the point that interests us here scholars have opted for a good sense solution based on a distinction between the facts narrated and the judgment passed on them by the narrator. The facts are located in the past, and Augustine sets them down quite simply, adding nothing and suppressing nothing. The judgment passed on the facts is, however, a judgment made in the present, that is, at the moment when the writer sees the past through new eyes: the eyes of an ascetic and a bishop to whom even a "little fault" is a "bitter morsel" to swallow.

Childhood

With this obvious distinction in mind, here are the facts. Augustine's sins as a child were negligence in study, little acts of cheating in play, little thefts from the domestic pantry, quarrels with playmates, and lies. He liked to win at games and could not stand being cheated. When he found that he had been cheated he became a bitter critic, as stern in blaming the subterfuges of others as he was unyielding, when discovered, in denying his own. He could not always find boys willing to play with him. Then he bought their cooperation with little gifts that he had gotten by small thefts.[2]

Such were the facts. Nothing unexpected, evidently, in any lively and outgoing child. We must not let ourselves be fooled by the famous exclamation: *tantillus puer et tantus peccator* ("a great sinner for so small a boy").[3] These words represent the later judgment of the writer, who does not mean that when he was a child he considered himself a great sinner.[4] Augustine is emphasizing not the seriousness of the sins but the seriousness of evil inclinations that if not corrected in time, would lead to sins of quite different kind from those of the child who stole nuts and was overly absorbed by games.

After describing his childish actions, Augustine asks: "Is that the innocence of childhood?" And he answers: "It is not, O Lord. For these same things are but transferred from our first subjection to pedagogues and teachers; and our playing with nuts and balls and sparrows, to our subjection afterward to magistrates and prefects, and gaining gold and manors and slaves."[5]

Adolescence

When Augustine entered his adolescence his sins became more serious. The main ones were these: the theft of pears from a neighbor's orchard, sins against chastity, a passionate liking for shows, and a quasi-connubial union with a young woman of Carthage.

The least serious was the theft of pears, even though the author of the *Confessions* reflects long and bitterly on it. His reflections nonetheless do not change the real character of the incident described. The action was indeed far from admirable, but at bottom it was no more than a boyish prank, though a prank which was motivated by the wicked desire to do something forbidden and dangerous.

Augustine's reflections focus not on the action itself but on the motive for it. Without a motive even Catiline would not have committed his crimes.[6] What then was Augustine's motive in doing what he did? Not gluttony, because he did not eat the pears; not need, because he had better ones at home. Perhaps his companions? It is a fact that outside of the bad company he would not have done what he did. But can the example and urging of others lead someone to commit a motiveless act? What, then, was Augustine seeking? What was it that he loved about this theft?

Augustine concludes to a *gratuitum facinus* (a crime committed for its own sake). It is this conclusion that causes his profound grief and leads him to write unforgettable pages on the "psychology" of vice and on the divine mercy that forgives even the sins we have not committed, inasmuch as prevenient grace keeps us from committing them.[7]

Augustine's sins against chastity were of quite a different order than the theft of the pears. "When, at sixteen years of age, I began to live idly at home with my parents while domestic necessities caused a vacation from school, the briars of lust grew over my head, and there was no hand to root them out."[8]

In fact, his mother was there. True enough, lest her son's studies be jeopardized, she did not go so far as to advise marriage. On the other hand, she constantly exhorted him to avoid fornication and, above all, adultery. But the boy was now sixteen and thought himself emancipated; he therefore scorned her admonitions and thought himself obliged to avoid putting them into practice. "I remember how she secretly admonished me with great solicitude, to keep myself pure from women, and above all to never defile anyone's wife. This seemed to me to be but the admonition of a woman, which I should be ashamed to obey."[9]

While engulfed in this tormoil of his senses, Augustine, now seventeen, went the next year to Carthage in order to continue his studies. Here the inexperienced and presumptuous young man from the provinces was sucked down into the whirlpool of the great city whose voluptuous ways had won it the name of *Carthago Veneris* (Venus' Carthage). "I came to Carthage, and there a cauldron of vicious loves was roaring on every side of me."[10] "I was much carried away with the stage plays, which were full of representations of my miseries and furnished fuel for my fire."[11]

In the beginning he joined the Catholic community and attended its liturgies. But even within the walls of the church he "dared to give way to concupiscence and to drive on the trade of procuring the fruits of death."[12]

Augustine the bishop does not hesitate to reveal to everyone these hidden and shameful sins. He does so with great humility and for the instruction of others. He does it in a precise manner and with an undeniable sense of modesty. He gives us no basis for letting our imaginations stray and attributing to him sins he did not commit or at least does not confess.[13]

The mother of Adeodatus

A year after his arrival in Carthage Augustine began to live with a woman by whom he had a son in the following year. The son was named Adeodatus; the woman is left nameless.

The judgment often passed on this episode was incorrect and has today been revised. It was not the act of a dissolute man, but on the contrary a bulwark against dissoluteness. The dissolute were rather those—and they were many—who gave themselves to vagabond vice and boasted of it. Carthage was well known for it. The stimulus to this kind of life came from the theaters and the celebrations in honor of the goddess Caelestis. Augustine gradually became aware of the whirlpool in which he was being sucked down and he wanted to escape from it and regain the freedom of an honorable life. He therefore committed himself to a stable union which, though not yet a true marriage, was at least an approximation to it, a kind of "second degree marriage."

The union was not sanctioned by Christian law and therefore Augustine deplored it. It did, however, meet with the approval of good people of the time, who regarded it as licit and honorable. Augustine in fact looked to it for *cum bona fama voluptatem*,[14] a sexual satisfaction accompanied by a good name. His action therefore represented not a sinking into the abyss of vice but, in this case, an emergence from it. It was an act of responsibility and a compromise born of the tug of passion and a moral sense of honor.

This sense of honor, which was something Augustine felt deeply, caused him to remain faithful to the woman for fourteen years, even though she was not his wife. "In those years I lived with one, not joined to me by lawful marriage, but chosen by the wandering heat of imprudent passion. Yet I had but one, and I was faithful to her."[15] "I was faithful to her"! A rare example of honorable behavior in his day—and not only in his day alone. Salvian tells us that such fidelity was almost unknown among the married fold of Africa,[16] and Augustine's sermons seem to confirm this judgment.[17] As for conjugal infidelity, Augustine had an example of that within his own family.[18]

This example of fidelity becomes even more astonishing when we reflect that Augustine was not yet baptized. The presence of the woman and his son Adeodatus created no trivial problems for Augustine, who was not rich and as a teacher had to move from city to city. He managed, however, with financial help from Romanianus; he kept the woman with him, loved her, was faithful to her, and suffered greatly when forced to separate from her.[19] All this signals a nobility of spirit, but also a very normal sexual construction.[20]

I consider it worth calling the reader's attention to this last point. The lengthy controversy that Bishop Augustine would later engage in with the Pelagians regarding disordered sexual passion was philosophical and theological in character and, contrary to what is frequently asserted,[21] not implicitly autobiographical.[22] The most serious sins of the young Augustine were not sins of sensuality but, as we shall see shortly, sins of pride.

5

Lover of Wisdom

ANOTHER side of Augustine's personality that is no less characteristic than his cult of friendship and that likewise elicits our admiration is his love of wisdom. The flame was lit in his soul at the age of nineteen while he was in his third year of rhetorical studies at Carthage. From that moment it dominated his thinking, inspired all his plans, and became the very reason for living.

Reading of Cicero's *Hortensius*

The program for the third year of rhetoric included the reading of Cicero's *Hortensius*, a philosophical dialogue containing a passionate exhortation to the study of philosophy. Augustine did not stop short at the literary side of the exhortation, as he usually did, but entered into its substance. He was immediately won over. He felt his heart inflamed by an almost unbelievable love of philosophy, with philosophy being understood not simply as knowledge of the truth but also as moral commitment, guidance for living, and love, quest, and possession of wisdom.

"When I was nineteen and a student of rhetoric, I read Cicero's *Hortensius* and fell so in love with philosophy that I immediately decided to devote myself to it."[1] These words are from the book *The Happy Life*, which Augustine wrote during his stay as Cassiciacum before being baptized. When he relates the same incident more than twenty years later in the *Confessions*, his words convey a deeper emotion, but his thinking has not substantially changed.

> The reading of this book changed my disposition and turned my prayers to you, O Lord, and quite altered my inclinations and desires. All my vain hopes immediately appeared empty, and my heart longed after the immortality of wisdom with incredible ardor. I had begun to arise that I might return to you.... O my God, how I burned with a desire to fly up from these earthly things to you. But I did not know what you would do with me. For *with you is wisdom;* now the love of wisdom in Greek is called *philoso-*

phia, and it was with such a desire that these writings inflamed me."[2]

The reading of the *Hortensius,* then, effected a radical and lasting religious change in Augustine. We naturally ask what the book said and how it could have had such a profound influence on the soul of a university student. The work is lost, but fragments of it have been preserved, chiefly by Augustine himself,[3] and from these we can form a not too inaccurate idea of the original book.

Content of the *Hortensius*

In this work Cicero sang the praises of true philosophy and refuted the self-styled philosophers who in fact taught error. The young student was struck by this approach that exhorted him to follow not one or other school of philosophy but philosophy itself.

> Some there are who seduce by philosophy, disguising and coloring their errors with this great, pleasing, and honorable name: almost all who were such, in the author's time, or before, are set down and described in that book. . . . I was for this one reason so particularly pleased with that exhortation of Cicero that it strongly excited and enkindled and inflamed me, not after this or that sect, but to love, seek, and pursue, and lay hold on and embrace wisdom itself, whatever it was.[4]

Cicero took as his starting point the fact that all, even skeptics, want to be happy.[5] He then showed that the essential condition for the happiness to which true philosophy leads is a moral life; in fact, to will evil is already to be terribly wretched.

> People who are certainly not philosophers but are nonetheless quite ready to speak out claim that all who live as they please are happy. . . . This is certainly not true. In fact, there is no worse unhappiness than to will what is not suitable. We are rendered less unhappy by not obtaining what we wish than by obtaining what we should not have wished for. In fact, disordered desire is the source of an evil greater than any good which fortune may bring.

Augustine quotes this passage in his book *The Trinity* and comments: "Very well said and very true!"[6] His comment is justified, for the passage shows the heights even of moral intuition reached by pagan philosphy.

Cicero continued: Therefore the ideal of the wise is to recognize that they have immortal souls, to devote themselves to the search for truth, to flee vice and practice virtue.

> If, as the ancient philosophers (even the greatest and by far the most illustrious among them) thought, we have an eternal and divine soul, then we ought to think that the more we act without turning aside from our way, that is, act in conformity with reason and with the desire of attaining greater wisdom, and the less we share in vice and human error, the easier will be the ascent and return to heaven. . . .
>
> Therefore . . . if we wish to pass without delay from our present dwelling to another that is infinitely superior, we must devote all our efforts and attention to such studies.[7]

In keeping with this ideal, which evidently has a strong religious tonality, Cicero emphasized the practice of the four cardinal virtues of which we have need amid the evils and attractions of the present life. In that other life for which we strive our happiness will consist in "knowledge" and in the "science" of the Author of all things.

> The great orator celebrates the merits of philosophy. Summarizing the lessons of the philosophical tradition that he sets forth in a clear and pleasing way, he says that all four of these virtues are necessary for us but only in this present life with its trials and errors. None of them will be needed once we have left this life, provided it is granted us to live where human beings are happy. For in order to be happy virtuous souls will need only knowledge and science, that is, the contemplation of that nature which is incomparably excellent and worthy of being loved: I mean the nature that created and ordered all other natures.[8]

Cicero also emphasized the avoidance of sensible goods—riches, pleasures, honors—which turn human beings away from the search for wisdom. Speaking of pleasure, he asks: "Should we seek bodily pleasures, those pleasures that Plato describes, truthfully and with perfect seriousness, as 'pitfalls and sources of all evils'?" The answer is clear: "The stronger our sensual impulses, the sooner they turn us from philosophy. Intense thought is incompatible with bodily pleasure. . . . What human being, overmastered by sensuality (the most violent of all emotions), can discipline the mind to thought or make reason prevail or concentrate on anything whatsoever?"[9]

         Chapter 5

Resolution

It is obvious that a philosophical ideal presented in this way would arouse the enthusiasm of a generous and noble young man like Augustine and bring about a profound religious change in him. We must also bear in mind that he read the *Hortensius* through Christian eyes, that is, that he located its teachings in the framework of the faith in which he had been raised. There can be no doubt on this point. One proof is the fact, already noted, that the only disappointment he felt as he read was that he did not find the name of Christ therein.

Augustine saw no opposition between the reasonings of Cicero and the teachings of the Catholic faith, and he was able to move, spontaneously and without conscious advertence, from the former to the latter. In like manner he passed spontaneously from the latter to the former when talking to his mother later on as Cassiciacum.

In this new setting, where the subject under discussion was the concept of happiness, Augustine asked: Are people happy, then, when they have whatever they want?

> My mother replied: "If they want and have what is good, they are happy; but if what they want is evil, they will not be happy even if they obtain it." I was filled with joy and said smilingly to my mother: "Mother, in one leap you have reached the heights of philosophy. You lacked only the words for developing your thought as Cicero did."

Augustine then repeated the words of the *Hortensius* that have already been cited from his book *The Trinity*, and continued: "At these words my mother uttered exclamations of delight, so that we forgot she was a simple woman and thought of her as an illustrious philosopher sitting among us."[10]

There can be no doubt that Monica derived her answer from her Christian wisdom. She certainly had not read the philosophers, nor do they seem to have greatly impressed her.[11]

Augustine's reading of the *Hortensius* through Christian eyes and the enthusiasm it roused in him made him forget its author's profound skepticism. Nor does he seem to have noticed, as he would notice with critical eye later on,[12] that Cicero offered two hypotheses—either death or immortality—regarding the lot of the soul and said he did not wish to choose between them. In any case, Augustine was not disturbed by the first hypothesis, which his faith assured him was false. Instead, he took seriously the ideal set before him and set about following it with tremendous fervor.

In a trice Augustine set aside the earthly prospects that until then had occupied his thoughts, and he began the gradual detachment from the "allurements" of the world that would lead him to the evangelical ideal of a consecrated life. He stopped hankering for riches,[13] he came to think of rhetoric as an empty pursuit concerned only with the cult of words[14]; and, finally, he began to see continence as good and desirable.[15] He resolved that once he had reached truth and wisdom, "I would relinquish all empty hopes of vain desires and deceitful follies."[16]

Augustine's reading of the *Hortensius* revealed to his admiring gaze the highest vocation of a human being. At that moment there was born within him the philosopher who later on, in the light and with the strength of the Gospel, would become the ascetic, the contemplative, and the mystic. But there was still a long and tortuous journey ahead before he entered upon the way of the Gospel. "But there were mists to confuse my course and, I confess, for a long time I kept my eyes on stars that sank into the sea and led me into error."[17]

We must follow Augustine in this long and wandering journey. Our guides will be the *Confessions* and the *Dialogues* of Cassiciacum.

6

Rationalist

IN one of these *Dialogues* we read the following:

> A kind of puerile scruple kept me from a critical approach to the truth. Subsequently I acquired greater self-confidence and dispelled this darkness of mind. I convinced myself that I ought to follow those who teach [the truth] rather than those who command [belief]. As a result, I fell among men who regard the visible light as worthy of the veneration paid to things supreme and divine.[1]

These words, which are our first information on Augustine's long wanderings far from the Catholic Church, also show us the root of his difficulties: he had taken a wrong approach to the basic problem of the relation between reason and faith. A confused conjecture—Augustine calls it a *"puerile superstition"* comparable to the fear of a a child who trembles in the dark without knowing why—led him to think that the quest for truth would be an offense against faith. In other words, he thought of faith as something mysterious and sacral, in the face of which reason has no choice but to bow down. The alternatives were therefore either to abdicate reason or to renounce faith. It hardly needs saying that this empty fear sprang from an impoverished religious development. Augustine was now an advanced student (in his third year at the university) and his ability singled him out among his fellows, but in the area of religion he had not moved beyond his mother's teaching and what he had heard in church at Tagaste or Carthage. He had not enjoyed a systematic religious formation that would have kept pace with his advance in secular culture and in age and prevented or quickly overcome false and dangerous notions.

His reading of the *Hortensius* helped free him from this ungrounded fear, but at the same time it inspired in him a disintegrative rationalism. He was persuaded that he must follow not someone who urged faith but someone who taught the truth; in other words, be a follower not of authority, which calls for faith, but of reason, which shows the way to the truth. That constant pair, reason and faith, presented itself to the nineteen-year-old

Augustine in terms not of collaboration but of opposition. A problem thus improperly set could not be solved. A youth of Augustine's temperament, conscious of his powers and eager for truth, could not fail to choose reason as against faith. That is what Augustine did.

In his desire to find wisdom he turned to the study of the Scriptures. The fact is noteworthy as a sign of his Christian formation. But for those who read it without proper dispositions Scripture can have some nasty surprises, and so it did for this nineteen-year-old university student. There were two in particular: a style that seemed excessively bare to a man whose taste had been molded by the refined language of Cicero, and a content that was excessively obscure for one who wanted things immediately clear and unmysterious.[2]

The first of these two difficulties was definitely superficial, although the careless language of the *Vetus Latina* (the old Latin translation), which was used in Africa, may explain to some extent the aversion Augustine felt. The second difficulty, however, was more serious. Scripture does in fact contain obscure points, seeming contradictions, and profound mysteries. But at least Augustine could have asked for explanations. The Church of Carthage no longer possessed a Cyprian, and Aurelian was still to come, but surely there must have been someone capable of helping him. And in fact we know that such a person was available, for Augustine himself speaks of him in the *Confessions;* I am referring to the Elpidius who bested the Manichaeans in debate.[3] But he either did not think of asking for explanations or could not bring himself to do so. He went his own way: the way of pride.

One day far off in the future Augustine remembered his experience and told the people:

> I myself was deceived for a while as a young man when I first approached the sacred writings. I did not go to them with the devout attitude of one who humbly sought but with the presumptuous mind of one who wanted to argue. . . . I dared to seek proudly what only the humble can find. How much more fortunate you are now! . . . You live like babes in the nest of faith and you receive spiritual food. I, alas, thought myself ready to fly, and so I left the nest and fell, because in fact I could not fly. But the merciful Lord

picked me up and put me back in the nest before passersby could
trample me underfoot.[4]

In this passage Augustine is referring to the divergent
genealogies of Jesus in Matthew and Luke. This was certainly
one difficulty, but not the only one. Coming as it did, however, at
the very beginning of the Gospel, it seemed to bar entry to the
thirsty pilgrim. What Augustine's other difficulties were we do
not know. We would surely not be far wrong if we were to think
here of the Old Testament and especially of the problems raised
by Genesis and by sacred history generally.

Manichaeans

At this time, while torn between desire and disappointment,
Augustine fell in with extremists who immediately satisfied his
expectations. They were Manichaeans; he listened to them and
was convinced; he abandoned the faith of his childhood and became one of them. All this took place within the space of a few
days,[5] odd as this may seem for an honest and intelligent young
man. The suddenness of his conversion can be explained only by
several concurring causes. The first of these was Augustine's own
interior dispositions; he was being driven by a burning desire to
find the truth, and he was at the same time irked by the disappointment he had felt on reading the Scriptures.

The Manichaeans made short shrift of Augustine's difficulties with Scripture, because they rejected the Old Testament in its
entirety and eliminated as interpolations everything in the New
Testament that referred to the Old. The genealogy of Christ was
one such interpolation. In any case, Christ had not assumed a real
body but only an apparent one, so that it was impossible for him
to have a genealogy.

Secondly, the Manichaeans claimed to be followers of truth:
"They said to me, 'Truth, truth,' and many there were who repeated this to me."[6] That was all the young Augustine wanted. It
is of this first meeting with the Manichaeans that he says later in
a well-known passage of the *Confessions:* "O truth! O truth! How
deeply even then did my innermost soul sigh after you, when

often and diversely and in many and large volumes, they sounded you to me in empty words!"[7]

In addition, the Manichaeans promised not to impose their faith on anyone, but nonetheless to free all from error by leading them to the attainment of "authentic and unveiled truth."[8] Beyond all else, it was this alluring promise that touched a secret chord in the soul of the young Augustine and made him a follower of the Persian "prophet."

> As you are aware, Honoratus [a friend whom Augustine himself had led into Manichaeism], we fell into their hands solely because they said they placed no reliance on constraining authority and instead would lead their disciples to God and free them from error by the power of reason alone. What other motive led me for nine years to scorn the religion my parents had instilled in me from childhood, and to follow those people as an attentive disciple but that I heard them tell us we were under the control of superstitious fear and were being required to believe before exercising our reason, whereas they did not urge anyone to believe before discussing the truth and gaining clarity of mind about it? Who would not have been seduced by such promises—especially a young man who was enamored of truth and whom discussions with educated people had rendered proud and a facile speaker?[9]

There can be no doubt that the attractions of rationalism were the primary reason why Augustine abandoned the Catholic Church and joined the Manichaeans. But here a distinction must be made between abandonment and the new allegiance: the former was unconditional, the latter was not.

7

Critic of the Catholic Church

AUGUSTINE joined the Manichaeans, but with reservations. What I mean is that he listened to what they had to say, believed their promises, felt a great sympathy with them—and waited. He waited for them to remove the veil of mystery that they cast over their teachings and to let the light of wisdom shine upon him. "I did not give them my assent but did think that under the veil of words they were hiding something important that they would eventually make known to me."[1] The reason for this attitude of prudent expectation was that the Manichaean missionaries "were more skillful and eloquent in refuting the teachings of others than they were firm and assured in demonstrating their own."[2]

This fact did not escape Augustine. He therefore joined them but remained in the rank of auditor, the lowest among the disciples of Mani, and did not, as he would have liked, pass to the level of the perfect Manichaeans, the elect. Only the elect surrendered "the hopes and occupations of the world" and professed poverty and complete continence.[3]

This valuable biographical information from the *The Value of Belief* is confirmed by the *Confessions* [4] and enables us to draw two important conclusions: Augustine's refusal to adhere fully to the Manichaeans and his readiness to devote himself unreservedly to the pursuit of wisdom once he should be sure of the path to take. By "unreservedly" I mean: embracing even poverty and complete continence.

But he never reached among the Manichaeans the certainty for the sake of which he had joined them. He did, however, reach another, though negative, certainty: that the way to be followed was not that shown him by the Catholic Church. In other words, he despaired of finding the truth in the Catholic Church,[5] and therefore he proudly departed from it with the conviction that it taught only "old wives' tales." He was a Manichaean with reservations, but he was an unqualified anti-Catholic. He thus became a bitter critic of the religion which until that time had been his and was still that of his mother.

This decisive departure from the Catholic religion was a major victory for the clever Manichaean propagandists. They "dealt with us like cunning bird-catchers who place limed branches by a pool to trap thirsty birds and then close off or cover over nearby waters—or use scarecrows to make them formidable—so that the birds will fall into the snares, not by choice but driven by need."[6] Such was Augustine's position: he accepted Manichaeism not because he was sure of it but because he was convinced he could not reasonably continue as a Catholic.

Supposed defects

Once a victim of Manichaean propaganda,[7] Augustine accused the Catholic Church first of all of fideism, that is, the authoritarian approach that demands faith without explaining the truth; an approach that is humiliating, irrational, and intolerable. It is knowledge, that is, gnosis, and not faith, that befits a wise human being.[8] And in fact Cicero and the Manichaeans urged knowledge, not faith, as the goal to be attained and the way to be followed. Augustine also criticized Catholics for maintaining an anthropomorphic conception of God, an unacceptable solution for the problem of evil, a materialist idea of the Incarnation, and an Old Testament faith.

If human beings were created in the image of God, as Genesis teaches, then God has a body like that of human beings. But that is a monstrous notion, as the Manichaeans easily showed,[9] and Augustine felt obliged to reject it. In fact, he rejected it in the name of piety toward God: "It seemed to me to be more reverent to believe you, my God, to whom I now confess your mercies to me, to be infinite on all other sides, though I was forced to acknowledge you finite on one side on which the substance of evil was set against you, rather than to think you to be on every side confined within the form of a human body."[10]

Consequently, he thought it impossible to agree with Catholics that God is the creator of all things, even the reality of evil. His very piety toward God and the idea of God's absolute goodness kept him from accepting such a doctrine." I thought I did better to believe that you had not created any evil than to believe that such a nature of evil as I supposed it to be was from you. For my ignorance took evil to be not only a substance but a corporeal one."[11]

Equally unacceptable was the Catholic idea of the Incarnation. If the Son of God really became incarnate by assuming a human body, he could not have avoided mingling with the flesh and being defiled by it. It would, therefore, be more prudent and pious to follow the Manichaeans in their docetism. "I was afraid to believe he was born in the flesh, last I should be obliged to think he was defiled by the flesh." Here Augustine feels obliged to add: "Your spiritual children, O Lord, will gently and lovingly laugh at my folly if they read these confessions. But that's the way I was."[12]

Finally, the acceptance of the Old Testament entailed the approval of wars, sacrifices, and the way of life of the early patriarchs. But all these should be repugnant to anyone professing a pure and spiritual Christianity. This argument was the old standby of the Manichaeans, who kept asking whether those were "to be accounted just men who had many wives at once, and who killed men, and offered up living creatures in sacrifice."[13] The correct answer, they felt, was obvious.

Obstacle to authentic Christianity

As a result of this propaganda Augustine saw the Catholic Church as an obstacle to an authentic, spiritual Christianity. A Manichaean of Rome, writing to him later on in an attempt to bring him back to the sect, reminded him of his former sentiments and cited some Old Testament precepts that he had found especially repugnant; among others, these included: "Place your hand under my thigh," "Kill and eat," "Increase and multiply." The writer then went on to praise Augustine: "I know you always had a horror of such things. I know you always loved sublime things that lift us from earth to heaven, things that mortify the body and give life to the soul."[14]

Augustine therefore accepted as valid the Manichaean criticisms of the Church and disdainfully parted ways with it. But we may ask: Before taking this serious and decisive step, did Augustine apply to himself the Roman adage, "Let the other side be heard?" Unfortunately, the answer is No. Yet a great Carthaginian apologist had written almost two centuries earlier that the Catholic Church often has but one desire, "that it not be condemned out of ignorance." Augustine, however, condemned it without a hearing. As he moved away from the truth, he thought he was advancing toward it.[15] Once more, pride was blinding him.

8

Manichaean Auditor

"I SOUGHT avidly, listened, believed rashly in all they said . . . urgently persuaded as many as I could of their teaching, and defended it with stubborn fervor."[1] That is how Augustine, in about 397, sums up a relationship with the Manichaeans that lasted from his nineteenth to his twenty-eighth years.[2]

After not a few discoveries[3] and a great deal of research,[4] we are fairly well informed today about the history and teaching of this religious movement that spread quickly in both the East and the West. For African Manichaeism, the identity of which with the original teaching of Mani there is no reason to doubt,[5] our principal source continues to be the works of Augustine, from his *The Morals of the Catholic Church and the Morals of the Manichaeans*, written at Rome in 388, down to his *Heresies*, which dates from 426. It is a source we may safely accept, although, given the polemical nature of Augustine's writings, they do not tell us everything about Manichaeism. that is, everything a historian would like to know.

During the nine years in which he was a follower of the Manichaeans Augustine acquired an extensive knowledge of their teachings from listening to their professors and reading their books. After his conversion to Catholicism, his disputes with their leaders were marked by care in reporting both his own words and those of his adversaries; moreover, when he was replying to their writings he cited these verbatim before giving his answers. It is to this scientific probity and polemical rigor that we owe our extensive and detailed knowledge of African Manichaeism.

A few points will suffice here with regard to Manichaeism generally. Its founder, Mani (known also, in Greek and Latin, as Manes, Manikkaios, Manichaeus), was of Persian birth, being born in Babylon on April 14, 216. After two "revelations" which he received when he was about twelve and twenty-four years old, he journeyed to India, then returned to Persia and received permission from King Sapor to preach his religion. He fell into disfavor, however, with Sapor's successor, Bahram I, was imprisoned, and died on February 26, 277, after twenty-six days of incarceration and torture.

Mani wanted to preach a universal religion and one that would be the most perfect possible: a religion of hope, light, and life. To this end he produced a syncretistic version of the then known religions. He regarded Christ, Zoroaster, and Buddha as his predecessors and "brothers," but he also claimed that his religion was superior to theirs. "All previous religions have flowed together into my religion and the wisdom that I have revealed." "From the outset my religion has been superior to all the others that have preceded it." He unhesitatingly prophesied that it would be universally received. "The hope that I proclaim will conquer the West and the East as well and will be preached in every tongue and in every city."[6]

In particular, Mani called himself "Apostle of Christ" and even claimed to be the Paraclete whom Christ had promised. "The Paraclete revealed to me all that has happened and will happen ... through him I have learned everything, through him I have seen all things; I have become one body and one spirit with him."[7] This claim reminds us of Montanus, just as the mythological cosmology of Mani recalls that of gnosticism. Manichaeism supposes Christianity and is meant to be an improvement on it. Manichaean gnosis, the last of the many forms of gnosticism, was also the most victorious and longest lasting of them. Although it was persecuted everywhere, it survived for ten centuries; as late as the 12th century it was doing battle against Christianity in Italy and France.

Summary of Manichaeism

Here is Augustine's summary of Manichaean teaching as given in his book *Heresies:*

> [Manes] posited two principles as diverse and opposed, eternal and coeternal, which have always existed; and following the ancient heretics he believed that there were two natures and two sub-

stances, that is, one good and one evil. Around this point they
elaborate a bunch of myths, speaking of a mutual struggle and
commingling, of a purification of good from evil, of an eternal condemnation for the evil as well as that good which cannot be purified, asserting all this in conformity with their dogmas. It would
take too long to deal with all these doctrines in this work.

As a result of these vain and empty fables of theirs, they were
obliged to say that the good souls, which are to be freed from the
admixture of the bad souls, that is, those of contrary nature, are of
an identical nature to that of God.

Therefore, while they readily admit that the world was made
by the nature of God, they also affirm that it had its origin in the
commingling of the good and evil that happened when the two na-
tures came in conflict with one another. Then to explain the purification and liberation of good from evil, they say that it came about
for the whole world and for all its elements by the powers of God
but also by their Elect through the drink they partake. They claim
that in this food and drink the substance of God is commingled just
as it is in the whole world. Now, in virtue of the kind of life that the
Elect of the Manichaeans lead, a holier and more excellent life than
the life of their Auditors, the divine substance is purified in their
Elect.

Indeed, their Church, according to their doctrine, is composed
of these two categories: Elect and Auditors. In all the other people,
even their own Auditors, this part of the divine and good substance
that, mixed into food and drink, is as it were bound and imprisoned, is according to them bound in a condition of greater impur-
ity—especially in those who propagate offspring.

Every portion of light is purified and brought back again into
the kingdom of God, as to its proper abode, by means of certain
vessels, which are the sun and moon. These vessels, they say, are
in turn constructed by the pure substance of God. They claim that
this corporeal light is the nature of God, the only light that is accessible to the eyes of living and mortal beings not only in these vessels in which they believe it exists in its purest state but also in
every other luminous thing where according to them it exists in admixture.

They say there are five elements that have generated their own
princes to the people of darkness, and these are called: smoke,
darkness, fire, water, and wind. The smoke gave birth to two-
footed animals, and they believe humans took their beginnings
from them; darkness gave rise to serpents, fire to quadrupals,
water to swimming creatures, and wind to flying creatures.

Five other elements were sent from the kingdom and substance of God to conquer these five evil elements, and in that struggle they have become intermingled with one another: air with smoke, light with darkness, good fire with bad fire, good water with bad water, and good wind with bad wind. As for the vessels we mentioned, that is, the two luminaries in the sky, they make this distinction between them: the moon is made of good water, and the sun is made of good fire.

After describing the obscene practices in which the Manichaeans engage at their gatherings, Augustine continues his summary:

They assert that the God who gave the Law through Moses and spoke through the Hebrew Prophets is not the true God but one of the princes of darkness. They read even the Scriptures of the New Testament in a false way, accepting what they like and rejecting what they do not like. They prefer instead certain apocryphal works, which they claim recount the whole truth.

In the heresiarch Manichaeus they see verified the promise of the Lord Jesus about the Holy Spirit. . . . That is why Manichaeus also had twelve disciples, in accord with the number of the Apostles, a number that is still observed today by the Manichaeans. They have among the Elect twelve whom they call Masters and a thirteenth who is their leader, seventy-two bishops who are ordained by the Masters, and priests who are ordained by the bishops. The bishops also have deacons. The others are called simply the Elect; but those of them who appear suitable are also to propagate and strengthen this error and to introduce it where it does not exist.

They claim that baptism in water obtains salvation for no one, and they do not believe they have to baptize those whom they have seduced.

During the day they offer their prayers toward the sun, wherever it happens to be in its orbit. During the night, they offer them toward the moon, if it appears; if it does not appear, they offer their prayers toward the North, by which the sun after its setting returns to the East.

They attribute the origin of sin not to the free choice of the will but to the substance of the opposing element. Dogmatizing that this is mixed in among human beings, they state that all flesh is the work not of God but of an evil mind that stems from the opposite principle and is coeternal with God.

They explain carnal concupiscence, by which the flesh lusts against the spirit, not as a weakness that is in us because of the corruption of our nature in the first man but as a contrary substance that adheres to us in such a way that when we are freed and purged it separates from us and lives immortally in its own nature. Since the flesh lusts against the spirit and the spirit is opposed to the flesh, they say that these are two souls or two minds, one good and the other evil, that come into conflict within the individual person.[8]

Readers of this doctrinal synthesis will be astonished that a man of Augustine's intellectual attainments should have accepted such a religious system. At the same time, however, they will find in it enough to explain his choice.

Positive features

Thus they will indeed find materialism, metaphysical dualism, and pantheism, along with an often repugnant mythological conception of the struggle between good and evil. But they will also find a radical and dramatic solution to the distressing problem of evil; a lofty ideal of perfection that leads human beings to free themselves from darkness and turn to the light; a sound and effective ecclesiastical organization; a committed and austere religious life, solemn liturgical celebrations, and lengthy and quite lyrical prayers. If we add to these the reasons indicated earlier—a "spiritual" type of Christianity and a gnostic rationalism—it is not difficult to understand how a young man who was intelligent and honest, but also full of himself and eager for a more than mediocre life, could have given credence to such a system.

There is no doubt that Augustine accepted the materialism and pantheism of the Manichaeans. At that time in his life, materialism represented the only way in which he could conceive of reality: "I could not conceive of the existence of anything else [except bodily substance]." [9] He saw pantheism, moreover, as the highest exaltation of human dignity and as explaining the teaching of the *Hortensius* that the human soul is "eternal and divine." "I thought that you, O Lord my God, who are the Truth, were only a bright and immense body, and I myself a little piece from that body."[10]

Furthermore, the metaphysical dualism that was the linchpin of the Manichaean system seemed to him the only possible solution of the problem of evil that was already causing him anguish. No wonder, since at the time he conceived evil to be not a privation of God but a positive substance. Given such a view of evil, dualism was the only answer he could give to the urgent (and insidious) question: What is the origin of evil? The question "greatly tormented me in my adolescent years; it pushed at me and thrust me—weakened by my efforts to solve it—into the arms of the heretics."[11]

In addition, Manichaean dualism freed human beings from the bitter consciousness of guilt by attributing this guilt not to individuals but to the evil substance that was in them and was waging war against the good substance. Such a solution could not but be pleasing to a proud young man who was having the sad experience of sin and at the same was ardently desirous of perfection. "It still seemed to me that it was not we who sinned, but I know not what other nature sinned in us. It pleased my pride to be free from guilt, and when I had committed any evil not to confess that I had done it. . . . I loved to excuse myself and to accuse I know not what was in me, and yet was not I."[12]

In addition to a doctrine that solved so many human and cosmological problems there was the austerity of the Elect, the real Manichaeans, who "gave an example of a chaste life and an admirable continence."[13] They were men wholly dedicated, according to their own testimony, to the victory in themselves and in the universe of the "reign of light." This austerity or, concretely, this following of the poor, chaste, and suffering Christ was the boast of Faustus, leader of the African Manichaeans,[14] who claimed to obey not only the precepts but the counsels of the Gospel.

In a word, Augustine believed that in Manichaeism he had found what he was looking for: wisdom without faith, morality without guilt, and Christian life without mediocrity and weaknesses.

There was still another motive that bound him to the Manichaeans: the warmth and intimacy that joined these people so closely with one another as members of a secret society that was known by few and opposed by many but was conscious of having a great message of salvation for all. A final factor in Augustine's attitude was the easy victories he won over unskillful Christians who tried as best they could to defend their own faith. This completes the list of reasons that made Augustine join the Manichaeans.

> Two things, both well suited to attract an inexperienced young man of my age, contributed more than anything else to setting me on strange paths. One was the friendship that became part of me, I know not how, as a result of a certain appearance of goodness; it was like a rope of many strands that got wound around my neck. The other was the harmful victory I almost always won in discussions with ignorant Christians who were trying to defend their faith as best they could. These repeated successes stimulated my youthful fervor, which for lack of reflection turned into the great evil of obstinacy. Since I engaged in this kind of controversy only after having heard of the Manichaeans, I generously attributed to their influence alone everything that I in fact derived from my own abilities or from my reading. Thus day after day their discourses made me eager for the fight, while my daily success in debate only made me all the more enamored of the sect. As a result, and to a surprising degree, I regarded everything they said as true, not because I saw the truth of it but because I wanted it to be true. This explains why, even if only step by step and cautiously, I became a longtime follower of men who preferred a beautiful stalk of grain to a living soul.[15]

Twisted ideas about God and human beings

He took part in their assemblies, celebrated the annual feast of Bema with them, recited the prayers to the sun, and—I have to record this but cannot pass it over—carried food to the Elect so that they in the work room of their stomachs might set free the divine substance present in the viands.[16] He actually believed

> that, when a fig is plucked, both it and its mother tree weep with milky tears. However, if some Manichaean saint should eat that fig (after it had been sinfully plucked by another and not by himself), he would digest it in his stomach, and from thence exhale angels: nay, rather particles of the deity, by groaning in prayer and sigh-

ing; and these portions of the sovereign and true God were imprisoned in that fruit till they were restored to liberty by the teeth and belly of some chosen saint.[17]

He even believed—and this is more unpleasant still—that "more mercy ought to be shown to the fruits of the earth than to human beings for whom they were made: for if anyone, who was hungry and was not a Manichaean, should have begged for something, I should have looked upon anyone who gave such a person a morsel as deserving capital punishment."[18]

9

Disillusionment

WHILE remaining loyal to the practices of the sect, Augustine, the austere Manichaean, was never certain of the truth of Manichaeism. He displayed an outward self-confidence and even arrogance: he made proselytes[1] and told his mother that one day she too would become a Manichaean.[2] Interiorly, however, it was different. Uneasiness, doubts, and difficulties—of a scientific, scriptural, and metaphysical kind—soon made their appearance.

After his final year at the university he returned to Tagaste.[3] Not long after—within a year—either because of the sudden death of a dear friend[4] or because of his desire "for a more eye-catching profession,"[5] he once again traveled up the valley of the Medjerda and opened a school of rhetoric in Carthage. In the interval he applied himself passionately to the study of the liberal arts. He read all the books he could put his hands on.[6] Chief among these were nine treatises, the *Disciplines,* of Varro, the most learned of the Romans.[7] According to the more common view of scholars, these treatises were devoted respectively to grammar, logic, rhetoric, geometry, arithmetic, astronomy, music, medicine, and architecture. Augustine studied philosophy in particular and had a special interest in astronomy; his curiosity, which became almost a stubborn passion with him, extended even to astrology.[8]

"I had read and remembered much of what was taught by the philosophers."[9] What were these works that he had read? Presumably the *Disciplines,* already mentioned, and other books of Varro, such as his treatise on philosophy; the philosophical works of Cicero; the manuals of Celsus (Celsinus?[10]) who "comprises in six large volumes the opinions of all philosophers who founded schools . . . nearly a hundred"[11]; the *Attic Nights* of Aulus Gellius, "an elegant writer with a great deal of fruitful knowledge"[12]; perhaps writings of Nicomachus of Gerasa, whose *Introduction to Arithmetic* Apuleius had translated into Latin[13];

and still others. In my opinion, he also read the works of representative Roman Stoics, or at least those of Seneca.[14]

Problems with Manichaeism

What Augustine learned as a result of this "uncommon erudition"[15] contrasted with Manichaean teaching on a point that had nothing to do with religion. It concerned astronomy.

I remembered many of the true things they [the astronomers] had spoken concerning the created world, and reason confirmed these things for me by mathematics, the regular succession of the seasons, and the visible evidence of the stars. I compared them with what Mani had said, who in his exuberant madness had written much about these things.

But the comparison did not favor Mani. "In his writings I could find no reasonable explanation of the solstices, the equinoxes, the eclipses, or any of the things I had read about in books of secular wisdom." Augustine then comments: "Yet I was commanded to believe his teaching, although it did not agree with the principles of mathematics and the evidence of my own eyes."[16]

These scientific truths are not part of religious faith. A person could therefore be ignorant of them or could even have false views about them without thereby being any less devout in dealings with God. Mani could have said nothing about them. But he did speak and write of them, and he proposed his views with the same authority with which he set forth his strictly religious teaching: the authority of an apostle of Christ and even the authority of one who identified himself with the Holy Spirit. Therefore, "when he was found to have erred in what he said about the sky, the stars, and the movements of sun and moon," he inevitably cast discredit on his entire religious teaching as well.[17]

Augustine cannot be gainsaid here. Yet Mani's reputation for holiness, which Augustine himself accepted, was such that it made the latter suspend judgment. He preferred to think that a careful examination of Manichaean teaching might well provide an explanation of the puzzle. He therefore awaited the arrival of Faustus, the learned man and bishop to whom his fellow religionists kept referring him.[18]

But difficulties pressed upon him from another quarter as well. A certain Elpidius made frequent public attacks on the Manichaeans of Carthage, citing passages of Scripture that spoke for a harmony between Old and New Testaments and were not easily refuted. These may have been essentially the same passages Augustine himself would later record in his book, *The Morals of the Catholic Church and the Morals of the Manichaeans*. In any case, Augustine considered the answer of Elpidius' respondents to be quite weak. And indeed it was; in fact, the respondents gave their answer only in private, as though they themselves were aware of its weakness. They "asserted that the Scriptures of the New Testament had been falsified by unnamed persons who wished to insert the Jewish law into the Christian faith." They were unable, however, to back this claim with uninterpolated copies of the New Testament.[19] Yet even in the face of these difficulties from Scripture Augustine preferred to keep a waiting attitude.

Then there was the dilemma with which Nebridius, Augustine's friend, presented the Manichaeans. Nebridius would ask them: What would the people of darkness (whom the Manichaeans regularly set over against God as an opposing mass) have done to God if God had refused to fight against them? If they answered (Nebridius said) that he would have suffered harm, then they would be admitting something they did not want to admit: that God is not inviolate and incorruptible.[20] If they answered that he would not have been harmed, then they would have to show why God should have accepted the combat. After all, it was so tragic and disastrous a combat that in it (according to Manichaeans) part of the divinity became mingled with the powers opposed to it, was reduced to a state of extreme wretchedness, and required help in order that it might be rescued and set free. In short, either they had to maintain that God is incorruptible, but then everything else they said would become meaningless; or they had to admit that he is corruptible, but that is so false and abominable an admission that no one would accept it. This argument made a great impression on everyone.[21]

Despite being wholly immersed in a materialism that confused his entire thinking,[22] Augustine began to think hard about his position, but he did not admit himself convinced. He still conceived God as "a bodily substance"[23] and evil as likewise a substance. It was therefore inevitable that he should regard metaphysical dualism as the only solution to the problem of evil. It was from this source, as from a poisoned well, that all other errors flowed.[24]

He therefore remained in the sect, hoping that his difficulties would some day be answered, and awaited Faustus as the great oracle. Meanwhile he wrote a treatise *Beauty and Proportion,* dedicated to a Roman orator, Hierius, whom he knew only by reputation but regarded as a model.[25]

Meeting with Faustus

Faustus came to Carthage in 383. Augustine listened to him, spoke with him, and found him to be eloquent, likable, sympathetic—but also so incapable of resolving Augustine's doubts that he would not even discuss them. Faustus' modesty pleased Augustine, who became his friend and offered to serve him as teacher of rhetoric. Interiorly, however, Augustine moved further away from Manichaeism or, more accurately, his confidence in the sect was badly shaken and began to wane.

> Once I had come to know this man well, all my efforts to make further progress in that sect fell to the ground. I did not cut myself off entirely from the Manichaeans, but since I could discover nothing better, I determined to remain content for the time being with what I had stumbled upon more or less by chance, until I could discover something more worthy of my choice.[26]

This light was not to present itself very quickly. To the disillusionment he had suffered were to be added others, until he was on the point of despairing entirely of human reason.

Not long after the meeting with Faustus, Augustine left Carthage and set out for Rome. His motives are known to us: he wanted to get away from a scholastic environment that he found intolerable because of subversive students,[27] and he wanted in addition to attain more desirable rewards. He had looked to Rome as a distant goal ever since he had dedicated his treatise on beauty and proportion to Hierius.[28]

We are familiar, of course, with the manner of his going. "The wind blew and swelled our sails and carried us out of sight of the shore." Monica remained behind, alone, "overwhelmed with grief," unable to believe the "deceit" and "cruelty" of her son.[29] The latter meanwhile was crossing the Mediterranean, accompanied by the prophetic good wishes of his friend Marcianus who, as Augustine was boarding ship, repeated to him a verse from Terence: "This day begins a new life and calls for new ways."[30]

Rome: final disillusionment

Rome did not give a favorable reception to this Roman from Africa who was destined to explain and praise its true glories.[31] On his arrival he suffered a serious illness[32] and two bitter experiences: the custom that Roman students had of abandoning the professor when the time came to pay the agreed fee[33] (a custom that was hard on Augustine's limited resources), and the discovery of the ineffectiveness of Manichaeism at the practical level.

In the eternal city he was a guest of the Manichaeans, who were numerous but remained hidden because of imperial decrees against them.[34] The emperors had in fact launched repeated attacks on them.[35] "At Rome I again associated with those deceived and deceiving 'saints': not only with their Auditors, one of whom was my host during my illness and convalescence, but also with those whom they call the Elect."[36]

Constantius, his host, who later became a Catholic,[37] was at that time an Auditor filled with enthusiasm for the sect and desirous of living to the full the ideal of perfection proposed by Mani. Even though a simple Auditor, Constantius exemplified the ideal. In pursuit of his purpose he intended to gather in his home, and support at his own expense, all who were ready to follow without reservation the precepts of the founder. Nor was his promise an empty one; he was a very rich man and could support a large number of people.

Obstacles to this proposed common life (a kind of Manichaean monastery) came from the very people who should have been for it: the bishops, who did not feel comfortable with those precepts. Finally, Constantius found a bishop, a rough, stubborn peasant, who came as first resident, gathered the Elect who were living in Rome, and set down a rule of life drawn from Mani's letter (the "Letter on the Foundation"). Many found the project intolerable and left. Others remained out of shame. The prescribed way of life began, with the guest Auditor insisting that the precepts be observed to the letter.

Meanwhile, rifts sprang up among the Elect as they accused one another of faults. It soon became clear just what these people were like who had declared themselves ready to observe the precepts of Manichaeism in their full rigor. When put to the test they muttered that the precepts could not in fact be observed. A rebellion was in the making. The guest Auditor summed up the situation in a dilemma: either the project was reasonable and should be carried out, or it was not reasonable, and the man who had imposed such precepts must be regarded as a fool. The rebellion intensified, and the voice of the majority carried the day. Each resident went his own way. Finally, even the bishop surrendered and fled in shame. It then became known that his life in the community was at odds with the rules he professed, since he had money for his own use and used to have food brought to him on the sly.[38]

This episode only confirmed the surprised disappointment Augustine had experienced earlier at Carthage when he observed the behavior of the Elect there.[39] His disillusionment was now complete; Manichaeism was henceforth a dead issue for him.

Yet the problem of wisdom remained. It even presented itself to him with greater intensity and urgency when he thought of the time he had lost and the disappointment he had experienced.

10

Toward Skepticism

AUGUSTINE now entered into a difficult phase that was psychologically very dangerous. Everything became questionable again, everything was undermined once more.

He did not even think of returning to the Catholic Church. He was rid now of his infatuation with Manichaeism but not of his anti-Catholic outlook. "I despaired of finding the truth in your Church, O Lord of heaven and earth. . . . The Manichaeans had turned me away from it."[1] He even despaired utterly of finding it there[2] because he was still convinced that the Catholic faith was "impossible to defend against the objections of the Manichaeans."[3] What a strange persuasion! But at least it helps explain the fact that for nine years he never thought of asking himself whether the Catholic Church might not have some answers to the Manichaean objections.

Two paths were now barred to him: Manichaeism and Catholicism. A third way was likewise barred, because the name of Christ did not appear there. There remained but one more path to follow, and it was the worst of all: the path of renunciation and distrust. That was the one Augustine now set out on.

The path not illumined by the name of Christ was that of pure philosophy. He had by now read all that Latin literature had to offer in the way of philosophical learning and ideas.[4] Nowhere in it had he found the answer to his interior problem. Here is what he says about it:

> Therefore, after the manner of the Academicians (as they are commonly represented), doubting of all things and wavering between all things, I resolved, once for all to leave the Manichaeans, thinking that I ought not even for that time of my doubt to remain any longer in that sect to which I already preferred some of the philosophers. Nevertheless, I refused absolutely to commit the cure of my sick soul to these philosophers because they were without the saving name of Christ.[5]

It is not easy to say just what philosophers Augustine had in mind. Certainly not the Epicureans, whom he detested. Only once, and in a moment of discouragement, did he refer to them, and then it was simply to say that he would have preferred Epicurus to the others, if Epicurus had not refused to believe "that the soul survived after death and was treated according to its merits."[6]

He had similar difficulties with the Stoics. Stoic morality—which was entirely concentrated on the promotion of the virtues, the control of the passions, the courageous and serene endurance of the blows of fortune ("Abstain and endure"), the defense of individual freedom, the interior life, and universal brotherhood—could not but please him. It was Stoic teaching on God and the soul that he could not accept. "Zeno took delight in his view of God and especially of the soul (a subject always of particular concern to philosophy): he claimed that the soul is mortal, that nothing exists apart from the sensible world, and that the only action in the world is the action of bodies (he regarded God himself as fire)."[7]

In fact, Augustine himself came close to this Stoic conception of a God who permeates the universe, informs matter from within, and pervades every living thing, when, after getting beyond anthropomorphism, he vainly tried to free himself from materialism. At that point he imagined God as "some kind of corporeal being, either infused into the world through local spaces, or else endlessly diffused beyond it."[8]

Respect for great philosophers

In my opinion, when Augustine refers to philosophers he thought superior to the Manichaeans, he means the great philosophers of antiquity: Pythagoras, who "was persuaded by a Syrian named Pherecides to believe in the immortality of the Soul,"[9] Plato, and Aristotle, whom he was later to have in mind in his little treatise *The Immortality of the Soul*. Speaking of the philosophers of his own day, he would say in *Against the Academics*:

> Nowadays we find almost no philosophers who are not Cynics or Peripatetics or Platonists. And for that matter there are Cynics only because there are people who find their delight in a free and

licentious life. As for learning and doctrine, as well as for morality which gives guidance to the soul, there have not been lacking very keen-minded and able men who showed in their discussions that Plato and Aristotle are so completely in agreement that only the ignorant or the inattentive could think them at odds. It took many centuries and many debates to develop a completely true philosophy, but this, in my opinion, is now an accomplished fact.[10]

When Augustine wrote these words, he numbered among the "very keen-minded and able men" Plotinus and Porphyry, whose works he read during the second year of his stay in Milan. But he already knew, from his reading of the *Hortensius* when he was nineteen, that the earliest philosophers—and the greatest among these—had taught that the human being has an eternal and divine soul. There is no doubt, then, that he had those philosophers in mind when he wrote the passage from *Confessions,* Book V, which I quoted above.

Yet despite his admiration for those great philosophers he was unwilling to put this trust in them. We already know the reason for this: they did not speak to him of Christ. At this point, he conceived the idea—a desperate solution to an insoluble problem!—that the wisest of all the philosophers were those who identified wisdom with a hopeless search for truth, a search for a truth that could not be found.

This outlook, though new, was neither superficial nor transitory. "When I had seen through the Manichaeans, I managed to escape from them. Then, once I had crossed that sea, for a long time it was the Academics who steered my boat as it was buffeted by every wind."[11] The words are from Augustine's *The Happy Life,* the first of his autobiographical writings (November 13-15, 386). The *Confessions* confirm this testimony.

In fact, the *Confessions* tell us that the temptation to skepticism attacked him in Rome and quickly became intense. "I began to think that the philosophers known as the Academics were wiser than the rest, because they held that we ought to doubt all things and asserted that nothing of truth could be comprehended by humans."[12] At that time, such seemed to him to be the authentic teaching of the Academics.

The Academics maintained that human beings can never obtain sure knowledge of the truths discussed in philosophy. . . . The whole duty of the wise, then, . . . is to search for truth. It follows from that the wise should not give their assent to anything, because they will necessarily be deceived if they give their assent to what is uncertain (and it is a crime for philosophers to err). Moreover, not only did they assert that everything is uncertain; they also offered many arguments in proof. They appear to have derived their thesis that truth is inaccessible from the famous definition of Zeno the Stoic. . . . To put the matter more briefly and clearly: truth is recognizable by signs that falsehood cannot show. But the Academics took great pains to convince themselves and others that such signs can never be discovered. They buttressed their view by pointing to the disagreements among philosophers, the mistakes made by the senses, dreams and madness, fallacious arguments and quibbles. They had learned from Zeno that there is no worse stupidity than assertions based on opinion. From this they developed the theory that if nothing can be perceived and if opinion is for fools, the wise should never put their seal of approval on anything.[13]

Drawn to the Academics

Yet the esteem in which Augustine held these philosophers kept him from believing that such was really their teaching. After all, the arguments against skepticism were so numerous and so telling—his book *Against the Academics* expounds them at length—that noble minds could not have failed to grasp them. He therefore assumed that their supposed skepticism was in fact only a way (the esoteric method) of concealing their Platonic spiritualism and defending it against the attacks of Stoic and Epicurean materialism.[14]

At the time, however, Augustine shared the common view and therefore looked upon these philosophers as exponents of his own state of mind. When he left Rome for Milan, the temptation to skepticism followed him. In Milan he went to hear Ambrose, but simply in order to see whether the bishop's eloquence lived up to its reputation; he had no interest in the teaching Ambrose was expounding. "I had lost hope that humans could find the path that led to you [God]."[15] A few months later, probably in June of 385, his mother also arrived in Milan. At this time, he says, "I . . . was in grave danger of renouncing the prospect of finding the truth."[16]

Ambrose noticed how pious a woman Monica was, and whenever he met Augustine he would praise her and congratulate the son on having such a mother. Augustine felt forced to comment: "He did not know what a son she had in me; for I doubted all these things and thought that the 'way of life' could not be discovered."[17] Nonetheless, when his mother arrived in Milan, he told her that while he was not yet a Catholic Christian, he was at least no longer a Manichaean.[18]

This would be good news to her, and it was as such that Augustine told it to her. But did the new conviction that had meanwhile taken hold of him—that there was no hope of finding the truth—put him in a better psychological state? We may doubt it. Augustine had good reason to speak of himself as being in "grave danger." For, while it is a serious matter to meet with error when seeking the truth, it is even more serious to stop looking for the truth because one is disillusioned at finding error. In any case, the new situation did have one advantage: it was the ultimate logical conclusion of a long journey into error. As such it could rouse in a perceptive mind the suspicion that one had taken the wrong road and must retrace one's steps by resolving one after another the misunderstandings with which the way had been strewn.

Such, at least, was the case with Augustine. He speaks of his state of mind at that time as a dangerous condition through which he must pass, like the crises physicians speak of, which, if surmounted, promise a passage from sickness back to health.[19] But before we contemplate Augustine on the road back, let us first look at him on the road of success—that is, professional success. In the Providence of God, the success was closely linked to the return.

11

"At Milan I found your devoted servant the bishop Ambrose"

DESPITE his interior state, now known to the reader, Augustine busied himself in an attempt to improve his professional status, now seriously compromised by the bad habits of the Roman students. He succeeded brilliantly by dint of acquiring patrons in pagan high society. We do not know whether he met the rhetorician Hierius, a Syrian to whom he had dedicated his first book while in Carthage,[1] or Ammianus Marcellinus, another Easterner, who at that time was writing his *History*. He did, however, get an introduction to Symmachus, prefect of the city, who took a liking to him.

Symmachus, a man of letters and a statesman, was one of the most representative figures of Roman paganism. In 382 he had, in the senate's name, tried to plead the cause of paganism by asking Emperor Gratian that the altar of Victory, which had been removed from the entrance to the Curia, might be restored to its place. He tried in vain, for the emperor would not receive him. In the following year he renewed the attempt under Emperor Valentinus II, who had succeeded his brother. This time Symmachus was given an audience, in which he pleaded the cause of old pagan Rome and made a powerful and moving appeal for tolerance and religious pluralism: "Not by any single way do human beings reach so great a mystery."[2] But Ambrose, who had meanwhile written a reply,[3] persuaded the emperor to deny permission.

About a year after this incident Symmachus, now prefect of Rome, was ordered to hire a professor of rhetoric for the city of Milan. Augustine learned of it, sought the position, and obtained it with the help of the Manichaeans.

> When a request was sent from Milan to Rome to the Prefect of the city to provide a professor of rhetoric for that city and to send him at public expense, I applied for the position through those same persons who were intoxicated with Manichaean vanities....

Symmachus, who was then Prefect, sent me, after testing my ability upon some subject of oratory.[4]

Symmachus realized that he was doing this African rhetorician
a great favor. The imperial court was located in Milan, and one
task of the professor was to pronounce the official panegyrics of
the emperor and the consuls for the year. It was an important
function and enabled the person charged with it to enter the circle
of high officers of state and to hope for further promotions. Augustine in fact was to think it certain that he would be given an
administrative post, perhaps the presidency of a tribunal.[5] At the
time, Symmachus had good reasons for sending to Milan as official professor a non-Catholic and even, since he was recommended by the Manichaeans, a man who was presumably
strongly anti-Catholic. We may think that these reasons, and not
solely the oratorical abilities of Augustine, influenced Symmachus' choice.[6] In the autumn of 384 Augustine left Rome,
which had not been a happy place for him. It is likely that he
passed through Furlo on the Via Flaminia and then continued on
the Via Emilia[7] to the Lombard capital, reaching this in plenty of
time to prepare his panegyric (January 1, 385) in honor of the consulate of Bauto, a friend of Symmachus.[8]

Catholic Rome had little to say to the soul of Augustine. As he
climbed the Aventine, he may have met Jerome hastening away
from the gatherings in the home of Marcella[9]; but if he did, it
meant little to him. Perhaps as he walked the Caelian hill he met
the cortege of elderly Pope Damasus; but if he did he would
hardly have spared him more than a glance of curiosity or even
contempt. His range of interests no longer embraced the affairs of
the Catholic Church; this had been so for many years now.

Milan

Not so at Milan. Milan was the residence of Ambrose, a man
too famous and influential to be ignored. Moreover, Augustine
was not simply a private professor now. He therefore betook himself to Ambrose. It was only a courtesy visit, but it left a profound
impression on the young professor.

And thus I came to Milan, to Ambrose the Bishop, known as one of the most excellent men of the whole world. . . . That man of God received me with a father's affection, and welcomed my coming with a bishop's kindness.

I began to love him, not at first as a teacher of truth, which I had no hopes of meeting with in your Church, but as a man who was kind to me.[10]

In Milan Ambrose was the center of an intense Catholic life, both intellectual and ascetical. These two aspects of the Milanese community corresponded fully to the dominant concerns in Augustine's religious outlook: intellectual probity and practical consistency. As we shall see when the time comes, they would eventually win him over.

Ambrose himself was an ascetic and a learned man. He had been bishop for ten years and was about fourteen years older than Augustine; he was also completely dedicated to God and to pastoral duties. The thirty-year-old professor did not immediately grasp the meaning of this life devoted to asceticism and the service of the Church. He regarded Ambrose "as a man happy according to worldly standards because so much honored by such important people"; at the same time, however, the celibacy that Ambrose practiced seemed to Augustine a real hardship.[11] He judged the man in secular terms; he observed the fact of celibacy but did not understand the reasons for it or the advantages it brought, still less its joys.

On the other hand, the man's eloquence attracted him without reservations. "I was delighted with his charming discourse; it was more learned than that of Faustus yet less soothing and enchanting in manner."[12] Until this time Faustus had been the only outstanding religious orator Augustine had heard, and the comparison therefore came spontaneously. In the *Soliloquies* he would later say that in Ambrose "an eloquence we had thought gone forever returned to life, and in a superior form."[13]

Ambrose belonged to an Aurelian clan and was the son of a rich senatorial family that was probably related to that of Symmachus. He had received the formation of a Roman aristocrat: grammar, Latin and Greek literature, rhetoric, and law.[14] As a bishop he read the Eastern Fathers,[15] the Neoplatonic philosophers,[16] and the pagan writers of antiquity.[17]

One of Ambrose's company was an equally devout and learned priest named Simplicianus.

> He appeared to me to be your good servant, for your grace shone in him. And I had heard that from his youth he had most devoutly served you. Now he was grown old, and I thought that in so long a time spent in your service, he must have experienced many things and learned many things. And so it was in reality.[18]

He had traveled a good deal, was a practiced theologian, had a good knowledge of Platonic philosophy, and had played a part in the conversion of Marius Victorinus, whose close friend he was. When Augustine visited him and told him that he himself had read some works of the Neoplatonists, Simplicianus congratulated him because "in the Platonists God and his Word are constantly implied."[19] Then Simplicianus told him the story of the great Victorinus' conversion.[20] Ambrose had received baptism from Simplicianus and "truly loved him tenderly like a father."[21]

Marks of Milanese Church

Around Ambrose and Simplicianus there had formed a circle of students who combined devotion to philosophy with the practice of Christian life.[22] We know something of Manlius Theodore,[23] Zenobius,[24] and Hermogenianus.[25] The first, and the most famous of these, was a "great admirer" of the Neoplatonists. Some years earlier, he had withdrawn into private life and in his country refuge had set himself to writing works of philosophy and treatises on classical metrics. Later on, he returned to political life and in 399 was appointed to the consulate, for which he won the congratulations of Symmachus and the praises of the poet Claudian.[26]

The Milanese Church was characterized not only by zeal for philosophical studies but also by a great enthusiasm for the Christian ascetical ideal. Ambrose was tireless in his praise of consecrated virginity, losing no chance to eulogize it and describe its exemplars. When he spoke of the Virgin Mary he waxed lyrical. One fruit of this fascination that marked his preaching was the many books he wrote that made him the most fruitful of writers on Christian virginity. Echos of this zeal for the evangelical ideal in its highest form were heard throughout Italy and even reached distant Mauretania. It was natural, then, that a strong spiritual movement should arise around the bishop of Milan. Many young women took the veil, coming from Piacenza, Bologna, and even Africa for this purpose.[27] Nor did young men lag behind. On the outskirts of the city there was a monastery "full of pious brothers"; Ambrose was its founder and spiritual guide.[28]

Once Augustine set out on his journey of return he would see this ecclesial community with new eyes and comment in amazement that "its members each followed a different path in the world."[29] In fact, during his stay in Milan he had two splendid examples of the religious fervor of the people and their attachment to their bishop.

The first was occasioned by the struggle against the Arians. The facts are well known. Toward the end of 384 an Arian bishop named Mercurinus, who changed his name to Auxentius (this had been the name of Ambrose's predecessor), came to Milan. In the spring of 385 Justina, mother of the young emperor Valentinian II and an Arian, asked that the Porcian basilica be given to Mercurinus. Ambrose was called to the court. A crowd of the faithful, knowing what was going on, milled around the palace, and the bishop had to be asked to calm them. He did, but won in return the withdrawal of the request.

In the following year, however, the request was repeated, and Ambrose decided not to yield. He locked himself in the disputed basilica and its adjoining buildings, together with the faithful and other bishops from the area, and sent a sharp refusal to the court. He rejected the compromises that were urged upon him, and even the siege laid to the basilica did not intimidate pastor or flock. In order to keep up the spirits of the people Ambrose addressed them without wearying and also introduced the Eastern practice of singing hymns (which he had composed) and psalms. This courageous resistance had its desired effect. On Good Friday, April 3, 386, the request was withdrawn and so were the troops.[30]

Among the faithful who had united themselves closely to the bishop was Monica. Augustine was not caught up in the general enthusiasm, but neither did he remain insensible to it. Here is how he himself remembered the incident.

> It was about a year, or not much more, since Justina, mother of Valentinian, the boy emperor, persecuted your servant Ambrose in favor of her heresy, into which she had been seduced by the Arians. The pious people watched night and day in the church, ready to die with their bishop, your servant. There also my mother, your handmaid, bearing a chief part in the solicitude and watchings, lived in prayer. Though cold as yet with regard to the heat of your Spirit, I was stirred up, nevertheless, by the concern and trouble of the whole city. It was then instituted that hymns and psalms should be sung after the manner of the Eastern Churches, lest the people should languish with the weariness of sorrow. This practice is retained to this day, and followed by many of almost all your congregations throughout the world.[31]

The second episode was the discovery and translation of the bodies of the martyrs Protase and Gervase. The Lord (Augustine writes) had preserved these bodies incorrupt in his secret treasury in order to bring them to light at the opportune moment and "restrain the rage of a mere woman, but one who was also an empress."[32] On this occasion many miracles took place. Augustine records in particular the cure of "a certain citizen who had been many years blind and was well known in the city." Then, speaking of the religious enthusiasm of those days (June 17-19) and the beneficial result for the Milanese Church in its struggle against Arianism, he continues: "The fame of this miracle was immediately spread abroad, and your praises were fervently celebrated, and the mind of that enraged woman, though it was not brought to the health of faith, was repressed from the fury of persecution."[33]

In telling these two stories Augustine does not fail to relate them to his own interior development. Using two biblical expressions, he tells us that he was "as yet cold with regard to the heat of your Spirit" and that "when the scent of your ointments was so fragrant, I did not run after you." The two metaphors make it clear that at that time he had not yet reached "the port of philosophy, from which one advances into the realm and solid land of happiness."[34] On the other hand, the metaphors do not imply that he was still far from it. In fact, when the two events just recorded occurred, he had traveled a good distance toward this goal.

12

On the Road Back

THE return journey was not to be as short and easy as the journey outbound. Augustine had abandoned the Catholic faith in the space of a few days; its recovery would take many years of tormented searching. It is always a lengthy, wearisome, and difficult task to dissipate a cloud of prejudices and solve a series of badly posed and badly answered problems. Such was Augustine's painful experience.

The road that led him away from the faith had been marked by certain milestones: rationalism, materialism, skepticism. On the road back he encountered the same errors and was compelled to overcome them one after another. The story of this conquest is the story of his conversion, which was, above all, the conversion of a great thinker. Yet the return journey would never have been undertaken if he had not first cast away the prejudices against the Catholic Church that he had acquired from the Manichaeans. There were two such prejudices in particular: the anthropomorphic representation of God and the unacceptability of the Old Testament. Ambrose removed these by his preaching.

Influence of Ambrose's sermons

The bishop of Milan contributed little or nothing to Augustine's conversion by way of private conversations; he contributed a great deal, on the other hand, through his sermons to the people. He never sat down with Augustine to discuss religion, as Simplicianus later did.[1] At a certain point, Augustine greatly desired such conversations with Ambrose, but the latter did not have the leisure or else, knowing the background of the African rhetorician, did not have the will to do so. The fact is that prior to his conversion Augustine spoke to Ambrose on only a few occasions, and then only briefly. In his writings he tells us of his courtesy call on the bishop after his arrival in Milan,[2] his consultation with Ambrose in his mother's behalf on the question of fasting,[3] and chance meetings with Ambrose in church or on the street, in which the latter spent the time praising Monica.[4]

At one point Augustine wanted to tell Ambrose of his interior "torments" and "dangers" but was unable to find the occasion. He "often" went to see him in his home, entered and waited, saw him always reading, and did not have the heart to disturb him.

I was unable to ask of him what I wished and as I wished, being shut off from his ears and voice by so many people to whose infirmities he ministered. And the time that he was not with them, which was but little, was taken up in refreshing either his body with necessary food or his mind by reading.

When he was reading, his eyes moved over the pages and his heart sought understanding, but his voice and tongue were silent. Often when we were present (for no one was refused entrance, nor was it the custom to give him notice of anyone's coming), we saw him reading in this manner in silence, and never otherwise. And having sat down in long silence (for who would dare to be troublesome to one so intent?) we departed. We supposed that for that short time which he had for refreshing his mind, free from the noise of other people's business, he was loath to be disturbed.[5]

He informed Ambrose of his own conversion in a letter in which he asked advice about the books of Scripture that he might helpfully read. Ambrose replied with the requested advice, but it proved rather unsuitable in practice.[6] If there had been someone available to teach Augustine at the time of which we are now speaking, he would have found his pupil well-disposed and very docile.[7] There was, of course, Ambrose, but he could not turn to Ambrose except with questions requiring only a short answer. "My perplexities required one perfectly disengaged, to whom they might be fully represented, and I could never find him so much at leisure."[8]

Despite the distance Ambrose kept outwardly, he made a decisive contribution to Augustine's return to the Catholic faith. He did so through his preaching, by which he removed the main obstacle: Augustine's distrust and—let me not mince words—contempt for the teaching of the Church.

Augustine went to hear the bishop every Sunday. At first he went, as I noted earlier, from a purely formal interest in the bishop's oratory and with little concern for content.[9] In time, however, as he realized that the ideas expressed were not what he had expected, he developed a growing interest in the content of these sermons.[10]

We do not know what sermons Augustine heard. The chronology of Ambrose's writings has not been established with certainty and, besides, many of the sermons Augustine heard may never have been written down or may have been lost. We do know, however, what it was in these sermons that caught his attention and gave him reason to hope. There were two themes in particular: the "spiritual" interpretation of the sacred books and the emphasis on the spirituality of God and the soul.

Corrected Augustine's thought

The spiritual or allegorical interpretation of Scripture rendered acceptable the Old Testament passages with which Augustine had found fault. Ambrose urgently recommended the Pauline criterion: "The written law kills, but the Spirit gives life" (2 Cor 3:6), and applied it extensively himself. His exegesis showed that many Old Testament passages, which, taken literally, seemed scandalous on account of their harshness or their candor, contained a deeper meaning hidden under the death-dealing letter. To this extent, Augustine's distrust of the Church appeared unjustified.

> I . . . heard one passage after another in the Old Testament figuratively explained. These passages had been death to me when I took them literally, but once I had heard them explained in their spiritual meaning I began to blame myself for my despair, at least insofar as it had led me to suppose that it was impossible to counter people who hated and derided the Law and the Prophets.[11]

But it was on the second theme especially that Augustine's thinking was turned upside down. The Manichaeans had accused the Church of a repugnant kind of anthropomorphism, but here was Ambrose emphasizing the absolute spirituality of God and the soul. "I often heard it said in the discourses of our bishop and in yours as well [he is speaking to Manlius Theodore] that when we think of God or the soul we should not think of anything corporeal."[12] The principle being invoked was the principle of Christian spiritualism. In keeping with it Ambrose interpreted the words of Gen 1:26: "Let us make man in our image, after our own likeness," as referring to the soul and not to the body. The words mean not that God is corporeal like human beings, but that human beings are spiritual like God. Human beings are in fact spiritual because their souls are gifted with intelligence and freedom and can cross the greatest possible distances in thought. Here we are in Italy, Ambrose would say, and in our minds we can see people we know, if there be any, who now live in Africa.

The example could not but be appealing to this most attentive and interested of Ambrose's listeners. The soul alone (Ambrose went on) can be united to God, and it will be all the freer in its quest, the more it rejects the demands of the body and of carnal lusts.[13]

Ambrose's words were a revelation to Augustine. He was overjoyed to learn that the Church did not teach what he had attributed to it; he was ashamed of having let the Manichaeans deceive him; he felt guilty of having asserted so much that was false without having taken pains to check it.

> When I discovered that the words that *man was created by you in your own image* were not understood by your spiritual children (whom by grace you have caused to be born again of their Catholic Mother) in such manner as to believe or imagine you to be bound by the form of a human body, . . . I was both glad and ashamed to find that for so many years I had been barking not at that which was indeed that Catholic faith but at the fictions of carnal concepts. For I had been so rash and wicked all that time as to be more ready to accuse and condemn that which I should have tried to learn by inquiry.[14]

The allegorical interpretation of Scripture and the spirituality of God and the soul were not the only two points that attracted Augustine's attention as he listened to Ambrose. There were others such as creation[15] and human freedom.[16] Creation explained the origin of the spiritual and material universe and cut the ground from under any and every form of dualism and pantheism; freedom located the origin of the evil we do within us and not in a nature different from us, as the Manichaeans taught, while the origin of the evils we suffer is to be sought in the impartiality of God's judgments.

In any case, it was not these further points but rather the initial two that unfroze Augustine's situation, so to speak, by stimulating him to a new hope. "I was . . . glad . . . to find that for so many years I had been barking not at that which was indeed the Catholic faith but at the fictions of carnal concepts."[17]

These words sound like a cry of victory, and in a sense they are. Above all, however, they give an inkling of a great and painful struggle. There were still many misunderstandings to clear up. As a result, Augustine continued to harbor a dangerous feeling of hopelessness, for this restless searcher, having found to his confusion that he had been tragically deceived, was now afraid of being deceived again. He was like a person who has had experience of a bad doctor and is now afraid to trust even a good one.[18]

The Catholic faith, as Augustine saw it at this time, "was not vanquished but not victorious either."[19] Its teachings were no longer indefensible, as he had thought; but this did not mean that they were true. Augustine wanted to see and be certain: as certain of religious truth as he was that "seven and three make ten." He had not gone so far into skepticism as to deny the evidence of the principles of mathematics: "I was not so mad as to think that even this could not be certainly known." Therefore he wanted the same evidence for the truths of faith as he had for the truths of mathematics. "I desired to have all other things equally demonstrable, whether material . . . or spiritual. . . ."[20]

He returned again to rationalism, but only for a time. He soon realized that while rationalism is true as a point of arrival, it is false and the source of many errors when it is taken as a point of departure. Meanwhile, wavering and uncertain, he decided to remain a catechumen in the Catholic Church, "which had been recommended to me by my parents" and this "till something certain should appear by which I might steer my course."[21] This particular psychological moment is set down in the book *The Value of Belief* in almost the same words as in the *Confessions:* "I decided to remain a catechumen in the Church to which my parents had entrusted me, until I either found what I was looking for or became convinced that it was not worth all the difficulties of the search for it."[22]

13

"I found a pole star in which to trust"

WE do not know when but we do know how Augustine was freed from his state of doubt. He himself tells us in an autobiographical secton of the book *The Value of Belief:*

> At times truth seemed impossible to discover, and then my thoughts were carried by a strong current toward the Academics. Yet at other times, when I reflected carefully on the liveliness, keenness, and perspicacity of the human mind, I thought that if truth eluded it, this could only be because it lacked a method for the search and that such a method would have to be given by some divine authority. The task, therefore, was to determine what this authority might be.[1]

Once Augustine had put aside his prejudices against the Church, his experience with the Manichaeans and his penetrating meditation on the human condition helped him gradually to develop a new conception of the relation between reason and faith. When he was nineteen, he had thought of faith as opposed to reason, that is, knowledge[2]; now he saw faith in terms of collaboration with reason. He no longer had to choose between the two but only to bring them into harmony. The motto now was to be, not "Reason *or* faith," but "Reason *and* faith."

The Manichaeans had demonstrated the necessity of such a collaboration by their own inconsistent way of acting. They had emphatically promised knowledge and had laughed at faith; but then, forgetting their promises, they had elaborated "a whole system of absurd inventions that could never be demonstrated and imposed them on their followers as things to be believed." Catholic teaching was preferable—and Augustine was in fact beginning to prefer it: "I found that it was with more modesty and without the least deceit that Catholic teaching required to be believed what was not yet demonstrated—either because it was really demonstrable though not to some or because it was not demonstrable."[3]

85

Furthermore, faith is an attitude inseparable from the human condition, for without faith there would be no history, no friendship, no family, no human association of any kind.

> You brought to my mind the incalculable number of facts that I believed although I had not seen them or been present at their development, such as the multitudes of historical events, accounts of places and cities that I never visited in person, and of other things that—because we wish to function in life—we accept on the word of friends, doctors, and people of all kinds. Lastly, you reminded me of how firmly convinced I was about the identity of my parents although I could know this fact only by believing what others told me.[4]

Here Augustine harks back to the appearance of an idea that was to be developed at length in his books. In the first of these he enunciates a general principle that he derived from ancient philosophy but that belongs in fact to the philosophical wisdom of every age: "As everyone knows, two things lead us to knowledge: authority and reason."[5]

In his third book *On Order* he sets forth the relationships between faith and reason in regard to their importance and their sequence in time. From the standpoint of importance, priority belongs to reason because it is better to see (that is, have knowledge) than to believe; from the standpoint of succession in time, however, the priority belongs to faith, since faith leads to knowledge. It is better, therefore, to believe in expectation of seeing than to fall into error or remain in the darkness of ignorance. In this teaching the reader will perceive the strong intellectualist element that is never missing from Augustine's thinking, even if the affective element is dominant.

> Authority comes first chronologically, while reason is first in order of importance. We give priority to one thing in action and to another in intention. The authority of trustworthy people seems more effective with the uninstructed multitude, while reason is more suitably used in dealing with the educated. At the same time, however, educated persons were ignorant before becoming educated, and no ignorant persons know the state of mind in which they should present themselves to their teacher or the kind of life that will render them docile. It follows from this that authority alone can open the door for all those who desire to learn the good in all its greatness and hidden depths.[6]

In another work, written in Rome, Augustine repeatedly stresses the same point.[7] He continues to do so down to that fine little book *The Value of Belief*, in which he sets out to demonstrate to his friend Honoratus "the rashness and wickedness of the Manichaeans in attacking those who accept the authority of the Catholic faith and, before they are able to contemplate truth that thought alone can grasp, first strengthen and prepare themselves for divine illumination by the exercise of faith."[8]

Augustine describes faith as medicine,[9] source of strength,[10] a nest,[11] a shortcut,[12] and a defense.[13] It purifies the interior vision and makes it stronger; it defends the weak against the attacks of the unbelieving; it nourishes and warms the faithful as long as their own wings are not yet ready for flight; it gives an effortless knowledge of the truths needed for salvation, even those that reason could attain on its own, but only with much labor; it softens the piercing brilliance of divine light and enables us to look at it in some measure. It was on these images, or some of them, that Augustine meditated while he was in Milan, as his soul gradually shed its uncertainty and approached the shores of the Catholic faith.

Authority of the Scriptures

Meanwhile, reflection on the value of faith led his thoughts to a further subject that, though different, was closely linked to the first: the subject of authority. Faith needs an authority on which it can rely. If this authority is to be valid and sure for all, it can only be the authority of God. Augustine recognized this authority in the sacred books. "In this way you thoroughly persuaded me that I ought not to find fault with those who believed in your Bible, which you have established with such great authority among almost all the peoples of the earth, but with those who did not believe it."[14]

The basis of this trust is certainty regarding divine providence, a certainty that the son of Monica had never lost[15] and that he would use later on in *The City of God* to shed light on the mystery of human history.

And so, since we are too weak to discover the truth by reason alone and for this reason need the authority of sacred books, I began to believe that you would never have invested the Bible with such conspicuous authority in every land unless you had intended it to be the means by which we should look for you and believe in you.[16]

The style and obscurities of Scripture were no longer a difficulty for Augustine.[17] He now adopted a contrary attitude that is frequently expressed in his writings:[18] the simple style of Scripture and the mysterious profundity of its content increase rather than lessen its authority, because they make it accessible to all yet penetrable by few. Its clarity of expression and everyday style are an invitation to all human beings to take refuge in its bosom, while the profundity of the mysteries it communicates invites the more able and more desirous to experience the joy of discovering hidden truths. "Its authority appeared to me so much the more venerable and worthy of a religious assent, in that it could easily be read by all, and yet preserved the dignity of its mystery in its more profound meaning."[19]

The fine castles Augustine had built at nineteen were crumbling one after another; he was acquiring that precious sense of mystery that would stay with him for the remainder of his life.[20] As though to underscore his reversal of positions, he ends this part of his story by saying to God: "These were my thoughts and you were with me: I sighed and you heard me. I wavered and you guided me. I walked in the way of the world and you did not forsake me."[21]

This humble trust did not fail to bear fruit. Shortly after, he took another and decisive step in the direction of faith, for he came to realize that the authority of the sacred books in which he was convinced he should henceforth look for wisdom supposed another authority: the authority that preserves and guarantees them. Where was this authority located? A lengthy and slow process of reflection persuaded him that this authority was the authority of the Catholic Church.[22]

Augustine was struck by the high esteem the Christian faith enjoyed throughout the world. On one occasion, when talking with his friends, he mentioned the materialist hypothesis that death is the end of everything; then, deeply stirred, he exclaimed: "But God forbid that it should be so. Surely it is no vain or empty matter that the towering authority of the Christian faith should have spread throughout the world."[23] This "towering authority"—which elsewhere becomes "the supreme authority"—is based on the properties of the Church as one, catholic, apostolic, unchanging, and fruitful.[24]

Authority of the Church

This new insight rid Augustine of another youthful misunderstanding and laid the foundation for another fundamental thesis of Augustinian apologetics. The misunderstanding was the one that caused the university student to oppose Christ to the Church in the name of a charismatic Christianity.[25] The thesis in apologetics asserts that the very life of the Church is a reliable motive of credibility. It is a thesis that Augustine developed against his former coreligionists, the Manichaeans.[26] It was while writing against them that he coined the well-known aphorism: "I would not believe in the Gospel if the authority of the Catholic Church did not bid me to do so."[27] The profound truth contained in the aphorism revealed itself to him in Milan while he was still looking for the pole star he should trust on his journey.

We do not know precisely when this revelation came, but it certainly preceded his reading of the Platonists. From this point on he no longer thought of himself as separated from the Church of Christ, and he once again accepted its authority as he had always accepted that of Christ. He was now delivered from doubt. We must nonetheless ask: How far is it possible to say that Augustine had already regained his lost faith?

The question has given rise to a great many studies and a great many differing views.[28] If we are to answer it, we must, in my opinion, make an important distinction between the formal motive of faith and the content of the faith professed. Augustine had recovered the first, but he did not as yet have clear ideas with regard to the second. In other words, he had accepted the principle of authority in matters of faith or, to use his own words, he had found "a pole star in which to entrust."[29] He had not, however, gained the needed clarity on some points, even fundamental ones, of the faith. His state was therefore one of simultaneous certainty and wavering.

The distinction is suggested, and even expressed, in the words of the *Confessions:*

> Such things as these I turned over in my wretched heart, burdened with corroding cares from the fear of dying without having discovered the truth. Yet the faith of *your Christ, our Lord and Savior,* professed in the Catholic Church, was strongly fixed in my heart, in many things indeed as yet unformed and fluctuating apart from the rule of sound doctrine, yet my mind did not forsake it, but rather more and more imbibed it.[30]

Philosophical and theological problems

At the philosophical level he felt himself still tangled in the meshes of materialism and dualism. He did indeed now maintain that God is "beyond corruption, hurt, or change," and he understood and believed that when we think of God and the soul we ought not to think of these as in any way corporeal.[31] Yet, no matter what efforts he made, he was unable to conceive an incorporeal being. A being without spatial extension seemed to have no existence at all.[32] This was his greatest torment, but it was accompanied by another hardly less great: the problem of the origin of evil. This was the terrible problem that had haunted him when he was nineteen and had led him—not indeed by itself but equally with other motives—to accept Manichaeism.[33] It was always with him, an obsession that drove him to look for an answer. Yet there seemed to be no answer but Manichaean dualism—which he now rejected![34]

On the theological level, too, there was still an area of shadows. One in particular covered the very heart of Christianity: the Incarnation. Strange though it may seem in a man who had been raised a Catholic, Augustine venerated Christ simply as

> a man of excellent wisdom and no way to be equalled; more particularly, because being miraculously born of a Virgin, he seemed to have attained to that great authority of lordship, by the divine care over us, to give us an example of despising temporal things for the attainment of immortality. But I could not in the least apprehend the meaning of the mystery of *the Word made Flesh.*[35]

Without realizing it, Augustine had the outlook of a Photinian.[36]

The fact is that the Manichaean docetism that he had professed for many years and had now decisively rejected, had confused his thinking. It had confused others as well. Even the sober-minded and reflective Alypius was convinced that Catholics who professed faith in the Incarnation were denying the existence of a soul and a human intelligence in Christ. On the other hand, he was also convinced that the deeds of Christ as narrated in the Gospel could not have been done by any but a rational creature. As a result, he advanced rather slowly toward the Catholic faith. "But," Augustine goes on to say, "afterward, finding that this was the error of the Apollinarian heretics,[37] he rejoiced in and readily entertained the Catholic faith. As for me, I must confess it was not till some time later that I learned to distinguish in 'the Word was made flesh' between the error of Photinus and the Catholic truth."[38]

But this unwitting ignorance did not prevent a global adherence to Christ and the Church,[39] any more than did his consciousness of being unable to conceive a spiritual being or to find a solution to the problem of evil.

The *Confessions* are explicit on this last point:

> I was still seeking whence came evil, and I could find no way to account for it. Yet you did not allow me by any of those waves of thought to be carried away from the faith, by which I believed that you were, that your substance was immutable, and you had care of us, and that there was a judgment to come. I believed too that in Christ your Son our Lord, and in the Holy Scriptures, which the authority of the Catholic Church recommended to us, you have appointed a way for our salvation unto that life which is to come after this death. These points, therefore, being safe and strongly settled in my mind, I inquired anxiously whence evil could come.[40]

If, then, Augustine cannot be said to have as yet been converted in the full theological sense of this term, he had certainly taken a decisive step toward such a conversion when he acknowledged and accepted the authority of the Catholic Church.

14

The Platonists

AUGUSTINE'S return to the faith was the return of a thinker who made distinct intellectual demands on himself. He was therefore unable to commit himself to the path of a dedication of God, as he wholeheartedly desired to do, unless he had first solved the speculative problems that haunted him. Two such problems were always present before his mind's eye and still unresolved.

Meanwhile he had been delivered from his false belief in the divination practiced by the astrologers. He had accepted this belief while at Carthage and had eagerly read their books, partly out of curiousity, partly from a need to find an explanation, other than free will, for the problem of sin. He could not be detached from this belief simply by the wise advice of the elderly Vindicianus, a well-known and deeply learned consul, or by the kindly teasing of his friend Nebridius. He kept trying to find a sure explanation of why some of the astrologers' predictions came true, and he could not find it.[1] He did find it in Milan, after he talked the matter over with Firminus, a dear friend who had been educated in the liberal arts and was a good rhetorician, and listened to the story Firminus had to tell him.[2]

He was unable, however, to end his preoccupation with the problem of evil, and it caused him great suffering. "What pangs did my heart then suffer in this labor! What groans did it send forth, O my God! And your ears were open to me, though I knew it not. And when in silence I earnestly sought, the secret contritions of my soul were loud cries to your mercy. You knew what I suffered, but no one else did."[3]

He was filled with this painful darkness when the Platonic philosophers came to his aid in the spring of 386. "You provided me, by means of a man much puffed up with the conceit of his own knowledge, some books of the Platonists, translated from Greek into Latin."[4]

"Admonished by these books to return to my own self, I entered into my inmost self. . . . I entered in and saw with the eye of my soul, above my mind, the Light unchangeable."[5]

Effect on Augustine's thought

This reading and experience, which undoubtedly played an indispensable part in the development of Augustine's thought, has attracted the attention of numerous scholars. These have brought a vast learning into play in order to determine who the unnamed person was that gave him the books,[6] who the Platonists in question were,[7] what books Augustine read,[8] and what influence these books had on his conversion.[9]

Plotinus and Porphyry are certainly the Neoplatonic philosophers most often mentioned by Augustine. He regards Plotinus as a Plato returned to earth,[10] knows the fortunes of his school,[11] and cites his writings, especially in *The City of God*.[12] On his deathbed, when the Vandals were devastating his world, he found consolation in the words of Plotinus.[13] Here is one passage on the Plotinian school:

> At that time the school of Plotinus was flourishing in Rome and was attended by many individuals possessed of quick and penetrating minds. Yet some of these let themselves be led astray by curious inquiry into magic; others, however, recognized that Jesus Christ, our Lord, is in his very person the changeless truth and wisdom they were looking for, and so they entered his service.[14]

The reference to magic seems directed at Porphyry and Iamblichus who gave Neoplatonism a sharply mystical and theurgic orientation.

Augustine considers Porphyry to be "a man of great learning," but in *The City of God* he is sharply critical of theurgy.[15] It is of interest, therefore, to learn what Augustine found in the Platonic books, what he did not find, and what he rejected.

He found, first of all, an exhortation to interiority, for this was an often repeated theme. "The soul must detach itself from all outward things and turn completely inward."[16] "Enter into yourself and contemplate" the changeless light of truth.[17] For Augustine this was a major discovery. Until that moment he had stopped short at sensible realities and the images of these that stormed in upon his soul. Now he was being urged to rise above both the realities and the images, to ascend higher and fix his attention on the light of truth that illumines the mind when it makes a judgment distinguishing truth from falsehood.

> Seeking to know why it was that I made a certain judgment when I judged, I found that there was above my changeable mind the unchangeable and true eternity of truth. I ascended this gradually from bodies to the soul . . . then to its inward faculty . . . and from there to the reasoning faculty.

> My rational faculty in me, perceiving itself to be changeable, raised itself to its own understanding . . . so that it might find by what light it was illumined when without the least doubt it cried out that the unchangeable is to be preferred to the changeable.[18]

Materialist conception of reality overcome

Augustine thus found the essential distinction between the sensible and the intelligible. But he made another discovery as well. He had believed that only corporeal realities existed.[19] Now, to his utter astonishment, he glimpsed a reality quite different from that which his senses perceived and represented, yet no less real and true, but on the contrary fully real and true: intelligible reality. "I asked, 'Is the truth then nothing, because it is not spread out through any space finite or infinite?' And you cried out to me from afar, 'Yes, in very truth, I AM WHO AM.' "[20] In fact, only that truly *is* which —like truth, for example!—remains unchangeable.[21] With this realization the materialist conception of reality, which had so long kept his mind in chains and suppressed its elan, was definitively overcome.

Along with the principle of interiority the Platonists presented him with the "principle of participation." According to this instructive principle all things come from God and are at once a participation in him and an imitation of him. In the human person, therefore, who not only exists but is capable of understanding and loving, God is present as creator, enlightener, and bestower of happiness. Or, as *The City of God* expresses it in a summary and clarification of Neoplatonic thought, God "is the cause of the created universe, the light whereby truth is grasped, and the source of the happiness we are to attain."[22]

Correct idea of evil

Finally, Augustine found in the Neoplatonists the correct idea of evil. He became aware, to begin with, that the Manichaean approach concealed a misunderstanding. (Another misunderstanding! His entire relationship to the Manichaeans had been a series of misunderstandings.) The first question to be answered in dealing with the problem of evil was not, and is not, the *unde malum?* *(Where does evil come from?)* but the *quid malum?* (What is evil?) for it is not possible to determine the origin of a thing without knowing first what kind of thing it is.

Augustine now learned from these philosophers that evil is not a substance but a privation and can therefore exist only in something good for which it represents a loss and corruption. Consequently, good can exist without evil—such a good is the supreme good—but evil cannot exist apart from something good, for then it would not exist at all.

> It became clear to me that those things also are good which are liable to corruption, which indeed could not be corrupted if they were the supreme good, nor again be liable to corruption unless they were good. For if they were the supreme good, they would be incorruptible; and if they were not good at all, there would be nothing in them that could be corrupted, for corruption injures, which it would not do if it did not diminish goodness. Either, therefore, corruption injures not at all, which cannot be said, or, as is certain, all things that are corrupted are deprived of some good. . . .
>
> Therefore, all things that have a being are good; and the evil whose origin I sought for so long is not a substance. . . . Thus I saw, and it was very clear to me, that you have made all things good; and that there is no substance at all which you did not make.[23]

The absurdity of Manichaean dualism had now been firmly established once and for all. Augustine would later spend many years of his life explaining and defending this principle against the Manichaeans. Then, when the Pelagians in turn came along and expounded a doctrine diametrically opposed to that of the Manichaeans, he would patiently and perceptively show that Catholic teaching passes untouched between the two opposing snares. But that is a subject for later discussion.

It hardly needs saying that Augustine would later expound with unparalleled mastery and originality these truths that he had come to understand through his reading of the Neoplatonists. They would become the foundation of his philosophical system. Thus we see a Latin thinker who was not at home with Greek and who read the Greek philosophers, at least at that stage of his life, only in Latin translation, nonetheless able as few others have been to master their thought while exercising a completely independent judgment. Augustine admired the Neoplatonists, but he was not their disciple.

Read through Christian eyes

It may be helpful to note that Augustine read these philosophers through Christian eyes, far more so than he had read the *Hortensius*. He had been prepared for such a reading by the Neoplatonist Christian circle he had met in Milan. In addition, both Neoplatonists and Christians admitted that Platonism and Christianity were in surprising agreement on many points. They even spoke of a dependence, but each side interpreted the dependence differently: Christians saw Plato as dependent on Moses and the prophets,[24] while Platonists saw our Lord as dependent on Plato. Ambrose rejected this last claim in a work, now lost, entitled *Philosophy*, in which "he wrote with great care and a wealth of detail against the stupid and arrogant people who claimed the Lord had profited from Plato's works."[25] According to Simplicianus, a certain Platonic philosopher (Marius Victorinus?[26]) used to say that the opening words of St. John's Gospel should be written down in gold ink and displayed prominently in all the churches.[27]

As a matter of fact, Augustine found—or believed he had found—in the writings of the Platonists the first part of the Johannine Prologue: the creation of the world, the struggle between light and darkness, the enlightenment of the soul that bears witness to the light but is not itself the light, the happiness of those who through participation in the fullness of the Word are renewed from day to day in wisdom. All this he learned "though the words were different and the meaning was expressed in various ways."[28]

On the other hand, he did not find in these books the second half of the Johannine Prologue, which is no less essential to Christianity than the first half and, from the standpoint of what is specifically Christian, is even more essential. Augustine points this out. "I did not read in them that *the word was made flesh and dwelt among us.*"[29] The haste and incompleteness of his reading did not enable him to see that this fundamental truth was not only not found in these books but was even rejected as a barbarian myth and openly declared impossible. This means that he did not read *Against the Gnostics* by Plotinus[30] or *Against the Christians* by Porphyry.[31] He became aware only later on of the profound opposition between Hellenism and Christianity.[32]

Augustine did, however, immediately perceive and energetically reject the polytheism of these writers. For while they accepted the oneness of God they did not exclude the worship of lesser deities; they admitted in practice and justified in theory the traditional idolatry.[33] We cannot say whether Augustine was alert to still other errors, such as metempsychosis.[34] On the other hand, he accepted certain doctrinal principles that he later rejected. It will be enough to mention the view of Porphyry that calls upon humans to flee everything corporeal *(corpus est omne fugiendum)*, as an essential condition for the attainment of happiness.[35]

It is perhaps worth calling attention to the fact that while Augustine accepted Neoplatonic spiritualities, he quickly corrected its exaggerations on essential points. The spiritualism that he followed and defended was Christian and not Hellenistic; that is, while energetically defending the spirituality of the soul, it regards the body as a creature of God and sees body and soul as together making up human nature and together providing the condition for full happiness.[36]

To use Augustine's own allegorical image, he behaved as the Israelites did when they left Egypt: just as they took with them the gold of the Egyptians,[37] so he made his own the good things in the books of the Platonists and abandoned their errors.[38]

What he found there was so sublime and enlightening that he thought he had now reached the goal he had longed for through so many years. He was mistaken. The goal was still distant.

15

"I took up Paul the Apostle"

ANOTHER obstacle, one to which Augustine had not given sufficient thought, now made itself felt: the obstacle of naturalism. Until now he had always been preoccupied with wisdom, but not with the way of reaching it. He had fallen in love with wisdom when he read the *Hortensius*, had lost the true idea of it while a Manichaean, and had now recovered it with the help of the Neoplatonists. He had not, however, asked himself by what path and by what means he was to gain possession of wisdom. This problem—the equally fundamental problem of mediation—had not had a place in his thinking. Neither Cicero, nor the Manichaeans, nor the Platonists had even raised it, to say nothing of answering it.

The Manichaeans thought of themselves as the "saviors" of God. The Neoplatonists proposed a rational and self-sufficient "ascent" to the realm of ideas. In this they were in continuity with an essential concept in paganism: had not Cicero said[1] and Horace sung[2] that human beings ask Jove for wealth and health but not for virtue? The attainment of happiness was therefore not mediated but direct; it depended not on divine aid but on natural human powers. Plotinus said while dying: "I struggle to restore the divine in me to the divine that is in all."[3]

As a result, when with the help of the Platonists Augustine glimpsed the authentic face of wisdom, he thought he needed only to turn to it, embrace it with all the energies of his soul, and take possession of it. He tried to do so but did not succeed. His heart's passionate yearning suffered a check, and he had to undertake a further search. A new problem had arisen.

Here, from his first book, is his own story of the phases of this new experience.

> Certain books . . . lit an unbelievable fire in me, unbelievable even to me when I think of it. I quickly entered wholly into myself. I turned my gaze . . . to the religion that had been instilled in me

from childhood and had become part of my very being; it was attracting me without my realizing it. And so . . . I took up Paul the Apostle . . . and read him with the utmost attention and devotion. . . .

Then . . . philosophy revealed its face to me so clearly that if I could have shown it, I will not say to you [Romanianus], who have always hungered for this unknown, but to that adversary of yours . . . he too would have straightway abandoned and despised his baths and pleasant gardens . . . and everything that roused in him the keen desire of pleasure, and he would have run to this beauty, as one filled with wonder and breathless ardor like a chastely passionate lover.[4]

The *Confessions* help us understand this initial autobiographical notice. Above all, they tell us that this unbelievable fire—the second one lit in the soul of Augustine[5]—led to an experiment in "ecstasy." Perhaps he had read that Plotinus "by an incredible act had four times attained to the vision of the end. For him the ultimate end was intimate union with the god who is above all things." The statement is from Porphyry, who admits to having the same experience on one occasion, when he was sixty-eight years old.[6] Or perhaps Augustine had not read these passages after all; perhaps the wisdom that revealed itself to him was so beautiful that he was carried along by it irresistibly and, driven by a strong impulse of awe-filled love, he desired to detach himself from all else and cling to it.

He ascended step by step from bodily things to the soul; within the soul, from the sense powers which we have in common with the beast to the activity of reason and from this in turn to the intellect that is enlightened by the changeless light. "And so, in the twinkle of a trembling glance, my mind reached that WHICH IS." "But," he continues, "I could not fix my gaze upon [invisible things]. In my weakness I was beaten back and returned to my old habits. I carried nothing with me but a loving memory and a longing after something whose scent I had, as it were, perceived, but was not yet able to feed upon."[7]

This experience, though ending in failure, was very valuable.[8] In it Augustine made two discoveries: of God as changeless Light and subsistent Truth, and of the impossibility for weak and sinful human beings to reach God by their own powers alone. The second discovery was not less important than the first. Augustine was beginning to grasp the difference "between those who see the place that they must reach, but do not see the way to it, and those who see the way itself that leads not only to the vison of that blessed country but also to the actual dwelling therein."[9] He had no choice now but to look for that way.[10] "So I seized eagerly upon the venerable writings inspired by your Holy Spirit, especially those of the apostle Paul."[11]

Reading Scripture with a new eye

When he was nineteen he had turned to Sacred Scripture after reading the *Hortensius*.[12] Now, at thirty-two he did the same thing. His reading of the Neoplatonists had made him enthusiastic for the goal by showing him its beauty, but it had not shown him any way to the goal except the inadequate and unsound way of reason and human nature as left to themselves. Therefore he turned once again to Scripture. This time he did so with success, because his interior dispositions had changed.[13]

As he read, he was aware of finding in St. Paul what he had read—or thought he had read—in the books of the Platonists. But he also found something those books had not contained: the ineffable mystery of Christ, the depths of which he did not yet realize.[14] In the pages of Paul, Augustine encountered Christ—not simply Christ the Teacher, whom he had always acknowledged, but Christ the incarnate Word, the Redeemer of the race, the source of grace. He also came to know the humility that confesses its own insufficiency and pleads for grace; the sacrifice of praise that offers thanks to God for his gifts; the pledge of the Holy Spirit, which is the basis for our hope of reaching the goal.

"I sought for the way of acquiring strength sufficient to enjoy you, and I could not till I embraced *the mediator between God and human beings, Jesus Christ. . . .* For *the Word was made flesh* so that your Wisdom, by which you have created all things, might become milk for our infancy."[15]

"Those other books have nothing of this. Those writings have not the feature of this piety, the tears of confession, *your sacrifice, a troubled spirit, a contrite and humbled heart*, nothing of the salvation of the people, of the Bridal city, of the zeal of the Holy Spirit, nor of the cup of our ransom."[16]

It was at the end of this long and wearisome journey on which so many errors had been clarified one after another, that the face of "philosophy" finally appeared to him. It was the "philosophy" of St. Paul, which contained both the truth the Platonists had reached and the truth proper to Christianity. It was the "philosophy" of God the creator "whose attributes—his eternal power and his divinity—have been visible since the creation of the world, being recognized through the things he has made" (Rom 1:20). It was the "philosophy" of Christ who is "the power and the wisdom of God" (1 Cor 1:24), his "image begotten before every creature" (Col 1:15), the one who "stripped himself and took the nature of a slave" (Phil 2:7) so that he might be "our wisdom and justice and sanctification and redemption" (1 Cor 1:30). It was the "philosophy" of the cross and Christian humility.

Augustine reproached himself for not having known this "philosophy" of humility before reading St. Paul. "Not being humble, I did not comprehend the humility of my God, Jesus Christ, nor did I understand what lesson his human weakness was meant to teach."[17] He would also reproach the Neoplatonists for being unwilling to accept it. "What reason did you have for not wanting to become Christians, except that Christ came in humility and you are proud?"[18]

The reproach was addressed in fact to all non-Christians, because the lesson of humility does not occur in the books of the other peoples: "not in the books of the Epicureans or in those of the Stoics, the Manichaeans, and the Platonists." "Everywhere you will find excellent precepts of morality and education, but you will not find humility. The way of humility . . . comes from Christ."[19]

Augustine had now overcome skepticism, materialism, rationalism, and naturalism. He had encountered Christ the Redeemer. He knew the goal and the way to it. We might say he had now been converted. And so he had—intellectually.

16

The Example of Antony

ACONVERSION, especially in the case of someone like
Augustine, who makes great intellectual demands
and at the same time has high moral aspirations, is a
complex and profound event. As such, it never has a
monocausal explanation.

If Augustine's sight had been set on a life in conformity with
the precepts of the Gospel, he would have faced few problems. As
a man who was austere and generous, faithful to the woman with
whom he lived, and a kind father, he could have received baptism, celebrated his marriage in the Church, and looked forward
to the "presidency" which he thought would not be long in coming. He would have been a good Christian, a good administrator,
and, in his free time, a good philosopher—one of many whose
names, if not whose works, history has preserved for us.

But he looked higher and contemplated a more demanding
life in which he would put aside earthly hopes and have the time
to devote himself unreservedly to wisdom. Such had been his intention at the age of nineteen: to seek wisdom and, having found
it, follow after it with his "whole" soul.[1] True enough, the intention produced no result, but this was due to the fact (this is his
own explanation) that he had not yet found wisdom. Scripture
had disappointed him,[2] the Manichaeans had not convinced him,[3]
and the Neoplatonists, though revealing the face of wisdom to
him, had also made him feel more strongly than ever the impossibility of gaining possession of it.[4]

Now, however, after his new and careful reading of the sacred books, he had reached a certainty that gave serenity: he
knew henceforth the authority in which he should place his trust,
he knew henceforth the true face of wisdom and the way to gain
possession of it. What, then, yet remained to be done? Nothing at
the level of ideas, everything at the level of the affections. The
need that had led him at nineteen to his noble purpose now made
itself felt anew and more imperiously—and there were no ex-

cuses left. "I could no longer claim that I had no clear perception of the truth—the excuse that I used to make to myself for postponing my renunciation of the world and my entry into your service—for by now I was quite certain of it."[5]

However, there were many powerful obstacles to his putting into practice this plan that would at the same time satisfy the felt need. Yet he was unwilling to be a Christian except on these terms. His friend Verecundus said the same thing of himself, but he was now married and therefore unable to adopt such a way of life.[6]

The obstacles to be overcome were three: wealth, honors, and women.[7] The first was in fact not really a great obstacle, the second was greater, the third the greatest of all.

After reading the *Hortensius* as a young man he had ceased to desire riches and would, if riches came, use little for himself and be generous with the rest.[8] Ambition for success held sway longer over his heart. It was the sole or principal motive that had taken him from Tagaste to Carthage, from Carthage to Rome, from Rome to Milan. But even ambition had taken second place to love of wisdom. His teaching career had become burdensome and distasteful. Simplicianus told Augustine of how, when Emperor Julian prohibited Christians from teaching literature, Victorinus, now a convert, gave up his post. Augustine thought this action as fortunate as it was courageous, since it gave Victorinus the opportunity to devote himself entirely to God. "I longed to do the same," Augustine comments, "but I felt bound, not by the chains of another's will, but by my own will, which had the strength of iron chains."[9] This enchaining will was his love of women.

He was determined to marry. In lengthy conversations with Alypius he had tried to persuade this friend that, even if married, they could together devote themselves to the pursuit of wisdom. Alypius denied this, but Augustine insisted, "pointing to the example of those who though married had studied wisdom and pleased God, and had faithfully kept and loved their friends."[10] A project for a "monastery" of philosophers never got started because of the anticipated refusal of the wives involved, but this failure again did not turn Augustine from his intention of marrying.[11]

The person most in favor of his marriage was Monica. She was an intelligent and practical woman and believed that only in marriage could her son live the Christian ideal that was drawing him ever more strongly.

It was Monica too—as the *Confessions* suggest without saying so—who looked out for a suitable young woman. Her choice fell on a girl of Milan. Augustine proposed and was accepted. The girl was still too young by two years for marriage, but the choice pleased him and he was willing to wait.[12] We may assume that the girl was everything that the prospective husband looked for in an ideal wife: "beautiful, chaste, obedient, educated, or at least easy for you to teach, and bringing enough of a dowry . . . that she would not be a burden for a husband needing leisure for study."[13]

Mother of Adeodatus

Why did he not think of regularizing his union with the mother of Adeodatus? From our modern viewpoint this would seem to have been the most logical solution and even the only just one. But it did not happen. Why?

The reader who wants to understand this obscure incident in the life of the still unconverted Augustine must realize, first of all, that the reason was not a lack of love. Augustine loved this woman who had been at his side for fourteen years and to whom he had always been faithful. The separation from her made his heart bleed. He tells us so in a profoundly moving passage of the *Confessions:* "When the woman with whom I was living was torn from my side . . . this was a blow that crushed my heart to bleeding, because I loved her dearly."

The reason, then, lay elsewhere, and the *Confessions* tell us what it was: she was an obstacle to his marriage: "The woman . . . was torn from my side as an obstacle to my marriage." But they do not tell us why she was an obstacle. We are therefore forced to hypothesize—an unsure and risky method, as everyone knows. Why, then, was she an "obstacle to my marriage"? Was the reason spiritual, economic, or social? All three suggestions are possible and have been made. The first, however, does not seem to me to be well-founded, and the second is insufficient. The real reason must have been social. If the mother of Adeodatus was, as she seems to have been, of lowly condition, civil law would have kept the marriage from being fully recognized.

In any case, it is not possible to accuse Augustine of either insensibility or fault. The former contradicts the evidence of the *Confessions*, and the second is not confessed. Yet if there had been a fault, Augustine, so scrupulously remorseful for his sins and so sincere in admitting them, would not have failed to say so. Nor would he have failed to reproach his mother as he does for other less serious attitudes, if he had seen something less than upright in her conduct. There was, then, no consciousness of a fault. The separation, though painful, must have seemed inevitable to all concerned. Even to inflexible Alypius. Even to the woman herself, who in any case must have seen from the beginning how the affair must inevitably end.

Certainly there were no illusions for the second woman with whom Augustine lived for a while when the first had departed and while he was engaged and waiting to marry the young woman from Milan in two years' time. This awareness makes the unnamed mother of Adeodatus all the more deserving of respect, since she gave Augustine everything and asked for nothing in return. When she realized that she was an obstacle to his becoming settled in life, she returned to Africa, leaving her son behind and "making a vow . . . never to know any other man."[14]

Prayer

Meanwhile things were coming to a head and turning Augustine's life in a new direction. The contrast between his interior aspirations and his daily habits was becoming sharper, more tragic, more rending. The voice of philosophy advised him, for the freedom of his soul, to renounce marriage.[15] To it was now added the stronger and more authoritative voice of St. Paul and the Gospel, which, without forbidding marriage, issued an invitation to a higher state, and did so in words pregnant with mystery: perfect continence is indeed a choice, but it is also a gift from God.[16]

A new idea was thus taking shape: if he was to attain to the goal he both desired and struggled against, he would need to rely not on his own strength but on the help of grace. He would have to pray. Ever since his youth he had asked God for continence, but he had added that he did not want the gift too soon: "Give me chastity and continence, but not yet."[17] Now he felt that he must pray to be granted it immediately.

Meanwhile he was increasingly persuaded that it would be better to consecrate himself to the love of God than to yield to his own passions, but he added, with an untranslatable play on the Latin words *vincere* and *avvincere:* "While I wanted to follow the first course and was convinced that it was right, I was still a slave to the pleasure of the second."[18] The bonds of passion, forged by habit, inflicted the *dura servitus* or "harsh slavery" of which the *Confessions* tell us. Liberation would come through a combination of two providential events: the story told by Ponticianus and the voice crying "Take and read!"

For reasons Augustine could not later recall, a man named Ponticianus, an African employed at the imperial court, came to visit him and was surprised to find the letters of St. Paul lying on a table used for games. He began to tell the story of Antony (whose *Life,* written by Athanasius, had been known in the West for some decades now) and the many monasteries in Egypt. He also told Augustine of the sudden conversion of two soldiers at Trier: after reading the life of Antony, they left their fiancees, consecrated themselves to God, and entered a monastery outside of Milan, of which Ambrose himself was the superior.[19] The story was new to Augustine and it astonished him. He had not even suspected that the consecrated life for men was such a vital movement in the Catholic Church; in fact, he did not know that such a thing even existed.

This discovery, the final one on his long journey of spiritual development, caused an interior upheaval and prepared the way for the resolution of the drama going on in his soul. On hearing such examples of conversion he was ashamed of himself, felt his own baseness, and knew that he had no excuses left. He felt a need of solitude and tears that he had never felt before. Hardly had Ponticianus left, when Augustine, followed by his inseparable friend Alypius, went out into the garden attached to the house, and gave free rein to his tears.[20]

We do not know how long this dramatic struggle of Augustine with himself went on. We do know, however, that the strug-

gle took place not at the level of Christian virtue, as a struggle between virtue and vice, but at the deeper level of the choice of a
way of Christian life, a choice between marriage and complete
continence. After many prayers and tears he chose complete continence.

The choice was hastened "when I heard the voice of a child—
whether of a boy or a girl I cannot say—singing repeatedly the refrain 'Take and read, take and read.' " He had not heard such
words used in any children's game and therefore took them as a
command from heaven. He got up, went over to where Alypius
was, opened the letters of St. Paul, and read the first verse on
which his eye fell: it was an exhortation to chastity (Rom 13:13).
At that moment his heart was filled with a light and certainty that
banished all the darkness of doubt.[21] The choice was made, and
made for good. "You converted me to yourself, so that I sought
for neither a wife nor any hope in this world."[22]

17

From *Against the Academics* to *True Religion*

THE long-desired goal had been reached, but Augustine did not feel satisfied. For him, as indeed for every convert, conversion was both a point of arrival and a point of departure. He had attained to faith, but he was impatient to plumb its content; for love of wisdom he had broken all earthly bonds, but he wanted to go further and embrace wisdom, take possession of it, and enjoy it permanently. What his dispositions were at the time he himself tells us not long after the event. In dedicating his book *The Happy Life* to Manlius Theodore he describes briefly the course of his interior development, and concludes:

> You can see what kind of philosophy it is that I have reached like a man sailing into a safe harbor. But the harbor is a very large one, and its very size can be a source of errors, although admittedly less serious ones. For I still do not know to what precise part of the shore I should sail and land, as being the only true place of happiness. What solid results have I achieved if I still suffer doubt and hesitation with regard to the problem of the soul? That is why I appeal to you as a humane and generous man, and in the name of the bonds uniting our souls, to stretch out your hand to me. . . . If you do me this favor, I think I shall be able with little effort to reach the state of happiness that I believe you already possess.[1]

At about this same time, he says to his mother in his dialogue *On Order:*

> We trust that you above all, Mother, will see to it that these good intentions bear fruit. For it was because of your prayers—of this I am sure and I bear witness—that God inspired me to value knowledge of the truth above everything else and to will, plan, and love nothing but this. Therefore I continue to believe that your prayers will win for us the great blessing to which your merits encourage us to aspire.[2]

Augustine thus saw himself with a twofold task, one intellectual, the other ascetical, both of them parts of an effort to ascend into the sphere of the mystical life. He felt himself to be hence-forth—and in fact he was—what his mother called him shortly before her death: a servant of God.[3] But he also continued to be what he had always been: a philosopher. Moreover, now that a firm choice had been made after long travail, he saw opening before him greater possibilities for the questing mind that was henceforth to be at the service of the faith. The thinker had been transformed into an apostle.

The thinker-become-apostle

His intellectual program is set down for us in the final pages of his first book, *Against the Academics:*

> Everyone knows that the stimulus to knowledge comes to us from two sources: authority and reason. I am utterly certain that I shall never diverge from the authority of Christ, for I know of none that could be greater. As for that of which keen reason is capable (for my state of mind is such that I ardently desire to gain truth by understanding as well as by faith), I am confident that for the moment I can find in the Platonists teachings which are not out of harmony with the sacred mysteries of faith.[4]

Augustine's ascetico-mystical program can be summed up in the words of the *Soliloquies,* where it is expounded at length. In order to see God, "the soul needs three dispositions: it must have eyes that it can use properly, it must look, and it must see. The 'eyes of the soul' are a mind free of every corporeal stain, that is, a mind already separated and purified from the desire for transitory things."[5] Ascetical effort is in the service of mystical insight.

Finally, his apostolic program (an apostolate of the mind) is indicated in his first letter. It is the ambitious program of a man who wants to give others renewed hope of finding truth. "In our time, when there are no philosophers left (I cannot think that the fellows going around in philosphers' cloaks are worthy of the name), it seems to me that people need to be given hope once again of finding truth, wherever the Academics with their subtle arguments have dissuaded them from seeking to understand things."[6]

Augustine immediately set to work. He continued in his teaching position until the now proximate Fall vacation (which

began around August 23), then he resigned his chair and withdrew into solitude in the Brianza region.[7] Here he prepared for his
baptism by an intense interior life, which as already indicated
was both intellectual and ascetical.

These two aspects mark the life of Augustine down to the
point when Providence turned it in a new direction. They are to be
seen, in other words, at Cassiciacum, Milan, Rome, and Tagaste.
If we are to grasp the true personality of the recent convert, we
must see this happy combination of aspects at work.

Cassiciacum

Augustine reached Cassiciacum, a country house placed at
his disposal by a friend named Verecundus, in the early days of
November. With him came his mother, his brother Navigius, his
friend Alypius, two fellow-citizens and disciples, Trigentius and
Licentius, his cousins Lastidianus and Rusticus, and his son
Adeodatus. Philosophical discussions began almost immediately
on November 9 or 10.

There were fifteen such discussions, all held in November
and focused on three fundamental points: certitude, happiness,
and evil. Meanwhile Augustine was reflecting in his own mind on
the necessity of purification and the immortality of the soul. The
result of the discussions and the thinking was four works,
Against the Academics, The Happy Life, On Order, and the *Soliloquies.* The subjects discussed, four of them metaphysical and
one moral, had their place in the great program of Christian philosophy that the new convert was boldly setting out to develop.

He began with epistemology, or the critique of knowledge,
which is at the basis of every philosophy. In the face of widespread skepticism, people had to recover the hope of finding
truth. Augustine therefore wrote against the Academics. He did
so, not, as has been claimed,[8] because he himself was still more or
less a skeptic, but because he wanted to remove, for himself and
others, every obstacle to the quest of truth.

The objections raised by the Academics did indeed still disturb him, not however because he found them cogent, but because of the great esteem in which these philosophers were held.
He thought it unlikely that thinkers like Carneades and Ar-

cesilaus had professed skepticism, a doctrine that cannot stand up to criticism. For it is quite clear that the mind adheres firmly and without the least doubt to many truths of a mathematical, logical, and sapiential kind. Similarly, with regard to sense perception (the Academics laid great stress on mistakes in this area), how is it possible to refute someone who claims to be conscious of perception and says, for example, "I am conscious that my ear takes delight in this sound"?[9] Thus self-consciousness (I know that I am, I know that I am thinking, I know that I am loving) does away with any possibility of skepticism.

With these arguments in mind Augustine concluded that the Academics did not really teach skepticism but rather used it as part of their esoteric method. They thought they could not convince people of the truth and therefore they chose to conceal it by proving fallacious the arguments of those who, like the Epicureans and Stoics, made knowledge of the truth a matter of sense perception.[10]

The residents of Cassiciacum discussed another and no less fundamental theme, happiness: its conditions, its nature, and its object. Their conclusion was that only in perfect knowledge of God could happiness be found.[11] They also confronted the serious and anguishing subject of evil. Do blessings and evil alike play a part in the plan of Providence? Augustine outlined an affirmative answer, but then, seeing that the discussion was becoming too difficult for the participants (and perhaps for himself as well), he turned their thoughts to the order to be followed in study and showed them how to rise from corporeal things to spiritual.[12]

The point, however, at which Augustine's passion for truth found explosive expression was in his reflections on the problem of death and immortality. There were now no other participants to make the discussion difficult, and he could launch out freely on the path of metaphysics. Here is the dialogue between himself and reason with which he introduces the decisive argument. (This, as everyone knows, is based on the presence of truth in the soul: since truth is immortal, so must the soul be.)

> *R[eason]*: Do not grieve: the human soul is immortal.
> *A[ugustine]*: How do you prove this?

R. By the principles you granted earlier, not, I think, without great circumspection.

A. I recall not having answered any of your questions lightly. But sum up for me briefly, please, and let us see where this long and winding path has brought us.

R. I shall do as you wish, but please pay close attention.

A. Go on, I am ready. Do you want me to die of suspense?[13]

Readers who look only at the general direction of these discussions will regard Augustine simply as a philosopher and even, as has been maintained, a philosopher not yet fully a Christian. If, however, we paid heed to all the details of the discussions, we find not only a Christian who believes in the Trinity, the divinity of Christ, and the sacred mysteries of the Church, but also an ascetic who is dedicated to an austere manner of life and anxious to reach the heights of contemplation. The *Confessions* only confirm and extend these areas of light.

His day began[14] and ended[15] with prayer. He spent half of the night in meditation,[16] often bathed in tears.[17] During the day his attention was given to philosophical discussions, household duties, and the instruction of his disciples Trigentius and Licentius. He spent little time at table, eating only what was strictly needed for allaying hunger[18]; he could even joke that the beginning and end of his meals coincided.[19]

Proofs of active interior life

Some proofs of this interior life are the lengthy prayer prefixed to the *Soliloquies* and the first book of this same work. He reveals here the degree of asceticism he had already reached and the wounds from which, with almost daily tears, he asked the Lord to free him.[20] These included especially the habits of his recent past, which were vividly present to his imagination and ready to test his constancy of purpose or, in any case, to make his weakness clear to him. Thus confronted with passions that were now overcome but not yet fully mastered interiorly, the new convert found no help but prayer, humility, and trust in God, for he was certain that God would, in his own time, lead him to the vision of ideal beauty to which he aspired. When his reason reminds him of his interior condition he answers in anguished tones:

Be silent, please! Be silent! Why do you torment me in this way? Why do you delve so deeply into my heart? I can no longer hold back my tears. I make no more promises, nor do I any longer flatter myself on my intentions. No more questions on that point! You say, do you not, that he whom I long to see knows when I shall have become healthy? Let him do as he pleases. Let him show himself when it pleases him: I submit wholly to his merciful care, for I am firmly convinced that he cannot fail to sustain those who put their trust in him. I shall make no statement about the health of my soul until I shall have seen his beauty.[21]

The glowing litany of love that opens the *Soliloquies* is born of that same anguish. All should read or reread that long prayer if they want to discover the real, the innermost Augustine of Cassiciacum. Here is a short sample from it.

God, you purify us and prepare us for divine rewards: be merciful to me. . . . Henceforth it is you alone I love, you alone I follow, you alone I seek, you alone I am ready to serve, for you alone rule justly, and I desire to be dependent on you. Command and ordain whatever you will, but heal and open my ears that I may hear your words. . . . Tell me where I should look in order to see you, and I hope that then I will be able to do all that you may command me. Lord and most merciful Father, receive back, I pray you, your fugitive slave. . . . Welcome me, your servant, as I flee from the things that welcomed me, a stranger, when I was fleeing from you! I know that I must return to you; open your door to me when I knock; teach me the way to you. . . . If those who take refuge in you find you by faith, grant me faith; if by virtue, grant me virtue; if by knowledge, grant me knowledge. Increase my faith, my hope, my love.[22]

In the *Confessions*, about twelve years later, Augustine records with pleasure and gratitude the "great blessings" he had received during the time at Cassiciacum and the ardent prayers he addressed to God there while meditating on the Psalms.[23]

Milan

When Augustine returned to Milan at the beginning of March in order to enroll for baptism, he continued his studies and interior ascension to God. He attended the baptismal catechesis, took part in the liturgical celebrations, and was moved to tears by the singing of sacred hymns. He meditated at length on the history of salvation, so full of mercy and mystery,[24] and visited the monastery of Ambrose outside the city walls.[25] Finally, he received baptism during the night of Holy Saturday, April 24-25, 387.

Meanwhile he continued his scholarly activity. He made some jottings, which never became more than an outline, on the immortality of the soul; they were intended as a prolongation of *Soliloquies*.[26] He conceived a vast encyclopedia of the liberal arts, along the lines of Varro, in which he would show the reader how to use material things as a stairway to God. Of the manuals making up such an encyclopedia he did write one *On Grammar*, which is lost. He began his book *Music* which would be completed, to the end of the part on rhythm, at Tagaste, and jotted notes for volumes on logic, rhetoric, geometry, arithmetic, and philosophy, but even these notes too are lost.[27] It is regrettable that he did not complete his projected encyclopedia, not so much for the information it might have supplied us on the liberal arts (this we can obtain from other sources) as for the rich teaching it would have given on the method for rising from these to God. Anyone who has read the sixth book of *Music* will certainly share this regret, even while being consoled thereby for the lack of the other manuals.

But perhaps Augustine had not realized the labor involved in writing at such length of ideas that he now considered puerile and trifling. He displays his uneasiness at the beginning of the sixth book of his *Music*, where he says:

> For five books now I have been dwelling at excessive length, and in really puerile fashion, on the study of rhythms that belong to time. But perhaps my benevolent readers will forgive this trifling when they consider the value of the work. I undertook it in order to help youths, and indeed men and women of any age, . . . to detach themselves, under the guidance of reason, and not hastily but by steps as it were, from their bodily senses and love of literature (to which it is difficult for them not to be attached), and, out of love for changeless truth, to unite themselves to God, the Lord of all things, who directs the activities of the human mind without the mediation of any creature.
>
> Those who read the preceding books, then, will find us in the company of grammarians and poets, not from any desire to remain in their company, but as a requirement of the journey.[28]

Meanwhile Augustine was looking for a place of residence where he could more easily implement his program of asceticism and study. The friends who were now living together and were bent on following Augustine in his "holy intention"[29] agreed that they should all return to Africa.[30] An important reason for this decision may have been the desire of Monica who, now that her mission was completed, wished to return to her hills and end her days where her mission had begun and her husband Patricius had been laid to rest.

But even apart from this legitimate desire of Monica, Tagaste may well have seemed the best solution. All the members of the little community of ascetics were from Tagaste. Moreover, Tagaste with its rich countryside and the many country houses scattered throughout it met all the desirable conditions: a place apart yet not isolated; far from the big cities but near the main arteries of communication. It was not that Augustine liked to travel. Far from it![31] But in addition to the tranquillity required for meditation and prayer, he needed a great many books and a good supply of writing materials. Besides, over there in Africa he still had his father's properties. And, in fact, one of these, a country villa, provided this first community of African cenobites with their first residence.[32]

Some months after his baptism, therefore, before summer's end and even before the beginning of September,[33] he set out on his return. This time he did not travel by public conveyance at the expense of the state but at his own expense, with less comfort and greater fatigue. The journey would have taken about twenty days. The route probably was the same one by which he had traveled north: the Via Emilia, the Via Flaminia, the Furlo Gap, Rome, and Ostia Tiburtina.

Rome

We do not know whether the company stayed a while in Rome before moving on to Ostia. To our disappointment, the *Confessions* are silent on this point and on the even more important question of whether Augustine returned to Rome after his mother's death. "I pass over many things because I am pressed for time. Accept my confessions and my gratitude, O my God, for many things that I am silent about."[34] He was in a hurry to tell of his mother's life and of what happened at Ostia before and after her death. We know, however, from other writings that after his mother's death Augustine returned to the eternal city with his friends and stayed there until after the assassination of the usurper Maximus,[35] which occurred, according to various sources, on July 28 or July 29 of 388.[36] Monica's death had occurred before November 13 of the previous year, when Augustine had not yet reached his thirty-fourth birthday.[37]

Why did he return to Rome? Had the annual sailing season ended? Did he want to find out about the religious life of Rome? Was it the presence of Maximus' troops in Italy? The sources provide little information. We do know that while in Rome he was interested in the life of the monasteries of men and women that had begun to flourish there for some years now; that he continued his studies in spirituality and philosophy; and that he began his defense of Catholic doctrine against the Manichaeans.

With regard to the monasteries, whose prudent administration and spirit of charity filled him with admiration, he wrote: "I became acquainted with many of them in Rome too; over each of them presided a person endowed with great seriousness, prudence, and knowledge of things divine, while the others who resided with this superior lived in charity, holiness, and Christian freedom. . . . This applied not only to men but to women as well."[38]

Ideas on spirituality

As I noted, he also developed his ideas on spirituality, writing a book on *The Greatness of the Soul,* and on philosophy, beginning his great book on *Free Will.* In the first of these two books he describes the stages of the spiritual life leading from purification to contemplation; these stages include: virtue, tranquillity, entrance into light, abiding in light. In the first stage the soul is liberated from control by the senses; in the second it is restored to health and interior tranquillity; in the third it is guided to the light of wisdom; in the fourth, which is proper to the perfect, it bathes in the radiance of that light.[39]

The philosophical question that most occupied him was the difficult and complex one of the origin of evil. He was endeavoring to grasp with his mind what he already professed by faith as a result of his submission to the divine authority. His attitude was that of the Christian philosopher. The general question included many more specific ones that he explicitly raised and answered. These had to do with the freedom by which the law is violated and from which moral evil comes into existence; the existence of God the creator of all things, including freedom; divine foreknowledge; the presence of evil in the world, that is, of the evil that human beings do not commit but suffer. Only the first of these questions was discussed at Rome; the others were discussed at Hippo in Africa, after Augustine's ordination to the priesthood.[40]

Meanwhile he also began his controversy with his former coreligionists, the Manichaeans.

> While residing in Rome after my baptism, I could not tolerate in silence the boasting of the Manichaeans about the continence or false and deceptive abstinence that led them, for the purpose of deceiving the ignorant, to prefer themselves to true Christians, with whom in fact they were not to be compared. I therefore wrote two books, one on *The Morals of the Catholic Church*, the other on *The Morals of the Manichaeans*.[41]

He revised the work and published it in Africa, probably in the following year.[42] The subject gave him an opportunity to go more deeply into a theme that he had very much at heart: love. The whole of the Christian law is in in fact based upon and summed up in love; it is love, too, that establishes the harmony between the two Testaments.

There is no doubt that during the approximately ten months of this second stay in Rome Augustine did not think only of visiting monasteries and writing books. He now saw Christian Rome itself with new eyes, and everything that could express and strengthen his faith was of interest to him. He knelt at the monuments *(tropaea)* of the Apostles, visited the tombs of the martyrs, and took part in the Catholic life of the city. We do not know whether he met Pope Siricius and became friendly with the ecclesiastical circles of Rome.

We do know, however, that his memories and love of the eternal city, which he never visited again, were indelibly impressed on his heart. They were dramatically revived at the time of Alaric's invasion of Rome. Occupied though he was on that sad occasion with defending Christianity from pagan attacks, he thought of Rome and, even though the city was now a smoking ruin, he hoped and predicted that it would endure. "Look," people were saying, "now that the world is Christian Rome has perished." Augustine answered: "Rome has been scourged, but not slain; it has been chastised, but not destroyed. Rome will not perish if the Romans do not perish. They will not perish if they praise God, but they will if they blaspheme him. What, after all, is Rome, if not the Romans?"[43]

Tagaste

After the death of Maximus Augustine paid his final respects to the tomb of his mother, on the marble slab of which Anicius Achenius Bassus would have the well-known epitaph inscribed in the early years of the fifth century.[44] The friends then left Italy forever, landed at Carthage, where they stayed for a few days,[45] then traveled up the valley of the Medjerda and settled at Tagaste.

In the cheerful and sweet-scented atmosphere of his native place, out in the open countryside where the trees were green and the birds sang, Augustine set about implementing the plan of life that he had conceived at Milan and thought out at Rome. Possidius writes:

> Once he had received the gift of grace he determined to return to Africa, to his own house and his own countryside, together with his fellow citizens and friends who had, like him, consecrated themselves to God. Having arrived there, he stayed for about three years. He renounced his possessions and, along with the others who joined him, lived for God in fasting, prayer, and good works, meditating day and night on the law of the Lord. The truth that God revealed to his mind in meditation and prayer he shared with others, present and absent, teaching them in his sermons and books.[46]

This passage brings out clearly the essential points in the Augustinian program: poverty, common life, asceticism, study, and apostolate. The purpose, as Possidius says, was to "live for God" *(vivere Deo)* or, as Augustine himself puts it more daringly, "to sink into the Godhead amid the peace of the contemplative life" *(deificari in otio)*.[47]

The little community made up of Alypius, Evodius, and Adeodatus grew to include others, and Augustine made it his task to teach them "to dwell at peace in themselves"; he would always regard this difficult science as the heart of monastic life. For this reason he did not accept the urgent invitation of Nebridius to move to Carthage.

Intellectual and apostolic program

Meanwhile he continued his intellectual and apostolic program. He wrote *The Teacher*, in the form of a dialogue with his son; he continued his controversy with the Manichaeans in *The Book of Genesis against the Manichaeans;* and he wrote that splendid little book, *True Religion.* The first of these three books gave him an opportunity to set down a basic thesis of pedagogy: God alone teaches the truth to human beings by enlightening them. The purpose of the second work was to give at least a provisional answer to the objections raised by the Manichaeans against Genesis. The third was intended as a short summary of Christian doctrine.

This last work had been promised and was now sent to his friend Romanianus, who was still entangled in Manichaeism.[48] Better than any work he had written up to this point it captures the thought and soul of Augustine. In it he shows "by numerous and copious arguments"[49] that the one true God, the Trinity, is to be honored by authentic religion. Authentic religion is to be found not among the pagans or the heretics, but in the Catholic Church, which alone is "orthodox," that is, "guardian of integral truth."

God leads human beings to salvation by the power of reason and the authority of faith. Reason brings them to God by way of the beauty of created things and in virtue of the light of reason itself. Even the vices of human beings lead them to God, although in a perverse way. Faith, on the other hand, reveals to them the divine plan of salvation that is carried out by means of history and prophecy: history for the past, prophecy for the future. Augustine concludes:

> Since this is the case, I encourage you, dear friends who are so close to me, and I encourage myself no less, to run with all speed to the goal to which God is calling us through his wisdom. . . . Let us not create for ourselves a religion that satisfies our imagination. . . . Let our religion not be a worship of earth and water. . . . Let our religion not take for its object the rational soul, however perfect and wise.[50]

The book contains in germ many ideas that will later be developed in *The City of God.*

The desire to plumb the content of faith more deeply was not limited to Augustine; it became a common concern. As a result, he found himself obliged to teach not only spiritual doctrine, but philosophy, theology, and Sacred Scripture. Evidence of this is a book with the unusual title *A Miscellany of Eighty-three Questions.* It arose out of the questions asked of him by the "brethren" and the answers he gave. The answers were originally written on small sheets of paper and were later collected and turned into a book.[51]

A true monastery

It has been asked whether the house in Tagaste was a true monastery, as the later one in Hippo would be. Possidius shows that he thinks it was. In fact, in describing the life led at Hippo he refers back to Tagaste: ". . . as he had done earlier when he returned home from overseas."[52] A good answer would be that the life at Tagaste was monastic in intention but not completely so in fact. By this I mean that to some extent the tranquillity that Augustine had so greatly desired, the *otium sanctum* (leisure of holy contemplation) to which he wanted to devote himself, was not fully attained.

The citizens of Tagaste were so proud and happy to have this great man in their midst (the fame of his way of life and his high genius had already gone abroad) that they could not refrain from besieging him with their demands. Augustine, always a kindly man, could not bring himself to disappoint them. The result was conflict with his ideal, and therefore deep uneasiness and suffer-

ing. Echos of it even reached Carthage, for Nebridius wrote to
him:

> Can it be true, my dear Augustine, that you are devoting your
> patience and energy to the business of your fellow citizens and still
> do not have the leisure you wanted so badly? Please tell me: who
> is bold enough to impose on you who are so kind? I am sure they
> do not understand the object of your love and ardent desire. Surely
> one or other of your friends could let them know your preferences?
> Why not Romanianus or Lucinianus? Well, let them at least listen
> to me. I will cry out and bear witness that you love God and want
> to serve him and be united to him. I wish I could attract you to my
> own country house, where you would be at peace. It wouldn't
> bother me to be called a tempter by your fellow citizens whom you
> love excessively and who have an excessive love for you.[53]

In this way the plan arose of establishing a monastery far
away from Tagaste. The choice fell on Hippo, a city by the sea.

Part II

The Pastor

18

"The servant must not disagree with his master"

AUGUSTINE therefore went down to Hippo, an ancient and wealthy Numidian city at the mouth of the Seybouse River; its full name was Hippo Regius, to distinguish it from Hippo Zarita in the Proconsular Province. He went with the intention of looking for a place where he could establish a monastery and of meeting a friend whom he hoped to win to the monastic life. He found, instead, an unpleasant surprise and, as he himself says, "violence" done to him.

Here is how, thirty-five years later, he tells the faithful of this incident that determined the course of his entire life:

> I came to your city when I was still a young man, as many of you know, and here I am, your bishop by the grace of God. I was looking for a place in which to establish a monastery and live with my brethren. I had abandoned all worldly hopes; I was no longer willing to become what I might have been, but neither was I looking to be what I now am. "I chose to be lowly in the house of the Lord rather than to live in the tents of sinners" (Ps 83:11). I kept far from lovers of the world, but I did not on that account regard myself as the equal of those who govern the peoples. At my Lord's urging I chose not a high place but the low and humble place where it pleased the Lord to say to me: "Go up higher."
>
> I was so afraid of the episcopate that once my reputation began to spread among the servants of God, I used to avoid places where I knew the bishop's chair to be empty. I was on guard against such a possibility and did what I could to work out my salvation in a lowly walk of life rather than expose myself to the danger of high office. But, as I said, the servant must not disagree with his master. I came to this city to see a friend, with the hope that he would join us in the monastery. I felt safe because a bishop occupied the see. But they laid hold of me and ordained me. Thus, via the priesthood, I came to the episcopate.[1]

We know the sequence of events from other sources. The bishop at the time was Valerius, a Greek by birth who had but an inadequate command of Latin and was now advanced in years. One Sunday in Peace Basilica *(basilica pacis)*, the beautiful cathedral of Hippo, he told the people how badly he needed the help of a priest. Meanwhile, ignorant of the storm that was about to burst on his head, Augustine stood among the faithful and listened. The presence of this man, certainly not completely unknown in Hippo, combined with the words of the bishop to excite the faithful. These were good people but highly emotional and somewhat rough in their ways; perhaps, too, they were irritated by the prostrate condition of their Church as compared with the Donatists. A tumult arose. They approached Augustine, seized him, led him to the bishop, and demanded amid uproar and loud shouts that he be ordained. Augustine's objections and tears were useless. "They laid hold of him and, as is usual in such cases, presented him to the bishop for ordination. They were unanimous in their desire that it should be done, and they repeated their demand heatedly and with loud cries. Augustine wept floods of tears. . . . But in the end he gave in to their wishes."[2]

Such occurrences were not infrequent in that age; Possidius speaks of them as "usual." Some other men ordained against their wishes were Paulinus of Nola[3] and Paulinianus, brother of Jerome and Nepotianus.[4] Possidius tells the same story of a man named Firmus, a convert of Augustine.[5] Twenty years later, the faithful of Hippo tried it once again with a rich aristocrat named Pinianus, but this time the affair turned out differently: neither he nor Augustine would yield to popular pressure.[6]

Torn between monastic and priestly ideals

Augustine himself tells us what his feelings were at the time of his ordination. His heartfelt and profound reluctance sprang from two considerations: the responsibility of the priesthood, which he thought beyond his strength, and what seemed to him an unbridgeable opposition between the monastic ideal, which he was unwilling to renounce, and the priestly ministry. He regarded the priesthood as "the most difficult, laborious, and dangerous office there is in the present life and above all at the present time." True enough, he also thought it "the most blessed in the eyes of God," provided it were carried out in the way prescribed by Christ—but he admitted he did not yet know what this way was.[7] He had written many books of philosophy, spirituality, and apologetics, yet he confessed he did not know. Surely, an admission that should make us think!

His consciousness of his own limitations made him weep. It was understandable, of course, that the people should not realize the true situation. But he realized it and reflected on his degree of preparation which, now that he had suddenly assumed the responsibility, seemed inadequate to the task. He regarded it as certain that the Lord indeed wanted him to be a priest "not in order to condemn him, but as an act of mercy." For this reason he felt even more keenly his obligation to make up for his lack of preparation.

> Now that I recognize my weakness I must carefully seek out all the remedies provided in his Scriptures and, through prayer and reading, ensure that my soul will be strong enough for such dangerous duties. I did not do this sooner because I did not have the time. Once I was ordained I thought I should spend my leisure learning the divine Scriptures, and I arranged things so that I should have freedom for this work. I really did not know as yet what I lacked for a task such as the one that now torments and consumes me.[8]

A special reason for his perturbation was the ministry of the word, which the bishop entrusted to him, thus departing from the general custom of the African Churches and opening himself to the criticism of his colleagues.[9] Augustine admitted that he held fast "with complete faith to whatever is necessary for salvation; but how am I to make use of it for the salvation of others, seeking not what is useful to me but what is profitable for the salvation of many?"

The instructions for carrying out this mission are certainly in the sacred books.

> If a man of God knows and assimilates these he can attend in a more orderly way to Church business or at least live with a more upright conscience amid the throngs of the wicked, or die rather than lose that life to which alone Christians of humble and gentle heart aspire. But how is this to be done if not by asking, seeking, and knocking, as the Lord tells us (Mt 7:7), that is, by prayer, reading, and tears?[10]

The result was that he asked and obtained a delay until Easter.

But there was another reason for Augustine's reluctance to accept the priesthood: the tension and even opposition between monastic life, which provides quiet for meditation, and the priestly ministry, which obliges a man to immerse himself in apostolic action.

Augustine had expressed his thinking on this point some years earlier in a letter to his friend Nebridius. Speaking there of familiarity with death (a theme no less Christian than philosophical), he maintains that

> God grants to a few, those whom he intends should rule the Churches, to look forward to death without fear and desire it ardently, and yet meanwhile to take upon themselves the labor of ruling the Churches. But, in my opinion, neither to those who are drawn to such a ministry by desire of worldly honor nor to those who, though private citizens, would like that kind of busy life does God grant the great blessing of attaining, amid the noise and agitation of assemblies and constant business, this familiarity with death that we are seeking. Yet both groups could well find absorption in God if they lived in a state of quiet peace.

> If I am wrong [he concludes], I am, if not the stupidest, then the laziest of all human beings, since unless I am carefree and at peace I am unable to taste and love the true good.

Interior and exterior detachment

Behind all this is Augustine's conviction that "if human beings are to achieve a complete freedom from fear that is not the result of insensibility or rashness or a desire for empty glory or a superstitious credulity, they must be greatly detached from the tumult of transitory things." From this detachment, both interior and exterior, comes "the solid joy that has nothing in common with any other joy."[11]

Augustine was thinking here of the courageous life of the wise man, of which the Neoplatonic philosophers had spoken so highly.[12] But he found this ideal to be in harmony with that of the Gospel. For this reason he accepted and followed it. As Nebridius put it, Augustine's writings echoed Christ, Plato, and Plotinus.[13] But he did not think and, given his recent past, could not think of himself as one of those to whom the Lord had given the gift of fulfilling a pastoral ministry and at the same time tasting that "solid joy" which was the object of his most deeply felt desires.

When God made his will known through the violence of the mob and the paternal insistence of the bishop, Augustine bowed his head and obeyed; he obeyed with tears, but he obeyed. He showed himself great in two ways: because he was unwilling and because he obeyed. But regret and nostalgia for the blessed state he had lost remained forever in his heart.[14]

Helping the Church

The experience thus forced upon him brought a radical change not only in his daily life but also, and more importantly, in his way of conceiving the service of God. The priestly dimension was now added to the monastic. At Milan he had discovered the Church as guarantor of the Scriptures; in Rome he had discovered her to be mother of all Christians; in Hippo he was now discovering that she needed the help of her own children. From this time forth he continued to promote monastic life but he also urgently recommended that monks accept the priesthood whenever the Church asked them to do so.

> If Mother Church asks for your service, do not accept from an eager desire to go out of the monastery nor refuse it from the tempting desire to do nothing. Instead, obey God with a humble heart. . . . Do not prefer the quiet of contemplation to the needs of the Church; for, if no one among the good were willing to help the Church in begetting new children, you yourselves would not have come to birth in her.[15]

This teaching, which shows the maturity Augustine's thinking on the point had reached, as well as a more profound sense of the Church, was to find its most incisive expression in *The City of God*. There he follows Varro's theory (which distinguished three kinds of life: active, contemplative, and mixed) and says that no one can completely separate the active and contemplative lives and that each kind of life must be on guard against equally serious dangers. He then concludes with this judgment:

> Love of truth seeks the quiet of contemplation (*otium sanctum*), while the urgency of love accepts the activity of the apostolate (*negotium iustum*). If no one imposes this latter burden

on us, let us apply ourselves to study and contemplation of the truth; but if it is imposed on us, we should accept because love urges us to do so. Yet even in this case we ought not to renounce completely the joys that truth brings, lest deprived of that sweetness we be weighed down by the urgency of love.[16]

Augustine regarded the love of truth and the urgency of love, despite the difference in their movements, as more easily harmonizable. Therefore this bold and fruitful innovator brought about and defended a fusion of the monastic and priestly ideals.

19

"Once a priest, he quickly established a monastery"

AUGUSTINE had gone to Hippo to establish a monastery and unexpectedly found himself a priest. The change of direction was a decisive one but it did not cause him to abandon his original ideal, as he told the people later on:

> Knowing my plan and desire to live in a monastery with the brethren, Bishop Valerius of holy memory gave me the plot where the monastery now stands. I began to assemble brethren of goodwill, men who would possess nothing, as I possessed nothing, and were ready to follow my example. I had sold my small property and given the proceeds to the poor; these men who wanted to join me did the same. We would all live from a common store, and that great and most fruitful property that is God would likewise become our common possession.[1]

These words are echoed in those of Possidius who, after telling the story of Augustine's forced ordination, adds that "once a priest, he quickly established a monastery near the church and began to live together with the servants of God according to the way and rule set down in the days of the holy apostles."[2] In words matching those of the Augustinian *Rule*, he indicates "the basic norm of this society," namely, "that no one is to possess anything of his own; everything is to be held in common and distributed to each according to need."[3]

It is easy to conclude that some of those who were living with Augustine at Tagaste likewise moved to Hippo; it is less easy to determine who they were.[4] Adeodatus was certainly not one of them, since he had died in the meantime.

The boy's father had left this moving recollection of him:

> We took with us [for baptism] the boy Adeodatus, born of my flesh and the fruit of my sin. You had given him every gift. He was barely fifteen and surpassed in intelligence many learned and respected men. I praise you for your gifts, O Lord my God, who are the Creator of all and have great power to reshape our deformities. . . . I praise you for your gifts.

> In a book of mine entitled *De magistro* [The Teacher],
> Adeodatus carries on a dialogue with me. You know that all the
> ideas expressed by the second speaker in his discussion are his, al-
> though he was only sixteen when it took place. I also experienced
> more admirable things in him. His intelligence inspired a sacred
> awe in me; but who except you could work such wonders? How-
> ever, you took him from this world early in life, and now I re-
> member him without apprehension, for there was nothing in his
> childhood or his youth or in any part of his life that need make me
> fear for him.[5]

As a consequence of the example and stimulus of the newly
ordained Augustine monastic life quickly spread throughout Africa. Only three years later Paulinus of Nola, writing to Alypius
who was already bishop of Tagaste, asked him to convey affectionate greetings to "the blessed companions and imitators of
Your Holiness, our brothers in the Lord (if they will allow me to
call them such) who are serving the Lord in the Catholic faith in
Carthage, Tagaste, Hippo. . . ."[6]

Church renewal through monastic life

With true zeal Augustine promoted, defended, and organized
monastic life, despite a lack of understanding by the clergy, opposition from the Donatist party, and the defects of the religious
themselves.[7] In this way of life he saw more than a lofty evangelical ideal that took over and validated the sapiential ideal of the
ancient philosophers, while at the same time making it available
to all social classes. He also saw in it an efficacious means of giving new life to the African Church. As he looked around him he
saw the sad situation in which this Church was living: paganism
still influential, Christian life lacking vigor in many respects, the
snares laid by the Manichaeans, the ruthless attacks of the
Donatists, and the infiltration of Arianism. He was inspired
rather than overwhelmed by the difficulties of the task and was
determined to renew this Church that had been the Church of
Cyprian and of Perpetua and Felicity. His purpose would be
served by the monastic movement, which would set a powerful
example and supply learned and devout priests.

His hopes were realized in the monastery of Hippo, and not
there alone, as Possidius tells us.

> The ideal lived by the holy servants of God, their continence, their austere poverty, became daily clearer to all. . . . The Church therefore greatly desired, and received, bishops and clerics from the monastery that owed its existence and progress to that great man. As a result the peace and unity of the Church was established and strengthened.

Augustine's first biographer, who had himself belonged to this monastery before becoming bishop of Calama, goes on to say: "I myself knew about ten holy and estimable men, men of continence and great learning, whom Blessed Augustine agreed to give to various churches, some of them very important ones." He then explains the reason for the rapid advance of African monasticism:

> Those in turn who were inspired by these holy men were scattered throughout the Churches of the Lord and there established monasteries. As their zeal for the prosperity of the Lord's word increased, they prepared for the priesthood brothers who were then placed in other Churches. Thus the teaching of the Church . . . spread by means of many and among many, not only in all parts of Africa but even overseas.[8]

Deeply convinced as he was that monastic life was a great storehouse of energy for pastoral activity, Augustine was unwilling to deprive either himself or his clergy of it when he succeeded Valerius as bishop of Hippo.

> When I became bishop, I realized that a bishop should show continual hospitality to those who visited him or passed through his diocese; otherwise he would be labeled inhospitable. But if such a custom were introduced into the monastery [he is referring to the monastery of laymen, the monastery attached to the church], problems would arise. I therefore decided to have a monastery of clerics right in the bishop's residence.[9]

We know a good deal about the life Augustine lived with his clergy. He himself spoke of it to the people in the year 425, in connection with a painful incident. A priest named Januarius had died and left a will; the will was in favor of the monastery but it was also contrary to the monastic rule. Augustine thought it necessary to intervene in order to avoid scandal and to put an end to the suspicions that were being extended to the entire community.[10] His first biographer goes into the affair in detail.[11]

The life of Augustine and his brother clerics was one of poverty, fellowship, and moderation, and was inspired by the first Christian community in Jerusalem (Acts 2:42-45; 4:32). Apart from the greater freedom of movement that clerics needed, the life was substantially the same as the one lived in the lay monastery that had been, and remained, his dearest ideal.

A completely common life

Poverty was understood as the surrender of all property, as a completely common life, as trust in God and joy in possessing him alone. Augustine, though bishop, was but one of many brethren: he wore clothing that came from the common wardrobe and took his meals at the common table. No exceptions were made in the matter of clothing.

> Let no one accept a gift of a cloak or a woolen tunic or anything else if not in order to put it in the common store; I myself keep in mind my determination to have everything in common and therefore I take what clothing I need from the common wardrobe. . . . Let no one offer me a valuable cloak that might be suitable for a bishop but is not suitable for Augustine, a poor man born of poor parents. . . . I want the kind of cloak I can give to any of my brothers who needs it; one that a priest or deacon or subdeacon can suitably wear. . . . If someone gives me a better one, I sell it as is my custom, so that, while the cloak may not be added to the common store, the price may be; I sell it and give the proceeds to the poor.[12]

There were thus no exceptions for clothing. On the other hand, there were exceptions in food, but the exceptions were for visitors and the sick. According to Possidius, "Augustine's fare was frugal; at times the vegetables were supplemented with meat for the sake of visitors and the physically weaker brethren; on such occasions there was always wine."[13] Meat and wine were consumed as an open challenge to the Manichaeans and in conformity with the teaching of the Apostle: "Everything created by God is good, and nothing is to be rejected if it is received with thanksgiving" (1 Tim 4:4).

"Fellowship" meant the daily exercise of charity, that is, mutual help and support, trust, and avoidance of offenses, ill will, and murmuring. As a help to eliminating this last-named ugly fault Augustine had two admonitory verses hung up in the refectory; moreover, he was inflexible in seeing that they were carried out and in severely reproving every violation.[14]

This whole way of life, in which poverty was marked by dignity and moderation by joy, had, in addition to its ascetico-mystical and apostolic purposes, a social purpose, namely, to reduce the needs of the members (in accordance with the noble principle of the *Rule:* "It is better to have fewer needs rather than more things") and thus be able to give more to others. And in fact, according to Possidius, Augustine "was always mindful of his fellow poor and, in order to give to them, drew upon the revenues that supported him and those who lived with him; he drew, that is, upon the revenues from the possessions of the Church or else upon the offerings of the faithful."[15] The key term is "fellow poor," *compauperes.* He felt himself to be "one of God's poor" or, as he also puts it, "one of Christ's least brethren."[16] He urged these same sentiments on his followers.

20

Theological Formation

THE will of the people of Hippo, which Augustine took for a sign of God's will, caused him to give a new direction to his monastic ideal by fusing it with the ideal of the priesthood. It also caused him to devote himself more urgently to his own theological formation. He had been planning to do so while at Tagaste, but he lacked the time. In his new situation he did not have any more time available, but the urgency was greater. He therefore devoted himself with extraordinary zeal to the study of theology or, concretely, to the study of Scripture and the writers of the Church.

He began by studying the credibility of the Catholic faith, and he produced as the firstfruits of his priesthood a fine work on *The Value of Belief.* The subject was a fundamental one and enabled him to attack head-on the Manichaean rationalism by which he and his friend Honoratus, to whom the work is dedicated, had at one time been deceived. It also enabled him to strengthen the conviction reached at Milan that faith has temporal priority over knowledge, because it is the way that leads to knowledge; to summarize the reasons for the credibility of the Catholic faith; and, finally, to establish the presupposition of theological research. The presupposition is this: If we are to understand the Scriptures, we must take as our guide not someone who rejects and condemns them (as noted earlier, the Manichaeans rejected the Old Testament) but rather someone who respects, safeguards, and explains them. "Who would seek an explanation of the abstruse and obscure works of Aristotle from someone hostile to them? . . . Who would set about reading and learning the works of Archimedes on geometry under the guidance of Epicurus who argued against them so stubbornly?"[1]

Augustine's study of Scripture was thus guided by faith and by Catholic writers. He would give impressive proof of this in his book *The Trinity* and, later on, in the Pelagian controversy.[2] Meanwhile, two years later, in 393, he would give a specimen of his progress in an address which, by an unprecedented exception, he was charged to deliver to the African bishops in their plenary council at Hippo. The address was published at the desire of his friends.

The book, entitled *Faith and Creed,* contains a succinct synthesis of Catholic doctrine, arranged according to the articles of the Creed. The book is important as documenting the formation of Augustine as a theologian. It shows signs of considerable progress in his knowledge of Scripture and the Fathers, but it also shows us how far he still was from the heights he would reach later on in his major works.

Early teaching on the Trinity

The progress and the distance are both clear in, for example, his teaching on the Trinity. The statement of the dogma and of the arguments from Scripture is clear and precise, but the explanation is still anchored to likenesses—really not very like—taken from corporeal things. The doctrine of relations and the psychological explanation are absent. The very fruitful insight into the Holy Spirit as subsistent Love is presented in an obscure and confused way. "Learned and spiritual men have written numerous books about the Father and the Son. . . . But the great and learned commentators on the divine Scriptures have not as yet discussed the Holy Spirit extensively and carefully enough to help us grasp easily what is proper to the Spirit in the Trinity." That is, they have not brought to light the personal trait by which the Holy Spirit is distinguished from the Father and the Son within the unity of God.[3] Some years later, when as a bishop he begins work on *The Trinity,* it is this point more than any other that he will have in mind. This difficult and fascinating question is certainly present from beginning to end of the work.[4]

Meanwhile he was also giving his attention to three other fundamental subjects: the explanation of Genesis, the Pauline doctrine of salvation, and the moral precepts of the Gospel. In this last-named area he began and completed a commentary on the Sermon on the Mount; he regarded the Sermon as "a complete program of Christian life."[5] But here again he would subsequently introduce corrections on many points and supply deeper perceptions. The *Revisions* make a number of observations, mostly on expressions that might convey an incorrect meaning. These observations are evidence of Augustine's insatiable search for the truth; they touch on many areas of theology, such as Christology, ecclesiology, anthropology, and the doctrine of sin. One example: the name "dominical man" *(homo dominicus)* given to Jesus Christ. Augustine had used it because he had read it in some Catholic commentators; now he recognized it as improper and wished he had not used it.[6]

Attempts at Scriptural interpretation

By and large, however, his attempt at the literal interpretation of Genesis and the commentary on Paul's Letter to the Romans were unsuccessful. As a layman he had already written two books of a *Commentary on Genesis against the Manichaeans,* in which he interpreted the text according to its allegorical meaning. Now, as a priest, he girded himself for the "extremely laborious and difficult" task of interpreting it according to the "letter," that is, "the historical sense." But, as he admits in the *Revisions,* "being a novice in the interpretation of the Scriptures I collapsed under the weight of such a vast undertaking." He did not complete even the first book of this commentary.

Later on, as a bishop, he attempted the task again, this time successfully. Over a period of years (400-15) he wrote the twelve books of *The Literal Meaning of Genesis,* which is one of his most important and demanding works. He had not published the incomplete work that resulted from his first attempt, and was thinking of destroying it, but then he decided to keep it as "what I think is a useful witness to my first attempts at explaining and commenting on the divine oracles."[7] Surely, all will be grateful to the bishop of Hippo for his humble and transparent sincerity.

Another area in which the newly ordained Augustine's efforts met with failure was a commentary on the Letter to the Romans. While with the "brethren" during a visit to Carthage, he was asked to explain some passages of the Letter.[8] Shortly afterwards he wrote a continuous commentary on the Letter to the Galatians[9] and then immediately decided to do the same for Romans. He planned several books but wrote only one. "Discouraged by the extent and difficulty of the task," he ended the commentary after the first few verses and "turned aside to other and easier work."[10]

He did not return to this project, as he did to the commentary on Genesis, but his study of the Letter to the Romans continued. He was attracted by the soteriological problems that the Apostle poses and resolves in this great letter, especially in chapters 7–9. We find an echo of this continued reflection in a miscellany of questions asked by the "brethren" and answers given by Augustine during the period from his return to North Africa to his episcopal consecration. I mentioned the title of this work earlier: *A Miscellany of Eighty-three Questions.*

> These questions were scattered about on a large number of sheets, because, in the period that followed upon my conversion and my return to North Africa, the brethren used to ask me questions when they saw me at leisure, and I dictated the answers without following any order. When I became bishop, I ordered that they be gathered together and turned into a book by being numbered in such a way that readers could easily find what they wanted.[11]

They were originally dictated without following any particular order, and we do not know the principle by which they were organized into a book. It is therefore impossible to determine the year to which any given question belongs, although all are from the period 388-96.

The questions deal with philosophy, theology, spirituality, and exegesis and are evidence of the many intellectual interests of the communities at Tagaste and Hippo. There are more questions on exegesis than on anything else; this too is significant. Especially important are the questions dealing with the Letter to the Romans. Here Augustine goes into the teaching of Paul on the Law, sin, and election to grace.[12]

This deeper analysis continues in the reply to the questions of Simplicianus, an important work from the beginning of Augustine's episcopate (397). "I had examined as best I could the questions you asked me about the Apostle Paul, and had put my answers in writing. But then, not content with my past study and explanation and fearing to have misled you by any carelessness, I made a more careful and attentive examination of the Apostle's own words and the tenor of his statements."[13] As a result of this new study he discovered and became fully convinced that accord-

ing to St. Paul even faith, and even the very beginning of faith, is
a gift of God, an election to grace.

> I made a strong effort to defend the freedom of choice of the
> human will, but the grace of God won the day, and I could no
> longer fail to understand the crystal-clear truth in these words of
> the Apostle: "Who sets you apart? And what have you that you
> have not received? But if you have received it, why do you boast as
> though you had not received it?" (1 Cor 4:7).[14]

Earlier, at least at one time, he had maintained that grace is
the divine response to our act of faith. This was an error—the
same error that would later be known as Semipelagianism. Augustine acknowledges the fact candidly and admits his change of
view.[15] On the other hand, he forcefully denies, with an appeal to
his early works, that he had changed his views on original sin, as
claimed by Julian[16] and others after him.

The main lines of Augustinian thinking on grace are henceforth fixed and will not be changed; any changes will affect only
marginal issues. For example, the question of whether the "I" of
which Paul speaks in Romans 7:24-25 is to be referred only to
human beings "under the Law" or includes human beings "under
grace" as well. "Later on [after 397[17]], after reading commentators on Scripture whose authority I esteemed highly, I
examined the passage more carefully and saw that the Apostle
could also be talking about himself."[18] "And this view is more
probable."[19]

It is not easy to say who the authors were of whom he is
speaking. We have some reason to think that he includes Ambrose, Hilary, the anonymous commentator on the Pauline Letters known as Ambrosiaster, Jerome,[20] and, among the older
writers, Cyprian. It is even more difficult to single out names of
Greek Fathers. On questions of ecclesiology he would have read
the Donatist writer Tyconius, whose "rules" he would adopt in
his *Christian Instruction.*[21] Later on, before beginning to write
The Trinity he read "all the Catholic exegetes of the Old and New
Testaments" that he could find.[22] During the Pelagian controversy he made a more careful study of the Eastern and Western Fathers on the question of original sin. In the book *Against*

Julian he summarizes a lengthy argument by saying: "The holy, blessed, and well-known commentators on the divine word— Bishops Irenaeus, Cyprian, Rusticus, Olympius, Hilary, Ambrose, Gregory, Innocent, John, and Basil, to whom, like it or not, I add the priest Jerome—to say nothing of commentators still alive, all condemn you."[23]

Theological method used

We are very well informed, on the other hand, about the theological method Augustine followed during the years that we are now discussing. He himself describes it for us at the beginning of his episcopate in the three books on *Christian Instruction,* which are an introduction to the study of theology, that is, concretely, the study of Scripture. These books are meant "as a help to the understanding of Scripture."[24]

Students who want to understand Scripture must approach it with the humble intention of discovering the author's thought (and not substituting their own for it) and with the firm conviction that the Scriptures are ordered to the twofold commandment of love as their goal and are summed up in it. To this end students must interpret the signs in which the Scriptures are expressed, both the signs unknown to them and the signs that are ambiguous. In case of the former, students must have recourse to the secular sciences: linguistics, textual criticism, grammar, history, and philosophy. Here is a worthwhile passage on philosophy: "If those known as philosophers—I am thinking of the Platonists in particular—say something that is true and in conformity with our faith, we should not be afraid of it but should . . . use it to our profit."[25] In other words, Christians should not reject anything true and useful that human beings have discovered, because truth, no matter where found, comes from God and belongs to Christ. Therefore it can and should serve to shed light on the message.

In the case of ambiguous signs (difficult passages) students must arm themselves with even greater humility and patience. They must constantly keep an eye on the rule of faith and on clearer passages, so that they may have before them a complete overview of biblical teaching. There are numerous more specialized rules that *Christian Instruction* explains and that there is no point in my mentioning here. Among these are the seven rules of Tyconius, which Augustine says are useful if applied "circumspectly"[26] and which he inserted into his work when, toward the end of his life, he decided to complete it (the fourth book).

By means of this program Augustine, during his years as a priest, made a careful study of the major themes of biblical theology and prepared himself for his long and difficult ministry as a bishop.

21

The Burden of the Episcopate

AUGUSTINE'S consecration as bishop was no less stirring an affair than his priestly ordination had been. Once again the bishop insisted, the candidate resisted, and the people launched their acclamations. There was one difference, however: the elderly Megalius of Calama, Primate of Numidia, who would have to do the consecrating, was against it.

The urgency Valerius felt about having Augustine as his coadjutor had a valid basis. Augustine's writings, his successful preaching, his victorious debates with the Manichaeans, and his tireless activity against the Donatists had won widespread fame for the young priest, both in Africa and abroad. There was reason, then, to fear that sooner or later some Church lacking a pastor would claim Augustine for its bishop and, in keeping with the customs of the day, would attempt to kidnap him. In fact, such an attempt had already been made; Valerius had thwarted it by persuading his ward to stay in hiding. Moreover, two friends of Augustine, perhaps from the very monastery in Hippo, had been requested for bishops' sees and had been consecrated: Alypius for Tagaste and Profuturus for Cirta.

To avoid the risk of losing this priest on whom all his hopes were set, Valerius used cunning. In complete secrecy he obtained the consent of Aurelius, Bishop of Carthage and Primate of Africa, giving as a reason—true as far as it went—his advanced years and uncertain health. He then asked Magalius to visit the Church of Hippo and there, in the presence of the bishops who had met for a regional council and of the people, he announced his intention. The people broke into enthusiastic acclamations, and the vaults of Peace Basilica echoed with them. "On hearing this announcement everyone rejoiced and enthusiastically demanded that it be done."[1]

On another occasion, when Augustine publicly chose his own successor, the secretaries recorded the acclamations and the number of times each was repeated. "The people cried twenty-three times 'Thank God! Praise Christ!'; sixteen times, 'Christ, hear us! Long live Augustine!'; then, eight times, 'You are our father! You are our bishop!' " Later, "the people cried out thirty-three times 'Thank God! Praise Christ'; thirteen times, 'Christ, hear us! Long live Augustine!'; eight times, 'You are our father! You are our bishop!'; and twenty times, 'It is right and fitting!' "[2]

The tumult was renewed almost every time Augustine finished a sentence. Something similar must have occurred on the occasion of which I am speaking here. The Catholics of Hippo had come to love their pugnacious priest and would never have consented to his being removed from the city.

Manner of episcopal consecration

This time, however, there were difficulties. Augustine reminded those present of the custom whereby only one bishop was allowed to a see, and he refused to let himself be consecrated. Magalius, moreover, was unwilling to perform the consecration, for he had lent an ear to accusations invented by the Donatists, among them that of casting love-spells. Thus the two men were in agreement, though for different reasons. But it took no great effort to make them agree on the opposite course of action. Augustine allowed himself to be persuaded by the exceptions to the rule both in Africa and in Churches overseas, and he finally yielded. (He did not know at the time that the practice to which he objected had been prohibited by the Ecumenical Council of Nicaea; later on, when he found out, he bitterly regretted what had happened.[3]) Magalius, for his part, soon realized that he had been deceived, and he publicly admitted his error.[4]

Augustine's consecration took place between Ascension of 395 and August of 397. It was commonly assigned, and many still assign it today, to 395, on the basis of Prosper's *Chronicon*. Others put it in 396,[5] on the basis of the fact that "the first two of the books I composed as a bishop"[6] were those written in answer to the questions of Simplicianus, who succeeded St. Ambrose. Recent writers do not consider the argument for the second date to be probative and accept the earlier date instead.[7] One thing is certain: in August 397 Augustine was bishop of Hippo when he signed the Acts of the Council of Carthage. Valerius was therefore dead and Augustine now had full responsibility for the diocese. He would have it for thirty-three years.

We know a good deal about this unusual bishop. We know his many activities as pastor and theologian and his interior dispositions. It will be helpful to turn our attention first to these dispositions, since they give insight into the soul of this man who was certainly an extraordinary person: a contemplative by inclination and a bishop by obedience.

He found his office a burden, a *sarcina*. He never liked it, even though he accepted it out of love and exercised it in a loving way. He wrote to the monks of Carthage in about 400:

> As far as my own comfort is concerned, I would much rather work with my hands at set hours every day, as in properly ordered monasteries, and have other times free for reading and praying or studying the Scriptures, instead of suffering the torments and perplexities caused by the questions of others. But we are servants of the Church and servants, above all, of its weakest members.[8]

And in fact he felt himself to be, and explicitly called himself, "a servant of Christ and, in his name, a servant of his servants."[9] His motto was: "To rule is to be useful" *(praeesse est prodesse)*. He accepted all the consequences of this motto, both for himself and for others. He went so far as to consider a non-bishop one who desired to rule but not to serve. And he tells us why: the word "bishop" signifies a responsibility, not an honor.[10]

The theme of service crops up continually in his thinking; it can even be said to be the root of his episcopal spirituality. He thinks of himself as first and foremost a servant of the Church of Hippo. "My first concern must be for the Church entrusted to me; I serve its interests and desire less to rule it than to be useful to it *(non tam praeesse quam prodesse desidero).* "[11] He would like to go to Tagaste to meet Pinianus and Melania who have come on from Rome, but he cannot, not because it is cold but because "the people of Hippo, whose servant the Lord has appointed me to be, are in trouble, and their bishop may not absent himself."[12] Whenever, he leaves Hippo on the service of the Universal Church, he tells the faithful the reason. Here is one passage:

> I beg you in the name of Christ not to let yourselves be cast down by my bodily absence. . . . The fact that my uncertain health will not let me perform all the services asked of me by the members of Christ (those members whom fear and love of him inspire me to serve) saddens me even more, perhaps, than it saddens you. Your Charity knows that I have never absented myself from your midst because of selfish caprice but only because of duty's call. That call has often obliged others of my holy brother bishops to face hardship on the sea and overseas. I have always had to abstain from such journeys not because of any evil disposition of soul but because of my ill health.[13]

The theme of service is present in the mind and on the lips of Augustine especially on the occasion of a colleague's episcopal consecration or on the anniversary of his own. On one such occasion he takes as the theme of his sermon these words: "Anyone who presides over a community must know, above all else, how to be servant of the many." To rule is to serve. His conclusion is that there are no bad bishops, because "if they are bad, they are not bishops." To anyone objecting that the man is a bishop because he sits in the bishop's chair, Augustine replies with dry, cutting irony, "yes, and a scarecrow stands in the vineyard."

At the same time, however, this stern and logical doctrine does not prevent the devout bishop from putting the faithful on guard lest they be scandalized by an unworthy holder of a see. On this occasion, as on others, he recalls the basic principle of sacramental theology and Church discipline (a principle clearly aimed at Donatist teaching): the exercise of a bishop's office does not depend on the man's moral qualities. A grape is a grape even if it grows amid thorns, and bread is bread even if served on an earthenware dish.[14]

The anniversary of his own episcopal consecration serves him, therefore, as an opportunity to remind himself of the burdensome responsibility he carries and to ask the faithful for the help of their prayers and obedience. "Help me by your prayers and your obedience to carry out these many serious and varied duties; then I shall have the joy of not so much ruling you as being useful to you."[15]

Augustine was justified in emphasizing how burdensome the episcopate was. A bishop had a far from easy time of it in fourth-century Africa and in a port city like Hippo. Foreigners came here from all parts; in its public squares educated people and peasants from the hinterland met; the people were affectionate but also rough and violent and rent by religious and social divisions. The difficulty was only increased when the bishop was a man of Augustine's radical temperament.

Time-consuming duties

A bishop's duties—preaching, catechesis, administration of the sacraments, care of the poor, the defense of the lowly and the underaged, the stewardship of the Church's goods, and, above all, the administration of justice—required time, dedication, and energy. In addition, there was the more wide-ranging task of defending the integrity of the faith against heresy and the unity of the Church against schism.

Particularly burdensome for Augustine—and, I suspect, not for him alone—was the administration of justice. To sit hour after hour in court, listening, admonishing, and making decisions, was a wearying and debilitating task. Yet Augustine did not spare himself but devoted a great part of his day to it, sometimes until mealtime, sometimes the whole day, fasting.[16]

He speaks of this task in a downcast letter to Eudoxius, abbot on the island of Capraia.

> We beg you to remember us in your prayers, for we believe that you pray very alertly and attentively, whereas our own prayers are weighed down and weakened by the darkness and confusion that secular involvement brings with it.... We are beset by so many problems that we can hardly breathe. And yet we are sure that if we persevere in the ministry in which God has designed to place us while promising his rewards, he in whose sight the groans of prisoners rise up will set us free of every care through the help of your prayers.[17]

Thus the bishop of Hippo felt greatly the burden of the episcopate and laid a heavy stress on the element of service that is an essential part of this office. At the same time, however, he also exposed the root from which the service springs: the root of love. "It must be love's function to feed the flock of the Lord."[18] These solemn words occur in a discourse that ought to be read in its entirety; in it Augustine is commenting on the Gospel of St. John, from which he derives the justification for his statement. The Gospel passage tells how before entrusting the flock to Peter the Lord elicits from him a threefold profession of love. "It is as though he were saying: 'Since you love me, what will you give me, what will you offer me?' . . . This is what you will give me if you love me: you will feed my sheep."[19] The words are as applicable to Augustine himself as they were to the Peter who had asked to remain with the Lord on Mount Tabor.

> Go down, Peter. You wanted to stay on the mountain, but, instead, go down: preach the word . . . toil, sweat, suffer torments . . . . The fulfillment of your desire is in store for you, Peter, but after death. For the moment he himself [the Lord] says to you: Go down to toil on earth, to serve on earth, to be despised and crucified on earth. The Life came down that it might die; the Bread came down that it might hunger; the Way came down that it might grow weary on the journey; the Fountain came down that it might thirst. Do you then refuse to toil? Seek not your own interests. Have love, proclaim the truth. Then you will reach eternity and find freedom from care.[20]

Augustine, therefore, looked upon the episcopate not as something desirable in itself ("it is unbecoming to desire it"[21]), but as a charge to be accepted as manifestation of love for Christ. This love must be humble, disinterested, and generous: humble, because the bishop realizes that the basis of salvation is not in being a bishop but in being a Christian; disinterested, because he must feed the flock of Christ as Christ's and not his own and must therefore seek the glory, lordship, and profit of Christ and not his own; generous, because it must be stronger than death.

For these reasons Augustine feared being a bishop and found his greatest joy in being a Christian. "I am fearful at what I am for you, but I draw strength from what I am with you. I am a bishop for you, a Christian with you. The former designates an office received, the latter the fountain of salvation."[22] He therefore asks the faithful to pray to the Lord for him, that he may be able to die for the flock entrusted to him: die in fact or in desire *(aut effectu aut affectu)*.[23]

Let us now look at such a bishop at work.

22

Minister of the Word

"**U**NTIL his final illness he preached the word of God in the church diligently, zealously, and courageously, and with clear and vigorous mind."[1] These words of the first biographer sum up almost forty years of ministry of the word. Despite his delicate health, weak voice, and insatiable desire for quiet study and meditation, Augustine preached a great deal. He preached not only in Hippo but in all the Churches of Africa to which he was invited or through which he happened to be passing, especially the Church of Carthage. When he was reviewing his writings at the end of his life, he bemoaned the fact that "wherever I happened to be I had to speak to the people and was very rarely allowed to remain silent and listen to others."[2]

We know that he regularly preached twice a week—on Saturday and Sunday—and often for several days running, sometimes twice a day. If we take into account five years as priest and thirty-four as bishop, the sum total of his sermons must have been very great, even allowing for frequent and lengthy journeys and not infrequent illnesses. The sermons that have come down to us represent less than half; for these we owe gratitude to the skilled secretaries who took them down. The others were either never published or are lost beyond recovery or are lying hidden in some library or other.

The sermons fall into three categories: commentaries on the Gospels and the first Letter of John; commentaries on the Psalms; and various other sermons that in turn can be divided into three categories: commentaries on Scripture, sermons on the liturgical seasons, and occasional sermons.

Augustine found preaching very fatiguing and a constant grief: fatiguing because of the physical effort it required (not infrequently he had to stop speaking because of weakness or loss of his voice[3]); a grief because it prevented him from devoting himself to study, as he would have liked. Moreover, he felt deeply the

149

disproportion between his words and his thought. All this is often voiced in his sermons:

> No one would like more than I the steady, tranquil repose of contemplation. Nothing could be better, nothing sweeter, than to study the divine treasure far from the noise of the world. Such study is sweet and good. On the other hand, preaching, reprimanding, correcting, building up, and attending to the needs of individuals is a great burden, a great responsibility, a great weariness. Who would not avoid such a burden? But the Gospel affrights me *(terret me evangelium).*[4]

Characteristics of eloquence

When he actually began to speak, the stark contrast between the brilliance of the truth that shone within him and the inadequate words that he spoke was a new source of grief.[5] And yet this grief, this interior tension, may have given rise to one of the most fascinating aspects of Augustine's eloquence.

Augustine did not have the exuberant copiousness of Gregory of Nazianzus, or the florid imagination of John Chrysostom, or the artistic gravity of Ambrose, or the Roman stateliness of Leo the Great. But more than any of these he had depth of thought, a flow of words that were sure and incisive, an immediacy and affective warmth in his exposition, and a poetic and mystical depth.

In 427, toward the end of his life, Augustine wrote a short treatise on sacred eloquence; it forms the fourth book of *Christian Instruction.* He says that he is not taking himself as a model, because he knows he lacks many qualities; in reality, however, the theory does reflect his own experience. Taking his cue from "a certain orator" (Cicero), he distinguishes three types of preaching: simple, ornate, and affective; to these correspond three styles: the simple, the moderate, and the grand. He was able to combine all three, and to pass with great ease from one to the other.

While he does not scorn the tools and rules of ancient oratory, he maintains that the Scriptures are the norm for sacred oratory. From Scripture (and from Cyprian and Ambrose) he takes his examples of each of the three styles. In his view, a sacred orator is one who "explains and teaches the Scriptures."[6] He ought to be able to speak both wisely and eloquently. If he cannot speak eloquently, let him at least speak wisely. "The better his knowledge of the Scriptures, the more wisely will he be able to speak. By 'better knowledge' I do not mean that he reads the Scriptures a great deal and learns them by heart, but that he understands them correctly and examines their teaching carefully, that is, that with the eye of the mind he penetrates to the very heart of the Scriptures."[7] If he is to speak well, he must know how to listen. If, therefore, "he does not listen to the word of God within himself, he will preach it in vain to others."[8]

This rule filled Augustine himself with a ceaseless desire to study the Sacred Scriptures and accounts for the eminently biblical cast of his sermons. He is a teacher but thinks of himself as a disciple. He wants to feed others from the same table at which he himself is fed. "In this bishop'a chair I sit before you as a teacher, but I am your fellow pupil under the one true Teacher."[9] "I offer you a food by which I myself live; I set upon your table the food with which I satisfy myself. I am a servant, not the master of the house."[10]

Augustine does not conceal from his people anything that he himself has learned from his meditation on the sacred books. He does not acknowledge two different teachings: one for the simple, the other for the learned. There is but a single source of Christian truth, and it must be made accessible to all, in order that all may slake their thirst at it. Consequently, the themes he takes up in his sermons are the same ones that he discusses in his books, no matter how demanding. The themes of the sermons are the same as those of *The Trinity, The City of God, The Literal Meaning of Genesis,* and his polemical works. They come from every area of theology and from every subject treated in the Bible: Trinitarian, Christological, ecclesiological, eschatological, moral, ascetical, and mystical themes. They are often imposed on him by the polemics of the moment; often, too, however, they are freely chosen for the sake of building up the faithful and of the joy he finds in plumbing the inexhaustible wealth of truth.

The sermons serve as a valuable commentary on his more extensive works and not infrequently shed a very useful light on these. Because he has to make himself understood by simple folk he is precise in his use of words and copious and detailed in his exposition, and makes frequent use of vivid images and examples that are almost always surprising and unforgettable. In other words, in his sermons Augustine practices both analysis and synthesis: analysis in order to communicate profound thought; synthesis, in order to summarize the thought in formulas so incisive as to sound at times like proverbs.

Here is but one example: his discussions of Trinitarian themes. The same themes occur in the sermons as in the major works: the inseparability of the divine operations outside of God *(ad extra);* the divine processions; the relations; the psychological explanation; the transcendence and mystical contemplation of the mystery; the intratrinitarian personal properties; the manifestations of the Trinity in the history of salvation. After *The Trinity,* the *Sermons on the Gospel of John* are the most important source for Augustine's thinking on this subject. He himself indicates as much when in the final book of *The Trinity* he cites a lengthy passage from the *Sermons* (99, 8-9), and this on an especially difficult and sensitive point.[11]

Similar remarks can be made on other subjects: the Incarnation, the Church, free will and grace, predestination. An observation is in place here: in the sermons we come upon mystical and poetical flights that are lacking in the other works, with the exception of the *Confessions.* It is the sacred text and the presence of the people that cause Augustine to take wing. As he speaks, he feels himself to be with his own family; he opens his heart to them, unveils his deepest thoughts, and soars upward, followed by the people, to God.

Scriptural commentaries in sermons

Consider the lyrical character of the psalms. The impassioned accents of the psalmists as they praise, thank, and invoke and admonish the faithful made their way deep into Augustine's heart from the time of his conversion.[12] From that point on the psalms became the habitual subject of his meditation and supplied him with the formularies for his daily prayer. Once ordained a priest, he projected a commentary on the entire psalter, with the aim of helping the people (who knew them by heart and sang them in church and at home) to understand their meaning and taste their beauty. He wrote the commentary chiefly in the form of sermons. The result was a vast work, in fact the most voluminous of all his works, and it occupied him from the beginning of his priesthood until well into his episcopate (392-415 and, for some psalms, even later).

A vast work, but therefore also an inexhaustible and fascinating mine of theological and spiritual teaching. In it he strikes all the notes of Christian life and devotion: from the depths where the sinner begs God's mercy to the heights where the contemplative praises God and exults before him. The Christological interpretation that Augustine regularly makes of the psalms helps to render his eloquence more ardent and relevant and his commentary more penetrating. In the psalms (he tells us) we hear the voice of Christ and of the Church, of Christ in the Church and of the Church in Christ. As everyone knows, this interpretation is based on a doctrine that is dear to Augustine and is expounded frequently and at length in the sermons on the psalms: the doctrine of the "whole Christ" *(Christus totus).*

Another mine of exegetical and doctrinal instruction is the *Sermons on the Gospel of John.* It was to be expected that here, as he followed the words of the evangelist, Augustine should reach the loftiest heights of theological and, secondarily, philosophical meditation. Even Plotinus helps him to understand the Gospel. The most sublime and difficult passages terrify him but they also stimulate his mind and intensify his desire to understand. In these cases he himself soars because he is able to be both profound and clear, original and simple. Read, for example, the sermons on the Prologue (especially the first, in which he contemplates the Word and explains how inanimate things have life in him) and those on Christ as the Teaching of the Father and, like the Father, himself eternal, even though begotten.[13]

To the commentary on the Gospel of John we must join the commentary on the First Letter of John or, more accurately, on the first verses of the First Letter. The commentary consists of ten sermons, all on a single theme: love. In my opinion, it is the best thing in Christian literature on this subject.

In the fourth book on *Christian Instruction* Augustine urges the Christian preacher not only to study Scripture but also to pray. "Be a man of prayer before being a preacher."[14] This, again, is a reflection of Augustine's personal practice. He prepared himself through meditation and prayer for his preaching. In a sermon's opening sentences (the exordium), which he always made very simple and spontaneous, he would urge the faithful to pray for him in order that he might be able to pay the debt he owed to them; or else he would tell them how glad he was that they had already been praying for him.

At times Augustine had to improvise. On these occasions he would abandon himself to the current of thoughts suggested to him by the sacred text and would emphasize those ideas that were a habitual part of his thinking and especially dear to him. This kind of improvisation occurred when, for example, a colleague invited him to preach and at the last moment suggested a subject that differed from the one Augustine had prepared; or when the cantor mistakenly intoned a psalm different from the one appointed or simply took the initiative and intoned one that he liked.

On the latter occasions Augustine took the occurrence as a sign of God's will. He therefore set aside the subject that he had prepared and took the new one now presented to him. "I was prepared to speak on a short psalm, and I told the reader to sing it; he sang a different one, perhaps because he became distracted. I prefer to follow God's will as shown to me in the reader's mistake, rather than to follow my own and use the discourse I had prepared."[15] "I did not prepare the sermon I am now giving. . . . God himself bids me speak on repentance, for it was not I who told the reader to sing the psalm he did."[16] In any case, the quality of the sermon did not suffer from its being improvised.

Popular in tone

Augustine's preaching is frankly popular in character. To begin with, although he does not scorn the tools of rhetoric, he aims primarily at holding a familiar conversation with the people who are thus attuned to their pastor and begin to seek, rejoice, and lament with him. This is a new kind of oratory, suggested to him by the same practical needs that had suggested a new kind of poetry to him in the alphabetic psalm he wrote as a primer against Donatism.

He also adopts word-forms and expressions from colloquial usage when he considers this necessary for clarity and effectiveness. "I would rather be criticized by the grammarians than be misunderstood by the people." Thus he says *fenerat* instead of *feneratur* (brings profit), *ossum* instead of *os* (bone), *sanguinibus* instead of *sanguine* (blood), etc.[17] He makes frequent use of assonance, alliteration, wordplay, and unpolished expressions. We today may find all this somewhat distasteful and be inclined to have our reservations. This is a legitimate reaction. But for Augustine they were all means in the service of his purpose, which was to impress the truth on the minds of his hearers.

The people gave him their eager and intelligent attention; they reacted, interrupted, and applauded. The speaker in turn profited by their reaction to digress in useful ways, but he did not allow himself to stray far from his main idea. The applause, even when frequent and prolonged, did not disturb him. On the other hand, he did not want people to be hypocritical, that is, to show approval that was at variance with their everyday life. If he had reason to suspect such a discordance, he would cry out: "I want good conduct from you, not applause!"[18] "I do not want the praise of those who live evil lives; I abhor and detest such praise; it is a cause of pain, not joy, to me. . . . You applaud me, but I ask myself: what kind of lives are these people living who now acclaim me?"[19]

When applause was a sign that the people had understood him, it made him happy and inspired him to continue with a difficult subject. This was the case, for example, with sermons on the Trinity.[20] He did not, however, conceal the fact that praise was a source of temptation to him and that he did not know how to deal with it. "If I tell you I do not want to be praised by those who live rightly, I am a liar. I do not totally desire praise, but neither do I completely reject it. I do not totally desire it, lest I be imperiled by human praise; I do not completely reject it, lest I be ungrateful to those to whom I am preaching."[21]

Augustine's preaching was very effective, often in remarkable and immediate ways. He himself tells us how he brought an end at Hippo to the feast known as *Laetitia* (Joy), which was in fact marked by obscene merrymaking.[22] He also narrates the story of the "great row" *(caterva)* at Caesarea in Mauretania.[23] Possidius records the unexpected conversion of Firmus.[24] More generally, the faithful sensed that their pastor's words were permeated by a sincere and selfless love for them, and they were unable to resist it. "What do I want or desire or long for? Why do I speak, why do I sit here, why do I live at all—if not that all of us may live together with Christ? . . . That is my desire, that is my honor and glory, that is my joy and possession. . . . I do not want to reach salvation apart from you."[25] It would be difficult indeed to hold out against such a strong and authentic love!

Even today, when we read Augustine's sermons on the printed page, they communicate something to us of his great spirit. To experience their full fascination we would have to have heard him, been near him, and lived with him. Such is the claim of Possidius, his first biographer, who lived with him for almost forty years. We can well believe him.[26]

23

The Goodness of Creation

PREACHING and the administration of justice did not exhaust the energies of the bishop of Hippo; he had enough strength left over to devote himself to a broader and more important activity in the service of the Universal Church: the defense of the faith. Circumstances led Augustine in this direction. Having been given the important office of priest at a time of profound change and violent controversy, he thought it his duty to play a part in events. He did so, without posturing and without wearying. He entered the lists against Manichaeans, Donatists, Pelagians, Arians, and pagans: not against individuals, whom he respected and loved, but against errors, in the presence of which he could not rest easy, no matter where they showed themselves.

No charge leveled at the Catholic faith found him without an answer, no opinion that was erroneous, or that he thought erroneous, went unrefuted. He defended the faith in spoken word, in letters, and in books. The first adversary to draw his attention was the Manichaeans.

Writings against the Manichaeans

Augustine's defense of the Catholic faith against the Manichaeans began, in desire, at Cassiciacum before his baptism[1]; it began in fact at Rome, immediately after his baptism.[2] It continued at Tagaste in the form of works devoted chiefly or even exclusively to the refutation of Manichaean doctrine.[3] Once ordained a priest he turned his attention primarily to his former coreligionists and began a lengthy series of works aimed at them.

I have already mentioned one book, *The Value of Belief*, which was directed against Manichaean relationalism. A second book, entitled *The Two Souls*, took up a basic Manichaean thesis: that the human being has two souls, one good and one evil, which are at odds with one another. The first of the two is a portion of God, the second a portion of darkness; from the latter comes all the evil human beings do, from the former all the good.[4]

157

At about the same time—specifically on August 28-29, 392—Augustine held a public debate with a Manichaean priest named Fortunatus. The latter had been living in Hippo for many years and had made numerous converts. He had the reputation of being a learned man. Catholics and Donatists, in agreement for once, asked Augustine to debate the truth of Manichaeism with him. Augustine accepted. Fortunatus, who had known Augustine from the days when they were coreligionists at Carthage, would have gladly declined, but his followers forced him to accept, since a refusal would have disgraced them. The debate was public and lasted for two days. The subject was one that was at the heart of Manichaeism: the origin of evil. On the second day Fortunatus admitted he could not give an answer, and he withdrew in good order. Augustine notes in his *Revisions* that Fortunatus "did not become a Catholic, but he did leave Hippo."[5] Possidius adds: " . . . and the authentic Catholic faith made its way into hearts and minds and won them over."[6]

Some time later Augustine came into possession of some controversial writings of Adimantus, who had been a disciple of Mani; in them he attacked the Law and the Prophets with the intention of showing that they were contrary to the New Testament. Augustine responded by citing Adimantus' words and then refuting them. The result was a book that has one peculiarity: some questions are answered twice. The reason is that the first answers, written on separate sheets of paper, got lost; by the time they were found, Augustine had written a second answer. He also answered some of the same questions in sermons to the people; others he did not answer at all, since the pressure of business caused him to put them aside and eventually forget them.[7]

Meanwhile he had been consecrated a bishop. A short time later, perhaps while answering the questions of Simplicianus, he refuted the *Letter of Mani known as "The Foundation."* This was an encyclical in which the basic principles of the Manichaean religion were set forth, a kind of catechism. It was read to Mani's followers so that they might attain to enlightenment and, by observing the precepts contained in it, might reach the life of glory. Augustine knew the letter well and refuted the first part of it, which was also the most important part, since the remainder stood or fell with it. In this part the founder of the sect proclaimed himself Apostle of Christ in the providence of God the Father. Augustine added some notes here and there throughout the remainder of the text as memory aids, should he ever decide to refute the rest of the work. He never did so,[8] but his method of working is worth noting.

Not long afterward he gathered up his energies for a weightier work. He had not yet finished writing his *Confessions* when he began a refutation of numerous "chapters" of Faustus, a Manichaean bishop. This was the same Faustus, "an African by descent, a native of Milevis, a delightful speaker and a clever mind,"[9] whom Augustine had met at Carthage and whom, while at Milan, he judged a better speaker than Ambrose if a soothing and seductive manner be taken as the criterion.[10] Faustus "wrote a book against the true Christian faith and the Catholic truth. I acquired it and the brethren read it; they asked and begged me, in the name of the love that makes me their servant, to answer it."[11] The result was a "sizable work" *(grande opus)* in thirty-three books, some quite short, others very long. The method Augustine followed was the one he had introduced in dealing with Adimantus: he first quoted what his adversary wrote and then gave his answer. It is due to this scholarly probity that Faustus' work has been preserved.

At this same period he wrote a book on *The Nature of the Good,* in order to demonstrate once again against the Manichaeans that God is immutable by his nature; that he is the Supreme Good; and that from him proceed all things, corporeal and spiritual, and that these are good to the extent that they are.[12]

Immediately afterward he wrote still another book. The occasion was a letter from Secundinus, a Manichaean Auditor, who wrote him from Rome, exhorting him in a friendly way to return to the sect. Augustine's motive in leaving the sect, he claimed, was desire for glory and fear of human beings; he could be saved only if he returned, for, otherwise, "How may an African be saved?" *(Quis Punicum salvabit?).* Secundinus accompanied this exhortation with a defense of his sect and an attack on the Catholic faith.

As we can easily imagine, Augustine answered immediately with a lengthy letter, which—because it lacks an address—is numbered among his books rather than his letters: *Against Secundinus, a Manichaean.* The text includes Secundinus' letter. Augustine regarded his answer as the best thing he ever wrote against "the scourge of Manichaeism."[13] It is in fact a short but comprehensive treatise of Catholic teaching on the creation of the world from nothing, on the divinity of Christ and our adoption through grace, on the nature and origin of evil, on marriage, and on freedom. The author refers his addressee to his book on *Free Will*, which, he says, "you can find at Nola in Campania, in the possession of Paulinus, a noble servant of God."[14]

His final labor in this area was his debate with Felix, one of the teachers of the sect, who had come to Hippo to make converts. He had stated in a discussion with Catholics that he was willing to let himself be burned along with the books of Mani if anything evil could be found in these. Augustine wrote to him and asked him either to answer in a public debate the question left unanswered by Fortunatus or else to leave Hippo.[15] Felix hesitated but then agreed to the debate. It was held in a church, in the presence of the people, on December 7 and 12, 404,[16] while secretaries recorded the proceedings. At the end of the second debate Felix acknowledged defeat, abandoned Manichaeism, and became a Catholic.[17]

This debate marked the end of sixteen years of sleepless labor in defense of the Catholic faith against a strong and well organized religious movement to which Augustine himself had adhered as a young man.

What did Augustine have against the Manichaeans? Certainly not their longing for wisdom, for that had been and still was his own aspiration; not their worship of God and constant prayer; not their keen sense of the problem of evil; not their assertion of the need of purification if a human being were to be delivered from darkness and clothed in light; not their intention of living an integral Christian life; not their ecclesiastical organization and the solidarity with one another that they felt and showed. He did not find fault with them on any of these counts, for they represented positive values that he himself had esteemed and still esteemed.

His criticism was directed at the major metaphysical, moral, scriptural, and methodological errors that the Manichaeans promulgated, and at the harsh accusations they nonetheless made against the Catholic Church. His pastoral duty of responding to these accusations and errors—a duty he had already felt and fulfilled as a layman[18]—impelled him, now that he was a bishop, to elucidate a wide-ranging metaphysical doctrine, explain the morality of the Gospel, defend the unity of Christian revelation, and provide solid apologetic arguments for it.

The credibility of the Catholic Church

Let me begin with the last point named. The much-praised rationalism of the Manichaeans forced Augustine to go more deeply into the relations between reason and faith. The principles into which he had gained insight during the long travail of his own conversion[19] were to be echoed, explained, and applied in all of his works. At every point these manifest a sapiential balance that is equally removed from rationalism and fideism. Faith precedes reason, but, in another way, reason precedes faith.

Therefore, "believe in order that you may understand" *(crede ut intelligas)*,[20] because understanding is the reward of faith. But the opposite also holds: "Understand in order that you may believe" *(intellige ut credas)*,[21] because it is reason that shows us "in whom we are to believe."[22] In fact, "we do not believe unless we have first thought that we ought to believe." On the contrary: "belief is simply thinking accompanied by assent. Not everyone who thinks believes . . . but all who believe think: they think when they believe and they believe by thinking."[23]

It follows from this that "faith too has its eyes," which perform two functions: they enable us to "see," in a way, that what we do not yet see is true; and they enable us to "see" with complete certainty that we do not yet see that which we believe.[24] In short, reason demonstrates that it is not foolish to believe and even that it is foolish not to believe.[25] The Church is therefore being wise (though the Manichaeans stubbornly accuse it of just the opposite) when it asks faith of its members before and above all else.[26] When it asks them for faith, it is asking them, not to renounce reason, but on the contrary to exercise it, both by grasping the motives of credibility that it offers them and by going more deeply into the content of the doctrine that it teaches them. It is in this way that the science of faith, or theology, is born.

> The task of this science is to beget, nourish, defend, and strengthen the salutary faith that leads human beings to a happy life. Many of the faithful do not possess this science, even though they have a deep faith. It is one thing simply to know what one needs to believe in order to reach a happy life (which cannot but be an eternal life), but quite another to know it in such a way as to make it useful for the good and to defend it against the wicked.[27]

"This then," Augustine concludes, "is the most proper norm to follow: bring the weak safely within the fortress of the faith and then fight for them with all the resources of reason."[28]

He himself was certainly one of the fighters of whom he speaks: "devout, learned, and truly spiritual men."[29] He explained the motives of credibility of the Catholic faith, answered the objections of the Manichaeans, and showed the inconsistency in their teaching.

Here is an important summary:

> Leaving aside the candid, genuine wisdom . . . that you do not believe exists in the Catholic Church, there are many other reasons that keep me within it. The consent of peoples and nations keeps me there; the Church's authority that is based on miracles, fed by hope, mantled by love, and rendered secure by age, keeps me there; the succession of bishops, the episcopal chair of the Apostle Peter and his successors, whom the Lord after his resurrection commissioned to feed the sheep, keep me there; the very name "Catholic," which this Church alone has rightly won, keeps me there. These many, powerful, and pleasant bonds associated with the name of Christian keep the believer within the bosom of the Catholic Church, even if the truth has not yet become clear because of our slow minds and unworthy lives. Among you, on the other hand, there is nothing similar that would invite and keep me; we hear only a promise of revealing the truth. If this promise were kept and truth were manifested in a way no one could doubt, it should certainly be preferred to all the reasons that keep me in the

Catholic Church. But as long as there is nothing but promises and the truth never appears, nothing will move me from the faith that binds my soul to the Christian religion with so many powerful ties.[30]

The Manichaeans promised a great deal but delivered little: little at the level of reason, nothing at the level of faith. Their founder proclaimed himself an apostle of Christ but offered no credentials. Christ had sent his apostles, and the apostles their successors. Via apostolic succession the Catholic Church went back to Christ himself and derived its authority from him. Mani had no way of tracing his line back. The Manichaeans therefore lacked both the divine authority that justifies faith and the truth that leads to knowledge. Their rejection of the Old Testament was incompatible with their claim to accept the New, since the harmony of the two Testaments is so obvious as to be undeniable. Augustine had been pointing out this harmony ever since his first work against the Manichaeans.[31] It was so evident that the Manichaeans found themselves compelled to fall back on the flimsiest of all arguments: the claim, unsupported by any proof, that the New Testament texts that refer to the Old Testament were interpolated.[32] The truth is that the Old Testament prepares in an obscure manner for the New, while the New explains the Old and brings it to completion. The Manichaeans had no grounds for calling themselves Christians.

At the end of this lengthy work against Faustus Augustine exhorts the Manichaeans as follows:

> If you wish to follow the authority of Scripture, an authority to be preferred to any other, then follow it as it has come down to us from the time of Christ himself, being handed on, preserved, recommended, and made illustrious throughout the world by the apostles and the sure succession of bishops in their sees. There you will see the obscurities of the Old Testament explained and its prophecies fulfilled. If you really follow the guidance of reason . . . you will understand or believe a truth that is given by nature to the human mind to keep it from being led astray by perverse doctrine, I mean the truth that the nature and substance of God is utterly immutable, utterly incorruptible. Then you will immediately cease to be Manichaeans, and sooner or later you will become Catholics.[33]

Absurdity of Manichaean pessimism

The bishop of Hippo had a good deal to find fault with in the Manichaeans not only on the specifically Christian level but also on the broader level of metaphysics (this level, too, then, has a Christian character). He faulted them for their materialism, pantheism, metaphysical dualism, and, as the ultimate consequence of this dualism, their pessimism. He himself had laboriously surmounted these errors in the course of his conversion, and he now taught the faithful how to avoid or overcome them. This pastoral zeal led him to stress certain points that provide the essential structure of his metaphysical vision: intelligible reality, the idea of God, creation, and freedom.

Everyone knows the Augustinian principle of interiority, that is, that the human mind is by its nature linked to intelligible reality and inevitably perceives this reality when it turns toward it.[34] One instance of such perception is the certitude those who live and think have that they indeed live and think.[35] This is a certitude that is impervious to doubt and cannot possibly be in error. "If I doubt, I am alive."[36] "If I am deceived, I exist."[37] Thus, truth dwells in the interior self,[38] and no one can fail to realize this.

This principle not only serves as a springboard for proving God's existence and the spiritual nature of the soul. It also serves to refute the skeptics and the Manichaeans. Against the former it safeguards the existence of certainty, against the latter the distinction between material reality and intelligible reality. This distinction is a basic one and a favorite theme of Augustine's preaching. We feel how greatly the pastor wishes his faithful to gain insight into spiritual realities (truth, justice, wisdom), so that they may escape the pull of materialism and ascend to God.

But it is no easy matter to rise above the body and the corporeal images that the senses transmit to the soul, and to gather oneself together in the part of the soul that is more remote from the body, there to discover with the mind's eye the intelligible light of truth. This is why Augustine constantly calls upon his hearers to enter into the interior self whose riches he never tires of explaining. In the interior self shines the image of God. "Where are human beings made in the image of God? In their intelligences, their minds, their interior selves, in that part of them by which they intuit truth, distinguish between justice and injustice, know the one who made them, and are able to acknowledge and praise their creator."[39] When human beings enter into themselves they become aware that they exist and think and love; there they seek Being, Truth, and Love, all of which are God.

It has often been claimed that Augustine emphasizes the idea of God as Truth and God as Love more than he does the idea of God as Being. It is difficult to establish this kind of "more" and "less," but one thing is certain: he speaks a great deal of God as first and supreme Being, and he does so in accord with both reason and revelation. Reason ascends from mutable beings to the immutable or supreme Being. Revelation, for its part, gives us the proper name of God, "I am who am," and thus transports us to the highest reaches of wisdom, where it invites us to meditate on the meaning of this name.

Augustine constantly harks back to this passage of Scripture. In his view, God alone possesses "true being, genuine being, authentic being," because he alone is Being. He is so convinced of this that he distorts language to express the inexpressible and calls God "Is." And he does this when speaking to the people! Commenting on the Book of Exodus, he asks in astonished tones:

> What does this mean? O God, our Lord, what is your name? He tells us: "My name is *Is*." But what does it mean to say, "My name is *Is*"? It means: "I abide forever, I cannot change." Things that change are not, because they do not abide. That which is abides. . . . This is why the immutable God deigns to make himself known by saying, "I am who am."[40]

Elsewhere, but again in a sermon to the people, Augustine exclaims: "Great is this *Is*, great indeed! What is a human being in comparison with it? What is a human being, no matter how great, in comparison with this mighty *Is*?"[41]

The idea of God as Supreme Being served, among other things, to attack the very roots of Manichaean dualism and show its absurdity. "The only thing contrary to being is nonbeing. Therefore there is no nature that is contrary to God."[42] This idea, which Augustine expounds in his first work against the Manichaeans, is often repeated as being a fundamental and decisive argument.

No one thinks that the fallen angels had a different nature deriving from a different principle and that God was therefore not their creator. We will more quickly and easily cast aside this impious error, the more accurately we understand the words that God spoke through his angel when he sent Moses to the children of Israel: "I am who am." Since God is the supreme essence, that is, supreme and therefore immutable Being . . . it follows that only a nature that does not exist can be contrary to the nature that exists in the supreme degree and through which all things have existence. Therefore no essence is contrary to God, who is the supreme essence and creator of all essences.[43]

The doctrine of creation flows from the idea of God as Supreme Being or, simply, Being. From the doctrine of creation comes in turn the doctrine of the goodness of things, and from the doctrine of the goodness of things the idea of evil as a privation of good. This chain of ideas undercuts the errors of the Manichaeans and displays the essential lines of a metaphysics that is in harmony with both reason and faith.

It is understandable, then, that in his polemical writings against the Manichaeans Augustine should put so much emphasis on the doctrine of creation. "The Catholic faith bids us believe, and reason teaches us with certainty, that the matter out of which things were formed could not have originated except from God, who is the source and creator of all things, not only those that have a form but also those that can have one."[44] This assertion is based on a dilemma: "Every good either is God or proceeds from God."[45] Things that change and are limited are not Being, Truth, Beauty, and Goodness, but they do participate in them. Therefore they are not God but they proceed from him. They do not proceed by emanation, because then they would possess the divine substance and be equal to God. They must therefore proceed from God by creation out of nothing.

This conclusion states a truth that is at once luminous and obscure, and therefore difficult, but it is the only truth that overcomes dualism, whether Manichaean or Platonic; it alone provides a reasonable explanation of the mysterious origin of things.

The debate with Felix the Manichaean is focused entirely on this argument. Augustine wants to show that the human soul proceeds from God but is not a particle of God. He therefore distinguishes between generating, producing, and creating, since one thing may proceed from another through generation, production, or creation.

> That which makers make they make either from their own substance or from something outside of themselves or from nothing. Human beings are not omnipotent; they can generate children from their own substance and as artisans they can make a box of wood, but they cannot make the wood; they can make a vase, but not the clay from which they make it. No human being can make anything from nothing, that is, make something be from that which does not exist. God, on the other hand, is omnipotent: not only does he generate his Son from his own substance, but he also creates the world from nothing and human beings from the earth. There is an immense difference between that which God generates from his own substance and that which he makes not from his own substance but from nothing; in the latter case he causes that which simply did not exist to exist and have its place among the things that are.[46]

The difference is that while the generated is equal to the generator, a creature cannot be equal to its creator. The reason for this difference is, in turn, that the generated is of the same nature as its source, whereas a creature differs in nature from its creator: it is limited, mutable, and defectible.

> You will ask me: "Why are things defectible?" And I will tell you: "Because they are changeable." "Why are they changeable?" "Because they do not exist in the supreme degree." "Why do they not exist in the supreme degree?" "Because they are inferior to the one who made them." "Who made them?" "He who exists in the supreme degree." "And who is that?" "God, the immutable Trinity. . . ." "Why did he make them?" "That they might exist. For existence, in however small a degree, is a good, since the supreme good is to exist in the supreme degree." "Out of what did he make them?" "Out of nothing."[47]

Two important conclusions follow from this doctrine: the goodness of things and the possibility of evil. Existence is a good. The things that exist are therefore good insofar as they exist. But because they have been created out of nothing they are changeable and can suffer evil, that is, they can suffer a privation of good. The privation cannot be total, for then they would simply cease to be at all, and so would the evil. Good, therefore, can exist without evil, but evil cannot exist apart from the good. Augustine emphasizes this point against the Manichaeans and later on, in order to clarify the ideas and respond to accusations, against the Pelagians.[48]

> The Catholic faith teaches that God alone is the uncaused nature, that is, the supreme and immutable Good. ... It teaches, further, that this supreme and immutable Good created the universe and all things in it as good, even though these things are not equal to their creator, since they are created out of nothing and are therefore mutable. There is, therefore, absolutely no nature that is not either God or God's creature; consequently, every nature, great or small, is good.
>
> At this point the question arises: What, then, is the origin of evil? I answer: it originates in the good, but not in the supreme and immutable good. Evils have their origin in inferior and mutable goods. ... But a nature would not be mutable if it came from God without having been created from nothing. Therefore God, the author of nature, is also the author of good. When things as a result of their condition suffer a privation of good they show, not by whom they were made, but from what they were made. This "what" is not something but utter nothing.[49]

Freedom and the existence of evil

The mutability of things is a key element in Augustine's teaching: it serves as a point of departure for proving the existence of God; it reveals the creatureliness of things; it explains the origin of evil. But the problem of evil is too complex and agonizing to let the bishop of Hippo be content with such a very general explanation. This is especially the case when evil affects human beings.

As a matter of fact, two evils are found in human beings: one that they suffer against their will (pain, death, disordered passions), and another that they deliberately bring about (sin). The Manichaeans explained both kinds of evil with the aid of their dualism, which, when applied to human beings, becomes the doctrine of the two souls. Augustine, on the other hand, explains these two kinds of evil by an appeal to freedom, in the abuse of which they have their origin. He grasped this explanation at

Milan prior to his baptism, as he listened to Ambrose; he sub-sequently explained and defended it throughout his life.

He had experienced within himself, with tragic intensity, the struggle between "two" wills, one of which remained firmly set in old habits while the other hesitated to free itself from these habits and follow new ideals.[50] He realized, however, that there was but a single soul and will and that it was the same "I" who willed and failed to will.

> It was I who willed it, and I who willed it not. It was the same I, but as yet I neither fully willed it nor fully willed it not. Therefore, I was in conflict with myself, and I was divided from myself. And this same division was indeed against my will; yet it did not man-ifest in me the nature of another mind, but the punishment of my own.[51]

He uses the same language when speaking to the people:

> Many confess their transgressions, but they lay them to the Lord God's account. When they are found to be sinners they say: "God willed it." . . . Perhaps you will tell me: "No one says such a thing! Who says, 'God willed it'?" Many people do. As for those who do not use these words, are they not saying the same thing when they say, "Fate did it to me; my stars did it"?

What these people ought to say is: "God created me as one pos-sessing free will. If I sinned, it was I who sinned. . . . I myself and not fate or fortune or the devil. Nor did the devil force me; I con-sented to his persuasion."[52]

The evil of sin is therefore not in things as such, for they are good. It is in the abuse of freedom, which uses good things in an evil way and thus produces a lack of rectitude, or moral disorder. "It is the act of a madman to shift to things the fault of those who use them badly."[53]

> In fact, when sin occurs, the evil is not in the object but in the way of acting, for evil natures do not exist. . . . Thus avarice is a de-fect not in gold but in human beings who love gold in a disordered way and disown justice, which they ought to prefer to gold, there being no comparison between the two. Lust is a defect not in bodies that are endowed with grace and beauty, but in the soul that loves bodily pleasures in a disordered way and disregards the vir-

tue of temperance by which we are united to things that have an even greater spiritual beauty and incorruptible sweetness. Vainglory is a defect not in human praise but in the soul that has a disordered desire for human praise and pays no heed to the testimony of conscience. Similarly, pride is a defect not in one who bestows power or in power itself, but in the soul that loves its own power in a disordered way and has contempt for an authority that is more powerful and more just. Those, therefore, who love any nature in a disordered way and who gain possession of it will become wicked through possession of a good and wretched through loss of a greater good.[54]

Therefore let no one go looking for the efficient cause of an evil will; its cause is not efficient: an evil will results not from something effective but from a defect.[55]

This defense of the essential goodness of things and this constant attribution of moral evil to a defect of the human will, which is free but defectible, are characteristic of Augustine's thinking in his controversy with the Manichaeans.

The same two themes recur, perhaps even more strongly, when the discussion shifts from the evil that human beings do to the evil that they do not do but suffer. Augustine, a man of keen sensibilities, had always been especially attentive to and acutely aware of this second kind of evil, which attacks and torments the whole person, soul and body. When barely an adolescent he already felt it to be a problem, and at the age of nineteen he went to the Manichaeans for a solution.[56]

Once he had passed through his Manichaean period, the problem came home to him again with great intensity. He heard Ambrose say that the cause of the evil we do is the free decision of our own wills and that the cause of the evils we suffer is the just judgment of God. He had trouble understanding this statement, especially in its second part. "When I willed or did not will anything, I was most certain that it was not any other thing but myself that willed or did not will. And I saw directly that herein lay the cause of my sin."[57]

But the other kind of evil, the evil that he underwent, especially because of the struggle within him between flesh and spirit, still left him questioning:

Who made me? Was it not my God, who is not only good, but goodness itself? Whence, therefore, have I this will to evil and repugnance to good, so that there is an occasion for my being justly punished? Who has put this in me and engrafted in me this root of bitterness, when all of me was made by my most sweet God?[58]

His questions were soon to be answered. He quickly became convinced that the best and even the only explanation of such evils is the Catholic doctrine of original sin, which locates in the free will of the first human being and in the just judgments of God the cause of the entrance into the world of the evils we suffer. From then on, that first abuse of freedom became a dominant motif in Augustine's dispute with the Manichaeans even before it played its important role in the controversy with the Pelagians.

In the debate with Fortunatus, which dates from the first years of his priesthood, we already find Augustine repeatedly asking, without ever receiving an answer, why God, whom nothing can harm, should have placed the soul in a condition in which it must suffer such great evils against its will. When his adversary, instead of answering, himself asked questions, Augustine said:

I see that you are unable to answer my questions and prefer instead to ask me questions. Very well, I shall give you an answer, provided you remember that you have not answered my own questions. I explained a moment ago, and I don't know how many times earlier, why the soul in this world is enveloped in wretchedness. The soul has sinned and is therefore wretched. It received free will but did not use this as it should have; it fell and was excluded from happiness and entangled in wretchedness.

In confirmation, Augustine cites Romans 5:19 ("As all have been made sinners by the disobedience of a single man, so all will be made just by the obedience of a single man") and 1 Corinthians 15:21 ("As death came by a man, so by a man resurrection from the dead"). When, his hard-pressed adversary admits he cannot answer, Augustine concludes: "I knew you had no answer, nor did I myself have an answer at the time when I listened to you Manichaeans on this question. That inability to answer served as a divine warning to me to abandon your errors and convert or, more accurately, return to the Catholic faith."[59]

Every evil, therefore, is either a sin or a punishment for sin; that is, it is either a free act of a defectible will or is the just punishment for such an act. This is the basic thesis of the work *Free Will*, which was written precisely in order to prove that both kinds of evil derive from free will[60]: one from free will as its direct cause, the other from free will as its condition. Later on, writing against the Pelagians, Augustine would repeatedly argue from the evils in the world to original sin, for he was convinced that only original sin can explain such great evils and that only the redemptive work of Christ can overcome them. In his final work he states an incisive principle that expresses a conviction matured over many years: "In the providence of God, who is just, no one can be wretched unless he or she has deserved to be wretched."[61]

The wonders of the world and the human person

The argument just mentioned[62] leads Augustine to paint a dark picture of the evils in our world, especially the evils that afflict children. On the other hand, it never causes him to forget the goodness of things and the value of the natural gifts God continues to bestow on sinful humankind.

I shall summarize here a long and powerful passage of *The City of God*, a passage that is among the most beautiful in this immortal work. The passage amounts to a poetic and mystical contemplation of the wonders found in the human person and in the universe. In it Augustine describes the power of human fertility, the harmony and beauty of the body, the inexhaustible capacities of the mind, the innate human ability to ascend to virtue, the discoveries of genius, the progress made in technology, the sciences, and the arts. All this serves as prelude to a discourse on heavenly beatitude and as a demonstration that while God punishes, and punishes justly, he also governs his creation with infinite goodness.

He begins, then, with the wonders of the generation and formation of the human body. God gave human beings the power to propagate themselves; he preserves this power in them and intervenes with his own ongoing action in order that "the seeds may develop and, from out behind the hidden and invisible veils that cover them, may evolve the beautiful forms that we see." "This work of his is so great and wonderful that when it is carefully studied not only in the human person—who is a rational animal and therefore the most beautiful and noble of all the living beings on earth—but even in the tiniest midge it fills the mind with astonishment and impels it to praise the creator."

The wonders of the body are inexhaustible: its sense organs, the arrangement of its members, its appearance, structure, and posture; furthermore the astonishing mobility of the tongue and the hands, which are so adapted for speaking and writing and for producing works of art and practicing the most varied trades.

A further source of wonder is the harmonious proportion between the various parts of the body; so marvelous is this that we cannot tell whether God in creating gave priority to usefulness or to beauty. Nor is this harmonious proportion found only in the external parts of the body, which anatomists study so eagerly. "If we could but know the numbers that determine this proportion, even the viscera, which have nothing attractive about them, would display a rational beauty so seductive that the mind . . . would judge it preferable to all the outward forms that the eye finds pleasing." Augustine also makes reference to the body's physical beauty, contemplation of which is disturbed, in our present state, by disordered passions. But a time will come when the body will be clothed in glory and "we shall enjoy each other's beauty without passion."

The wonders increase as we pass from body to spirit. The mind, which is asleep in infants and awakens and develops with the years, is capable of knowledge and art; the will is capable of virtue. "The very capacity for acquiring such goods is already itself so great and wonderful a good that we can never understand and speak of it as it deserves." "In addition to the art of living rightly and reaching endless happiness . . . has not the human spirit invented an infinity of other arts? . . . Think of how far human diligence has gone in the manufacture of clothing and construction of buildings! Think of the progress it has made in agriculture and navigation, of the refinements in sculpture and painting!"

Augustine goes on to list, with growing wonder, the discoveries of human genius in the sciences and arts. He even mentions "the poisons, weapons, and machines human beings have invented for use against their fellows" and the acuteness of mind with which philosophers and heretics have defended their errors. "Finally, who can adequately esteem the brilliance with which philosophers and heretics have defended their errors and falsehoods?"[63]

But all these things, splendid and marvelous though they be, are but consolations allowed to mortals. At this point Augustine lifts the veil and turns his gaze to the blessed immortality that God promises to human beings through Christ. Need it be said that the elderly Augustine—he was seventy-two or seventy-three when he dictated this passage—was far removed from the Manichaean pessimism that he had always rejected? The Pelagian controversy forced him indeed to emphasize the fall and its deadly consequences. Nonetheless he always preserved the deep optimism he had gotten from philosophy and the faith, that is, from the doctrine of creation and redemption, two luminous and pivotal elements in his doctrinal synthesis. I leave it to others to say whether this passage from *The City of God* may not be usefully compared with the passages of the *Pastoral Constitution on the Church in the Modern World* in which Vatican Council II speaks of the innate dignity of human beings and the value of earthly things.[64] I shall be satisfied to have set forth Augustine's thinking.

24

Augustine a Misogynist?

I N the doctrinal synthesis that Augustine constructed in response to the Manichaeans there is one part on which readers will surely want further information: sexual ethics. It has become customary to speak ill of the bishop of Hippo on this point (and not on this point alone!). His early adherence to Manichaeism, it is said, had a deleterious influence on him even after his conversion; as a result, his teaching on marriage acquired a gloomy and pessimistic tinge and, in particular, seriously belittled the dignity of women. Critics also refer to his personal experience, that is, to the fact that as a young man he kept a concubine for fourteen years and then, because he wanted to marry a younger and richer woman, suddenly abandoned her without shedding a tear.[1]

Readers of the present book already know that this last assertion is unfounded and even in open contradiction to the testimony of the *Confessions*. With the other assertions in mind I shall here provide a brief explanation of the essential points in Augustine's teaching on marriage. Readers can then judge for themselves whether this teaching deserves praise or blame; in any case, they will see what Augustine's theological outlook in this area really was.

Marriage: a natural institution

The first point to be made is this: Augustine resolutely defends marriage as a natural institution that God willed from the beginning of the race's existence and that flows from the essentially social nature of the human person.[2] Even had there been no sin, the human race would have maintained itself in existence through the sexual collaboration of man and woman. This truth is so evident today that it is difficult to believe it was ever doubted. And yet it was. Spiritualistic interpretations of the "Increase and multiply" ordinance in Genesis were current even among Christian writers. In a book he wrote as a layman against the Man-

175

ichaeans[3] and in another from the first years of his episcopate[4] Augustine himself avoided taking a position on the subject. Not long after, however, a careful study of the Scriptures convinced him that the words of Genesis were to be taken literally.[5] From then on his views were firm and unwavering. Here is how he puts it in *The City of God,* after having expounded the views of the spiritualists:

> We, on the other hand, resolutely maintain that increasing, multiplying, and filling the earth in accordance with the blessing of God, is a gift of marriage, which God instituted from the very beginning, prior to sin, when he created human beings male and female, with sexual differences that are evident in the flesh. . . . It is utterly clear, therefore, that God created them male and female, with bodies of different sexes, so that they might beget children and, in this way, increase and multiply and fill the earth. It would be most absurd to deny all this.[6]

This firm and well-reasoned position represented a major doctrinal advance on the side of marriage and therefore of the dignity of women in particular; thenceforth it had an established place in theology. Many years later, when Julian calumniously accused him of teaching that the devil had invented marriage, Augustine could answer dryly: "God created the sexes," and he added: "Even had there been no sin, children would have been born through the union of the sexes."[7]

The second essential point in Augustine's teaching has to do with the resurrection of the dead. No one today would maintain that the risen body will be asexual or that women will not rise as sexed beings. At that time, however, there were those who did maintain this view, mistakenly basing it on some passages of Scripture.[8] Augustine joined in the discussion and explained:

> I regard as more reasonable the view of those who maintain the resurrection of both sexes. . . . Risen bodies will be freed of defects, but their nature will be preserved. Female sexuality, however, is not a defect but belongs to nature. It will indeed be thenceforth free of conjugal union and childbirth; the organism will however continue to exist, not any longer for its old use but clad in a new beauty that . . . will serve to glorify the wisdom and goodness of God who created what did not yet exist and then rendered incorrupt what he had created.[9]

This was another, and long, step forward on the road to establishing the dignity of women and of marriage.

Equality of man and woman

The third step on this same road was taken when Augustine presented his copious teaching on the goods, or blessings, of marriage. The fourth was his unyielding defense of the complete equality of man and woman in regard to the duty of observing premarital and marital chastity.

With regard to the third step it will be enough here to remind the reader of the well-known trio that Augustine so often repeats and explains: children, fidelity, sacrament. In his view these are the three advantages or blessings of marriage: the virtuous generation of children, mutual fidelity, and indissoluble union.

> Marriage has its advantages: that children are not simply begotten, but are begotten virtuously, legitimately, chastely, and socially; that, once born, they are raised without unjustified preferences and in a salutary and persevering way; finally, that both partners observe mutual fidelity and respect the sacrament of union.[10]

Because of his views on this subject, he makes it a point, when speaking of virginity, to put consecrated persons on their guard against belittling the dignity of marriage:[11]

> I warn men and women who profess complete continence and holy virginity to prefer their own state to marriage, but at the same time not to regard marriage as evil. We know that the Apostle says, not insincerely but truthfully, that "he who gives his daughter in marriage does well, but he who does not give her in marriage does better" (1 Cor 7:38). . . . That is the principle of the Lord and the apostles, the true and sound principle: to choose what is better without condemning what is less good.

He then adds this telling image: "Let those who decide to remain single not flee marriage as though it were a pit of sin; let them rather move beyond it, as a good but lower hill, to the mountain of complete continence."[12]

The fourth step mentioned above, which directly concerns the dignity of women, is the assertion of the complete equality of the two sexes in regard to the duty of fidelity. Young men (Augustine insists) have an obligation to remain chaste, just as they expect their future wives to be chaste; husbands must themselves observe the same conjugal fidelity that they require of their wives.[13] Let them not say: "But we are men!" And let them not appeal to civil law, which strictly punished adultery by women but either punished less strictly or simply ignored adultery by husbands. Augustine attacks the first excuse with the formidable weapon of irony.[14] He attacks the second with a distinction that would be habitual with him: civil law is one thing, the law of heaven is another. Certain things are allowed by civil law but not by the law of heaven.[15] He himself had appealed to civil law and not to the law of heaven when as a youth he had taken a concubine; now, as a bishop, he teaches the faithful to look to the law of heaven and not civil law.

In order to understand Augustine's debate with the Manichaeans we must recall what they taught. They summed up morality in their theory of the three seals: the seals of the mouth, the hand, the womb. The first seal prohibited blasphemy and the consumption of meat and wine; the second forbade the killing of animals and the uprooting or harming of plants; the third forbade reproduction. Manichaean Auditors, though not forbidden to marry, were repeatedly urged to avoid begetting children on the grounds that it was sinful.

Such a dissociation of reproduction and sexual activity was, to Augustine's mind, a most obvious condemnation of marriage, since this is by its nature ordered to procreation. He repeats this point frequently, while appealing also to the "matrimonial registers" (tabulae matrimoniales) that explicitly recalled this ordination.[16]

In his defense of marriage against the Manichaeans Augustine was obliged, therefore, to speak not so much of sexual activity in itself as of the intrinsic connection between it and reproduction. That is what he does, but he does not on this account forget that marriage includes more than this relationship. Marriage also establishes a natural society of man and woman; this is the first of all societies, and it is based on love.

As a member of the human race and by nature a social entity, every human being has a great natural blessing: the powerful instinct of friendship. God willed that all human beings should originate in a single human being in order that they might be bound together in a society not only by similarity of race but also by the ties of kinship. The basic natural union within human society is that of man and woman. God did not even create them separately and then unite them as former strangers: rather he drew woman from man.[17]

I assert ... that marriage between man and woman is a good. . . . But it is legitimate to ask: Why is marriage a good? It seems to me to be such not only because of the procreation of children but also because of the natural society it establishes between the two sexes. Otherwise the name "marriage" could not be given to the union of elderly persons, especially if they had lost their children or never had any. In fact, even if the ardor of love diminishes with the years, in a happy marriage, however long, an ordered charity *(ordinata caritas)* remains ever alive between husband and wife.[18]

Disordered passion

The question of sexuality was not to the fore among the Manichaeans, since their primary concern was to avoid procreation as being a sin against the godhead. This question did, however, come to the forefront in the Pelagian controversy, where its context was the broader question of the origin of evil and in particular of disordered passions in the human person. These are disordered, not simply because they are passions but because they are not subject to full control by reason and are therefore a hindrance to moral goodness and the cause of the interior struggle of which Paul gives such a dramatic description in his Letter to the Romans (7:14-25).[19] According to Augustine—and the teaching of the Catholic Church—this struggle is a consequence of sin; according to the Pelagians it is part of the native human condition and would have been experienced even if there had been no sin. A case in point is sexual passion.

If we are to understand Augustine's position, we must bear in mind the clarifying distinctions he makes. Two in particular are fundamental. He makes a sharp distinction between the sense faculty, which is good, and disordered passion, which to the extent that it is disordered is evil. The biblical name for disordered passion is concupiscence. "The sense power is one thing, disordered concupiscence is another. You must carefully distinguish the two if you do not want to go badly astray."[20] Concretely, sexuality is good and even a reason for astonishment to one who reflects on it. Sexual passion, on the other hand, *to the extent that it anticipates and resists reason* is evil.

Here as elsewhere Augustine offers a helpful example: a lame man. A lame man owes his ability to walk to his motor faculty, which is something good; that he walks with a limp he owes not to the faculty as such but to the defect in it, and the defect is an evil. Therefore, as we need not approve of the evil because of the good, neither should we condemn the good because of the evil.[21] This is the essence of Augustine's reply to Julian in the long and exhausting controversy on marriage and sexuality.[22]

A second distinction further explains and supports the first. In this area, and indeed in this area above all others, Augustine distinguishes between the human condition before sin and the human condition after sin. There would have been sexual activity even in the earthly paradise, but the restraint of shame would not have been needed nor would there have been the struggle between "flesh" and "spirit" that marks sexual activity after sin. The act of reproduction would have been accompanied by sensual delight, but a delight that would not have needed provocation or have experienced resistance, but would have obeyed the "calm" and "peaceful" command of reason.[23] After sin the grace of Christ helps human beings return, though not completely here on earth, to that blessed condition of perfect balance in which there existed between spouses "a faithful union based on chaste love, a reciprocal devotion between body and soul, and an effortless obedience to the divine commandment."[24]

Sexuality and reproduction

Stripped of unnecessary detail, such are the essential lines of Augustine's thought on the subject. His thinking shows two constant concerns: first, to assert, in the name of the human personality and of right order, the priority of right reason or of true love over the impulses of instinct and, second, to insist on the essential ordination of sexuality to reproduction.

If we apply his argument not only to sexuality but also to the spiritual nature of woman—and some have made this application on the basis of a passage in Paul (1 Cor 11:7)—Augustine's teaching proves to be once again clear and clarifying. Woman, like man, has been created in the image of God. "The human person was made in the image of God at a level where sex plays no part, that is, in the spiritual soul. . . . The image of God resides only in the part of the soul that is united to the eternal reasons, which it contemplates and from which it draws inspiration, a part that women evidently possess no less than men."[25]

It hardly needs saying that Augustine's thought on sexuality reflects the influence of Platonic philosophy. The influence does not come, however, from Platonic dualism, for, contrary to what is often asserted, Augustine decisively surmounted this dualism and effectively disproved it.[26] The influence is rather that of Platonic moral teaching, which regards bodily pleasures as an obstacle to the ascent of the spirit, since these pleasures are "the baits and enticements of the vices."

Augustine is convinced that although the Bible (like reason) rejects Platonic dualism, it contains the same moral teaching as Plato, but in a clearer and more profound way. Consequently, when Julian argues that sexuality "as it now is" (namely, removed from the calm control of reason) is a good and not a defect in human nature, Augustine admonishes him in sorrowful tones: "I beg you, do not regard pagan philosophy as more virtuous than our Christian philosophy, which is the only true philosophy." He reminds Julian of a lengthy passage in Cicero (one of the passages from the *Hortensius* that made such a deep impression on him when he was nineteen[27]) and concludes:

> Thus speaks a man who for lack of faith knew nothing of the happiness of paradise, nothing of the resurrection of the dead. We should blush as we listen to these utterly true arguments of the pagans—we who have learned from our true and holy philosophy, which consists in true devotion, that the flesh has desires contrary to the spirit and the spirit desires contrary to the flesh.[28]

It is clear, then, that Platonic philosophy did not inspire Augustine's thought but simply confirmed it; he did, of course, consider the confirmation very timely when dealing with a Christian adversary. His thinking depends essentially on the teaching of the Bible, and it is in the light of this teaching that it should be studied and judged.

Augustine interpreted 1 Corinthians 7:7 as making a concession (but this interpretation may be described as common to the Fathers); as a result, his sexual ethics seems rather stern. But we should not forget that the strictness is balanced by the "conjugal love" on which he lays so much emphasis.

Thus he teaches that when the use of marriage is motivated by passion alone, that is, when it is separated from the intention of procreating, it is not an inherently praiseworthy act, because we cannot describe as praiseworthy the domination of reason by passion. Such an act is nonetheless allowed for the sake of conjugal fidelity; he therefore calls it a "venial" fault.[29] This means for Augustine that, provided it remains open to conception (a condition expressly mentioned), the act is permitted for the sake of preserving a good. It must be added, however, that conjugal love can make such an act even praiseworthy and meritorious.[30]

There can be no doubt that Augustine greatly advanced the theology of marriage. Other advances and other valid doctrinal contributions are certainly possible. Justice demands, however, that Augustine be given his due and that his teaching be accurately reproduced.[31]

25

The Message of Ecclesial Communion

WHILE defending the Catholic faith against the Manichaeans. Augustine was already fighting zealously on the Donatist front as well. The sad rift that the Donatist schism had caused in the unity of the Church had already lasted through almost a century of ups and downs. This is not the place to retell the story with its deeds and misdeeds. The schism erupted in 312, but its roots went back to the persecution of Diocletian and even further back to Cyprian's theology of baptism. It erupted, took organized form in a "party," and spread throughout Africa despite the laws suppressing it. In a short time most of the African Churches, of which there were a good many (over 600), had two bishops, two clergies, and two groups of Christians: the Catholics and the "party of Donatus."

The history of this sad affair has been told many times.[1] Optatus and Augustine gave a theological interpretation of it, while modern scholars like Frend and Brisson emphasize (in a not fully convincing way) the sociopolitical aspect.[2]

The situation at Hippo was especially sensitive: in the town itself Catholics were in the minority (from his church Augustine could hear the voices of the Donatists in theirs), while roundabout, as in Siniti and Fussala, they had completely disappeared. In general, the Catholic Church throughout Africa was in a state of exhaustion.

"It began to raise its head"[3] when Aurelius was consecrated bishop of Carthage and Augustine became a priest of Hippo. The year 393 saw the celebration at Hippo of a plenary council that dealt with the reform of the African Church. Immediately after it, Augustine began his great work for unity and peace among Christians. He began in the town that had chosen him its priest, but he soon included all of Africa in his sphere of action. Sermons, letters, and books mutiplied at an astonishing rate.

183

The reply to the Donatists

Augustine's first work on the subject was his *Psalm against the Donatist Party*. It was a popular alphabetical song in the form of a responsorial psalm (the soloist sang the stanza, the people repeated the refrain). For pastoral reasons it was based on rhythm instead of on classical metrics, and it had a suggestion of rhyme. It is one of the earliest and most interesting examples of popular poetry.

Its purpose was to teach the history of Donatism to the illiterate person in the street and to explain why the Donatist stand was wrong. It begins thus: "It is a shameful thing to hear a dispute and then base judgment on respect of persons. The unjust can never possess the kingdom of God. It is intolerable that anyone should tear the robe of another; how much more deserving of death are those who rend the peace of Christ? Let us ask, without any self-deception, who has committed such a crime." To this the people answered: "Lovers of peace, judge now the truth."[4]

Augustine was next called upon to refute a letter of Donatus who, according to Majorinus, had been bishop of the schismatics at Carthage and, by reason of his imposing personality, had given the sect its name. This work is lost.

He also wrote a long letter, his first on the Donatist question, to his "beloved lord and honorable brother, Maximinus," Donatist bishop of the neighboring town of Siniti, who had been accused of rebaptizing a Catholic deacon.[5]

Once Augustine was consecrated bishop, his activity against the Donatists became more intense. We may distinguish two main periods: before and after the conference of 411, of which he was a convinced and tireless promotor. Around 397 he wrote a work, in two books, entitled *Against the Donatist Party;* this too is lost. From 400 to 406, the period of his greatest activity, he replied to all writings emanating from the adversary: those of bishops Parmenian of Carthage and Petilian of Cirta, of Cresconius the grammarian, and of anonymous other Donatists. The works written in response to Parmenian, Petilian, and Cresconius comprise nine books in all and are the major treatises on the Donatist question.

Later on he wrote a book on *The One Baptism, against Petilian*, which added nothing new from a doctrinal standpoint and which he wrote simply in order not to violate his own rule of allowing nothing to pass unanswered, even if this meant tedious repetition. In this context he remarks in the *Revisions:* "While I was multiplying my efforts in frequent discussions against the Donatists, a layman came to church with some of the arguments, partly oral, partly written, which they believed favorable to their cause. I supplied a very short answer. This little book was entitled *Against What Centurius Brought from the Donatists.*"[6] The book is lost, but it is worth mentioning here as an illustration of the rule Augustine had set for himself. He was anxious to lose no opportunity for spreading the truth and unmasking error.

During this same period he wrote a fundamental work: the seven books *On Baptism, against the Donatists*. His aim in this work was to deprive them of the authority of Cyprian, to whom they regularly appealed. Nothing could be less favorable to schism than the example of Cyprian, for despite his convictions and his bitter dispute with Pope Stephen he never separated himself from the unity of the Church. Augustine than goes on to demonstrate the validity of baptism conferred by heretics, since this was the heart of the theological problem.

Augustine also wrote a *Letter to Catholics against the Donatists,* and several other works that are lost: *Proofs and Testimonies against the Donatists; Against an Anonymous Donatist;* and *Admonition to the Donatists regarding the Maximinianists.* These three were very short and journalistic in style; they nonetheless show the bishop's zealous efforts to supply everyone with accurate information on the controversy, and to do so in whatever way he could.

The Conference of 411

Augustine believed above all in the effectiveness of frank and open oral discussion. He knew from experience that truth has an irresistible power for those who sincerely love it. He therefore sought every opportunity for dialogue with the other side, but he often sought in vain. Soon after being consecrated a bishop he wrote to this end to Proculeianus, his Donatist counterpart at

Hippo,[7] but the effort was fruitless. Fruitless, too, were similar requests made to Crispinus, Donatist bishop of Calama,[8] and to a bishop Honoratus, whose see is unknown to us.[9] The conference of Carthage was thus the fulfillment of a great plan.

During the days of the conference he worked tirelessly. He spoke to the people[10]; he promoted a bold proposal that would remove every possible obstacle[11]; he accepted the delaying tactics of the other party in order not to compromise his main objective[12]; and he skillfully led the discussion, bringing to bear all his great abilities as a controversialist. To the people he spoke of the beauty of unanimity, recommended calm, and asked for prayers, fasts, and good works. Success crowned the aims and efforts of Augustine and the Catholic bishops. Marcellinus, the magistrate presiding at the conference, and the emperor himself issued an edict of union.

But an edict of union was not yet a union, and it could even be in many ways an obstacle to union. Actual unity demanded intelligent and patient work to preserve for the Catholics the fruits of their success, while at the same time making it easier for the Donatists to acknowledge the truth that had been demonstrated to them. Augustine therefore set to work.

He wrote a short summary of the acts of the conference, "a useful work that makes it easy for everyone to find out what was accomplished and also has numerical references at the head of each article, thus enabling readers to consult the parts of the acts that interest them, while avoiding the long and wearisome discussions."[13] He also addressed what he calls "a rather lengthy and carefully written book" to the Donatists, in which he responded to the calumnies spread by their bishops about the attitude of the imperial commissioner and explained clearly what had taken place at the conference. He did the same thing in briefer form in a synodal letter addressed to the Donatists in the name of the Catholic bishops who had gathered in council at Zerta on June 14, 412.[14]

He then addressed a book to Emeritus, a Donatist bishop who had been one of the strongest defenders of the sect at the conference; Augustine described his book as "rather useful" because "it explains with convenient brevity the arguments confuting the Donatists and showing how completely they were defeated."[15] At the same period he wrote a handbook for Count Boniface on *The Correction of the Donatists*; in it he summarizes the history of Donatism, shows the suitableness of juridical intervention, and emphasizes the kindness of the Church as it calls back those who have gone astray and embraces them.[16]

Later on, in 418, he traveled to Caesarea in Mauretania at the request of Pope Zosimus. There he spoke to the people on the unity of the Church (the well-known *Sermon to the People of the Church of Caesarea*) and held a public discussion with the Donatist bishop Emeritus, in the presence of the faithful and bishops of the province.

Finally in about 420-421 he wrote two books against Gaudentius, Donatist bishop of Thamugadi and one of the seven who had defended the sect at the conference of Carthage. Gaudentius had written two letters to Dulcitius, the tribune charged with carrying out the imperial edict against the Donatists of Africa; the letters were a response to the tribune's warning that he should return to the unity of the Church and not carry out his dreadful plan of setting fire to his church and burning himself and his followers in it. The tribune asked Augustine to answer the letters; he did so. His first book came into the hands of Gaudentius who, according to Augustine, responded by "not adducing any new argument but showing rather that he could neither answer nor remain silent." "Intelligent readers could see this for themselves by comparing his writings and mine. But it was my policy not to leave any letter unanswered. As a result, my one book became two."[17]

The reply to Gaudentius marked the end of Augustine's anti-Donatist labors. These had lasted for thirty years and had been crowned with success. The painful fact of Donatism did not immediately disappear, but the sect was declining. Monceaux says quite rightly that "Augustine won out because he knew what he wanted and used the necessary means; he was able to recruit the allies he needed according to time and circumstance and to carry them with him in the victorious campaign of which he was the animating spirit."[18]

True principles, false conclusions

In the Manichaean controversy Augustine was defending and studying in depth the general foundations of the faith; he was dealing with metaphysical questions. The Donatist controversy was a domestic dispute between two Christian Churches, and the need here was to study and defend particular aspects of the nature and structure of the Church. Here were two Churches, united in their acceptance of the Scriptures, the creed, and the sacraments, but deeply divided on important questions concerning the sacraments and the Church. Catholics and Donatists, appealing to St. Paul (Eph 4:5), were in agreement that there is but one God, one faith, one Church, and one baptism. "You have reminded us that it is written: 'There is one God, one faith, one baptism, one incorrupt and truly catholic Church.' All this I grant, although the actual wording is somewhat different. But since I grant it, what is its relevance to the question that divides us? What you wish to infer cannot really be inferred from those words."[19]

Augustine accuses the Donatists not of accepting false principles but of drawing false conclusions from true principles. There is but one baptism, but this does not mean it cannot be administered validly (provided it be administered properly) outside the Church. There is but one Church, but this does not mean that it comprises only saints. There is but one faith, but this does not mean that even if unaccompanied by charity, it suffices for salvation.

In response to the Donatist views, which were openly sectarian, this watchful shepherd does two things: he accumulates an extensive documentation on the origin of the schism, and he explains the mystery of the Church. With the documentation he seeks to establish what really happened and deprive the schism of any valid historicial basis. With the explanations of the mystery he seeks to go more deeply into the theology of the Church and the sacraments and, in so doing, to deprive Donatism of its theoretical basis.

In addition, he wants the people to have a grasp of both the history and the doctrine.[20] He frequently reviews the history of Donatism and brings out its internal contradictions, or what he sees as such. Even more frequently, however, he recalls Donatist teaching and shows its lack of theological foundation. It is important to Augustine to show that in the mystery of the Church, which consists essentially in the communion of the sacraments and the communion of the saints, the faithful have the sure basis for their faith, the source of love, the secret of freedom, and the power of salvation. The Donatists misunderstood both of the communions in question.

A communion in the sacraments

With regard to the first of these communions, the Donatists agreed that baptism administered in the Church is the sacrament of salvation and that sacred ordination gives its recipient a share in the hierarchic ministry of the Church. But they made the validity of the sacraments depend on the ecclesial holiness of the minister, something the "traitors" did not possess because they had separated themselves from the Church. The "traitors" were, concretely, the Catholics. When, therefore, a Catholic came over to Donatism, that is, in their view, the true Church, he or she was rebaptized; the baptism administered by Catholics was not a true baptism. This teaching and practice created a gulf between the two Churches.

As Augustine wrote to a Donatist bishop named Maximinus, who was reported to have rebaptized a deacon, "to rebaptize a heretic . . . is surely a fault, but to rebaptize a Catholic is criminal."[21]

In keeping with the Roman tradition that had been reaffirmed by Pope Stephen and by the Councils of Arles and Nicaea, Augustine himself accepted as valid both the baptisms and the ordinations conferred by the Donatists as brothers and sisters and called them such. In explaining the theological ground of these two different attitudes he put the emphasis on the Christological aspect of the sacraments and introduced an important distinction. It was the first of many that proved necessary in order to bring clarity into the rather confused ideas of the Donatists. It was the distinction between a true (or valid) sacrament and a fruitful sacrament. "It is one thing not to have the sacrament at all, and another not to have it fruitfully."[22]

Let me give a quick summary of his teaching. The sacraments of the Church are Christ's sacraments. He instituted them; they are administered in his name and by his authority. Because they belong to him and not to Donatus they imprint a character; it is through his merits that they are what they are. "Baptism is baptism not by the merits of those who administer it, but by reason of the holiness and truth it has from him who instituted it."[23] Christ is the primary minister of baptism. Therefore "when Peter baptizes, it is Christ who baptizes; when Paul baptizes, it is Christ who baptizes; when Judas baptizes, it is Christ who baptizes."[24] For this reason the Catholic Church does not rebaptize anyone already baptized, no matter where or by whom. It does not rebaptize lest it cancel out "the inscribed name of the commander," "the seal of the king." Rather it respects the name inscribed, approves it, and declares it its own. It combats and seeks to remove only error and division, so that what was formerly an occasion of condemnation may become a source of salvation.[25]

On the other hand, the simple fact of having a true or valid baptism does not mean that one is in the Church, as was claimed by the Donatists who turned Augustine's admissions into reasons for rejecting union. If we have baptism (they said), we have the true Church; why then all the anxiety about union? Augustine answers: It is not enough to have baptism; one also needs the grace proper to baptism, namely, the love that the Holy Spirit pours out into our hearts. But anyone who breaks unity and does not live in a Catholic peace does not have love. The Church is not only a communion in the sacraments; it is also a communion of saints. There is thus a double unity at a double level: one on the objective level of the means of salvation and another on the subjective level of love.

A communion of saints

At this point Augustine introduces another key idea and another fundamental distinction. The key idea is from eschatology. The Church is the people of God that is on a journey to an eternal destiny; in the future and the beyond this people now on pilgrimage through time will reach immortality and full holiness. We must therefore distinguish between the present Church and the future Church, not as between two different Churches but as between two phases of a single Church. The Church without blemish, of which the Apostle speaks, is the future, not the present Church. Here on earth the Church is indeed holy, but not all of its members are holy; it is the body of Christ, but a "mixed" body, that is, made up of good and wicked. The Church is like a net that pulls in good fish and bad fish; it is a threshing floor containing both chaff and grain. "The Church of the present age is like a threshing floor. I have said it often and will say it often again: it contains chaff and grain."[26] Grain and chaff—the good and the wicked—live together, outwardly one but spiritually distinct. "Bodily" —that is, external —separation will be effected at the end of time. This teaching contains in germ the magnificent idea of the two cities that Augustine will later develop when he offers his synthesis of Catholic doctrine in response to the pagans.[27]

As a result of this key idea and distinction Augustine feels compelled to emphasize another and no less important truth on which Christian freedom depends: the presence of sinners in the Church does not prevent or detract from the innocence of the good. The good derive their holiness and their security from Christ. For just as it is Christ who baptizes in every baptizer, so it is Christ who rules in every ruler, and it is always Christ who teaches in every teacher.

> Therefore, as I have often said and now strongly insist, no matter what we are, you are safe who have God for your Father and the Church for your Mother. The goats graze now with the sheep, but they will not be found at the right hand. The grain is now threshed with the chaff, but the chaff will not be put in the storehouse. Good fish and bad swim together in the Lord's net, but not all will be placed in the baskets. Let none glory in themselves, even if they be good; let none flee from God's gifts, even if these be found in the wicked.[28]

Augustine's main conclusion, however, is that if one is to be safe one must remain in unity. Christ teaches the truth, but he teaches it from the chair of unity. God "has located the teaching of truth on the chair of unity." When seated on this chair, which is that of "the teaching of salvation ... , even the wicked are forced to teach what is good. For in fact what they teach is not their own but God's."[29] Christ forgives sins, but he does it within the unity of the Church. The power to loose and bind was received by Peter who personifies the unity of the Church: "He, one individual, received it for all, in order that all might be united."[30] When Peter received the keys of the kingdom of heaven, "the united Church" received them in him. The greatness of the "prince of the apostles" is measured by the fact that at that moment he embodied "the universality and oneness of the Church."[31]

The same principle applies to government. It is Christ who governs the Church, but he does so in unity with the shepherds, who make one with him. "All good shepherds are in the one Shepherd and make one with him. When they feed, it is Christ who feeds. . . . Therefore the One is in them and they are in the One."[32] It follows from this that no matter who governs, be he good or wicked, the faithful form "a single flock, which is safeguarded by a single shepherd."[33]

The Church as mystical body of Christ

Only persons who remain in unity are united to Christ and only they who are united to Christ have the Holy Spirit, because only lovers of unity possess love. "Those who do not love the unity of the Church do not have the love of God in them."[34] Augustine can legitimately be called the apostle and theologian of unity. By making the necessary distinctions he constructs an indispensable ecclesiological and sacramental synthesis that makes it possible to do justice to all the data of Scripture and Tradition. By so doing he recovers the pneumatological positions of Cyprian and penetrates to the very root of unity.

The Church is the mystical body of Christ, and the Holy Spirit is the soul of this body.[35] Just as the soul gives life only to those members that are part of the body, so the Holy Spirit gives life only to those who belong to the mystical body of Christ, which is the Church. "The Catholic Church alone is the body of Christ. . . . Outside of this body no one receives life from the Holy Spirit. . . . It follows that those who are outside of the Church do not have the Holy Spirit. . . . Yet one who enters the Catholic Church without inner conviction likewise does not receive the Spirit."[36]

The faithful show that they recognize the body of Christ if they do not neglect to be the body of Christ. Let them become the body of Christ if they want to live by the Spirit of Christ. Only the body of Christ has life from the Spirit of Christ. Brothers and sisters, do you understand what I am saying? You are human beings; you possess a spirit and a body. By "spirit" I mean what is usually called "the soul," which makes you human beings; you are in fact composed of soul and body. You have, therefore, an invisible spirit and a visible body. Tell me, then: what is the vital principle of your being? Does your spirit draw life from your body, or your body from your spirit? What will and must those respond who are alive (if they do not respond, I doubt they are alive)? "My body draws life from my spirit." Well, then, do you want to have life from the Spirit of Christ? Then you must be in the body of Christ. . . .

If you want to live, you have a place in which to live and one who will give you life. Draw near and believe, enter and become part of the body of Christ: then you will have life. Do not disdain to belong to the interconnected members; do not be infected members that cause the others to blush. Be beautiful, be strong, be healthy, remain united to the body, live by God for God. Toil on earth that you may reign in heaven.[37]

For Augustine, then, a love for the Church and a harmonious coexistence within its unity are the measure of the gifts of the Holy Spirit: "Let us be convinced, brothers and sisters, that we possess the Holy Spirit to the extent that we love the Church of Christ."[38] To "love the Church" means to be integrated by love into its structure, which is a structure of unity and harmony (two properties that result precisely from love).

It is this conviction on Augustine's part that inspires his anguished calls for unity. In these passages he usually speaks of the Church as both mother and dove: a dove that laments,[39] a mother who weeps and waits and calls. Here is the beautiful and impassioned appeal with which he ends his psalm against the Donatists. In it the Church addresses her children:

My children, what complaints do you have against your mother? Tell me, for I want to know: Why have you abandoned me? You accuse your own brothers and sisters, and I am greatly wounded. . . . What have I done to you, I who am your mother everywhere in the world? I exclude the wicked if I can; if I cannot, I must put up with them. I put up with them until they repent or are separated from me at the end. Why do you abandon me, and why must I be tormented by your final death?[40]

Touching appeals of this kind are not infrequent in Augustine. Batiffol remarks that "no one has spoken more movingly of the Church's motherly heart than the son of Monica."[41] Augustine's deep feeling springs from his unshakable presupposition that the Church is necessary for salvation. He makes his own the well-known words of Cyprian: "There is no salvation outside the Church."[42] Thus, speaking in 418 to the people of Caesarea in Mauretania and having in mind Emeritus, Donatist bishop of the place, who was present, he repeats Cyprian's thought in a form that is no less forceful and compelling: "Outside the Church you can have everything—except salvation." He continues with examples: "You can have the dignity [of bishop], you can have the sacrament [of baptism], you can sing Alleluia, you can answer Amen, you can hold the Gospel [in your hand], you can have and preach the faith in the name of the Father and of the Son and of the Holy Spirit. But nowhere except in the Catholic Church can you have salvation." You can even be a martyr outside the Church, but you cannot have the martyr's crown.[43]

Augustine is evidently not speaking in these passages of a *conscious* belonging to the Church, such as would be required in the case of the Donatist bishop, since such a man could not have been ignorant of the truth, especially after the conference of Carthage. Augustine does not deny that there are Christians who in good faith are separated from the Catholic Church, although he did not adopt as broad a view in this matter as we do today. There are separated Christians who "defend their opinion . . . without stubborn bad will, especially when their views are not the result of their own bold presumption but have been inherited from their parents . . . and who, on the other hand, carefully and diligently seek the truth and are ready to be corrected when they have found it." Such people, according to Augustine, "are not to be accounted heretics."[44] Heretics are those "who resist the teaching proper to the Catholic faith when it has been taught to them."[45]

The principle enunciated by Augustine and Cyprian applies only to the last-named. It follows from this that there are different ways of belonging to the Church: full communion, which consists in being integrated into the Church's oneness and having charity; partial communion, which consists either in being in the unity without having charity (sinners in the Church) or in having charity without being in the unity (the just who are outside the Church).[46]

But is it possible to identify this Church that is one and holy, body of Christ and temple of the Holy Spirit, dove and ark of salvation? It certainly is, says Augustine. This Church has two aspects that are inseparable, one visible and another invisible: the Church is a historical fact, and it has an eschatological dimension. In dealing both with the Donatists and with the Manichaeans Augustine uses two arguments in particular in order to establish the identity of the visible Church: universality and apostolicity.[47]

The whole of Scripture shows the necessity of universality; Augustine gathers up the passages and repeats them often and emphatically. But if the Church is universal, it cannot have taken refuge in a corner of Africa and have continued to exist only in the "fragment of Donatus."[48] No, it is the *Catholic Church* and cannot fail to be recognized.

Furthermore, the Church is built on the foundation of the apostles, even if the apostles in turn rest on another foundation, which is Christ, "shepherd of shepherds" and "foundation of foundations."[49] The true Church of Christ is therefore recognizable by its apostolic succession. "The surest and really the most advantageous way" of ascertaining this succession is to list the successors of Peter "to whom, as the representative of the entire Church, the Lord said, 'On this rock I will build my Church, and the gates of hell shall not prevail against it.' " And in fact Augustine does list all the bishops who had succeeded to the "chair of Peter." He concludes: "No Donatist bishop is to be found in this succession." (At this point he adds an interesting point of historical information: "The Donatists did, however, send someone on the side who acted as bishop to a few Africans in Rome and there propagated the sect known as the Montenses or Cutzupitae." We do not know the explanation of these names.)

With the stubborn Donatist in mind, Augustine continues, in a reaffirmation of his own position: "Even if a traitor [i.e., a man guilty of having handed over the sacred books to the pagans] secretly made his way into the series of bishops that runs from Peter to Anastasius, present occupant of the see, this would not in any way harm either the Church or Christians innocent of that fault."[50]

The doctrinal synthesis that the bishop of Hippo elaborated in connection with the Donatists controversy led to a major development of Catholic dogma and itself entered largely into theology. In particular, Augustine received from Cyprian and passed on to others a strong and heartfelt love of the Church that can still be felt in the pages of his works. Even today we can hear the echo of his anguished appeal: "Let us love the Lord our God, let us love his Church: God as our Father, the Church as our Mother; God as Lord, the Church as his handmaid, for we are the children of his handmaid. But this marriage is cemented by great love: no one can offend the one and merit the friendship of the other."[51]

26

The Cross, Grace, and Christian Freedom

The Pelagian Controversy

BY the time Augustine brought thirty years of debates with the Donatists to an end, he had already been involved for ten years in another controversy. This, the controversy with the Pelagians, had the Universal Church for its arena; it was also more difficult from a doctrinal point of view, and the error Augustine was combating had more serious historical consequences. In the beginning, he remained on the sidelines. He was not personally acquainted with the promotors of the new ideas, nor did he take part in the Synod of Carthage that condemned Caelestius, a disciple of Pelagius, who had been accused by Paulinus.[1] He restricted himself to refuting the new ideas in sermons and conferences,[2] his attention being focused at this time chiefly on the great conference with the Donatists.

Before long, however, he was drawn into the fray in person. Marcellinus, the imperial representative, was worried about the growing unrest the new controversy was causing, and in 412, the year after the conference with the Donatists, he asked for Augustine's views. The latter's answer to Marcellinus' questions is contained in the work *The Merits and Forgiveness of Sins*, the first and most important of his writings against the Pelagians. Aurelius, bishop of Carthage, also asked Augustine to intervene. In June 413, in the Basilica of the *Maiores* at Carthage, he preached a major sermon on the baptism of infants. His spirit, his method, and his aims emerge from the words of the peroration:

> Let me therefore, if possible, persuade my brothers [the Pelagians] not to call us heretics. We could perhaps apply that name to them, since they call such important points into question, but we do not do so. Let their devout mother [the Church] support them in order to heal them, and carry them in order to teach them, lest she be obliged to weep for them as dead children. They really go too far; their attitude is hardly tolerable, and to tolerate it further is in-

197

deed a sign of her great patience. Let them not abuse the Church's patience; it is in their best interests to accept correction.

We exhort them as friends; we do not dispute with them as enemies. They speak ill of us, and we put up with it; but let them not speak ill of the rule of faith and of the truth, nor contradict holy Church which labors daily for the forgiveness of original sin in infants. This is a well-founded work. Those who hold divergent positions on other questions that have not yet been completely thought out and not yet answered with the full authority of the Church may continue to do so; error in those areas may be tolerated. But they must not go so far as to shake the very foundation of the Church. That must not be. Perhaps our patience is not yet reprehensible; we ought nonetheless to worry lest we be accused of negligence.

What I have said will be enough for your Charity. Those of you who know these people should deal with them in a friendly and fraternal way, calmly and lovingly, even though they grieve you. Let piety do now what it can; afterward, impiety cannot meet with love.[3]

From this time forward he entered into the controversy with all the advantages of his theological background, his personality, and his experience. He engaged once again in intense activity, even more so than in previous disputes, because the issues here were more serious. Once again the sermons, letters, and books poured out, this time until death cut the cord.

In order to convey a clearer idea of this activity, I shall divide it into three periods or, more accurately, three sectors as determined by the adversaries with whom he was dealing. The three individuals or groups were: Pelagius and his disciple Caelestius; Julian; the monks of Hadrumetum and Marseilles. The first period was marked by calm and positive theological exposition; the second by inflamed polemics; the third by clarifications within the household of the Church.

Augustine's first work, *The Merits and Forgiveness of Sins*, is fundamental because it contains the first biblical theology of redemption and original sin. It called forth in turn another and no less fundamental work that deals with the difference between law and grace. Marcellinus, the magistrate to whom the first work was dedicated, told Augustine of his puzzlement at a statement in it. He read there that while human beings can avoid sin with the help of grace, no one in this world is in fact without sin. "In response I wrote a book entitled *The Spirit and the Letter,* in which I made a detailed study of the Apostle's words, 'The letter kills but the spirit gives life.' "[4]

In this book Augustine distinguishes in fact between law and grace and explains the relations between the two. The law, that is, the letter, is given so that we may seek grace; the spirit, that is, grace, is given so that we may observe the law. Law commands and is an occasion of death; grace aids and is a source of life. Grace has its power from the love that the Holy Spirit pours out in our hearts. Only the divine gift of charity, without which human beings cannot be good and with which they cannot be wicked, leads them to salvation. *The Spirit and the Letter* is a key work for understanding Augustine's teaching on grace.

Some years later (415) Augustine had occasion to reply to a work of Pelagius that had the programmatic title *Nature*. His reply had a no less programmatic title, *Nature and Grace*. The two theological outlooks here confronted could not be summed up more succinctly and effectively. "I answered in order to defend grace and not in order to attack nature, which is liberated and governed by grace."[5] At this same period he gave his response to the *Definitions* (apparently a set of axioms) of Caelestius, an energetic and active disciple of Pelagius. Augustine's work was entitled *Perfect Justice*. In it he showed that Christian perfection can in fact never be perfect in this world, since the divine command that we love God with our "whole" heart is an ideal to which we aspire, not a goal we actually reach. This is another basic thesis in Augustine's anthropology.

In the interim, while Pelagius was in Palestine visiting his friend John, Bishop of Jerusalem, he was accused of heresy, tried by the Synod of Diospolis, and acquitted. News of the acquittal pained and amazed the bishop of Hippo. He asked that the Acts of the synod be sent to him, and he examined them carefully. He then wrote a work showing that while the fourteen bishops of the synod had acquitted Pelagius, they had also condemned Pelagianism. Pelagius was acquitted because he had cleverly hidden his true views and not acknowledged as his the doctrine that had been challenged. Augustine's book was entitled *The Acts of Pelagius* and was addressed to Aurelius, Bishop of Carthage.[6]

The condemnation of Pelagius' teaching followed soon after. It was published by Pope Innocent I on January 27, 417, when he approved the decrees of two African councils: those of Milevis (416) and Carthage (417).[7] It was to this judgment that Augustine was referring in the famous words spoken at Carthage: "The acts of two councils dealing with this matter were forwarded to the Apostolic See, and an answer had come back. *The case is finished (Causa finita est)*. God grant that the error too may be finished!"[8] He returned to the point three years later, saying that the pope's reply "removed all doubt on the question."[9] The condemnation was solemnly confirmed by Innocent's successor, Pope Zosimus, in his letter *Tractoria*, written in the spring of 418. Augustine commented: "Pelagius had fooled the synod in Palestine, but he did not manage to fool the Church of Rome."[10]

Some time after the renewed condemnation by Pope Zosimus, and while still at Carthage, Augustine was asked by three aristocrats, Albina, Pinian, and Melania, to write a work denouncing the deception practiced by Pelagius. Pelagius talked of grace, but he meant freedom and law. In addition, both he and his disciple Caelestius denied original sin, which was an obvious truth of the faith. Augustine's work was entitled *The Grace of Christ and Original Sin*.[11] The controversy had now entered a second phase in which exposition gave way to polemics. This phase was marked by bitterness, and it lasted a long time.

Julian and eighteen other Italian bishops refused to subscribe to the *Tractoria* of Zosimus. They wrote the pope two letters, composed by Julian, in justification of their stand. These contained a profession of faith and harsh accusations against their adversaries. Among the accusations were charges of Manichaeism, the denial of free will, and the condemnation of marriage; the bishop of Hippo was named as one of those who held such views. Pope Boniface therefore sent the two letters to Augustine and asked him to reply to them. He did so with a work in four books, *Against the Two Letters of the Pelagians*. It was dedicated to the Bishop of Rome who had requested it.[12]

Shortly before this, Augustine had written another work, this time at the request of Count Valerius of the court of Ravenna, by way of answer to the third of the accusations just mentioned. The work was entitled *Marriage and Desire,* and it became the starting point for an endless debate. The first (originally the only) book of the work came into the hands of Julian, the chief accuser. He quickly wrote a reply in four books, dedicating them to a man who shared his views, "Turbantius, my dear colleague in the priesthood." Some of Julian's friends thought the reply too lengthy; they made a summary of it and sent it to Valerius, who in turn sent it on to Augustine. Augustine replied by adding a second book to his *Marriage and Desire.*[13]

Some time after, in about 421, the complete text of Julian's four books reached Augustine, who realized that the extracts originally sent to him did not always reflect the real thought of his adversary. He therefore decided to write a fuller and more careful reply; the result was the six books of his work *Against Julian.* Of these four discussed, one by one, the four books of Julian; two formed an introduction in which Augustine set forth and developed the argument from Tradition.[14]

Meanwhile, the second book of Augustine's *Marriage and Desire* had reached Julian; the latter, having written four books in reply to Augustine's first, now wrote eight in reply to his second. These were dedicated to Florus, another bishop who shared Julian's ideas. Alypius happened to be in Rome and saw the second reply; he had it copied and sent it to his friend, asking him to reply to this new attack and refute its theses point by point.[15] Augustine, though now seventy-four years old, set to work. He dictated six books, but death overtook him and the work remained unfinished.

While carrying on this bitter debate with Julian, Augustine was also forced to take a position on the difficult and sensitive question of the harmony between grace and free will. A letter of his to Sixtus, a Roman priest,[16] was copied in Rome and read in Africa in the monastery at Hadrumetum, where it greatly disturbed the monks who interpreted Augustine's defense of grace as a denial of freedom. In order to put an end to the discussion, which was turning into a quarrel, the abbot addressed the bishop of Hippo. The latter, always ready to serve others, replied with two letters[17] and a work that once again had a programmatic title: *Grace and Free Will.*

In this book he shows that Scripture teaches both truths and that both must be maintained, even if we do not grasp how they are to be harmonized.[18] The clear and well-documented explanation given was not enough, however, to resolve all difficulties and calm all spirits. Some concluded from it that Christian asceticism had no room for *disciplina* (fraternal correction), but only for prayer. There is no need of correcting those who are living an evil life; we need only pray that they be granted the grace of changing their ways. The abbot turned to Augustine once again, and he replied with a further book *Correction and Grace*.[19] It is the most important of all his works for understanding his systematic theology of grace.

These two works—*Grace and Free Will* and *Correction and Grace*—which were written to bring peace to the monks of Hadrumetum in Africa, were a source of great uneasiness to the monks of southern Gaul and more specifically to those of Marseilles and Lerins. Prosper and Hilary, two laymen, informed Augustine of the lively opposition there and asked him to reply to the objections.[20]

The result was two more works, the final ones from his pen: *The Predestination of the Saints* and *The Gift of Perseverance*. In them Augustine shows that the beginning of faith, conversion, and perseverance in the good are gifts from God and not the work of free will, as his opponents in Gaul were claiming. Divine predestination is therefore a gratuitous gift, but it is also a source of serene confidence, as Augustine is at pains to emphasize.[21]

"Lest the cross of Christ be rendered ineffective" (1 Cor 1:17)

Augustine considered Pelagianism to be a form of arrogant naturalism. On the one hand, it denied original sin and the necessity of grace and, on the other, asserted human sinlessness (*impeccantia*) and autonomy before God, thus striking a double blow at the heart of Christianity. In other words, it stripped all meaning from the cross of Christ and the idea of our redemption. It was this unclouded insight that caused Augustine to labor so unceasingly.

Pelagius' book, *Nature*, had been sent to him by two young aristocrats, Timasius and James, who had consecrated themselves to God as a result of Pelagius' exhortations but then had realized his errors and had separated from him.[22] Here is Augustine's judgment on the book:

> The book you sent me I have read from beginning to end . . . quickly but nonetheless with great attention. In it I see a man filled with burning zeal against those who sin but—instead of blaming the human will—seek to excuse themselves by blaming human nature. He is overly incensed against a pestilential habit that even pagan authors condemn when they exclaim: "Wrongly does the human race complain about its own nature." The author defends these very words with all the talents at his disposal. I fear, however, that in so doing he has put himself with those who "have zeal for God, but not an enlightened zeal" (Rom 10:2-3).[23]

The people Augustine has in mind avoid one error at the cost of falling into an opposite error. In speaking of "pagan authors" he is surely thinking of the well-known verse of Horace,[24] but out of respect for the author of the book with which he is dealing he does not name him. He does, however, refer to a passage of St. James that is not any less severe in the part of it that he does not quote.

> The writer seems to speak with insight, but his wisdom is of the kind that makes ineffective the cross of Christ (1 Cor 1:17). "This wisdom is not from above" (James 3:15); I do not add what follows in St. James[25] lest I seem to insult our friends, whose sharp and lively minds we would prefer to see on the right path and not departing from it.

After paying this tribute of loving respect to his adversaries, Augustine states the theme of his reply in these solemn terms:

> The author of the book you sent me is inflamed with zeal against those who would defend their sins by invoking the weakness of human nature. We ought to have the same or even greater zeal in seeing to it *that the cross of Christ is not rendered ineffective.* It is rendered ineffective, however, if we in any way allow that justice and eternal life can be won apart from the mystery of Christ. Yet that is precisely the position defended in this book. I do not say it is defended consciously, lest I be forced to say that its writer is not a Christian at all, rather, in my opinion, the author defends it without realizing it.[26]

Given Augustine's premise, we can understand what his attitude to the Pelagians is bound to be: he will not deny what they assert, but he will assert what they deny: redemption, grace,

Christian freedom. His reproach to them is that they deny these great and essential truths of revelation, and not that they assert, as they do, the goodness of things, the blessings of marriage, the holiness of the law, the responsibility of the sinner, and the justice of the saints.

> When we insist that the Pelagians . . . must not deny original sin, or deny that the justifying grace of God is given freely and not in accordance with our merits, or deny that human beings, no matter how holy or virtuous, are not so just that they do not need, even after baptism and as long as they live, the forgiveness of sins— when we insist that they not deny these truths or regard those who believe them as cut off from the grace of the Savior . . . they produce clouds of smoke in the form of other questions with which they hide their error in dealing with simpler folk or folk slow of mind or less acquainted with the Scriptures. Such clouds of smoke are: praise of creatures, praise of marriage, praise of the law, praise of free will, and praise of the saints. As if any of us reviled these things and did not rather exalt them by praising duly their creator and Savior! But. . . .[27]

The entire theological and pastoral work of the bishop of Hippo can be regarded as summed up in this "but." His main effort was to show that we must not defend some truths by denying others but must rather maintain and affirm all of them together in the higher unity that is Christian doctrine. When we do not see the deeper explanation of this unity—and this happens frequently in dealing with such a sublime subject—we must fall back on the sense of mystery that should never be lacking in the Christian soul.

The error of the Pelagians, then, was their onesidedness: they affirmed the goodness of nature and the power of freedom, but they denied the necessity of redemption and the efficacy of grace. They boasted of their distance from the Manichaeans, but they failed to see that they were falling into the opposite but no less serious error. Catholic doctrine, on the other hand, followed a path between the two extremes. "What does it profit these new heretics—enemies of the cross of Christ and opponents of divine grace—to be clean of the Manichaean error if they die from the sickness of their own error?"[28]

Augustine perseveringly defends this position with its harmonious synthesis of contraries, as he shows that the Catholic

Church is equally distant from the Pelagians and the Manichaeans,[29] just as in another day it had been equally distant from the Sabellians and the Arians.[30] The demands of debate obviously cause Augustine to lay greater emphasis on the truths that are being denied, but he does not assert them at the expense of the others, although, again owing to the thrust of polemics, these remain in the background. This is clear to attentive readers of his works who do not let themselves be upset by the use of language that is not always technical and is often oratorical, or be influenced by the liveliness of a debate in which matters essential to Christianity are at stake.

Augustine's aim was to bring home the doctrine of redemption. Original sin and redemption are two closely linked truths: they stand or fall together. By denying the first, the Pelagians also denied the second. Augustine saw this and repeated it in every way he could. His program was to assemble the passages of Scripture on redemption, use them to show that Christ is essentially a redeemer, and conclude that those who have no need of redemption do not belong to Christ.

> It will be simpler to heap up as many [texts] as can be found or as many as seem sufficient to show that the Lord Jesus Christ came into this world solely . . . in order to give life, save, redeem, and enlighten those who dwell in death, weakness, slavery, prison, and the darkness of sin, under the power of Satan, prince of sinners. . . . Once this has been abundantly shown, the conclusion will be that those who have no need of life, salvation, liberation, redemption, and enlightenment can have no part in the saving work of Christ.[31]

It follows that either infants need Christ—and therefore are in sin, which, in the case of infants not yet able to exercise reason, cannot be personal sin—or they do not belong to him. This dilemma sums up Augustine's theology of the relations between original sin and redemption.

The redemption wrought by Christ is therefore necessary for all, inasmuch as none can be justified before God except by the one mediator between God and human beings. "This is what it means to 'render ineffective the cross of Christ': to maintain that human beings can be justified without it, justified by means of the natural law and free will."[32]

Redemption is universal in scope; that is, it has been accomplished by Christ in behalf of all human beings, even those who in fact are lost, even Judas. Judas "threw away the sum of money for which he had sold the Lord but was unable to appreciate the price for which the Lord had bought him."[33] Throughout the Pelagian controversy Augustine repeatedly affirms the universality of redemption as an irrefutable argument for the universality of the fall. We must keep this clear universalism in mind if we want to avoid misinterpreting those texts in Augustine that give a restrictive explanation of the well-known Pauline passage on the universal salvific will (1 Tim 2:4).[34]

Redemption, moreover, does not consist solely in the example of virtue that Christ has given; it also includes ransom, reconciliation, and liberation. It was accomplished by the sacrifice of the cross, which was a proper, freely offered, and perfect sacrifice.[35] Thus, while the Pelagians set imitation over against imitation—the imitation of Christ by the just against the imitation of Adam by the wicked—Augustine laid his primary emphasis on the opposition between rebirth in Christ and birth in Adam.[36]

As a result of this contrast, the focus of the discussion shifted from redemption to justification, another central point in Christian teaching. One of Augustine's concerns was to introduce clarity into this concept, which is broad, profound, and complex. He noted that the biblical terms for it—rebirth, adoption, salvation, charity—display part of their meaning when referred to the present life and their total meaning when referred to the future life. In other words, Christian justification and the life of the Church are essentially, though not exclusively, eschatological realities. Justification in this life is authentic, real, and interior insofar as it includes the forgiveness of sins, for this forgiveness is "full and total," "full and complete,"[37] and entails both the presence of the Holy Spirit, who pours love into hearts, and deification. But justification will be complete only in heaven, when mortality is eliminated by the resurrection, and "God will be all in all."

In explaining the far from easy idea of justification Augustine introduced valuable distinctions that were not always understood at the time and have not always been understood since then. There is, for example, the distinction between the forgiveness of sins, which is given in baptism and is total, and the renewal of the old self, which is not total but progressive. This renewal will be complete only after the resurrection, which itself is an effect of baptism, but one that is future, not present. There is also the distinction between the evil of sin itself, which is forgiven, and the evil of the inclination to sin, which remains. It remains, however, not as a reason for condemnation but as a reason for struggle.[38] This distinction led Augustine to write a book entitled *The Christian Struggle.*

Grace and freedom

Another subject that Augustine was very concerned to explain and bring home to readers was freedom and grace. Without freedom there is no human dignity; without grace there is no salvation. Any error on this subject cannot fail to have serious consequences. He had defended freedom against the Manichaeans; now he had to defend grace against the Pelagians. Once again his aim was to show that Catholic teaching keeps a course between two extremes.

First of all, he removes a misunderstanding. Contrary to what the Pelagians say, grace, as understood by Christians, is not freedom, although freedom, like creation, is a very precious and utterly gratuitous gift. Nor is grace the same as revelation or the law, although both of these are signs of God's immense goodwill toward us. Nor is it simply justification, although this is God's supreme gift. Grace is the help that removes "ignorance" and "difficulty" and thereby leads human beings to justification, supports them in the struggle against evil, makes it possible for them to persevere in goodness, and ensures their salvation. In short, to use an Augustinian definition, it is "the inspiration of love."[39] For in order to do the good it is not enough to know the good; one must also experience its attraction and love. If it is merely known but "its attraction is not felt and it is not loved, there will be no action, no acceptance of it, no virtuous life."[40]

Having once explained the true concept of grace (the grace that later theologians will call "actual"), Augustine goes on to show that grace does not deny freedom but is rather its source. When he speaks of freedom in the Pelagian controversy, he is thinking of Christian freedom. It is this that concerns him, this that he emphasizes. His inspiration and motto during this long battle was taken from the words of Jesus: "If the Son sets you free, you will be truly free" (Jn 8:36). There are four great Christian freedoms: freedom from sin, freedom from the inclination to sin, freedom from death, and freedom from time. Augustine never tires of praising and defending these. Here is a forcefully worded and compact summary that takes as its point of departure the relation Paul establishes between law and faith.

> Do we therefore use grace to overthrow freedom? Never! In fact, we even uphold the value that is free will. Just as the law is not overthrown by faith but rather upheld by it (Rom 3:31), so free will is not overthrown but upheld by grace. The law cannot be observed except by a will that is free. Yet from the law comes knowledge of sin, whereas from grace comes the health of the soul that is free of the vice of sin, from the health of the soul the freedom of free will, from the freedom of free will love of righteousness, and from love of righteousness the fulfillment of the law. Therefore, just as the law is not overthrown but upheld by faith, because faith asks and obtains the grace by which the law is observed, so free will is not overthrown but upheld by grace, because grace heals the will and the healed will freely loves righteousness.[41]

The idea of Christian liberty is so deeply rooted in Augustine's soul that he sees the entire history of salvation as a history of freedom. In the beginning, before sin, human beings had two freedoms: "the power not to sin" and "the power not to die." Sin brought the loss of these as its punishment. Christ won them back by his redemptive work. When human beings share in the fruits of redemption through grace, they gradually regain those freedoms. They will regain full possession of them at the end of time when "the power not to sin" and "the power not to die" will be replaced by two immensely greater freedoms: "the inability to sin" and "the inability to die," that is, the gifts of perfect justice and of immortality.[42]

Speaking of Christian freedom, Augustine tells the people: "The first freedom is to be free of serious sin." He goes on to say:

> When human beings begin to be free of these sins . . . they begin to raise their heads in the direction of freedom. The freedom they now have is only the beginning of freedom; it is not perfect freedom. "But why is it not perfect freedom?" someone may ask. Because "I experience in my members another law that is in conflict with the law of my mind" (Rom 7:23). . . . There is partial free-

dom and partial slavery. Freedom is not yet total, not yet pure, not yet complete, because we are not yet in eternity. . . . When will freedom be truly full and perfect? When all enmities cease; when "the last enemy, death, is overcome" (1 Cor 15:26).[43]

While Augustine habitually speaks of Christian freedom, which is his main concern, he does not ignore or neglect the primarily philosophical subject of freedom of choice. For it is freedom of choice that concretely grounds the responsibility of human beings for their actions and makes these actions worthy of praise or blame, reward or punishment. In order to defend this freedom along with grace, he wrote the work mentioned earlier, *Grace and Free Will* (or *Grace and the Free Choice of the Will*).

Having reached this point, however, he repeatedly says that the question is a difficult one and that few can come to grips with it. He means the question of how freedom of choice can be harmonized with the action of grace. He exhorts his readers, therefore, to hold fast to the *fact*, even if they are unable to understand the *how*.[44] The fact is that God created us without our cooperation but will not save us without our cooperation—"he who created you without you does not justify you without you: he creates beings who do not know they are being created, but he justifies only those who will to be justified."[45] Therefore grace does not exclude freedom nor freedom grace. "Freedom of choice is not destroyed because it is helped [by grace]; rather it is helped because it is not destroyed."[46]

With this principle as a basis Augustine repeatedly exhorts his readers to prayer, action, and confidence. He often reminds them that God does not abandon us if we do not abandon him,[47] and he sets as a seal on his teaching about grace this solemn aphorism that sums up so many pages of his writings: "We live in greater safety if we give everything to God *(tutiores vivimus si totum Deo damus)*."[48]

Despite what has at times been said, this attitude does not mean a discrepancy between the pastoral and the theological approaches to predestination.

Speaking as a theologian, Augustine, the Doctor of Grace, expounds and explains the seemingly opposed statements of Scripture (as he understands them after long study), namely, the universality of redemption (and therefore God's love for all human beings) and the divine predilection of the elect; the responsibility of the sinner and God's greater mercy to the just. In his pastoral dealings with the faithful, this teaching provides him with motives for combating both the negligence that omits to do good and the presumption that ascribes salvation to our own merits. It allows him as well to emphasize both human activity and trust in God.[49]

When reason attempts to fragment the mystery, he reminds it that the divine plan may be unfathomable, but it is not unjust. "God is good, God is just. Because he is good he can save everyone without merits of theirs."[50] "Since it is written that 'all the ways of the Lord are mercy and truth' (Ps 25:10), his grace cannot be unjust nor can his mercy be cruel."[51] According to the teaching of Paul, one thing is certain: there can be no injustice in God (Rom 9:14). The rest is mystery, and before mystery we can only bow down. Augustine knows this and bows down. He exhorts others to do the same.

> You seek reasons; I will tremble before the abyss. . . . You build syllogisms; I will stand amazed. You go on debating; I will believe. I see the depths, I do not succeed in reaching the bottom. . . . Have you come to examine? Believe me, if you have come to scrutinize the inscrutable and to trace the trackless, you are already lost. . . . It is like wanting to see the invisible and speak the ineffable.[52]

I am well aware, of course, that others have interpreted, and continue to interpret, Augustine's doctrinal synthesis on grace, and especially the part of it that deals with predestination, as a pessimistic and hopeless vision of reality. I can only say that such an interpretation does not reflect either his spirit or his writings. Since the character of the present book does not permit me to deal with the subject very extensively, I have indicated the main headings of an interpretation I regard as accurate and allowed readers to study for themselves some of the texts on which it is based.

For the same reason I have explained Augustine's own interpretation of Pelagianism and have not discussed the revaluations of that movement that are to be found in modern studies of the question, some of them quite recent.[53]

27

The Controversialist

WE have been reviewing the work of a man who for so many years was always writing against someone (the titles of Augustine's books that begin with the Latin word *Contra*—"Against"—are numerous indeed). My readers would surely like to know the spirit and method with which Augustine carried on these countless battles. Their desire is understandable, and I shall try to satisfy it.

Augustine was undoubtedly a formidable controversialist. He developed his ideas through study and defended them forcefully, clearly, and ably. He does not get lost in details but goes directly to the heart of the question. With sure insight he sees the consequences of an erroneous principle and demonstrates them with inexorable logic. As a consummate dialectician, he is able to spot the ambiguities in an adversary's argument and put the other on the defensive by pushing him into unavoidable dilemmas. In Augustine's eyes there is but one way of being consistent with oneself, and that is to yield to truth; such a submission does not humiliate us, it exalts us. He is certain of his own faith and has the skill to marshal all possible arguments in its defense. If an opponent lacks arguments and gives an empty answer, Augustine reminds him, in ironical tones not unmixed with pity, that there is no worse plight than to be unable either to speak or to remain silent.

Yet Augustine the controversialist is motivated and sustained by love. His is a tender and passionate love both for truth (he has unfailing confidence in its power to draw human beings) and for the erring. It is a demanding love, but it is also humble, generous, honest, and constructive.

He never forgets his own experience of being astray, and the memory compels him to be modest and patient. Thus he tells the Manichaeans:

> You are treated harshly by those who do not know how difficult it is to find truth and avoid error . . . who do not know what

211

a rare and arduous thing it is to rise above bodily images with the aid of the mind's sweet devotion . . . who do not know the price that must be paid to heal the eye of the interior self so that it can at least see its own sun . . . who do not know the painful effort required if one is to succeed in understanding God in even the smallest degree. . . . Finally, you are treated harshly by those who have never gone astray in the error in which they see you entangled. For my part . . . I cannot be so harsh . . . but must show you the same patience my friends showed me when I was following your teachings.[1]

These are the sentiments that determine his attitude.[2]

Confidence in the power of truth

The consciousness of his own past errors is awakened again in the debate with the Pelagians. In the most painful phase of this controversy, when it is not the Pelagians but the monks of Gaul who object to his teaching on grace, he openly admits that at one time he entertained the same erroneous view that they now profess. "When the observations of my readers enable me not only to be better informed but even to correct my views, I consider this a favor from God; this is a service I look for especially from the Church's teachers." But this conscious modesty does not keep him from reminding his opponents that they too must be on guard against error, since, after all, they too can go astray. "Those who think me mistaken must be willing to meditate diligently and repeatedly on what I have written, for it is they who may be mistaken."[3]

The same confidence in the power of truth is to be seen in the Donatist controversy. Augustine reminds the Donatists of the rule that governs theological discussion in the Church, where they should have remained. As long as obscurities have not been clarified we can and should discuss the matter, but—and this is the rule—"without dark clouds of sacrilegious pride, without arrogance of mind, without disputes inspired by envy and jealousy; but rather with holy humility, Catholic peace, and Christian charity."[4] There is no doubt that this was the atmosphere he desired should permeate the discussions with them. He looked upon the Donatists as his brothers and sisters and loved them as such. "Whether they like it or not, they are our brothers and sisters.

They will cease to be our brothers and sisters only when they no longer say 'Our Father.' "[5]

The Donatists did not like this and reacted with scorn. There was, of course, a certain logic in their attitude: since they did not acknowledge the validity of baptisms administered by Catholics, they did not regard the latter as brothers and sisters in Christ and did not wish to be regarded as such by them. The only thing Catholics could do to please them was to show no concern or interest in them. There was thus a psychological barrier, but Augustine did not lose heart. He did everything he could to break down the barrier, and he succeeded. The weapon he used was love. "Let them say what they want against us; for our part, let us love them even if they do not want our love."[6]

The love that would have everyone possess the truth in common led to respect and generosity toward adversaries. Augustine gave a moving proof of this in his dealings with the Donatists. (I say this even though it was precisely in the Donatist controversy that Catholics had to make the unpleasant choice of falling back on the power of the state.) He showed them signs of sincere and unhypocritical deference. "He who searches consciences knows that I act with a sincere intention and with sentiments of Christian humility, even if this is not evident to the majority."[7]

At the Council of Carthage in 401 he was a convinced backer of the conciliar decree that the Donatist clergy should be received into the Catholic Church without losing their clerical rank.

He even went much further at the great conference of 411, where he proposed that Catholic bishops should pledge themselves in a written statement to Marcellinus, the presiding magistrate, to yield their sees to their Donatist colleagues should they be defeated in the debate, while not demanding the same of the Donatists should the Catholics emerge victorious. Thus, if the Catholics won, the Donatist bishops would share the episcopal dignity with the Catholic bishops: either the present Catholic and Donatist bishops would hold a see jointly or, if this were unacceptable to the people, both would resign and make way for the election of a new, single bishop. The almost thirty bishops present, with only two dissenting voices, enthusiastically embraced this proposal, and the solemn document was drawn up. In it we read:

How can we draw back from offering this sacrifice of humility
to our Redeemer? Did he not descend from heaven and take human
members in order that we might become his members? Shall we be
afraid to descend from our episcopal chairs in order to keep his
members from being torn apart in a cruel division? We need only
be faithful and obedient Christians; let us seek to be such at all
times. We have been consecrated bishops for the service of the
Christian communities; let us therefore do an episcopal work that
is useful for the Christian peace of Christ's faithful. If we are indeed profitable servants, how can we endanger the eternal interests of the Lord for the sake of our temporal dignity? Our episcopal
dignity will have been more fruitful for us if we lay it aside in order
to unite the flock to be scattered. Can we have the effrontery to
hope for the honor promised us by Christ in the world to come if
our ecclesiastical rank is an obstacle to the unity of Christ in this
world?[8]

No one can fail to recognize in this passage the great soul and
effective style of the bishop of Hippo. There are some, however,
who accuse him of insincerity in speaking as he did. The reason
may be that the formulation of the proposal made his hearers
hopeful or even certain that fortune would smile on the Catholic
side. If this is indeed the reason for the accusation—and I for my
part can see no other—I must say that I fail to see the force of the
argument. That is, I do not understand how the certainty of success renders the proposal insincere. The idea was that, even if the
Catholics should win, the Catholic bishops would accept one of
two outcomes: either they would have the Donatist bishop sharing the governance of their diocese with them or they would both
retire from the episcopate and let a third party be elected in their
stead. Both consequences demanded renunciation and would not
have been accepted unless the bishops had a keen sense of responsibility and an unselfish love of the Church.

Some years later, Augustine looked back to the making and
acceptance of the proposal as having been in the circumstances
"a sweet memory," and he repeated the deeper pastoral reason
for it: "If I decide to keep my see and thereby cause the flock of
Christ to be scattered, can the misfortune of the flock really bring
honor to the shepherd?" Stern words, these, that show the ultimate consequences entailed in ministerial service. "What you are
for your own sake [namely, a Christian] and I for mine, we should

be at all times; what I am for your sake [a bishop] let me be if it helps you and not be if it harms you."[9]

Love was also the source of Augustine's generosity to his adversaries. The Donatists spread calumnies against him,[10] spoke of him to their followers as "a wolf that ought to be killed for the safety of the flock,"[11] and even tried to do away with him.[12] Yet he would never allow this personal side to play a part in the debate. He would say to the faithful:

> Put aside any consideration of me personally. Say to them only this: "Brothers, stick to the question. Bishop Augustine is a member of the Catholic Church, has his own charge, and will have to render an account of it. I regard him as a good man. If he is a bad man, that is his business, but even if he is a good man, I do not base my hope on him." . . . Therefore do not fight them in order to defend me.[13]

It would be difficult to be more generous than that.

Exacting scholarship

Augustine's scholarly probity was as great as his generosity. He carefully investigated the provenance of writings before giving an answer to them; he read them attentively and reported faithfully what they said. This method forced him into a great many lengthy and useless repetitions, but he adopted it because of his concern for objectivity. Sometimes his scrupulousness caused him even to write a new work when he found that the text to which he had previously replied did not reflect accurately the thought of his adversary. That is what happened in connection with the work entitled *Against Julian*.[14]

Augustine went to every length to keep a discussion from being obscured, to the adversary's advantage, by doubts about the authenticity and fidelity of the writings he was examining. Such doubts would have made it easy to avoid the main point at issue and go wandering off into digressions. He wanted his readers to be able to go straight to the core of the problem and pass judgment without distracting irrelevancies. For this reason he set before them both his own text and that of his adversary, even if the latter might be, as it often was, long, inconclusive, and even offensive. It is to this concern for scholarly probity, this indifference to his personal interests, that we owe so many of the Manichaean, Donatist, Pelagian, and Arian writings that have come down to us. As we read these documents today, we may come to different conclusions from those of Augustine, but we cannot fail to thank him for having passed the documents on to us.

Lively polemics

Before ending these remarks on Augustine as controversialist, I must point out that at times the polemics become very lively indeed. I am thinking in particular of the *Unfinished Work against Julian*, which contains Augustine's answer to the final defense of Pelagianism. Julian, a prolix writer, fought with all the means available to an aggressive disputant and did not shrink from accusations, insults, and calumnies, even coarse calumnies. The elderly Augustine paid Julian back in the same coin, showing him that such tactics could not hide weak arguments.

Julian repeatedly charges Augustine with Manichaeism. The latter shows the falsity of the charge and then turns it back on his adversary who, without realizing it, has with his doctrine become a valuable ally of the Manichaeans.[15]

Because of Augustine's teaching on concupiscence, Julian calls him "prosecutor of the saints and patron of asses." Augustine answers: "What are you talking about, you slanderer of Catholics and fellow-traveler with the Manichaeans? What are you talking about? Even you, ass-brain, should blush to talk so stupidly. . . . Why can't you understand, you ass, that human beings cannot be born sinless while asses can?" He then cites a passage from Ambrose and concludes: "If you yourself do not have the soul of an ass, recognize that concupiscence is natural to the beasts but a punishment for human beings."[16]

Julian claims that via Alypius Augustine has sent more than eighty African horses to the court of Ravenna in order to curry favor and win an imperial verdict against the Pelagians. Augustine answers:

> Either you are speaking slander or you don't know what you are talking about. Therefore you are either a liar or a fool. If you made it all up, what could be more malicious? If you believed some-

one who told it to you, what could be more stupid? Then in an act of impudence or, better, utter madness, you had the nerve to write it down and were not afraid that your books might make their way to places where my colleague Alypius had been received . . . and where your brazen lies would be read and make you either a laughingstock or an object of contempt.[17]

Elsewhere, seeing inconclusive arguments being advanced against him, he exclaims: "Where is the logic you're always boasting about? If you are so learned and so sharp, why can't you see these things? And if you do see them, why do you set traps for the unlearned and the simple?"[18] Or, in a drier tone: "If you have nothing to say, be quiet if you can; unfortunately, you're incapable even of that."[19]

These are but a few examples of the lively exchanges that marked an endless controversy. Only once was Augustine profoundly disturbed by what was said; on that occasion he became his old self. It was when his caustic adversary went beyond acceptable limits and attacked Augustine's mother with coarse insults. Augustine answered:

> You have insulted even the memory of my mother, a woman who never did you any harm, never entered the lists against you. A sure sign, is it not, that you have succumbed to the evil spirit of slander? You have not feared what is written: "Slanderers shall not possess the kingdom of God." . . . For my part, I think your parents, Catholic Christians, are to be honored, and I am happy for them that they died before seeing you turn heretic.[20]

We can hear in these words the deep emotion of a man who has been attacked in his deepest feelings (few have loved their mothers as Augustine did). We glimpse also the self-control of a controversialist who reacts to the offense simply by reminding his adversary that slanderers will not escape divine wrath.

In the remainder of this work, however, the controversy is fierce and cutting in its tone, as Augustine returns blow for blow. The tone is surprising. The controversy with the Pelagians had begun in an atmosphere of calm and respect. Augustine spoke of the Pelagians with appreciation and esteem: he praised their lives,[21] acknowledged the acumen and fruitfulness of their writings,[22] and admired their intellectual talents.[23] In the beginning, he refuted the error without mentioning its authors.[24]

Toward Pelagius himself he showed special goodwill; thus in his first writing against the Pelagians he says: "I have read some books of Pelagius, who, they tell me, is a holy man and has made no little progress in Christian life."[25] On receiving from Pelagius a letter filled with praise of him, Augustine replied very courteously, though without entering into the merits of the issues: "Beloved master and desired brothers, may the Lord reward you with his blesssings, and may these be yours forever and bring you to live eternally with him who is eternal."[26]

He showed no less goodwill toward Julian. Writing to Julian's father, Memorius, who had asked him for a copy of his books on *Music*, he speaks of "our son and fellow deacon, Julian," "our companion in the service of Christ," and expresses a keen desire to see him. He therefore asks the father to send his son to Hippo.[27] Even in the heat of controversy, he calls him (in the work *Against Julian*) "beloved son Julian,"[28] although the polemical tone is by now more intense. The liveliness increases in the second reply, the *Unfinished Work against Julian*. Why?

I think that there were two reasons for the change. First of all, Augustine had given up any hope of persuading his adversary, who was now openly and contumaciously rebellious; he could now only carry on with his duty, which was to unmask error and defend the faith. He did so with the resources given him by dialectic and experience. Second, having decided, in his concern for objectivity, to present his reader with Julian's complete text, filled as it was with accusations and frenzied blows, he had no choice but to respond with equal force and energy. Had he not, he would have left his readers, especially the simpler and more defenseless among them, at the mercy of Julian's deceptive arguments and insidious blows; lacking an adequate response, these could not but have made an impression.

Love for his adversary and for the Church

Henceforth, and not through the fault of Augustine, controversy degenerated into diatribe; the only alternatives were not to answer at all or to give tit for tat. Augustine chose to reply in the same coin he received, since in his view the defense of the faith required it. Yet he had in his heart a great love for his adversary.

Modern readers may think he would have done better to choose the first alternative or, at most, to issue a brief document succinctly outlining the main theses against Pelagianism and referring his readers to the major work that preceded for further details. Augustine in fact chose the second alternative. We do not know whether he did so on his own initiative or at the persuasion of friends. We do know that friends were urging him to take this course, in particular Alypius, the friend who was dearest to him and had the greatest influence on him.

In any case, the fact that a man over seventy, burdened with many concerns, should have devoted the hours of the night (during the day he was dictating other works[29]) to composing such a long, tedious, and difficult answer cannot but make us marvel at the physical stamina, intellectual energy, and indomitable love of the Church that it supposes. Whatever the reader's judgment on the *Unfinished Work against Julian*, it has the merit of having preserved the text of Julian himself and given us Augustine's final answer to the views of the Pelagians.

The reply repeats the usual themes and here and there develops them further. Above all, it states and develops a new thesis that turns back on Julian himself the accusation of Manichaeism he had previously urged against the Catholics. According to Augustine, by its denial of original sin Pelagianism unwittingly becomes Manichaeism's best ally. This thesis has given rise to long and lively discussions that have in large measure been the vehicle for the historical unfolding of the theology of grace.[30]

28

Ecumenism

I T is common knowledge that the decline of Donatism had two causes: its theoretical refutation and the intervention of the imperial government. Augustine's involvement in both was important, but it is also the object of criticism from modern scholars. It has become almost obligatory today to accuse him of harshness toward the Donatists and a lack of ecumenical spirit and, above all, of being the first theoretician of the Inquisition.[1] In my opinion, these judgments are based partly or wholly on an inaccurate grasp of the facts. I shall therefore continue to explain these. I have already described Augustine's refutation of Donatist theory; I turn now to the question of governmental intervention and Augustine's attitude toward it.

Early government intervention versus the Donatists

The government had already intervened several times with legislation imposing unity, but this had produced little fruit. The first edict of unity was issued by Emperor Constantine in 316. The Donatists responded with stubborn violence. Its agents were bands of fanatics—men of the lowest type, known as "Circumcellions"—who roamed the countryside bringing terror, destruction, and death everywhere. Their battle cry, *Laus Deo* ("Praise God!") was more fearful than a lion's roar to their unfortunate victims.[2] They stole or destroyed the crops ("Solids they carried away, liquids they poured out"[3]); they assaulted, beat, mutilated, and killed human beings. They dealt cruelly even with themselves, often committing suicide in order to win the martyr's crown. "They live as bandits, die as circumcellions, and are honored as martyrs."[4]

This violent resistance led to the issuance of an edict of toleration in 321. The Donatists breathed more easily and spread rapidly, but they did not change their violent ways. In the face of this situation, Constantine's successor Constantius pursued his father's policy; that is, he tried the method of persuasion, but in vain. The Donatists forgot that they themselves had appealed to the power of the government and they now denied the emperor any right to intervene in religious matters. "What has the emperor to do with the Church?" Since peaceful efforts had failed, Constantius in 347 revoked the edict of toleration and reinstated the edict of 316 with its demand for union. Macarius, commissioner for Africa, applied the law with severity, producing many victims whose coreligionists honored them as martyrs. The repression lasted no more than a year, but it remained notorious. The Donatists inveighed in their writings against the cruelty of "the days of Macarius" and bestowed on Catholics the nickname of "Macarians."

The situation was reversed in 362 when Emperor Julian repealed the decrees of his predecessors and showed open favor to the Donatists. Eager for revenge, the "Donatist party" shed Catholic blood in various places. But things soon changed again, for emperors Valentinian and Gratian began once more to protect the Catholic Church. Their laws, however, do not seem to have been strictly enforced, and there followed years in which the two Churches consolidated their positions and produced their best controversialists: Optatus of Milevis and Parmenian. Theodosius the Great succeeded to the throne and began to act more effectively. He issued many laws against heretics, among them that of 392 which imposed a fine of ten pounds of gold on any cleric guilty of heresy. The law was applied against the Donatists in Africa, at least in cases in which they abetted violence.[5]

Early view of Augustine

The year 392 brings us to the time of Augustine. Shortly after being ordained a priest, he realized that repressive laws could not by themselves restore lost unity; he even thought they could prove harmful, since they could produce outwardly conforming Catholics in place of open schismatics. What was needed was diligent and persevering catechesis. People had to be enlightened about the origins of Donatism and its lack of coherence both historical and theological. They had to have Catholic teaching explained to them and be shown that truth and love alike call for unity.

He set to work immediately. Soon after his ordination he wrote to Maximinus, Donatist bishop of Siniti (near Hippo):

> Let us put aside the useless accusations that the two parties level against each other out of ignorance. Do not keep bringing up "the days of Macarius," and I will not keep bringing up the cruelty of the circumcellions. The former does not affect you, nor the latter me. . . .
>
> Let us deal with the matter objectively, as reasonable men who appeal to the authority of the Scriptures. As far as possible, let us calmly and peacefully ask, seek, and knock, so that we may obtain and find and have the door opened to us. Who knows? Perhaps God will bless our united efforts and prayers, and the great and shameful wickedness that covers Africa will begin to disappear from our land.

He wants the discussion to proceed freely, unaffected by fear either of the secular authorities or of the circumcellions:

> I shall not take any steps as long as the soldiers are here, lest any of you think I want to carry on the discussion amid an uproar that is alien to the cause of peace. I shall wait until they have departed; then all my hearers will realize that my aim is not that people should be forced against their wills to join a particular communion, but rather that they should come to an understanding of the truth through peaceful inquiry. On our side, there shall be an end to fear of the secular authorities; on yours, let there be an end to terrorizing by the circumcellions.[6]

Augustine defended this ecumenical attitude and won acceptance of it from the Fathers of the many regional councils he attended. It was accepted, for example, by the Councils of Carthage of 401 and 403. But Augustine's words and those of the councils found no echo among the Donatists. The latter did not answer letters or agree to discussions or stop spreading a climate of distrust and hatred. In 403 the council invited them to take part in a public conference; it proposed a method that would assure free discussion and impartial judgment. The invitation fell on deaf ears. The Donatists replied scornfully that the children of the martyrs could not deal with the descendants of traitors. Violence increased. The circumcellions even tried to strike at Augustine himself[7]; they attacked Possidius[8]; they committed a horrible crime against Maximinus, bishop of Bagai.[9]

The Donatist question came up for reexamination at the council of 404, but attitudes had now changed. All were in agreement that imperial intervention was needed; the only thing to be discussed was its extent. Some—the older bishops—said that a decree of suppression should be requested; others, Augustine among them, maintained that nothing more than a decree of protection should be sought. By such a decree the imperial authorities would have to protect Catholics against Donatist violence and ensure the free circulation of ideas. To this end all that was needed was to apply the Theodosian law of 392.

This second view prevailed, and a delegation left on its carefully defined mission. But before it reached the emperor, the latter had learned of Donatist cruelty through other channels and had issued a decree of suppression. Donatism was condemned, and Donatists were commanded to return to the Catholic Church. Such was the decree of Honorius of 405. The law prescribed that the Donatist heresy "not only could not resort to violence but also could not exist without incurring punishment. In order, however, to show Christian restraint even toward those who did not deserve it, the penalty established was not capital punishment but a fine, while their bishops or ministers were subject to banishment."[10]

Later view of Augustine

What was Augustine's attitude toward this law that the Catholics had not requested and did not want? We may suppose that his first reaction was negative. We know, however, that at least subsequently he welcomed it and defended it as opportune. He had changed, and the change was to have no small historical consequences. It will be profitable, therefore, to determine clearly the reasons for his new outlook and to define its limits.

Three reasons persuaded Augustine to accept and defend the law; the authority of his episcopal colleagues, the abundant fruits of the new law, and his own fuller theoretical grasp of the pedagogical function of fear of punishment.

We know as a matter of fact that at the Council of Carthage in 405 the Fathers sent two clerics to the emperor to thank him for the steps he had taken and that they wrote to the provincial governors and city magistrates asking that these measures be implemented. Scholars have no doubt that Augustine was present at this council, even if the summary of its acts does not mention him. It was certainly on this occasion, then, that his colleagues used the eloquence of the facts to persuade him that the law was a good one.

> I had to admit the cogency of the examples my colleagues put before me. Initially, I had been of the opinion that no one should be brought forcibly into the unity of Christ and that we should act solely by word, fight for the cause by discussion, and convince others by reason, so that we might avoid having in our midst as pretended Catholics those whom we had formerly known as open heretics. But I had to yield to my colleagues, who no longer simply opposed me with words but rather presented me with factual proof. The most powerful argument against me was the example of my active city which had belonged totally to the Donatist party but had now converted to the Catholic Church out of fear of the imperial sanctions. We now see that city so set against the murderous spite of your sect that one would think it had never belonged to it. The same thing had happened in many other cities, the names of which the bishops gave me.[11]

In fact, the movement of conversion met with resistance, but it was nonetheless impressive. This was especially true after the great conference of 411. "It is no longer isolated individuals but many whole cities that we see becoming Catholic, motivated by a heartfelt abhorrence of schism and a fervent love of unity."[12] Augustine describes their feelings and especially their joy. Thus he writes in his treatise, *The Correction of the Donatists,* which was addressed to Count Boniface:

> If you could only see how satisfied the people are with Christian unity and how they come in large numbers to listen enthusiastically and sing sacred hymns! You would see assembled crowds of the faithful listening attentively and rejoicing to hear the word of God. Many of them remember their past error with great sorrow, and they experience great joy in meditating on the truth now known to them. They feel great contempt and disgust for their former teachers, as they realize the lies these men used to tell about our sacraments. If you could only see how many others say that they had wanted for some time to become Catholics but did not dare, since they were surrounded by hotheaded fanatics.[13]

These facts provide the basis for Augustine's theory. With regard to one of his works (now lost) against the Donatists, he writes in his *Revisions:* "In the first of these books I said that I disapproved of schismatics being forced into ecclesial communion by the secular arm. And at that time I did indeed disapprove, because I did not as yet realize all the evil things they would do with impunity, or all the improvement that the vigilance of the authorities could inspire in them."[14]

Value of fear of punishment

There is no doubt that the fear of punishment (where the law is a just one) has the twofold function of keeping people from evil and leading them to virtue. It stimulates the lazy, supports the weak, and helps everyone to overcome one fear by means of another: a wrongful fear by a proper fear. Augustine writes:

> I am not saying that people can be compelled to be good! I am, however, saying that fear of a punishment they are not ready to accept can cause people either to abandon the ill that keeps them from the known truth or to recognize truth they had not known. In other words, fear may spur them to reject the falsehood for which they were doing battle or to look for the truth of which they had been ignorant or, finally, voluntarily to admit as true that which they were previously unwilling to admit.[15]

That is how it worked out with the Donatists:

> As soon as these laws took effect in Africa, those who were looking for the opportunity or were deterred by fear of reprisals from desperados [the circumcellions] or were afraid of being rejected by their relatives immediately entered into the communion of the Catholic Church. There were many others who lived in heresy solely as a result of family tradition without ever having previously made an effort to understand or examine the reason for the schism. Now they became convinced after serious reflection that they had no solid reason for suffering the misfortunes that threatened, and they therefore became Catholics without any difficulty. It was in fact their anxiety that opened their eyes, whereas the previous lack of anxiety had had no salutary effect. The example and new conviction of all these converts was followed by others less capable of understanding on their own the difference between Donatist heresy and Catholic truth.[16]

The Donatists, however, had a different version of the facts. They complained about the repressive laws; they accused the Catholics of cruelty and the state of abusing its power; they regarded themselves as martyrs and claimed that the persecution of their Church was a sign of its truth. Augustine answers all these complaints with an abundance of arguments. From Scripture he derives facts and reasons showing that not all coercion is evil. There is a coercion that leads to good, and this kind is to be approved. He appeals, for example, to the evangelical *Compelle entrare* ("Make them come in") by which human beings are led to the banquet of truth and peace. This differs from the coercion practiced by the Donatists, which leads to evil.[17] Nor should the Donatists boast of being martyrs, for it is the motive and not the suffering as such that makes a martyr.

It was essential therefore that the law should have the good for its object and that fear of punishment should be accompanied by enlightenment of minds. Augustine never separates these two aspects: law and instruction should go hand in hand. "If we simply inspired fear and did not instruct as well, we would be unjust tyrants. On the other hand, if we instructed without also inspiring fear in people who are so hardened in ancient habit they would advance too slowly on the path of healing."[18] It must be understood that the victory is always a victory of truth and not a victory of one group of human beings over another. The law has therefore the pedagogical function of capturing attention and helping toward the acknowledgment of truth. "Do you think we should be self-congratulatory at the victory over error? No! The victory belongs to the truth. After all, what do we matter?"[19] The answer shows great insight. It is the answer of the Gospel: We are unprofitable servants.

Critique of Augustine's outlook

How are we to judge Augustine's outlook? We are desirous of freedom and especially of religious freedom. Moreover, long experience has shown us the abuse possible in this area. We are therefore perplexed at Augustine's attitude and have serious reservations about it. On the other hand, if we are to avoid judging him unjustly, we must keep in mind certain points often forgotten.

The first is that he is dealing with a particular case in a particular part of the world and that this case had its own special historical and ideological context. He does not adopt the same attitude toward other errors such as Pelagianism. Donatism was unique in that it was a social as well as a religious disorder. The first need was to free the adherents of the "party" from terrorization by their coreligionists. Augustine's writings repeatedly emphasize this point. The great need was to let proven and acknowledged truth have its way. Augustine writes to the Donatists after the conference of 411: "You used to say: 'If only we could gather together in one place! If only we could hold a conference and let the truth appear!' Well, we've had our conference; error has been shown up and truth has appeared. Why, then, do you still avoid unity? Why do you still show contempt for the truth?"[20]

The second point to be kept in mind has to do with the limits set to state intervention. Augustine constantly urges humane treatment and absolutely rejects the death penalty, even in the case of common crimes. This is something worth noting. He writes to Marcellinus: "As a Christian judge, you must do your duty in the spirit of a loving father; be angry at wrongdoing but do not forget to be humane."[21] He praises Marcellinus for not having used torture in drawing up the case against the guilty. A short time later he writes to him again:

> I ask that the punishment to be inflicted on them, even though they have admitted to terrible crimes [the murder, blinding, and mutilation of priests], not include the death penalty. I ask this not only for my own peace of conscience but also in order that Catholic moderation may be evident to all. . . . In view of the cruelty they have practiced, any sanction short of death will appear an act of mercy.

Then, realizing that not everyone may approve of his views, he adds: "Some of our people, deeply disturbed as they are by the atrocities committed against them, may think that such a course of conduct is inappropriate and amounts to weakness and indifference. But once the feelings of the moment have passed . . . the full extent of the Church's kindness will be clear to all."[22]

The emphasis is the same in a letter to Proconsul Apringius, a brother of Marcellinus:

As a Christian I beseech the judge, as a bishop I exhort the Christian. . . . The interests of the province are one thing, those of the Church another. . . . Join me in fearing the judgment to be passed on us by God our Father, and show forth the mildness of our Mother [the Church]. . . . Deal kindly with the wicked. In a monstrous act of cruelty they tore the limbs from a living body. By acting mercifully you can see to it that the limbs they used in their unspeakable crimes will be preserved for some useful work.[23]

Sadly enough, the theoreticians of the Inquisition took over certain principles of Augustine without heed to their content, limits, and spirit. He would never have countenanced the funeral pyres of later ages. Thus even if we today adopt a different position on certain aspects of this sensitive issue, we cannot fail to recognize his great moderation and goodness of heart. We cannot justly lump together with the overhasty proponents of recourse to the secular arm this man who always preferred an open heretic to a false Catholic and maintained that men and women cannot believe against their will.[24]

29

"A vast and difficult task"

PAGANISM, though dying, still had its defenders. Philosophers and men of letters were nostalgic for a now irretrievable past; they lauded the social and spiritual values of the old religion and condemned the new.

The indictment of Christianity embraced its dogma and its moral code, its history, credibility, and effectiveness. The Incarnation was said to be absurd, the morality of forgiveness and love of enemies impossible and harmful, the change of outlook from Old Testament to New ridiculous, the hope of a future life empty, and resurrection from the dead sheer madness.

These charges—one or other of them, if not all at the same time—were heard frequently. Augustine often mentions them and does not fail to respond to them.[1] The terrible disaster that fell on Rome in August of 410 was not indeed the original cause of the accusations but it did give them a new harshness and a specious justification in the eyes of many. "Meanwhile Rome was destroyed by the invading Goths under the leadership of Alaric; it was a terrible disaster. The adorers of a multitude of false gods—the people we usually call 'pagan'—tried to blame the Christian religion for the calamity and began to blaspheme the true God more harshly and bitterly than they had previously done."[2]

The pillage of Rome by the barbarians and the fires that destroyed a city that had gone unscathed for so many centuries and was regarded as invincible gave new life to pagan hatred of Christianity and pagan accusations against it. But the events shook Christians as well, for they had shared the conviction that Rome was eternal. There had even been apologists who promised the return of the Golden Age once the empire was converted to Christ. The condition for such a return was verified: the Church was no longer persecuted; the emperors had become Christians. But now in place of a Golden Age came the destruction of Rome.

The dismay was deep and widespread. Augustine could see it in the faces of the refugees who sought a haven in Africa, and there were many of them. He felt obliged to intervene in order both to refute the pagans and to give support to Christians. "Inflamed with 'zeal for the house of God,' "[3] he took up the cudgels. He did so first of all in the form of letters and sermons in which he sketched a response for his Christian readers and hearers and urged them to stand firm against pagan charges, to show increased generosity in face of the growing need, and, above all, to keep their eyes fixed on heaven in accordance with the promises of Christ. He reminded them that Christ had not promised security for the earthly city and for things human. On the contrary, he had even predicted their destruction. Nor did the martyrs die in order that monuments of stone might remain undisturbed. "Did Peter die at Rome and was he buried there in order that the stone walls of the theater might not collapse?"[4]

Augustine himself was deeply moved by the destruction wrought in the capital of the empire. "Dire news has come to us: destruction, fire, pillage, killings, torture. Yes, we have heard much, bemoaned it all, wept often, been hardly consoled."[5] But he would not have Christ blamed for the situation and he would not have Christians lose faith and trust. He therefore taught them to give a firm, consistent answer to the pagans. "They say, 'See, it is in Christian times that Rome has been burned and destroyed.' Give them this answer, 'Troy, the mother of Rome, was also destroyed by fire. If the gods were unable to defend Troy, how could they defend Rome? In fact, this fire is not the first but the third that history records.' "

The timid, who were often Christians of weaker convictions, did not like such stern and candid language. They began to murmur: "If only he would stop talking about Rome!" Augustine got wind of this and gave them his answer. He refused to admit that his words were insolent. "Far be it from me to insult anyone! God keep any such idea from my heart and conscience!" He protested his love of Rome. "Did I not have many brethren there? Do I not have them there still? Does not a large part of Jerusalem, the pilgrim city [of God], dwell there?" But he repeated his point forcefully. "My intention in not remaining silent about Rome is to insist that what they say about our Christ is false: that he is responsible for Rome's destruction and that their gods of stone and wood were her defenders."[6] In any case, he was convinced that Rome had not been utterly destroyed but simply punished. "A city is made not of walls but of its citizens."[7] "If the citizens do not perish, the city does not perish."[8]

In his *Letters* he dealt with deeper and more complex problems such as the credibility of the Christian faith, the non-impossibility of the Incarnation, the wise pedagogy that marks revelation, and the social effectiveness of Christianity.[9] Once occasion for such discussion was provided by a Roman aristocrat named Volusian, a pagan and skeptic, yet not unmoved by the phenomenon of Christianity. He was a friend of the tribune Marcellinus, who in turn was a close friend of Augustine. Attracted by Augustine's reputation, Volusian told him of his difficulties with Christian teaching; they were the difficulties heard regularly from educated pagans. Marcellinus added further difficulties of his own, and Augustine answered both men.

The two letters are essentially two lengthy treatises. Having written them, the author believed he had accomplished his task, or at least that he could accomplish it, should anything more prove necessary, by means of further letters intended for a large readership. But Marcellinus was not satisfied and urged Augustine to write a sustained work. "I entreat you to write several books on these points. By removing all doubts, such books will be exceptionally helpful to the Church, especially in this present age."[10]

Origin of *The City of God*

This request from a friend who was also a very good Christian gave Augustine the push he needed for carrying out a monumental plan he had long had in mind. The result was *The City of God:* a laborious, gigantic work that is at one and the same time a defense of Christianity, a philosophy and theology of history, a political theory, and a treatise on spirituality. The author himself speaks of it in his preface as "a vast and difficult task." At its end he voices his confidence that he has fulfilled the commitment he made in undertaking "this huge work." In the midst of so many other occupations, he labored at it through many years, from 413 to 426, publishing sections of it at intervals. In 414 he published the first three books, in 415 books four and five, in 417 books six to ten. He was at work on book fourteen in 418-19. The last books are to be assigned to 425-26 when the author was already a year or two past his seventieth birthday.

Although the work took so many years to finish and was published at various times, it reflects a plan that was present from the beginning. Augustine sets forth this plan at the end of the first book[11] and harks back to it frequently in the course of the work.[12] The plan is at once simple and monumental: it embraces the history of the human race (genesis and palingenesis), is summed up in the story of two human beings (Adam and Christ), and has its concrete focus in two loves (love of self and love of God).

The work has two parts, one polemical (the first ten books) and one doctrinal (the last twelve books). The first part is a refutation of paganism, the second an exposition of Christian teaching. There are five sections in all, two in the first part, three in the second. Books I-V show the *social* impotence of paganism, that is, the inability of the cult of the gods to secure earthly prosperity. Books VI-X show the *spiritual* impotence of paganism, that is, the inability of pagan worship to ensure eternal happiness. The second part of the work is divided into three sections (of four books each) that describe successively the *origin, history,* and *destiny* of the two cities, the city of God and the city of this world. Each of the twenty-two books develops its own special theme within the section and part to which it belongs. The overall structure is faultless,[13] although there are many digressions in response to needs of the moment.

Method

The method too is simple, though not an easy one for the author to apply. It consists essentially in developing three key points: opposing Christian wisdom to the pagan wisdom on which the adherents of the old religion relied; bringing out what was valid and praiseworthy in pagan wisdom; and showing that all this is found more perfectly in Christianity.

The first of these points is announced in the preface of the work, which is written with great care and makes a solemn programmatic statement.

> The most glorious city of God, considered, on the one hand, in the course of history ... and, on the other, in the stability of its eternal dwelling ...—such, dear son Marcellinus, is the subject of this work. I have undertaken it at your request and to fulfill the promise I made to you that I would defend this city against those who prefer their own gods to its Founder. A vast and difficult work, indeed, but God is our helper!
>
> I am aware of the strength I will need if I am to show the proud how mighty is the virtue of humility, which attains to heights that lie beyond all the unstable and ephemeral grandeurs of earth and are reached not by usurping human pride but only by a gift of divine grace. For the king and founder of this city of which I plan to speak has revealed, in the Scriptures of his people, this decree of the divine law: "God resists the proud and gives his grace to the humble" (1 Pet 5:5). Yet souls swollen with pride attempt to appropriate for themselves this divine privilege, and they love to say in praise of themselves that they "spare the submissive and subdue the proud" (Virgil, *Aeneid* 6:854).[14]

Augustine therefore constantly opposes divine wisdom to human wisdom, life in accordance with God to life in accordance with human standards, and the freedom given by grace to the domination exercised by concupiscence. He is here engaged in an activity of demolition that smashes away at paganism and often ridicules it.

But this negative activity by itself is not enough and would even be unjust. It is impossible to ignore the valid and praiseworthy results of pagan wisdom. Augustine was all the less able to ignore them because he was, and thought of himself as, a Roman.[15] He therefore acknowledges them gladly and with gratitude, and he wants to retain them. To this end he writes abundantly on the ancient masters of the Roman spirit: on Titus Livius, Sallust, Varro, and Cicero. With their aid he intends to confound his comtemporaries and flay their moral corruption. He openly acknowledges the virtues of the ancient Romans, "avid for praise, liberal with money, thirsty for glory, content with an honest fortune." He praises above all their love of their country, which they wanted to be free and strong. By reason of that love they avoided many vices and exercised many virtues, especially the virtue of putting the common good before their individual good: they scorned private wealth in order that the public treasury might be full. These virtues should be an example even to Christians, provided they understand how worthy the heavenly city is of being loved if those person loved the earthly city so much.[16]

The greatness and stability of the empire depended on those virtues and not on the worship of the gods, which was a school of immorality and could not therefore be the source of prosperity. It was not the pagan gods or fate, but the true God who in his own time and manner gave the Romans their empire. "Beyond doubt, it is divine providence that establishes human kingdoms."[17]

Basic principle

This basic principle, which sheds light on the Augustinian conception of history, is restated, with rich detail and broad vision, in a passage that must be accounted among the finest and most concentrated in *The City of God*.

> This supreme and true God, then—who with his Word and his Holy Spirit is Three in One; this only God, the omnipotent creator and author of every soul and every body, and in whose blessedness all participate who are truly and not illusorily happy; who made the human person as a rational animal composed of a body and a soul and who, when human beings sinned, determined neither to let them go unpunished nor to abandon them without mercy; who has given being to good and wicked alike as he has to the stones, vegetative life as he has to the plants, sense life as he has to the animals, and intellectual life to them as he has otherwise to the angels alone; who is the source of every rule, every form, and every form of order; from whom come measure, number, and weight; from whom comes everything that has a nature, a genus, a value of whatever kind; from whom come also the seeds of forms, the forms of seeds, and the movements of forms and seeds; who gave flesh its beginning, beauty, health, and fruitfulness, the arrangement of its members, and the salutary harmony among the members; who gave even the irrational soul its memory, feeling, and instinct, and in addition endowed the rational soul with spirit, understanding,

and will; who has not failed to give a harmonious proportion of parts and as it were a kind of peace not only to heaven and earth, not only to angels and humans, but even to the organs of the smallest and most worthless animals, the least feather of a bird, the flower of the field and the leaf of the tree—this God cannot conceivably have decided to leave the kingdoms of the world with their relations of domination and enslavement outside the laws of his providence.[18]

The only reasonable course, then, is to acknowledge this one true God and to worship him according to the Christian religion, which, while not denying human virtues, offers men and women a share in the life of that city that "has truth as its king, charity as its law, and eternity as its measure."[19] It will be profitable here to reread the well-known address to the Roman people that constitutes—ideally—the high point of the first part of *The City of God*.

> Desire, rather, these blessings, O noble soul of the Roman people, descendants of the Reguli, the Scevolas, the Scipios, the Fabricii! Yes, desire these blessings and have the skill to distinguish them from the base vanity and treacherous malice of the demons. If you naturally possess any praiseworthy quality, it will be purified and made perfect only by true devotion; wickedness destroys it and completes its ruin. Choose now the path you must follow in order to win—not in yourself but in the true God—praise that is free of any falsehood.
>
> In former times you won glory among the peoples, but by a hidden judgment of divine providence the true religion was not there for you to choose. The day is at hand; awaken now, as you have at times awakened in some of your members in whose perfect virtue and sufferings for the true faith we now glory. They struggled to the end against hostile powers, they overcame them by their fearless deaths, and "by their blood they gave us a homeland." To this homeland I invite you: come, I beg you, join its citizens whose asylum, as it were, is the forgiveness of sins. Pay no heed to your degenerate fellows who slander Christ and Christians by holding them responsible for our sad age, whereas they themselves yearn for the days when they enjoyed not a peaceful life but unhindered vice. Yet those days never satisfied you, even as regards your earthly homeland.
>
> Lay hold, now, of your heavenly homeland; it will cost you little, and yet you will truly reign there for ever. In that homeland you

will find no Vestal fire, no rock on the Capitol, but the only true God "who will set no limits for you in space and time, but will give you a kingdom that has no end."

Cease looking for your false and lying gods, reject them with contempt, and run to true freedom. . . . Claim your freedom against the unclean spirits. . . . You have done well spontaneously to refuse citizenship to actors and comedians. Now awaken fully! The divine majesty is not appeased by acts that defile human dignity. How can you rank with the holy powers of heaven the gods who are jealous of such honors as these, when you exclude from Roman citizenship the very people who offer the gods these honors!

Incomparably more glorious is the city on high where the victory belongs to truth, where holiness is our true dignity, where happiness is found in peace, and where life is eternal.[20]

This address deserves a lengthy commentary, but readers will want to provide that themselves.

Social influence of Christianity

In regard to the social influence of Christianity Augustine has launched a no less well-known challenge in his reply to Marcellinus.

Let those who claim Christ's teaching is hostile to the state produce an army of soldiers such as Christ wants; let them produce provincial governors, husbands, wives, parents, children, masters, slaves, kings, judges, and even tax payers and tax collectors such as Christian doctrine prescribes. Then they may declare this teaching hostile to the state instead of admitting that if it were observed, it would provide the greatest safety of the state.[21]

The challenge is spelled out in many passages of *The City of God*, especially in the first five books, which have for their purpose to show the moral superiority of Christianity.

It will be enough to mention Augustine's defense of true freedom, his praise of the Christian emperor, and his call for justice. Here is a strong statement on this last subject.

Take away justice and what are kingdoms but great bands of highway robbers? And in turn are not bands of highwaymen just little kingdoms? Are they not groups of men under the command of a head, bound together by a social contract and sharing their booty according to a law accepted by all? If such a pestilent band accepts new felons and grows to the point where it occupies territories, sets up its own centers, takes control of cities, and subjugates people, it openly takes for itself the title of kingdom. The title is henceforth assured it in the eyes of all, not by any lessening of the greed that impelled it but by its ability to proceed now with impunity.[22]

The method mentioned earlier is followed again when Augustine deals with the pagan philosophers, who are the main focus of his attention in the second section (Books VI-X) of the first part of *The City of God*. He energetically contrasts Christian doctrine with their teaching, which is powerless to resolve the deeper problems of life, and especially the problem of a way of salvation for all. Christian doctrine provides a sure norm for judging the validity of the philosophers' teaching.

> I therefore prefer to all others, and consider as being closest to us, those philosophers who recognize that the supreme and true God is the author of all things, the light by which we know, and the good to which our actions tend, and that he is for us the source of nature, the truth present in all teaching, the happiness that crowns life. These include the Platonists in the proper sense of the term, as well as philosophers of any other school . . . the Ionian school . . . the Italian school . . . the wise men and philosophers of other nations—Atlantic Lybians, Egyptians, Indians, Persians, Chaldeans, Scythians, Gauls, and Spaniards—who have grasped and taught these doctrines.[23]

Augustine's unswerving attitude was first of all one of clear opposition: we and they; our doctrine and theirs. With regard to creation in time he writes: "The arguments of the philosophers will not move me from this belief. . . . Reason may not be able to refute them, but faith should laugh at them."[24]

But his attitude, though unswerving, was not blind. Unlike Tertullian, he was not prejudiced against philosophy. Quite the contrary! He had read the philosophers and continued to read them; he valued their methods and acknowledged the many truths they had expounded. He accepted these truths joyfully and incorporated them into his Christian vision. That is precisely the gigantic task he undertakes in *The City of God*. His aim is to examine the truths spoken by the philosophers, refute their errors, answer their difficulties, and construct a doctrinal system that is in harmony with the faith. And, we must admit, he is faithful to this aim. Thus he takes a good deal from the philosophers, but he rejects as much again. The dehellenization process is real and thoroughgoing. Thus he rejects the coeternity of creation and God, the opposition between soul and body, the preexistence of souls, the theory of reminiscence, and metempsychosis. On a more strictly religious plane, he rejects the supposed impossibility of the Incarnation and resurrection and any autonomous ascent of human beings to God (that is, the denial of grace).

He devotes a good deal of space in *The City of God* to the subject of mediation. This was a vital problem. Pagan wisdom offered a solution based on magic or, to give it a less invidious name, theurgy[25]; Apuleius had written of this in *The God of Socrates* and Porphyry in the *Return of the Soul*. Augustine now subjects these works to a detailed examination. I said earlier, and I repeat it here, that his sympathies were with the Platonic philosophers, whom he considered closer than any others to the Catholic faith. "No one has come closer to us than the Platonists."[26] At the same time, however, he recognizes and rejects their errors no less than those of other philosophers. Thus his debate with Apuleius and Porphyry is long and closely argued. He admits that the problem is real but rejects the solution offered as absurd. God is indeed inaccessible, and human beings cannot reach him without a mediator; but no demons—not even the good demons whom Christians call angels—can provide this mediation.

God is immortal and blessed; human beings are mortal and wretched. A mediator must share the qualities of both: he must be immortal and blessed like God, mortal and wretched like human beings. "We must look for a mediator who is not only a human being but also God, so that by means of his blessed mortality he may raise human beings up from their mortal wretchedness to a blessed immortality."[27]

At this point Augustine introduces a lengthy discourse on Christ the mediator in order to show once again that Christian doctrine, and it alone, provides the solution to a problem felt by all. Christ alone is that universal way to salvation which Porphyry claimed could not be found. "Apart from this way, which has never been lacking to the human race (it was foretold as a future event, and is now proclaimed as already having come to be), no one has ever been rescued, no one is rescued now, and no one will ever be rescued."[28]

Thus the first part of Augustine's hard and laborious task ends with a vision of Christ as the center of human history. But his genius and zeal were not satisfied with a negative polemic against the pagans.

30

The Two Cities

THE idea of the two cities came to Augustine at an early stage in his Christian life. We already find it, in a sketchy form, in the book *True Religion,* which he wrote as a layman in 390; ten years later it is set down more explicitly in *The Instruction of Beginners* and reaffirmed in *The Literal Meaning of Genesis,* where he promises to write *The City of God.*

To explain how Augustine conceived this cherished idea that is so fundamental to his doctrinal system there is no need of appealing, as some do, to Manichaean dualism that supposedly continued to exert no small influence on his unconscious mind. All we need do is go back to the Scriptures. These speak in express terms of the struggle between light and darkness, spirit and flesh, good and evil; above all, they speak of the final separation of the upright from the wicked. There is plenty here to explain Augustine's own conception. The Manichaeans wrongly deduced from the biblical texts (or used them to confirm) an absurd metaphysical dualism that Scripture in fact condemns. Augustine, on the other hand, delved more deeply into these texts and integrated them into a vast conception that is based on the ethical and eschatological dualism taught in the Scriptures.

Taking its cue from the Scriptures, Augustine's practice—not exclusively indeed, but principally[1]—is to explain Catholic teaching by narrating the history of salvation. In his *True Religion* he already notes that "the entire human race, like the life of any individual human being, is governed from Adam to the end of the world by the laws of divine providence and shows itself to be divided into two groups: one is the multitude of the wicked . . . the other the generation made up of the people of God." Then, focusing on the idea of the "people of God," he explains that the history of this people from Adam to John the Baptist is contained in the Old Testament. The Old Testament is in turn a type of the New, in which the history of the new people begins; this history will continue until the judgment, when the Lord returns in glory. Then "the people made up of the just . . . will arise so that the remnants of the old humanity may be transformed into the new; the people made up of the wicked, the people that from the beginning of history to its end have embodied the old humanity, will likewise arise, but in order to plunge headlong into the second death."[2]

In *The Instruction of Beginners* the two peoples become two cities.

> Two cities, one of the wicked, the other of the just, continue on their way from the beginning of human history to the end of the world. At the present time they are intermingled at the level of bodies but are distinct in spirit. In the world to come, on the day of judgment, there will also be a bodily separation between them. All those human beings who love pride and temporal power . . . and seek their own glory by subjecting others are members of one and the same society. . . . In like manner, all those human beings and angelic spirits who humbly seek the glory of God instead of their own and who serve God devoutly belong to a single society.[3]

These ideas that are scattered throughout Augustine's writings come together in his principal work. In a magnificent vision he identifies the history of the world with the history of two cities, the two cities with two human beings, the two human beings with two loves, and the two loves, not with two realities (good and evil), but with two different or even opposed and freely adopted attitudes toward the same reality.

The two loves

In a passage familiar to all, Augustine says: "Two loves thus established two cities: love of self unto contempt of God built the earthly city, and love of God unto contempt of self built the heavenly city." He then goes on to explain the divergent workings of these two contrary loves:

> The one city glories in itself, the other in God. . . . The one . . . is controlled by the lust for power; the other inspires human beings to mutual service, leaders by commanding, subjects by obeying. The one, in its lords, loves its own strength; the other says to its God: "I will love you, Lord, who are my strength."
>
> In the one, the wise, who live by human standards, have sought the goods of the body or of the spirit or of both, but those who could have known God "have failed to glorify him as

God. . . ." In the other there is but one wisdom: the devotion that gives the true God the worship due to him and that awaits its reward in the society of the saints—human beings and angels together—so that God may be all in all.[4]

This justly famous passage explains the origin and program of the two cities. It also raises a major difficulty: how can love of self and love of God be opposed if it be true that only love of God makes possible an authentic love of self? The opposition does indeed have something mysterious about it, and Augustine often speaks of it to the people. In his writings we find two series of texts: one that, like the one just cited, emphasizes the opposition between love of God and love of self; the other that emphasizes the happy and necessary coincidence of the two. "In some inexplicable way those who love themselves and not God do not love themselves; and those who love God and not themselves love themselves."[5]

Light can be shed on this enigmatic situation by appealing to another pair of concepts that Augustine uses in order to bring out the contrast between the two cities: social love and private love. "Two loves . . . one looking toward the neighbor, the other centered on self . . . have marked the limits of the two cities established among human beings . . . and one city is the city of the just, and the other city is the city of the wicked."[6]

This radical opposition becomes intelligible only if we realize that "social" love means for Augustine a love of the common good, while "private" love is a love of the particular good, that is, a good possessed or desired to the exclusion of others. Thus social love unites, private love divides and, by dividing, begets pride, avarice, and greed, which are the roots of all evils. It is called "private" because it is turned in on itself and "deprives" the person of communion (which is true wealth) with God and other human beings. Sin is a love of the part instead of the whole; it is factiousness and privation.[7] That was true of the angels; it is also true of human beings. It is from these roots that the city of the wicked springs; this city is established on the foundation of private love and therefore has for its banner confusion and discord. The city of the just, on the other hand, loves and seeks the common good; in the enjoyment of this good it finds reciprocal communion, in communion unity, and in unity happiness.[8]

Social love, then, is love of God but also love of self and others in God, who is the common good of all. Private love, on the contrary, is a love of self that, because private, is in conflict with the love due to God and other human beings; it is therefore a disordered love.

The collision of these two loves produces the drama of history. Augustine looks upon history with the eyes of both a believer and a thinker. Theology and philosophy are not separable areas for him, nor can reason alone grasp the intelligibility of history. He deals with the two areas without separating them; that is, he sets forth the teaching of revelation, but he explains and defends it with the tools of reason. In the vast drama that is history he distinguishes five acts, as though it were a classical tragedy: creation, the fall, the Law, the coming of God, and final outcome. In each act he deals with one of the great problems that history raises and compels us to face: the origin of things, the existence of evil, the struggle between good and evil, the victory of good over evil, and the ultimate ends of things. Over all of them shines the light of Providence, for Providence, being wisdom and love, is the soul, master, and ultimate explanation of history.

Creation in time

In his exposition of the divine plan of salvation as made known in revelation Augustine overturns many positions taken by the pagan philosophers, especially with regard to the beginning and end of history. At the beginning stands creation, for there is no history without contingency and no contingency without creation. The author of *The City of God* believes that the Neoplatonists accepted creation, but he is aware that they did not accept creation in time and even declared it to be impossible. Divine revelation, on the contrary, teaches creation in time or, as Augustine says more accurately, with time. He proudly opposes this doctrine to the teaching of the philosophers and defends its content.[9] God created all things at the beginning of time; he created not because of any lack or necessity but freely and out of pure love; he created "because he willed to do so" and "because he is good" and created things are good.

> There are three things we ought to know about creatures . . . namely, who made them, by what means he made them, and why he made them. . . . If then we ask, "Who made it?" the answer is "God." By what means did he make it? He said: "Let it be!" and it was. Why did he make it? Because it is good. There is no maker more perfect than God, no art more effective than the Word of God, and no reason better than this: A good God created what is good!

Things are good because God is good and created things are good.[10] "The [biblical] words 'God saw that it was good' make it clear that God did not create out of necessity or for his own advantage but solely out of goodness or, in short, because it is good!"[11]

The arguments of the philosophers against creation in time are invalid. When reflecting on God's creative action we must not let our imaginations mislead us into thinking that in God as in human beings acting and not acting are different and successive states. No, God "is able to act while resting and to rest while acting, and he can apply to a new work a plan that is not new but eternal." If he first did not create and then created, " 'first' and 'then' are undoubtedly verified in things, that initially did not exist and then existed. In God, however, there is no subsequent will that alters or replaces a previous will. In him one and the same immutable and eternal will causes created things first not to have been, as long as they were not, and then to be, when they began to exist." Not everyone can understand this, Augustine says, but for those who can, creation in time shows in a marvelous way that God created things "out of disinterested goodness," since without them he is already blessed in an eternity that has no beginning.[12]

God created not only the universe and human beings, but the angels as well. He created them all as good, but not all remained good. In fact, "while some of them remained constantly united to the common good, which is God himself, united, that is, to the eternity, truth, and love that are God, others found their delight rather in their own power, as though they were their own good, and so they fell from the heights of the common good, the source of happiness, back upon that which they had in themselves. They substituted their arrogant ostentation for the sublime glory of eternity, their empty cleverness for the certainty of truth, and their isolated interests for the charity that unites all indivisibly, and so they became proud and envious deceivers." Thus there came to be two groups of angels: the good and the bad. As Augustine carefully points out, the distinction between them was not a difference in nature, for the nature of all of them was and remains good, being the work of God, "author and good creator of every substance." The difference was due "to the difference in their wills and desires."[13]

Human beings, too, were created good; they were created in the image of God and are therefore the summit and crown of the visible universe. Augustine stresses this point. He does so for polemical and, we might say, autobiographical reasons,[14] but he does so above all for philosophical, theological, and mystical reasons. The creation of human beings in the image of God is a fundamental thesis, an irreplaceable supporting column, and a luminous summary of Augustinian thought.

Sin and suffering

Yet, though they were so honored, human beings sinned as did the rebellious angels. In their sinning, evil entered the world and with evil, division. The two cities make their appearance in the history of Cain and Abel, who are their prototypes and as it were their founders: the one a wicked fratricide, the other an innocent victim. From that moment the two cities travel the roads of history, united insofar as they share a common stage, but divided in ideals, actions, and expectations.

Augustine follows their career in Sacred Scripture and in secular history, down to the coming of Christ and on to his own times. He sees them traveling side by side but always in opposition. The opposition often turns into open persecution and the inflicting of injustice.

> Thus in this world, and in the evil days that run not only from the time when Christ and his apostles were present among us in body but even from the time of Abel, the first just man, killed by his

wicked brother—from then to the end of the world, the Church goes its pilgrim way amid the persecutions of the world and the consolations of God.[15]

But while it is true that sufferings unjustly inflicted by the earthly city sadden the city of God on its journey, it is also true that each city experiences both good and evil in this world. The difference between the two cities is the use they make of these blessings and evils; a different spirit animates each.

> There is a difference between the sufferers, even if their sufferings are alike; virtue and vice differ even when subjected to the same torment. In the same fire gold shines and straw smokes; under the same flail the stalks are crushed and the grain is set free; the oil does not mingle with the dregs even though it flows under the weight of the same press. So too the same force [of tribulation] tests, purifies, and clarifies the good, but condemns, destroys, and annihilates the wicked.[16]

The different use made of suffering depends on a difference in basic direction, and this in turn depends on a difference in ultimate end. Augustine devotes a good deal of space to this subject, presenting the two conceptions (pagan and Christian) of happiness, peace, and justice, and showing how they are opposed.

Happiness

The pagan view locates happiness in the blessings of the body or in those of the soul or in both together, but always in the present life, the present world, the here and now. The Christian view, on the other hand, locates it in the world to come, that is, in eternal life that is known through faith, expected in hope, and attained through grace-supported love. The opposition between the two outlooks is clear, and it is only the beginning.

The pagan view is a delusion, for happiness cannot be obtained through the goods of the body, which are uncertain, transient, often attacked by suffering, and finally removed by death, nor through the blessings of virtue, which in order to be virtue must struggle against evil (think, for example, of temperance, fortitude, justice, and prudence!), nor finally through the blessings of family, friendship, civic life, or national life. Only in the city of God is true and secure happiness to be found, because happiness there is complete and everlasting. This true happiness is not to be had on earth; here we possess it in hope, not in reality. "Present reality unaccompanied by that hope brings only a false happiness that is in truth great wretchedness."[17]

A further opposition marks the very concept of virtue—of virtue generally and justice in particular. In answering Julian Augustine discusses at length the important question of the virtue possessed by unbelievers.[18] I have no room here to discuss the question in detail and will say only this: Augustine acknowledges and praises the virtues of the ancient Romans, who maintained "a certain uprightness of their own that was adequate for establishing, extending, and preserving the earthly city."[19] He also accepts that no human being, however wicked, can fail to perform some good works in a lifetime.[20] But he also holds that a virtue whose operations are not referred to God is not a true virtue.

In order to determine whether or not an action is virtuous, it is not enough to inquire into its object; the intention must also be taken into consideration. The intention is either explicitly evil (then the entire action becomes evil) or it is virtue sought and exercised for its own sake (and the action is then simply "pride and empty show") or it is God (and the action in this case has all the properties of true virtue).[21] It follows from this that true virtue belongs to the city that lives a divine and not a merely human life.

Justice

All this holds in a special way for justice. The pagan philosophers had written a good deal about justice, and the author of *The City of God* likewise has a good deal to say about it. The reader can go back over what he says, or at least those passages I have cited.[22] In Book XIX his intention is to show that there is true justice only when human beings are subject to God. The natural order demands that body be subject to soul and soul to God. If this second submission is lacking, the first cannot be exercised in its full measure. Therefore, while the soul may indeed command the body, there will be no true justice unless the soul in turn obeys God. This is another and perhaps the most profound cause of the opposition between the two cities. "The city of the wicked rebels against the authority of God who commands it to offer sac-

rifices to him alone; in that city, therefore, the soul does not domi-
nate the body nor reason the vices through rectitude and fidelity;
consequently it lacks true justice."[23] On the other hand, true justice is found in the city "whose founder and governor is Christ."[24]

Using Cicero's definition of a republic, Augustine shows that
the Roman "republic" was never truly such, because, lacking as it
did the worship of the true God, it also lacked true justice. But
where there is no justice, neither is there law. Consequently the
Roman people did not exemplify Cicero's definition; they were
not a multitude united through consent to a law and through a
community of interests. Augustine is evidently speaking here not
of positive law but of the natural law that has justice for its object
and is indeed identified with it. "Law" here is a philosophical and
theological concept, not a juridical one.

The Roman republic can indeed be called a republic ("thing
of the people"), but only if one changes the definition of people.
That is what Augustine does.[25]

The difference in definitions of justice gives rise to a further difference in the ideas of domination and peace. One city seeks in
fact the glory of dominion and it is itself dominated by its passion
for dominion; the other city serves even when it commands. "But
in the house of the just who live by faith and still journey far from
this heavenly city, those who command are at the service of those
whom they seem to rule. For it is not the passion for domination
that inspires their rule but the desire to be of use, not the proud
desire to be master but the concern to be of service."[26] In this city,
then, those who rule preserve the natural order willed by God,
who had decreed that "rational beings made in his image should
exercise dominion only over irrational beings: not human beings
over other human beings, but human beings over the animals."[27]

Peace

Finally, there is a vast difference in the respective conceptions of peace. Every human being, every people, every living
thing desires peace. It is impossible not to love peace. Even those
who make war love and seek peace. "Even laborious wars are for
the sake of peace."[28] But what is peace? In Augustine's view
peace includes two elements: order and security. Everyone is

familiar with his definition, for it has become the traditional one: peace is "the tranquillity of order." When the definition is applied to human beings, it becomes: peace is "orderly agreement" (*ordinata concordia*). The peace of a house consists in the orderly agreement of its inhabitants in commanding and obeying; the peace of a city consists in the orderly agreement of its citizens, again in commanding and obeying.

The city of the world can attain to this peace, even amid murderous fratricidal conflicts. But the city of God has a peace of its own, which is true peace and the source of every other peace save that which marks such wickedness as has not yet been punished. I mean peace with God and the peace of human beings with one another in God. "Peace between mortal human beings and God takes the form of orderly obedience, in faith, to the eternal law." From this peace flows the peace of the heavenly city, which is "the perfectly ordered and perfectly harmonious society of those who enjoy God and one another in God."[29]

All this will be verified, however, only in the next world when death has been overcome and the "social life" of the saints is complete, secure, and everlasting. God will then be all in all. For it is from him that the heavenly city, which includes angels and human beings, derives

> its origin, form, and blessedness. If we are asked whence it comes, we answer: "It is God who made it!" Whence comes its wisdom? "It is God who enlightens it!" Whence comes its happiness? "It is God whom it enjoys!" Because it subsists in him it has being; because it contemplates him, it is enlightened; because it is united to him it is blessed. It exists, lives, and loves: it flourishes in the eternity of God, shines luminously in the truth of God, and rejoices in the goodness of God.[30]

The city of the wicked, on the other hand, will not enjoy peace when it enters its final stage. Its fate will be just the opposite: eternal suffering without possibility of death.

The last books of *The City of God* are devoted to the question of final ends. The author rejects the theory of an "eternal return" and defends the future resurrection against the ridicule of the pagans by showing that Plato and Porphyry meet and are reconciled in the Christian synthesis. Against erroneous views held by Christians he also defends the eternity of the respective destinies of the two cities. The work ends with the beatific vision in which God is enjoyed. "There we shall rest and see; we shall see and love; we shall love and praise. That is what will come endlessly at the end."[31]

Identification of two cities

A few observations are in place here. The Augustinian conception of the two cities is undoubtedly a magnificent one but it also raises numerous questions that many scholars have tried, and are still trying, to formulate exactly and clarify. I shall mention one of them. Does this radical explanation of the two cities— one destined to rejoice with Christ, the other to suffer with the devil—leave sufficient room for a "human city," a "political city," or, as others describe it, a "spiritual earthly city," or—whatever the name—a third "city" in between?

Lack of space prevents my going into the question fully here. Let me say, however, as a help to readers who may go on to read Augustine's masterpiece for themselves, that the two cities constitute a "mystical"[32]—that is, spiritual and ideal—concept. The concept undoubtedly applies to human history, in which the forces of good and evil are at work. It would, however, be a serious mistake to identify the two cities with the Church and the state respectively. The earthly Church as an institution is a vehicle for the values of the city of God, but not everyone in the Church belongs to this city; such an identification can be made— and Augustine often makes it—only when the term "Church" is taken in a spiritual and eschatological sense: the Church thus understood includes all the elect and only the elect.[33]

Still less can the state be identified with the city of Satan. Despite the interpretation sometimes given of his thought, Augustine does not regard the state as being the result of sin, even if some of its manifestations and functions (coercion, for example) are connected with sin. The state, like the household (*domus*)[34] and the city (*civitas*),[35] springs from the social nature of human beings and has tasks and goods proper to it. Augustine sums up the tasks in the threefold function of commanding, providing, and serving[36]; he sums up the goods in the supreme blessing of peace.[37] Even the heavenly city profits by this peace.

> Unhappy the people that is separated from God! Yet even such a people loves a certain legitimate peace, which is proper to it but which at the end it will no longer have because it has made poor use of that peace before that end. Meanwhile it is our concern as well that it should enjoy this peace during the interim of the present life, since as long as the two cities are intermingled, we too profit by the peace of Babylon. . . . This is why the Apostle urges the Church to pray for the kings and authorities of Babylon and adds: "in order that we may be able to live a tranquill and peaceful life in all devotion and charity."[38]

It must be added, however, that through the goods proper to it the city of God in turn makes no small contribution to building this peace and thus to establishing the state on the basis of justice and promoting the prosperity of society. Not without good reason did Augustine's masterpiece exert a major influence on medieval political thought.[39]

Not everything that the medieval thinkers proposed and defended can be attributed to Augustine. It is impossible, nonetheless, to minimize what he did to show the social and political effectiveness of Christianity.[40]

31

A Tireless Worker

REFLECTING on the vast body of work produced by Varro, Augustine remarks in *The City of God:* "He read so much that we are astonished he found time to write, and he wrote so much that we have difficulty believing anyone has read him through."[1] We may say the same of Augustine himself. His works are so numerous and extensive that we are astounded he could have written them all. It seems impossible that a bishop absorbed in the pastoral care of a diocese, which if not large was certainly difficult, could have found time to write so much, especially when this care imposed so many more important duties, of which two—preaching and the administration of justice—were particularly trying.

We have already seen what the administration of justice entailed for bishops of that age and for the bishop of Hippo in particular.[2] I shall mention here one episode that occurred toward the end of his life (September 26, 426): the designation of his successor. The pastor called his people together and asked them to approve his choice of Eraclius, a priest, as future bishop of Hippo. The official acts of this session were drawn up and have been preserved. The devout old man had two purposes in view: to prevent the lamentable agitations and disputes that had occurred in so many other dioceses at the election of a bishop and to be able to entrust to the newly elected successor some part of his own work, and specifically the administrative part.

Some years earlier he had asked and obtained from his people that he might be left free five days a week, because he had pressing tasks to complete. The agreement was recorded and approved, but it was not respected for long.

> We agreed that for five days of the week no one was to trouble me so that I might occupy myself with the study of Scripture, as my brothers and fathers—my colleagues in the episcopate—had charged me to do at the two councils of Numidia and Carthage. The agreement was put in writing and you approved it with your

acclamations. . . . But the agreement was respected for only a short time. . . . Now I never have time free for what I want to do; morning and afternoon I am absorbed by the affairs of the people.[3]

In 426 Augustine made a new attempt; this time, it seems, he was more successful. He asked the faithful to turn henceforth to Eraclius in all the countless matters they had in the past brought to Augustine himself. The faithful approved. Augustine thanked them with the profound emotion of one who feels an intolerable burden being lifted from him.

Journeys

To the episcopal duties of the diocese of Hippo were added those, no less burdensome, that Augustine's concern for the Church of Africa imposed on him: participation in councils (which were scheduled for every year, even if they were not always held) and invitations from his colleagues. These duties forced him to travel often: land journeys only, as I remarked earlier,[4] but long and uncomfortable ones that also took up a great deal of time. On about twenty occasions he traveled to Carthage by one of the three routes that led from Hippo, which was 175 to 210 miles distant from Carthage, depending on the route: the coastal route, which was the shortest, or the one via Tagaste to Sicca Venerea, which was the longest. The journey could last from eight to ten days, not counting further detours.

He also journeyed to Cirta, to Calama, several times to Milevis, to Thiava, to Tagaste: all of them towns in Numidia, but not just a stone's throw away by any means. Cirta, to the southeast (the modern Constantine), was about 90 miles distant, and Milevis, native place of Faustus the Manichaean and Optatus the Catholic adversary of Donatists, about 125 miles. The journey took far longer than an hour or a day. Once, at the request of Pope Zosimus, Augustine traveled from Carthage to Caesarea in Mauretania, over 600 miles distant, and from Caesarea he journeyed back to Hippo, another 430 miles; he was sixty-four years old at that time. Some years later he and his friend Alypius, bishop of Tagaste, traveled to Tubune to meet Count Boniface, who was in charge of defending the outermost boundary of the *pax romana*. Tubune was a fortress located in the south on the edge of the Sahara. If they went from Carthage via Theveste (Tebessa) and Thamagudi (Timgad) the journey was over 370 miles long, and the return trip to Hippo another 250; if they went directly from Hippo by way of Cirta and perhaps Tagaste the round trip was not less than 500 miles; Augustine was seventy at this time.[5]

Writings

And yet this man who was so busy and so much a part of the pastoral life of the African Church for almost forty years wrote so much that he became a proverb. Possidius, his first biographer, already expressed this widespread astonishment. "He dictated and published so many books and preached so many sermons (which others took down and he revised), either to refute heretics or to explain the canonical books for the edification of the holy children of the Church, that a student would have difficulty getting through them all and learning their contents."[6]

Isidore of Seville wrote that if anyone claims to have read all of Augustine's works that person is a liar.[7]

The student who seeks to explain this astonishing fact cannot appeal solely to Augustine's natural gifts—intelligence, memory, imagination, sensibility, love of wisdom—which were indeed many and exceptional. He must appeal as well to the moral qualities Augustine had developed in himself, to his working methods, his stamina, his literary training, and, in no less a degree, his supernatural gifts.

Driven as he was by a desire to feed on wisdom and to meet the needs of the Church, Augustine never knew what it meant to waste time. He was a formidable worker who could make good use of the smallest periods of time. He refers not infrequently to the "drops" of time that "trickle" upon him in his work. "Brother, I think you know how much work I have in hand and how very few are the drops of time that trickle down upon me; were I to use these for other things I would feel I was neglecting my duty."[8] And he exclaims in the *Confessions:* "Drops of my time are precious to me."[9]

He had a keen and profound sense of the tension between what he wanted to do and what he was able to do, between desire and reality. He never succeeded in doing all that he wanted, and yet he always did more than he should have been able to do. He was an ascetic and had reduced his material needs to the minimum so that he might have more room for thought and action. His free time was always busy. "My leisure is filled with great labor."[10]

Working methods

He ate little[11] and slept less. At Cassiciacum he had adopted the custom of spending half the night—either the first part or the second—in meditation.[12] We may be certain that this habit did not slacken in the years of his episcopate. We know in fact that in his late old age—when he was 74 to 76 years old—he worked day and night dictating books, "insofar" (he adds with a sigh) "as I have any relief from the other business that is constantly descending on me from all sides." The step he had taken of entrusting the administrative side of his task to his designated successor had therefore been only partially successful.

The two works on which he was simultaneously engaged at this time were the *Revisions* and the *Second Reply to Julian*. When Quodvultdeus, a deacon, asked him to write a book on heresies, he said he could not do it because he was busy dictating the two works just mentioned, one by day, the other by night. Julian had written eight books against one of Augustine (the second book of the work *Marriage and Desire*), but only five of these had been sent to Augustine from Rome. He therefore adds, with his accustomed affability: "When I have finished replying to the fifth, then, God willing, and if the other three have not reached me, I am ready to begin the book you ask for. I shall work on both at once, that is, your book and the revision of my writings, devoting the hours of the night to the one and the hours of the day to the other."[13]

Augustine's first biographer tells us that this was not an isolated episode but his habitual practice. After saying that Bishop Augustine did not like to get involved in temporal affairs, Possidius continues:

> Once he had arranged these matters in orderly fashion, his soul immediately fled them as bitter and troublesome and returned

to the higher interior things of the spirit: the study of divine truth, the dictation of what he had discovered, and the correction of what he had dictated. Thus he went on, working by day and keeping watch by night.[14]

This exceptional application to work was accompanied by a practical and effective method of studying. He took notes as he read and meditated. "I meditate on the law of the Lord, if not day and night, then at least in my smallest moments of leisure, and I put my meditations in writing lest my memory betray me."[15] Sometimes he would make notes in the margin of the codex. These might later be collected by disciples, perhaps even without the master knowing it, and would end up being turned into a book. This was the case with the *Annotations on Job*, which are "a source of enjoyment for the few readers capable of understanding them."[16] In other instances, the marginal notes prepared the way for the dictation of a work that might otherwise have never been written.[17] Or again they might serve as a reply to someone who remembered Augustine's old profession and thought himself justified in importuning him with "countless questions on literature." "I have answered your questions, not only those in the present letter but also practically all the others that I was able, even if only in the form of short annotations on the pages listing your queries."[18]

Notes

In general, before writing a book Augustine made notes for the purpose. There were cases in which the book was never written; then the notes were either lost (as for most of the books in his projected *Disciplines*[19]) or reached the hands of readers and replaced the book itself (thus the *Immortality of the Soul*[20]).

When brethren in the community in which he was living or in others where he was passing through asked his views on important questions of philosophy, theology, or exegesis, he would write or dictate his answers on sheets of paper lest his words be lost. In fact, some of his works are collections of such sheets. I am referring to the *Miscellany of Questions in Response to Simplician*[21] and the *Explanation of Some Statements in the Apostle's Letter to the Romans*,[22] two works which are very important for this reason (and for others as well).

One fact in particular needs mentioning. When Augustine preached in church, whether at Hippo or at Carthage or anywhere he might be, secretaries took down his words with surprising accuracy. He was then able to revise the sermon and allow it to be published. In other words, as he spoke he had in mind not only his hearers but his prospective readers. This is why so many of his sermons have survived and form no small part (even if not the principal part, as for other Fathers) of his literary heritage.

Some other factors in Augustine's productivity were his long and careful training in rhetoric and the indispensable collaboration of his fellow religious. His training enabled him to speak and to dictate letters and books with great ease; his brethren helped him by organizing the volumes in his library,[23] consulting books, and comparing texts.

In my opinion, however, we must look higher for the ultimate explanation of his prodigious activity.

Part III

The Mystic

32

Lover of Beauty

WE do not understand Augustine the man and much less Augustine the pastor and theologian unless we realize that he was also a mystic, and a great one. With penetrating insight his first biographer reminds us of this fact. Speaking of Augustine's activity as a writer Possidius remarks: "He resembled the devout Mary of the Gospel, that figure of the heavenly Church, of whom it is written that she sat at the feet of the Lord, intently listening to his words."[1]

It is not necessary to review here the question, discussed—and substantially answered—in decades past, of the meaning to be given the word "mystical" when it is applied to Augustine. Almost all the scholars who have studied the subject give the term "mystical" its strict sense here. Some even regard Augustine as the prince of Christian mystics. Others consider him to have been simply an "intellectual" or a "great enthusiast."[2]

The controversy is a long-standing one and is due to a lack of agreement on the concept of mysticism. The essential point at issue is whether or not there is a place in this concept for an intellectual vision; in other words, whether intellectualism and mysticism, philosophical approach and infused contemplation are mutually exclusive or can be convergent. Most scholars maintain a possible convergence and give as a prime example the experience of Augustine. "Augustine is for me the Prince of Mystics, uniting in himself, a matter I do not find in any other, the two elements of mystical experience, viz. the most penetrating intellectual vision into things divine, and a love of God that was a consuming passion."[3]

Before we follow Augustine in his mystical ascents it will be profitable to take a closer look at his poetic genius. For Augustine was a poet as well. I make this claim not because he wrote verses (these were few and not of high quality) but because he had a poet's sensibility and imagination. He was a passionate lover of beauty. His very first work was devoted to this subject and was entitled *Beauty and Proportion*. The book has not survived, but the passage in the *Confessions* in which he mentions it shows the things that occupied his thoughts when he was twenty-six.

> I was in love with earthly beauties. . . . I said to my friends, "Do we love anything but what is beautiful? And what is beauty? What is it that attracts us and attaches us to the things we love? For if there were not in them a gracefulness and beauty, they would not attract us." And I observed and made note of the fact that in the bodies themselves there was one thing that made them a whole and therefore beautiful; and another that had its beauty from being aptly suited to another, as a part of the body is to the whole, or a shoe to the foot, and the like. These speculations gushed forth in my mind out of my inmost heart, and I wrote certain volumes, *Beauty and Proportion*—I think two or three. O God, you know, for I have forgotten. I do not have them; they have been lost, I know not why.[4]

Consequences of love for beauty

Because he loved beauty he loved light, "the queen of colors," and singing and harmony. At Milan he wept as he listened to the sacred hymns of another poet, Ambrose, being sung by the faithful; at Hippo he was deeply moved when he heard his own people singing the psalms. Such singing fascinated him. At times the fascination seemed to him to be excessive, and he considered doing away with singing, which he himself had introduced, and substituting for it a type of recitation closer to declamation than to song, such as was used (he says) in the Church of Alexandria.

> But when I remember those tears that I shed at the singing of the chants of the Church in the beginning of my recovered faith, and also how much I am now moved, not with the singing but with the things that are expressed in song when they are declined with a clear voice and a most suitable modulation, I acknowledge once more the great benefit of this practice.[5]

Of the many works he planned to write on the liberal arts, the only one he completed in addition to his *Grammar* was the one on music, the science of rhythm.

> A consideration of words will show us the power that rhythm exercises in all movements. Such an analysis leads up a ladder as it were and mounts step by step to the divine secrets of truth. On

this ascent wisdom shows her most cheerful and pleasant side and with all the prudence at her disposal helps those who love her. For this reason, when I first retired from the world and my soul was free of more serious and urgent duties . . . I planned to write an introduction to the study of truth. I wrote six books on rhythm alone, and planned (I admit) perhaps another six on melody, in the hope that I would eventually have the leisure to write them. But once the burden of ecclesiastical duties was laid on my shoulders . . . all those delightful prospects faded away, to such an extent that I now have trouble even finding the manuscript.[6]

It was in the perspective of rhythm that Augustine saw the universe, the human person, and history. No reader of the *Confessions* can forget his interior pilgrimage in search of God. "I asked the earth. . . . I asked the sea. . . . I asked the sky, the sun, the moon, and the stars." And all of them replied, "We are not your God." "My asking was my attention to them, and their answer was their beauty."[7]

Earth and the heavens also cry out that they did not make themselves. . . . Therefore, you O Lord, who are beautiful, made them, for they also are beautiful; you who are good, for they also are good; you who ARE, for they also are. But they are not beautiful and good as you are beautiful and good, nor do they have their being as you, their Creator, have your being.[8]

God is "beauty at once so ancient and so new."[9] He is the "father of beauty,"[10] "in whom all beauty has its source."[11] He is "source, principle, and author of goodness and beauty in all that is good and beautiful."[12]

But the privileged dwelling of beauty in our universe is the human person with its perfect body, marvelous memory, capacity for the arts, its love, virtue, and wisdom. "What do we praise in bodies? Nothing else but beauty. What is corporeal beauty? The right proportion of the parts, together with a certain charm that color lends."[13]

"People go a great way to see and admire the heights of mountains, the vast billows of the sea, the broad reaches of rivers, the compass of the ocean, and the motions of the heavenly bodies. But they pay no attention to themselves."[14] The same can be said of artistic beauty. It too comes to us, through the hands of artists, from the eternal Beauty. Yet while human beings derive from this Beauty the norm for judging their artistic productions, they do not accept the same norm for making right use of these productions.[15] They do not accept it because they are forgetful of themselves. Yet virtue consists in true beauty. "In the final analysis, what is our justice or the other virtues by which we live rightly and wisely if not the beauty of the interior self? Certainly it is in virtue of this beauty and not of any bodily likeness that we have been made in the image of God."[16]

Augustine looks at history too in terms of rhythm: history is a vast poem written by the pen of a supreme artist.

> He, the unchanging creator and ruler of changeable things, knows much better than human beings do what is suitable for each age [of history]. He knows what he needs to give, add, remove, take away, increase or diminish at a given moment, in order that the beauty of the universe, which is made up of things suited to their own time, may unfold and reach its completion like a concert performed by a supreme artist. Then those who adore God as he should be adored in the time of faith may rise from this created beauty to an eternal contemplation of absolute beauty.[17]

But history also contains evil. Augustine is well aware of it and suffers from it; the only explanation he can find for it is the beauty of the whole. A painter knows where to use black in order that the painting as a whole may be beautiful. Shall God not know where to put sinners so that his creation may be properly ordered?[18]

Soul of a poet

This esthetic sensibility, combined with insight into the highest truths, often makes Augustine's discourse soar like great poetry. He has the ability to convey true and profound sentiments in vivid and effective images. He is able to express spiritual realities so that they do not lose their immaterial purity, but also to give passionate voice to the things of earth so that without losing their concrete density they become a sign of the divine and a ladder to it. He has the rare ability to liberate the most abstract truths from their abstractness and present them in such a way that they manifest their vibrant reality and radiate warmth and power.

All this can be seen especially in the sermons and in the *Confessions*. The touch of his imagination transforms humans, restless unless they find rest in God, into dry blades of grass[19]; love into a weight that carries human beings wherever they go[20]; earthly life into a sound between two vast silences: the silence of what is no longer and the silence of what is not yet[21]; wealth into a pauper's dream:

> A beggar, lying on the bare ground and trembling from the cold, falls asleep and dreams of treasures; in his dream he rejoices and grows arrogant, and will not spare even a glance for his own father who is clothed in rags. As long as he has not awakened he is rich; but the greater the empty joy he experiences in sleep, the more, when he awakens, will he suffer from reality.[22]

The generations of human beings on earth are leaves of a tree that is always green. "The tree is always clothed in green; but look at its foot and see all the dry leaves you trample on."[23] Faith becomes a "nest" in which the little birds prepare for flight; those who claim to understand before they believe are like little birds who want to fly before they have acquired feathers. Augustine applies this image to himself as a presumptuous young man of nineteen: "I myself was deceived for a while. . . . I, alas, thought myself ready to fly, and so I left the nest and fell, because in fact I could not fly. But the merciful Lord picked me and put me back in the nest before passersby could trample me underfoot."[24] Christ becomes a tree planted beside the river of temporal realities. "Do you feel yourselves being swept toward the falls? Hold fast to the tree."[25]

Examples could be multiplied almost endlessly, for Augustine's warm imagination was exceptionally rich. Frequently it is the poetry of the psalms, which he admired so greatly, that supplies him with appropriate images; often it is an incident from the Gospels that stirs him and gives wings to his imagination. Thus the episode of the woman taken in adultery: the accusation, the answer, the flight of the accusers; Jesus is left alone with the poor woman: mercy and wretchedness. "They all went away. He was left alone with her in her loneliness: the creator and the creature, mercy and wretchedness."[26] That confrontation contains the whole drama of salvation.

It is when Augustine speaks of God that his poetry soars to unparalleled heights, as in this passage of the *Confessions*:

> What then is it that I love when I love you [my God]? Neither the beauty of the body nor the graceful order of time, nor the brightness of light, so agreeable to these eyes, nor the sweet melodies of all kinds of songs, nor the fragrant scents of flowers, ointments, or spices, nor manna and honey, nor limbs agreeable to carnal embraces—none of these things do I love when I love my God. And yet, when I love him, it is true that I love a certain light and a certain voice and a certain fragrance and a certain food and a certain embrace; but they are the type that I love in my inner self, where my soul is flooded with the light that no place can contain, the sounds that no time can carry away, the scent that no current can disperse, the relish that no eating can diminish, and the embrace that no satiety can break. It is this that I love when I love my God.[27]

Poetic prayers

The same profound concepts, the same vivid images occur when he speaks of God's action within him.

> Too late have I loved you, O Beauty so ancient, O Beauty so new, too late have I loved You! ... Those things kept me far from you, which, unless they existed in you, would have no being. You have called, you have cried out and pierced my deafness. You have lightened, you have shone forth and dispelled my blindness: you have sent forth your fragrance, and I have drawn my breath and pant after you. I have tasted you, and I hunger and thirst; you have touched me, and I am all inflamed with the desire of your peace.[28]

Then there is the poetry of the long and impassioned prayer that opens the first book of the *Soliloquies*. It is a prayer with the spaciousness and majesty of a symphony. Its substance is philosophical and theological and its inspiration mystical, but the feeling that animates it, the rhythm that controls it, and the form in which it is expressed turn it into poetry, and marvelous poetry at that. I wish I could cite it in its entirety.

First, there is an introduction: "O God, creator of the universe, grant that I may pray to you as I ought." Then, contemplation of God at work in the sensible world: "You created from nothing this world whose sovereign beauty is evident to every eye." Next, in a magnificent crescendo, an invocation of God as source of the intelligible world: "O God, father of truth, father of wisdom, father of true and supreme life, father of happiness, father of the good and the beautiful, father of intelligible light, father of our awakening and enlightenment, father of the pledge that bids us return to you, I invoke you."

He turns again to contemplation of the divine being "in which there is no discord, no confusion or change or need or death, but only supreme harmony, supreme clarity, supreme constancy, supreme fullness, supreme life, to which nothing is lacking, in which nothing is superfluous." And to contemplation of divine providence "according to whose laws the heavens move . . . the soul is guaranteed freedom of will . . . all blessings come to us and all evils are kept far off." Then a sweeping conclusion: "Hear me, hear me, hear me, my God, my Lord, my King, my Father, my Maker, my Hope, my Reality, my Honor, my House, my Homeland, my Salvation, my Light, my Life. Hear me, hear me, hear me in the way that you alone have and so few know."[29]

If this is not poetry, than I know not where to find it.

33

A Letter to God

AUGUSTINE was a profoundly religious man, and for him esthetic contemplation inevitably became mystical contemplation. The prayer just cited is but one example. The *Confessions* is a much more extensive and better example. He wrote it at the beginning of his episcopal career, in his forty-fourth to forty-sixth years.[1]

He may have been persuaded to do so by friends, among whom in this case was Paulinus of Nola, a friend of both Alypius and himself. Another motive may have been the desire to dissuade these friends from praising him so often and so generously. Again, he may have felt a need of interior strength in the hard labors of the apostolate or a way of peopling the solitude in which his new responsibilities placed him. This last-named reason surely played some part. Augustine cultivated friendships as few other men have, and yet, once consecrated a bishop, he was in fact a man very much alone. He was surrounded by a flock who loved him but did not understand him; he was far from the friends most close to him; his episcopal duties made it impossible for him to fill his solitude with the study of Scripture and so he sought relief in writing a conversation with God.

The *Confessions* is in fact a long letter to God, in which the author speaks of everything that concerns and interests him: the facts of his life, the mysteries of grace, the profound questions of philosophy, the interpretation of Scripture, his interior ascents, and the wonders of creation. It is therefore a work at once of autobiography, philosophy, theology, mysticism, and poetry. Its many-faceted richness makes Augustine's letter to God a work of world literature, much read in the past and read even more today.

Contrary to what is often thought, the *Confessions* is not simply a confession of sins. Augustine does indeed confess his sins and does so with ruthless honesty and deep humility, but this is only one aspect, and not even the principal aspect, of the work. Augustine's *Confessions* has far wider horizons: it embraces the three dimensions—past, present, and future—of his own life, the divine gifts of creation and salvation, and the mysterious plans of providence. The dominant note is therefore praise. The same is true of the Scriptural verb *confess.* Augustine himself frequently explains that there is a twofold *confessio:* the *confessio pec-catorum* (confession of sins) and the *confessio laudis* (confession of praise). The two, moreover, are closely connected, inasmuch as to confess one's own sins is already to praise God.[2]

Personal opinion of confessions

Here is what he says, toward the end of his life, when he sends Darius a copy of the *Confessions:*

> Here, then, my son and my illustrious lord, who are a Christian not in outward seeming only but in Christian charity as well—here is the copy of my *Confessions* that you requested. In them behold me and do not praise me as being something other than I really am; believe what I say about myself in them, instead of believing what others say of me. Look at me in these books and see what I was in and of myself, and if you find anything pleasing in me, then join me in praising not myself but him who I desired should be praised for what he did for me. It is he who made me; I did not make myself. On the contrary, I was lost, but then he who had made me remade me. Once you have seen from these books what I really am, pray for me that I may not fall back but be able to continue advancing. I know what I am saying, I know what I am asking. . . . I ask that not only you would pray for me, but all those too who wish me well when they hear you speak of me.[3]

Some years earlier, when reviewing this already famous work, he wrote in his *Revisions:*

> The thirteen books of my *Confessions* praise the just and good God for all my actions, bad as well as good, and they raise the minds and hearts of my readers to him. Such, at any rate, was the effect they had on me while I was writing them, and they have the same effect on me now when I reread them. What others think of them is their business. I know, however, that they pleased and still please many of my brethren.[4]

This passage tells us in so many words that the *Confessions* were favorably received; it also tells us in more veiled terms that there were criticisms and reservations. Among the critics were the Manichaeans, Donatists, Pelagians, and pagans. All these for one reason or another did not accept—indeed, could not accept—the judgments and sentiments Augustine had expressed in this work. They even used it in varying degrees to attack, accuse, and reject its author. Pelagius' reaction is well known. In his book *The Gift of Perseverance* Augustine writes:

> Which of my works has been more often read or more enjoyed than my *Confessions*? This was published before the Pelagian heresy made its appearance, and in it I said, and said often: "Give what you command, and command what you will." Pelagius heard one of my brothers, an episcopal colleague, cite these words in Rome; he could not stand them, but contradicted them so violently that he almost quarreled with the person who cited them.[5]

Less well known, but sadder, is the case of Julian, who used the *Confessions* as the basis for an attack on Augustine's mother.[6]

But not all the criticisms were from outsiders; some came from the "brethren." Augustine seems to have anticipated these as he wrote, and he turns from time to time to the strong, the less gifted of mind, and the proud; that is, to those who would be conscious of not having committed the sins he was confessing, or who would not understand what he was saying, or who would pretend to understand what in fact they did not understand. He asks the first group not to scorn him or, above all, not to be less thankful to the Lord as though he had been less generous to them.[7] He urges the second group to be content with understanding what they did understand and, for the rest, to ask God for the gift of understanding.[8] He leaves the last group to fan the earth with their breath, stirring up the dust into their own eyes.[9]

The *Confessions* is certainly not an easy book to read. If we are to grasp its various aspects and especially if we are to understand its style and tone, we must enter deeply into the soul of its author, a man who combines strict intellectual standards with profound mystical aspirations, a lively sense of sin with an awestruck expectation of salvation.

Story of his conversion

In his *Confessions* Augustine undertakes to tell us of himself. He does not tell us everything, but only what fits in with the perspective he has chosen: his conversion to faith and to the service of God. What does not contribute to this is irrelevant and is omitted. As a result, to our great regret we find him dismissing some periods that we regard as important, such as his second stay in Rome, with a few words: "I pass over many things, as I am hastening much."[10] Similarly, he omits the name of the friend whose unexpected death afflicted him so deeply,[11] and he says almost nothing of his life as a professor in Carthage, although this lasted eight years.[12]

Even in what he does tell us we must distinguish between the facts themselves and the judgments he passes on them. The facts have to do with Augustine the subject of the story; the judgments are those of Augustine the teller of the story. There are two Augustines, but both are true and authentic. The author of the *Confessions* faithfully reports the facts as they happened and to the extent that memory has collected and retained them; when he is certain he tells us that he is certain; when he is in doubt he tells us that he is doubtful; when he does not remember he tells us that he does not remember. His judgments on the facts, however, are suggested to him by a conscience that has been formed and made sensitive in the school of the Gospel.

Everyone is familiar with the theft of the pears; much has been written on it, and what has been written has often not been to the point. Augustine narrates the incident itself in careful detail and without exaggeration, and he includes the circumstances that lessened his guilt. In his sixteenth year, at night, after continuing their games out of doors, until late evening as usual, a group of young men, Augustine among them (he reminds us that if he had been alone he would never have done the ugly deed), went and shook the pear-tree in a neighbor's garden. They carried off a large number of pears, not because they needed them or were greedy or from any other reason, but simply to throw them to the pigs.[13]

Such was the fact. Everything else comes from Augustine the theologian, philosopher, and penitent, who weaves long and beautiful meditations around the fact in an effort to discover the reason for this "gratuitous sin" that he committed because he enjoyed "doing wrong for no other reason than that it was wrong."[14]

The reason for this reflective dimension of the *Confessions* that is interwoven with the narrative and is even more extensive than the story proper is this: Augustine sees and relates the facts of his life as part of the universal panorama of providence. The panorama has for its focal point God and the human person as an inseparable pair. He asks what God is for the human person and the human person for God; he passes quickly from the one to the other and uses the one to shed light on the other. This vision, which is at once theocentric and anthropological, becomes the basis for philosophical, theological, and mystical discourse.

Philosophical interpretation

The philosophical discourse is concerned with God and creation, providence and evil, human beings and their aspirations, time and eternity. Neoplatonism comes to his aid in developing these themes. Augustine takes over the major metaphysical theses of Neoplatonism and makes extensive use of them; he does so, however, not as a disciple, but as a master in his own right, for as he uses them he also corrects them and moves beyond them. He subordinates them in particular to the Christian idea of God and the doctrine of creation. It is in ascending from creatures to God that he gains full certainty.

> I said, "Is the truth then nothing, because it is not spread out through any space finite or infinite?" And you cried out to me from afar, "Yes, in very truth, I AM WHO AM." And I heard as the heart hears, and there was no room left for doubt. And I could more easily doubt that I was alive than that Truth is not; which is clearly seen being understood by the things that are made.[15]

Augustine views the human person as three-dimensional, since it is, knows, and loves. He therefore attains to God as absolute Being, supreme Wisdom, and primal Love. All else that has being, truth, and goodness proceeds from God, not by way of generation (for then it would be equal to him), but by way of creation from nothing. All these other things are inferior to him: they are and yet they are not.

I looked into the other things that are below you, and I saw that they neither altogether had being nor altogether lacked being. That they had being indeed, because they are from you; and that they were lacking in being because they are not what you are; for that truly *is* which remains unchangeable.[16]

Because God is changeless, he "does not exist in degree but is absolute being"; he exists beyond measure, he is what he is.[17]

So determined was Augustine to enter more deeply into the doctrine of creation that he devoted the final books of the *Confessions* to a commentary on Genesis. But the question arises: why does he add these last three books to the *Confessions*, since these books represent—or so it seems—a shift from autobiography to doctrinal exposition? And why the choice of Genesis?

The answer, it seems to me, is to be found in the fact that his friends asked him to continue his *Confessions* by "confessing" his now customary way of ascending to God. In response, he describes the daily effort at purification that he has adopted in order to reach God; he also shows his readers (surely a valuable autobiographical datum!) how his love feeds on the word of God, and he offers a commentary on some chapters of Scripture to illustrate his own method of meditating on God's word.

The choice of Genesis is due, in my opinion, to the truths that this book of Scripture contains, chief among them the truth of creation, which is the essential basis for a conversation—and that is what the *Confessions* is—between human beings and God.[18] Augustine wants to know how God in the beginning created heaven and earth, and he confesses that he has acquired three major certitudes: that God alone is eternal, because he alone is not by nature subject to change; that everything which is not God has received its being from him; and that no creature, however perfect, is coeternal with God. He confesses these certitudes and resolves the difficulties, which are neither few nor easy, against creation and especially against creation in time or, more accurately, with time.

The doctrine of creation yields the idea of God as both transcendent and immanent. On this point the *Confessions* is an exceptionally rich lode of statements: God is "most hidden and ever-present," "most high and most near," "internal and eternal," "more inward to me than my inward self and higher than what was highest in me."[19] The same doctrine of creation yields another and no less luminous truth that permeates, animates, and guides the entire *Confessions:* the truth of providence. "You have as much care of each one of us as if you had no other in your care, and as much care of all as of each single one."[20] It is in the light of this truth that Augustine tells the story of his own life. Even evil has its place in the plan of providence, not because evil is God's doing but because he who is just and good makes it serve his order. He is "disposer and creator of all things natural, but of sin, only the disposer."[21]

Sinners can therefore act against the will of God but they do not on that account fall outside of his plan. The idea of order reigns supreme in many of Augustine's works, those especially that deal with the distressing problem of evil.

Theological interpretation

Discussion of this problem causes Augustine to lift the veil and move from the level of philosophy to that of theology, where he deals essentially with the problem of grace and salvation.

The problem of salvation has a starting point, which is the fact of sin, and a goal, which is the presence of grace. The movement of sin is contrary to that which leads human beings to possession of God. The way to God, which Augustine reviews so frequently, runs from exterior things to interior and from inferior to superior, or, in less abstract language, from the world to human beings and from human beings to that which transcends them, namely, God. Readers will recall Augustine's two precepts: return into yourself, rise above yourself. The movement of sin is just the opposite. Sin "is not a substance but a perversion of the will that separates us from the supreme substance, from you, O God, and turns us back toward inferior things; rejecting the goods it has that are interior it gorges itself on exterior goods." The result is alienation and tragedy: genuine alienation is the only real human tragedy.[22]

These deep convictions form the basis for Augustine's teaching on grace, which is often expressed in pairs of opposites: slavery and freedom, ugliness and beauty, dispersion and unity, emptiness and fullness, death and life, restlessness and rest. These are also some of the many antitheses that make up the fabric of the *Confessions*. The resolution of the oppositions comes from Christ, for Christ the mediator is the sole hope of humankind. In him our tragic state is overcome and our dilemmas are resolved. He is immortal and just; by becoming mortal while remaining just, he gave human beings who are both mortal and unjust the power to become just and immortal.[23] On one occasion Augustine exclaimed before the people: "O Word, who exist before time, who made time and were born in time although you are eternal life! You call beings who are temporal and make them eternal!"[24]

The loftiest expression of the mystery of grace is therefore to be found in the final paragraphs of Book X of the *Confessions*, the longest and most profound book in the entire work. In this passage the young bishop, who felt crushed under the weight of his new responsibilities and was meditating a flight from them, voices his firm hope and confidently agrees to continue his burdensome ministry.

> How have you loved us, O good Father, who have not spared even your own Son but have delivered him for us all! How have you loved us, for whom he, who did not consider being equal to God a thing to cling to, became obedient to death, even to death on a Cross. He who alone was free among the dead, having the power to lay down his life and the power to take it up again, became in your eyes, on our behalf, both a victor and a victim, and therefore a victor because a victim. He became in your eyes on our behalf, both the Priest and the Sacrifice, and therefore the Priest because of the Sacrifice. He made us your children instead of servants by being born of you and becoming our servant. And therefore do I justly repose a strong hope in him, that you will heal all my maladies through him who sits at your right hand and intercedes with you for us; else I should despair. For many and great are these my infirmities; they are many and great, but greater is your medicine.[25]

Mystical interpretation

It is from these theological heights that Augustine the mystic soars higher still. The *Confessions* was written as a book of spiritual "elevations," and that is what it truly is. The sentiments of prayer are to be found on every page. The *Confessions* begins with a cry of astonishment at the greatness of God and the condition of human beings as sinners who nonetheless desire to praise him; it ends with a longing for the endless peace that is fullness of life and the permanent possession of God. Augustine's prayer springs from his philosophical and theological vision and is indeed inseparable from it.

> Oh, that I might rest in you! Oh, that you would come into my heart and inebriate it, that I may forget my sins, and embrace you, my only good! What are you to me? In your mercy let me speak. What am I to you that you should demand my love and, if I do not love you, should be angry and threaten me with grievous woes? Is it then a slight woe not to love you? Ah, for your mercies' sake, tell me, O Lord my God, what you are to me. Say to my soul: "I am your Salvation." So speak that I may hear. . . .
>
> The mansion of my soul is too narrow to receive you: let it be enlarged by you. It is all in ruins: be pleased to repair it. It has within it such things as will offend your gaze: I confess and know it, but who shall cleanse it? Or to whom besides you shall I cry out?[26]

This felt need of interior purification, which Augustine expresses at the very beginning, leads to the lengthy examination of conscience that is set down in Book X. The presuppositions behind this examination are not those of the Neoplatonists and Pythagoreans, for Augustine rejects these; they are those of the Gospel: All things are good and praiseworthy, but if we violate proper order and attach ourselves to them with the glue of love, they hold us back on our journey and turn us toward nonbeing.

> Let my soul for these things praise you, O God, the Creator of all things, but allow it not to cleave to them with the glue of love through the senses of the body. They go on the way they were going, that they might not be, and leave the soul wounded with pestilent desires because it would have them still be and longs to repose in them, but they abide not and run away. And who can follow them with any bodily sense when they are gone, or hold them fast while they are at hand?[27]

Augustine recalls St. John's threefold command, that we should abstain from "the lust of the flesh, the lust of the eyes, and the pride of life,"[28] and he uses this as the basis for a detailed and unsparing examination of conscience. This examination has for its purpose to acquaint the reader, in a frank and humble way, with the results of Augustine's ascetical efforts to overcome the attraction of the senses, curiosity, and pride, the three sources of temptations that are a hard test for the spirit as it endeavors to ascend to God.

In connection with the attractions of the senses Augustine sketches with fine psychological insight the contrast between the lover of beauty and the ascetic—two types that dwelt side by side in Augustine himself. The lover of beauty delights in the beauty of the corporeal world but is in danger of stopping there; the ascetic does not deny this beauty but seeks to use it as a ladder by which to mount up to a higher beauty. By reason precisely of this ascetical effort, the opposition turns (though not always completely) into a friendly collaboration.

> How innumerable are the things made by every kind of art and workmanship: in clothes, shoes, vessels, and such like handicrafts, in pictures also and every kind of statutes, and these far exceeding all necessary and moderate use and pious signification, have human beings added to the allurements of the eyes—outwardly following what they have made, inwardly forsaking him by whom they themselves were made and destroying what they were made to be.
>
> But I, O my God, and my glory, even from these things do now sing a hymn to you and offer a sacrifice of praise to him who offers his sacrifice for me. For all these beautiful patterns, which pass from souls to the skillful hands of artists, are derived from that beauty which is above the soul, after which my soul sighs day and night.

But this ascent to eternal beauty is not easy nor is it attempted by all lovers of beauty.

> But those who fashion and admire these exterior beauties, while they take from that first beauty the rule of judging them, do not take from it the rule of using them. And there he is, and they do not see him, so as to stop there and go no farther, and keep their

strength for you, and not scatter it abroad upon wearisome pleasures.

Often Augustine himself does not succeed fully in this endeavor:

> As for me, who am speaking and discerning these things, I am also apt to have my steps entangled in these beauties, but you pluck them out, O Lord, you pluck them out, because your mercy is before my eyes. For I fall miserably into these snares, and you draw me out again mercifully—sometimes without my perceiving it because I have only lightly fallen upon them, and sometimes with pain to me because I had stuck fast in them.[29]

Another opposition that the ascetic sought to overcome was between the desire to know, observe, and experiment (Augustine had this inquisitiveness in a high degree; it led to his strong enthusiasm in youth for the theater and astrology) and the duty, now a habit, of devoting his mind to serious matters.

> I do not now go to the circus to see a dog chasing a hare; but in the field such a course presented to my sight, when I chance to be passing by, takes me off, perhaps, from some thought of great moment, and draws my attention toward that chase, not so as to make me turn aside with the body of my mount, but with the inclinations of my heart. . . . What, when I am sitting at home, a lizard catching flies or a spider entangling them in her nets, often fixes my attention upon them? . . . I go on from them to praise you, the wonderful Creator and ordainer of all things; but it was not with this thought that I first began to observe them.[30]

The most difficult opposition, however, had to do with praise. Praise is a source of pleasure; Augustine, who received a great deal of praise, quoted Persius to express his own reaction to it: "My heart is not hardened."[31] But the desire to be praised, or vainglory, or self-complacency, is a subtle and dangerous vice. On the other hand, a praiseworthy way of life is not to be abandoned because it wins praise, nor may a bishop not want his ministry to be valued. The bishop of Hippo, a man of sensitivity and born for friendship, felt how difficult it was to steer a course between these two extremes. In order to succeed in this, he prayed a great deal, cultivated an awareness of his own sentiments and desires, and made it his goal to love the truth above all else.[32]

Journeying toward the fullness of being

Augustine's ascetical endeavors were always supported by mystical aspirations. For him this meant escaping the devouring coils of time and journeying toward the fullness of being. Here is how he concludes his well-known meditations on time; the passage displays convergent ideas from three different sources: Plotinian philosophy, Pauline Christology, and the poetry of the psalms.

> But because your mercy is better than lives, behold, my life is but a distraction, and your right hand has held me up in my Lord, the Son of Man, the Mediator between you, the One, and us who are many, in many ways and in many things—that by him I may lay hold of that by which he has laid hold of me, and may be gathered up from my former life, to follow the One, forgetting what is behind; not distended to future things and that which are before; not distractedly but intently I press on to the prize of my heavenly calling, where I may hear the voice of your praise and contemplate your delights that neither come nor pass away.
>
> But now my life is wasted with grief, and you, O Lord, my Comfort, my Father, are everlasting; but I am divided among the times, of whose order I still know nothing. My thoughts and the deepest recesses of my soul are torn asunder by tumultuous varieties, until such time as I shall flow together into you, purified and melted by the fire of your love.[33]

This humble and sincere longing was at times fulfilled by an extraordinary gift of divine favor. Augustine tells us as much in veiled yet transparent words. Speaking of his daily meditations, of which the *Confessions* provide a sample, he says:

> Often I do this [survey this world through senses and memory]. It gives me great pleasure, and as often as I can have leisure from necessary duties I repair to this pleasure. Neither can I find in all these things, which I run through consulting you, any safe place of repose for my soul but in you, where all my dissipations may be recollected and that nothing of me may go astray from you. And sometimes you do admit me into a most unusual affection of devotion within my interior, to I know not what sweetness, which, if it were to be perfected in me, I know not what there could be in the next life which the present did not possess. But I fall back again into the things below, by the weight of my misery; and I am again engulfed in the things I am accustomed to, and am held fast by them. . . .[34]

34

"Lord, one and only God, Triune God"

"I began my work on the Trinity, the supreme and true God, when I was a young man and I have published it in my old age."[1] So says Augustine in a letter to his friend Aurelius, bishop of Carthage, in which he tells of his experiences in composing this famous work. In fact the work was not produced in a single continuous period but was long meditated and written at intervals. He dictated it from time to time and then stopped with Book XII still unfinished; the difficulty of the subject and the pressure of more urgent tasks prevented him from going further.

"For the moment I have no desire even to work on my *Trinity*, which I have had in hand for a long time, for it has cost me a great deal of effort and I suspect that few will understand it. Other writings that I hope will be useful to a broader public have a prior call upon my energies."[2] His friends were impatient, but he resisted their importunities, aware of the responsibility accepted by someone writing on a subject in which "error is more dangerous and research more laborious."[3]

> I am distressed when I think of Horace's saying, "The word once spoken cannot be taken back." That is why I delay longer than you like or find tolerable the publication of books on Genesis and the Trinity, since they deal with very sensitive questions. It is inevitable that they will contain ideas deserving of censure, but at least the errors will be fewer than they would have been if I had released the books in great haste and without proper consideration.[4]

But his friends grew tired of waiting and took action: they managed to acquire and circulate the books already composed. A cleric of the monastery or a secretary or even the librarian himself must have been in on the plot. Augustine was deeply grieved and planned not to complete the work but to complain about the incident in other writings and refuse to acknowledge as his the books that had been circulated before he thought them ready for publication. His friends, however, insisted that he finish the work; among these friends was Aurelius, whom he greatly respected.

As usual, Augustine gave in; he finished Book XII, added the Preface to the first five books, composed three more, corrected the books already circulated—"not as I would have liked, but as best I could, so that they would not be too much in disagreement with the copies stolen from me and now in the hands of others"— and sent the whole to Aurelius with permission for it to be "heard, copied, or read" by anyone who wished.[5] Thus, a work that had been over twenty years in the writing (from 399 to after 420) was finally published. Against the friends who had used unorthodox means to force his hand Augustine took but one revenge: he asked that his letter to Bishop Aurelius, in which he explained what had happened, be added to the work "as a separate preface."

The books so laboriously composed form a mighty work not only of theology and philosophy but of profound mysticism as well. In fact, it was mystical as well as theological motives that inspired the work. In the last book of the *Confessions* Augustine is filled with astonishment as he speaks of the trinitarian mystery. "Who can understand the omnipotent Trinity? Who of us does not speak of it, if indeed it be the Trinity? Rare is the soul that speaks of it with knowledge of what it says." He goes on, however, to suggest a way of reaching some little understanding of the mystery.

It would be well for us to consider these three things as they are in us. These three things are far different from that one Trinity; but I mention them only that we may test ourselves and realize how far different they are. Now the three things of which I speak, are: to be, to know, and to will. Indeed, I am, I know, I will. I am a being who knows and wills. I know that I am and that I will, and I will to be and to know.

Let those, therefore, see this who can, how life is inseparable in these three: one life, one mind, one essence; finally, how inseparable is the distinction; and yet, there is a distinction. All people each have it before them. Let them look at themselves and see, and let them tell me.

But when they have discovered and said something about these things, they must not think that they have found that Unchangeable which is above all these things; which is unchangeable, and knows unchangeably, and wills unchangeably; and whether all three are in each one so that all three belong to each, or whether both ways at once, in an admirable manner, simple, and multiple—infinite to itself, yet a limit to itself; unchangeably the Self-same in the superabundance of its Unity—who can easily conceive this? Who can in any way express it? Who would rashly pronounce upon it?[16]

Completes the teaching of the earlier Fathers

What Augustine sketches in this passage is the program for his work on *The Trinity*. In fact, he began this work shortly before or shortly after finishing the *Confessions*. As a theologian he wanted to clarify certain points on which the earlier Fathers had given inadequate explanations. There were three such points in particular: Why is it that although we confess that the Father is God, the Son is God, and the Holy Spirit is God, we may not say that Father, Son, and Holy Spirit are three gods but must rather say that they are one single God? Why is it that although the operations of the Trinity *ad extra* (operations having their term outside of God) are inseparable, yet only the Son became incarnate, only the Father's voice was heard on Tabor, and only the Holy Spirit descended on the disciples in the upper room? Finally, what are the personal properties of the Holy Spirit and why is the procession of the Spirit not a generation?[7]

In order to answer these questions Augustine undertakes to expound, defend, formulate, and illustrate the entire dogma of the Trinity. He expounds it by examining the manifestations of the Trinity in the economy of salvation (examination of Scripture: Books I-IV); he defends it (against the arguments of the Arians) by a fuller analysis of the doctrine of the relations (Books V-VII); he improves the formulation with the aid of the doctrine of terminology (Books V-VII); he illustrates the great mystery through a study of the human person which, being created in the image of God, is itself a mysterious trinity (Books IX-XV). Such is the work's vast theological program; it is profoundly original and yet faithful to a tradition that I have no room to examine here. I wish simply to make the point that the work is indeed in the line of the tradition.[8]

My main concern here is to show that from beginning to end Augustine writes as both theologian and mystic. While *The Trin-*

ity is not, in its literary form, a conversation with God, as the *Confessions* is, but rather a detailed, patient philosophical and theological study, such a conversation does go on in the soul of the man who dictates the books. His intention as he dictates is to ascend himself, and lead his readers, to contemplation of the august mystery, for he is convinced that Christian life is trinitarian or it is not Christian. And in fact our joy will be full only when we enjoy the Triune God in whose image we have been created.[9]

Human beings must therefore order their entire lives to remembering, knowing, and loving the Trinity, so that it will be present to them and they may contemplate and enjoy it.[10] The study of the human person, which occupies so many books of the work, is simply an exercise for attaining to knowledge of the Triune God—a knowledge that is not purely theoretical, but experimental, affective, and beatifying. For this reason the quest is marked by the critical discernment of a theologian, but also by the dispositions of a contemplative, namely, a keen and disinterested love of truth, an assiduous study of Scripture, a profound sense of the mystery, and a humble and trusting ascent to the goal.

> It is also necessary—may God grant it!—that in providing others with these books to read I myself should make progress, and that in trying to answer their questions I myself should find what I am seeking. Therefore, at the command of God our Lord and with his help, I have undertaken not so much to discourse with authority on matters known to me as to know them better by discoursing devoutly of them.[11]

The contemplative spirit that is present throughout the work finds untrammeled expression in the final prayer, in which the author asks God for the grace of seeking him tirelessly, remembering him always, and knowing and loving him so as to find happiness in him.

> Lord our God, we believe in you, Father, Son, and Holy Spirit. . . . Directing my efforts in accordance with this rule of faith, I have sought you as best I could and as you gave me the power. I have desired to see with my understanding that which I believed; I have studied much and labored greatly. Lord my God, my only hope, hear me lest I weary and cease to seek you; grant rather that I may always earnestly seek your face. Grant me the strength to

welcome me when I try to enter; where you have closed the door to me, open it when I knock. Grant me to be mindful of you, to understand you, to love you! Grant me these three gifts in increasing measure, until you have wholly remade me.[12]

The work itself is structured in such a way that its readers, taking faith as their starting point, will come to see themselves as created images of the Trinity and, by means of a prolonged exercise of their intellectual powers and a serious effort at purification, will rise step by step to wisdom, which is the most profound image of the Triune God in us and one that will be made complete and perfect when we know God face to face.

Treatise on soteriology and pneumatology

The overall work is thus possessed of an internal logic that leads the reader not only through the stages of the philosophical and theological inquiry but also through all the stages of the spiritual life. Few have realized it, but the work contains in fact a treatise on the mission of the Son, or soteriology; it contains a spacious exposition of the action of the Holy Spirit, from whom comes the sanctification of the Church; it contains a repeated teaching on the necessity of faith and purification if we are to reach the vision of God; finally, it contains a lengthy and enthusiastic study of the knowledge of God and the nature of wisdom.

The treatise on soteriology includes all of Book IV and a large part of Book XIII. The focus of the treatise is on love. The mission of the Son was to lead believers to contemplation of the Father. "This contemplation has been promised us as the goal of all our actions and as our eternal fullness of joy. . . . When we come to eternal life we shall gaze upon him who said to his servant Moses: 'I am who I am. You shall tell the children of Israel: He who is has sent me to you.' "[13] The Son accomplished his mission by showing us the Father's love. We were separated from God and though we wanted to return to him we had to become convinced that he truly loves us. "We had to be convinced of how greatly God loves us, lest despair keep us from seeking him; we had to be shown what state we were in when God so loved us, lest we grow proud of our merits."[14] That is what Jesus accomplished by his redemptive work in which, through the true, utterly free, and perfect sacrifice of the cross, he became the mediator of unity, freedom, and life.

But our loving God expects us to respond with love, and it is the function of the Holy Spirit to put this love in our hearts. At this point Augustine studies the necessary relation between the procession of the Spirit within the Trinity and the mission of the Spirit in the history of salvation. The result is a spacious treatise on pneumatology and supernatural anthropology that is in fact the most original part of the entire work: The Holy Spirit is given to us because he is Gift; he pours love into our hearts because he is Love; he sanctifies us because he is the Holy One; he establishes the communion of the faithful in the Church because he is Communion: he is the Gift, the Love, the Holiness, and the Communion of the Father and the Son.[15]

This trinitarian vision leads Augustine to discuss at length the nature of our justification or, to use another terminology, the idea of salvation. The discussion centers on the human being as created in the image of God and on the effects that sin and the gifts of the Holy Spirit have on the image. Augustine paints a picture of these contrasting effects that is immensely rich in detail. A full and complete forgiveness is the immediate effect of baptism; renewal, which is progressive and never complete, continues throughout life and calls for Christian ascetism. "Contemplation is the reward of faith, and it is in view of this reward that faith purifies our hearts. . . . Proof that this contemplation requires purity of heart is given above all in the verse, 'Blessed are the pure of heart, for they shall see God.' "[16]

Interior renewal progresses as human beings advance in wisdom. As we know, this word, which is such a favorite of Augustine, is extremely rich in meaning, for the idea of wisdom covers the whole range of philosophy, theology, and mysticism. It means the presence of God in us, and knowledge, and love, love being manifested in and nourished by devotion. The reader will be familiar with the Augustinian distinction between science and wisdom: "The intellectual knowledge of eternal realities belongs to wisdom, rational knowledge of temporal realities belongs to science."[17] The second is ordered to the first, which is the higher of the two and constitutes the supreme dignity of the human person.

It is in wisdom, therefore, that the image of the Trinity is to be sought. The image consists in the fact that human beings remember, know, and love, and it reaches its highest level when memory, knowledge, and love have God for their object. The image therefore becomes like its original as memory becomes richer, knowledge more profound, and love more complete. It follows from this that "the likeness of God will be complete when that vision of God will be complete of which Paul the Apostle says, 'Now we see in a glass darkly; then we shall see face to face.' "[18]

The ways of affective knowledge of God

We will be helped in understanding this Augustinian teaching if we bear in mind that the *memoria Dei* (remembrance of God) has a metaphysical and not merely a psychological meaning: it means the presence of God in human beings even when they are not mindful of it. Moreover, the God who is present is present with his creative power, his illumining light, and his gift of indwelling.

The goal of wisdom, then, and especially of mystical wisdom (as understood by Augustine), is far off and difficult to reach. Its attainment requires patient and persevering effort. Augustine's work on the Trinity tries to get readers to commit themselves to this effort. Book VIII, which is of a more mystical character than the others, constitutes an introduction to the entire second part of the work. It describes the ways of affective knowledge of God; such knowledge does not exclude but rather requires theoretical knowledge.

The ways are those of truth, goodness, justice, and love, all of which in God are supreme and subsistent realities. With the aid of these ideas we can come to know not only what God is not (this is already a major attainment) but also, even if very imperfectly, what he is. To be successful, however, the quest must be accompanied by a sincere ascetical effort that frees us of the impurities caused by disordered passions.

> Understand then, if you can, O soul weighed down by a corruptible body and burdened with many and varied earthly thoughts—understand, if you can, that God is Truth. For it is written that "God is light": not the light that our eyes see but the light that the heart sees when you hear the words, "he is Truth." Do not seek to know what truth is; if you do, the obscure mists of corporeal images and the clouds of phantasms will immediately make their presence felt and darken the serene light that flooded over you in the moment when I said "truth." Yes, you were immediately dazzled as by lightning when the word "Truth" was spoken. Stay there if you can. But you cannot; you fall back into the ordinary, the earthly world. What then, I ask you, is the weight that pulls at you if not that of the impurities caused by the birdlime of passion and by your strayings on your pilgrimage?[19]

The same procedure is applied to the other ideas mentioned earlier. "Once again, understand if you can. You certainly love only the good. . . . This thing is good, and so is that. Eliminate the 'this' and 'that,' and gaze, if you can, on good as such; then you will see God, who does not have his goodness from another good, but is the goodness in every good."[20] We see God above all, however, in love of others.

> Let no one say, 'I do not know what it is to love.' Love the brothers and sisters, and you will love this love itself. In fact, you have a better knowledge of the love with which you love than you do of the brother or sister whom you love. By that very fact God is better known to you than your brother or sister is; better known because more present to you; better known because more interior to you; better known because more certain. Embrace God who is love and you will embrace God with love.[21]

After this magnificent prelude the second part of the work begins; it is arranged in such a way as to lead the reader to the highest goals. Augustine explains:

> If we think back to the point in these books at which our minds began to glimpse the Trinity, we will light on Book VIII. In that book we tried as best we could, with the help of my analyses, to elevate our attentive minds to an understanding of that supreme, immutable nature that is other than our own minds. . . . But this ineffable light dazzled our gaze, and we realized that our weak minds

could not yet grasp it. Therefore, in a digression inserted between what we had in mind to say, we turned aside to our own minds, wherein we human beings are made in the image of God, and we found an object of study more familiar to us on which we might focus our attention with less fatigue. Thus from Book IX to Book XIII we dwelt upon our creaturely selves in order that with our minds we might see, via created things, the invisible perfections of God.[22]

In the books that follow, Augustine intends to complete the journey. But at the end he realizes, as all the great mystics do, that he has not yet reached the goal. "Now, having exercised our minds on inferior things as long as was necessary, or perhaps longer than was necessary, we seek to rise to contemplation of the sovereign Trinity that is God—but we are unable."[23]

It is from this experience of impotence that the final prayer, already cited in part, springs. Augustine finishes his work with the conviction that he has said little and perhaps said that little badly.

"Lord, one and only God, Triune God, may your faithful be grateful for everything that I have said in these books that is from you; may you and they forgive me for whatever in them comes from myself. Amen."[24]

35

The Final "Confessions"

AUGUSTINE is a man who tells us a great deal about himself; in fact, we know almost everything about him. Before his baptism he tells us of himself in the valuable prologues to the dialogues written at Cassiciacum; he tells us of himself at greater length and on a broader canvas in his *Confessions;* and he tells us of himself in his *Revisions,* which we may with good reason think of as his final "confessions."

Readers should not be deceived by the Latin title *Retractationes,* which they might misunderstand as equivalent to the English "Retractions." The Latin verb *retractare* does not mean "retract," "recant," "disavow," but rather "discuss again," "reexamine," "review." The *Revisions* is a very original kind of work, in fact the most original we have from the pen of this prolific African writer. In the literary world, writers in their later years will often go back over their writings and, with a definitive edition in view, approve, disapprove, and correct. Augustine was unable to do that sort of thing because his writings were too numerous and too scattered. Instead he wrote another book to tell his readers what he thinks of his works and how he would like them to be read. "I have written this book to be put into the hands of those from whom I cannot recover my published works for correction."[1]

To this end he reread "with the severity of a judge and, as it were, the pen of a censor"[2] his entire literary output, which had appeared uninterruptedly and at a dizzying pace for forty-four years, or from a few months after his conversion to a few days before his death.

The *Revisions* is inspired not by vanity or pride but by a religious sense of responsibility. Augustine wants to judge himself lest he be judged by God. He knows that a book of this kind will cause surprise and will not lack for critics, but this is unimportant to him. In reviewing his *Confessions* he says: What others think of them is their business; in his own intention they had served, and served still, to raise the mind and heart to God; that was enough to justify their composition and reading. In like manner he says of the *Revisions:* "Readers may place their own interpretations on this undertaking. For myself, I have had to apply here as elsewhere the Apostle's words: 'If we judge ourselves, we will not be judged by the Lord.'"

He also recalls what Christ says about the account to be given of every useless word and what St. James says about the duty of being ready to listen and slow to speak. He is aware that he himself, on the contrary, has written a great deal and spoken a great deal. He laments that "whenever I was present and the people had to be addressed, I was rarely allowed to be silent and listen to others and thus be 'ready to listen and slow to speak.'"[3]

An indispensable guide to his works

He therefore writes a new set of "confessions," this time not about his life but about his writings. He tells the reader the subject of each, its occasion, its place in the chronological order, and the key to interpreting it properly. He wants his readers not to follow him where he has erred, but also not to attribute to him errors he has not committed. The work is both an examination of conscience and a defense and proves to be an indispensable guide to the literary production, thought, and soul of this man who is over seventy when he writes it.

His intention was to review his books, letters, and sermons, but the pressing occupations of his last years did not allow him to complete the project. He regarded this review as "very necessary,"[4] but he thought it even more important to answer the difficulties of the monks of Marseilles and the aggressive reply of Julian. If he had gone solely by his own preferences he would certainly have chosen differently. His first concern, however, was for the Church. As a result, we do not have the priceless guide to the letters and sermons that he had intended to provide. How unfortunate for us!

Augustine had been planning the *Revisions* for a long time. He begins the work by saying in the Prologue: "It is many years since I began to plan and make ready for the work that I now undertake with the help of the Lord, since I am convinced I must not put it off any longer."[5] It appears that he was thinking of it as early as 412, or fourteen years before he actually began it. In that year he wrote to Marcellinus the Tribune:

> Even if an opinion of mine cannot be defended with solid arguments, it is in any case only mine, not that of an Author whose thought may not be legitimately criticized, even when we do not understand it and therefore have the impression that it is untenable. I admit therefore that I try to be one of those authors who write because they grow in knowledge and who grow in knowledge by writing. If, then, through carelessness or inadequate learning I have set down an opinion that calls for correction not only by others capable of discovering the fault but also by myself who have the duty of adverting to it, at least later on, when I have gained sufficient understanding, such errors ought not to cause surprise or pain; they are rather to be forgiven, and others should rejoice not that the mistake was made but that it has been disowned.
>
> Those who would have others be in error so that their own mistakes may remain hidden are indulging in an ugly kind of self-love. How much better and more useful it is for a writer if others do not err as well, so that their warnings may rescue the writer from error or, if the writer does not want to surrender the error, at least others will be free of it! If God grants my wish and allows me to write a book in which I bring together all the statements in my writings which with good reason I find displeasing, then it will be seen that I am impartial toward myself.[6]

The idea of such a book may have been suggested by the Pelagians and their distorted use of his youthful writings, or by those others who accused him of an improper hesitation with regard to the origin of the soul. In any case, the real reason was his awareness of his own fallibility and the resultant need of continually reexamining his ideas in the light of truth.

> You wish me well, but you labor in vain if you answer those who reprove me out of malice or ignorance or with good reason by telling them I am so infallible as never to have erred anywhere in my writings. The cause you defend is indefensible, for you will be refuted by my own judgment on myself. It is no pleasure to have my closest friends judge me to be what I am not.

In fact, he thought that Cicero's compliment, "He never spoke a word he wished had been unsaid," applied to fools rather than wise men. Therefore, "if we have not succeeded in always speaking so carefully that we have nothing to regret, let us regret what we know we should not have said."[7]

Reveals Augustine's soul

Such was the outlook that gave birth to the *Revisions*. This work is not only a bibliographical source of extraordinary importance, nor simply a valuable doctrinal work that sheds light on the development of Augustine's thought from the philosophical, theological, exegetical, and literary standpoints. It is also, and not least, an autobiographical document of the first order. In it Augustine reveals his soul: his apostolic zeal, his kindness and affability, his love for the truth, his humility, his devotion to others to the point of complete self-forgetfulness. All these things emerge when we look beyond the simple, lean style and read the work with this dimension in mind.

We find proof in this work that Augustine looked upon himself as, and was in fact, the servant of all. Most of his books were written on request, and the request was often persistent, demanding, impatient. "I replied on orders from my brethren."[8] "Under pressure from my brethren, whom I could not refuse, I corrected . . . completed and published [the books on the Trinity]."[9] "The venerable elder, Aurelius, bishop of that Church [Carthage] bade me write something on this subject [the work of monks], and I did so."[10] "It was expected that I would write on holy virginity, and I did so without delay."[11] "A friend . . . brought me this book [of Petilian] and strongly urged me to reply to it; I did so."[12] "Some of my brethren, very zealous Christians, obtained a copy of this [Marcionite] book and sent it to me without delay for an answer; they urged me not to put off my answer, and so I refuted it in two books."[13] He would rather not have regarded as his own a set of annotations that he had jotted in the margins of his copy of Job and that some friends had collected, but "I could not refuse their wish."[14]

These are but some examples. The petitioners varied, but the response was always the same. Augustine regarded no sacrifice as too great if he could only be useful. The *Revisions* thus makes clear his pastoral concern to reach everyone: the "humble throng of the uneducated and illiterate"[15]; those who knew little Latin[16]; the busy or hurried folk who had little time to read or found reading too difficult.[17]

Above all, this work reveals the serene and dignified humility of a man who is not ashamed to acknowledge the effort it cost him to go deeply into certain subjects, or that he had written unsuccessful books, or that that he had sometimes failed of his purpose. Had he been a different kind of person he would surely have eliminated from among these works some that had been fruitless attempts or even failures. Instead he preferred them to remain "as witnesses . . . to my first attempts at explaining and commenting on the divine oracles."[18] Thus he kept a work on lying, which in the author's own judgment was "obscure, complicated, and irksome," even though later on he wrote another book on the same subject with a similar yet different title, *On Lying* (the earlier book had been *Against Lying*).[19]

The same outlook finds expression in the frank admission of hesitations, errors, and changes of view. One hesitation, which is defended as well as admitted, concerns the origin of souls. An error, likewise admitted but corrected, has to do with the beginning of faith. Of changes, finally, there are many, and not always for the better; these are concerned especially with points of exegesis.

On the other hand, Augustine's attitude of sincere honesty does not prevent him from defending himself against tendentious interpretations; in fact, it even urges him to do so. He defends himself with dignity and firmness.

We may recall, for example, his defense of his work on *Free Will*, which the Pelagians misused. He reminds his adversaries of an elementary distinction that they seem to have overlooked. "It is one thing to ask whence evil comes, another to ask how one may return to one's original state of goodness or attain to a higher state." In his *Free Will* he had been discussing the first question, not the second. "Let the new Pelagian heretics . . . not boast, therefore, that I am on their side." However, despite the purpose of that work, he had also spoken, if only in passing, of grace. He pulls together these passages and concludes: "Here, long before the Pelagian heresy made its appearance, I spoke as though I were already engaged in debate with them."[20]

He offers a similar defense of other writings, this time works against the Manichaeans. In these he had repeatedly used a definition of sin that emphasized the freedom of the will and seemed to exclude the possibility of original sin. He observes in the *Revisions* that the definition is valid because it defines sin alone and not that which is also a punishment of sin. "Without free will there is no sin, actual or original."[21] The former is free in itself, the latter is free only in its source. Some readers may think that it is Augustine's defense and not the Pelagian interpretation that is tendentious. This is perhaps to forget that Augustine does not say he had these distinctions in mind when he wrote against the Manichaeans; he says only that they are valid and can therefore be used to reconcile the various facets of Christian doctrine as he understands and defends it, whether against the Manichaeans or against the Pelagians.

Humility and dignity

In any case, my only point here is that humility and dignity go together in Augustine's outlook; they even spring from the same source. The *Revisions* is a remarkable document.

Humility and dignity: this is a combination often inculcated by Augustine. We know the emphasis he places on humility, which is inseparable from charity: it is the foundation of charity,[22] its dwelling,[23] and the way to it.[24] But humility is not synonymous with weakness: "Where there is humility, there is grandeur" (*Ubi humilitas, ibi maiestas*).[25] These two attributes are rooted in love of the truth, for it is this love that reveals to human beings their distance from the ideal and, at the same time, the source of their own true worth.

This love and these attributes regulated Augustine's own relations with others and marked his friendships. He cultivated friendship with great enthusiasm; he wanted it to be intimate, warm, and effusive, but also free, that is, candid and sincere. "Be-

tween us there must be not only love but the freedom of friends;
you on your side and I on mine should not remain silent about
anything in our letters that may be a cause of displeasure."[26] He
is writing here to Jerome, who was rather annoyed by criticisms
of some of his interpretations of the Bible. But Augustine's attitude remained the same no matter who his interlocutors or correspondents were: he demanded for himself the same freedom he
granted to others. He acknowledged his own mistakes, and he
wanted others to do the same for theirs. "No one can be a true
friend to another human being without being first of all a friend of
truth; if love of a friend is not disinterested it is not love at all."[27]

36

"Love, and do what you will"

READERS of Augustine stand amazed at the frequency and variety with which he discourses on the ever new theme of love. "Brothers and sisters, I can never speak enough of love."[1] In his eyes, human activity, revelation, and history all have love as their center. We have already seen this for history, which Augustine sums up in two cities, and these in turn in two loves.[2] But we must go more deeply into this whole subject.

Love: the most profound and mysterious element

Love is the most profound and mysterious element in the human person, in whose inward self love is concentrated along with truth, from which love is inseparable. "Interiority" points not only to the presence of truth in the depths of the soul but also to the revelation of love, which issues from those depths to become the source of the spirit's dynamism, the unavoidable relationship with God, and the unconscious but indestructible cleaving of the spirit to being, truth, and goodness. Human beings are, they know, and they love; they love as a result of knowing and they know as a result of loving. The "word" spoken by the mind is "knowledge joined to love." "When the spirit knows and loves itself, its word is united to it by means of love. And because it loves knowledge and knows love, the word exists in love and love in the word, and both together in the spirit which loves and speaks the word."[3]

Love affects the soul as weight does the body. This comparison, which is philosophically valid and poetically beautiful, occurs often in Augustine's writings and is rich in meaning.[4] "Weight," as understood here, pulls a body not necessarily "downward," but rather to its proper place—the place that is in keeping with the nature of the body and in which the body comes to rest.

The body tends toward its own place by its own weight. Weight does not tend downward only, but to its own proper place. Fire tends upward, a stone falls downward. They are driven by their own weights and seek their proper places. When oil is poured under water it rises to the surface; if the water is poured upon oil, it sinks to the bottom. They are driven by their own weights, they seek their proper places. Things which are out of their proper place are restless; put them in order again, and they are at rest.

After the comparison, the principle: "My weight is my love, and whenever I am borne, my love carries me there."[5]

It is from this hidden interior force that all the passions are born, for these are but modulations of the single movement of love.[6] The same is true of the virtues. "Virtue is simply love of the good that ought to be loved. To choose this good is the work of prudence; not to let oneself be separated from it by any difficulty is the work of fortitude, by any enticement the work of temperance, by any feeling of pride the work of justice."[7] He repeats this idea in a letter to Jerome[8] and more briefly in *The City of God:* "It seems to me that a brief and accurate definition of virtue is 'ordered love' (*ordo amoris*).[9] Vice is also love, but this time a disordered love. It is therefore love, and not knowledge, that determines the moral quality of human beings: they are good or wicked, just or injust, not because of what they know but because of what they love.[10]

Love: center of divine revelation

An author with this conception of the primary and irreplaceable function of love can easily make love the center of divine revelation and Christian life. That is what Augustine does. Starting from the biblical idea of God as Love, a theme he never tires of meditating on, he sees creation and salvation as manifestations of a divine love that does not suppose the goodness of things but establishes or creates this goodness. "There is in God a supremely holy and just goodwill, a love of his creatures that springs not from need but from goodness."[11] We may paraphrase a well-known sentence in the *Confessions*[12] and say that God does not love creatures because they are good, but they are good because he loves them.

In addition, Augustine regards love as the content of Scripture, the goal of theology, the summation of philosophy, the soul of pedagogy, the secret of politics, the fruit of wisdom, the inspiration of grace, the essence and measure of Christian perfection, and the gift on which all the other gifts of the Spirit depend. A broad program indeed, the elements of which are brought before us in countless passages of Augustine's writings. Here are a few. "Scripture commands nothing but love."[13]

> Those whose hearts are filled with love understand without error and observe without wearying the manifold, abundant, and wide-ranging teaching in the sacred writings. The Apostle even says: "Love is the fulfilling of the law" (Rom 13:10).... When you understand anything in the Scriptures, it is love that is manifesting itself to you; when you fail to understand, it is love that is hiding itself from you. Those, therefore, who possess charity possess both what is manifest in the divine words and what is hidden in them.... What is the greatness of love? It is the soul of the Scriptures, the power in prophecy, the salvation that comes from the sacraments, the solid foundation of knowledge, the fruit of faith, the wealth of the poor, the life of the dying....[14]

Love: fruit of the Spirit

Among the fruits of the Spirit charity or love is the one on which all the others depend.

> For this reason, when Paul the Apostle wishes to contrast the fruits of the Spirit with the works of the flesh, he begins with love: "The fruit of the Spirit is love," and then presents all the other fruits as flowing from love and closely connected with love. These other fruits are "joy, peace, patience, kindness, goodness, faithfulness, gentleness, self-control." And in fact how can we have a well ordered joy if we do not love the good in which we rejoice? How can we be truly at peace unless we love one another? How can we be patient and persevere in the good unless we love fervently? How can we be kind if we do not love those whom we help? How can we be faithful in a salutary way if we do not have the faith that works through love? How can gentleness be of profit to us if it is not inspired by love? And how can we refrain from that which contaminates unless we love that which ennobles? Rightly, then, does our good Master emphasize love so much and consider the commandment of love as enough by itself. Without love all the rest is good

for nothing, while love is inconceivable without all the other good qualities thanks to which human beings become good.[15]

The Holy Spirit draws souls to Christ by inspiring in them the love that enlightens the mind, inflames the will, and gives rise to desire. Here is a well-known passage on this subject from the sermons on St. John's gospel:

> When, therefore, you hear Christ saying that "no one comes to me unless the Father draws him," do not think that you are drawn against your will, for the soul is drawn by love. We should not worry that people . . . may find fault with these Gospel words of Sacred Scripture and say to us: "How can I believe voluntarily if I am drawn?" I answer: You are drawn not by your will alone but by pleasure. What does it mean to be "drawn by pleasure"? "Delight in the Lord, and he will grant you the desires of your heart." The heart too has its pleasure, for the bread of heaven is sweet to it. If the poet can say: "Each is drawn by his pleasure" (not by necessity but by pleasure, not by obligation but by delight), with how much greater justice can we not say that they are drawn by Christ who find their delight in truth, in beatitude, in justice, in eternal life, and, in short, in all that is Christ? If the bodily senses have their pleasures, why should not the soul have its pleasures? . . .
>
> Show me a heart that loves, and it will understand what I mean. Show me a heart that yearns, a heart that hungers, a heart that journeys thirsting in this wilderness, a heart that longs for the fountain in the eternal homeland, and it will understand what I mean. If I speak to a heart that is cold, it will not understand what I mean. . . .
>
> Show a green branch to a sheep, and you draw it. Show nuts to a child, and it is drawn; it runs whither it feels drawn; it is drawn by its love, it is drawn without being wounded, it is drawn by the cords that bind the heart. If, then, these delights and pleasures draw earthly lovers when shown to them—for it is true that "each is drawn by its pleasure"—shall we not be drawn by the Christ whom the Father reveals to us? After all what does the soul desire more ardently than truth?[16]

Both naturally and by grace, love is the source of the spirit's dynamism; it regulates thought and gives rise to action. Augustine gives incisive summary expression to this dynamism in the aphorism: "Love, and do what you will." He used it first in 394-95[17] and a second time around 415.[18] In both instances the context is one of instruction. "Here, once and for all, is a short precept:

Love, and do what you will. If you are silent, be silent out of love; if you correct, correct out of love; if you forgive, forgive out of love. Make sure the root that is love is within you, for from that root only good can come."[19]

Love: primacy in our lives

But this famous aphorism undoubtedly has a broader meaning, although not any of those often given to it. It does not signify that love is autonomous in relation to the moral law; nor does it serve to justify the suppression of the Donatists.[20] It signifies only that love has a primacy in our lives that belongs to it on three basic counts: its power to make truth operative and in control of our thoughts and affections; its power to assimilate the lover to the good that is loved; its ability to be itself a luminous and fruitful source of knowledge.

First, how is love defined? "True love consists in adhering to the truth so that we may live justly."[21] "True love": there are therefore a true love and a false love. False love is a love of self that is not first of all a love of God. False love is a love for others that does not lead them to God but takes them away from him. False love is a love that does not use creatures in an ordered way but seeks to enjoy them in place of God. Few have insisted on this distinction as often and passionately as Augustine.

He emphasizes, then, the fact that it is love that brings the lover to deeper knowledge of truth. "We do not enjoy what we know unless we love it . . . and we do not persevere in knowing what we love unless our knowledge is accompanied by love."[22] On the one hand, then, it is true that "what is completely unknown cannot be loved." On the other hand, it is also true that "when we love something that is known in some degree, the power of our love brings us to a better and deeper knowledge of it."[23] It follows from this that "no good is perfectly known unless it is perfectly loved."[24]

Passing now from loved object to loving subject, we see immediately that love has the power to assimilate the lover to the properties of the beloved. It follows that "each individual is what his or her love is." This is a principle from which Augustine does not hesitate to draw all the pertinent conclusions. "Do you love the earth? You will be earth. Do you love God? Shall I say: You will be God? I dare not say it on my own, so let us listen to the Scriptures: 'I said: You will be gods, and all of you will be the children of the Most High.' "[25]

The deification of human beings through love of God is a thesis that emerges from the Pelagian controversy and completes and crowns Augustine's teaching on justification.[26] "While a soul lives in wickedness it is dead; once it has become just, it shares in a life distinct from its own, since it is by ascending to God and being united to him [through love] that it is justified by him."[27] What, then, is justification? It is deification. "He who justifies deifies. . . . We have become gods, but by his grace as adopter, not from his nature as begetter."[28] This deification is attributable to the power of love. In fact, "the loved object must give a share in its properties to the lover,"[29] as flame does to fire and light to the air.

The Augustinian axiom, "Love, and do what you will," has thus both a philosophical and a theological meaning. From the philosophical standpoint it expresses in a concise and effective way the primacy of love; in so doing it is far removed from pure intellectualism, on the one side, and exaggerated voluntarism, on the other. From the theological standpoint it underscores the indispensable demands of charity and shows the unique part that charity plays in Christian perfection.

In fact, charity is the only virtue that one cannot possess and at the same time be wicked, since it is the only virtue that renders the human being formally good. "Have love, and you will have everything else; without it nothing else you may have will profit you."[30]

Love, and love alone, enables us to distinguish between good actions and bad actions, even when they are otherwise indistinguishable because of their external similarity. Its presence renders actions good that are seemingly wicked, just as its absence renders actions wicked that are seemingly good. "The actions of human beings are not distinguishable except as rooted or not rooted in love."[31]

> Enter into your own conscience and question it. Look not at
> what emerges externally but ask what is the root that lies hidden in

the earth. Has the desire of money taken root in you? If so, you may have the appearance of good works, but truly good works there cannot be. Has charity taken root in you? If so, be sure that no evil can spring from that root. Pride caresses, love corrects. Pride dons garments that will please human beings; one who loves deals blows in order to correct with discipline. Chastisement inspired by love is more profitable than alms inspired by pride. Brothers and sisters, return into yourselves. In everything you do look to God as your witness.[32]

Progress in love

Above all, love is the measure of Christian perfection and the power that makes interior ascents possible. "Initial love is initial justice; love growing is justice growing; great love is great justice; perfect love is perfect justice."[33] The theme of the full equivalence between love and perfection was dear to the patristic tradition and has come into its own again in the documents of the recent Council; Augustine shows inexhaustible variety as he makes it the center of his spiritual teaching. According to him, progress in love depends on three factors.

The first is the intensity of our desire. The divine commandment of love and the capacities of the soul itself point to a totality that can never be achieved here on earth. Christian life is therefore marked by a basic tension. "If you want to be what you are not as yet, you must always be dissatisfied with what you are. . . . Be ever increasing, ever journeying, ever advancing; do not stop on the way, do not turn back, do not stray from the path."[34] He who created you wants your entire being.[35]

"No measure is set for the love of God; the only measure here is to love without measure. We need not worry about loving him too much; we need only fear loving him too little."[36] In these words Severus, a disciple and friend of Augustine, sums up concisely and accurately the thinking of his teacher. The latter turns this principle into a norm of conduct for himself. Listen to this moving prayer from the *Confessions*:

> Give yourself to me, O my God, restore yourself to me. I love you, and if it is too little, let me love you more. I cannot measure out my love, so as to know what is yet lacking in it to make it enough; that so my life may run to your embrace, and never turn away until it be hidden in the secret place of your face. This only I

know, that it is never well with me except when I am with you—not only without but within myself also—and all abundance that is not my God, to me is only poverty.[37]

The second factor that determines progress in love is selflessness or disinterestedness. If love is not selfless it is not love. "What is not loved for its own sake is not loved."[38] Augustine formulated this principle early in his life and always remained faithful to it, writing of it with special enthusiasm and penetration. Here, for example, is a passage in which he contrasts "chaste" fear and servile fear, the latter being opposed to disinterested love, the former being inseparable from it.

> What of the two fears I mentioned? There is a servile fear and a chaste fear. There is a fear that you may be punished and a fear that you may lose justice. The fear of punishment is servile fear. There is nothing laudable about fearing punishment; the most iniquitous slave and the cruelest bandit fear it. No, it is no great thing to fear punishment, but it is indeed a great thing to love justice. Do those, then, who love justice have no fear? They do indeed fear: not, however, punishment but the loss of justice.
>
> Be convinced, brothers and sisters, and ask yourselves what it is you love. Some among you surely love money. In fact, will I find any who do not? Now, precisely because you love it you will understand what I am saying. You fear a loss. Why? Because you love money, and the more you love it, the more you fear to lose it. Well then, those who love justice are filled with an even greater fear, for they fear to lose justice more than you fear the loss of your money. Theirs is a chaste fear, a fear that lasts for ever; love does not remove or dismiss it but rather embraces it and clings close to it as a companion.
>
> We are journeying to the Lord so that we may at last see him face to face. Chaste fear keeps us close to him; it does not disturb but strengthens us. An adultress fears that her husband may come; a chaste wife fears his leaving her.[39]

We must love God "freely," that is, without looking for a reward. This fundamental principle of Augustinian spirituality has given rise to various interpretations, on the assumption that love of God must exclude desire of a reward. I suggest, however, that the key to Augustine's meaning is not far to seek. He provides it repeatedly. First, the principle: "As for us, brothers and sisters, let us love God purely and chastely. A heart is not chaste that serves God for the sake of a reward." Then, the explanation:

What does this mean? Are we not to be rewarded for our service of God? No, we shall have a reward, but our reward is the very God whom we serve. He will be our reward, because we shall see him as he is. Observe how your reward is assured, for what does our Lord Jesus Christ say to those who love him? "He who loves me keeps my commandments; and he who loves me will be loved by my Father, and I too will love him." What will he give us? "And I will show myself to him."

If you do not love, this promise means little to you. But if you love, if you yearn, if you freely serve him who has freely redeemed you (for you had no prior merits that he should redeem you), if the benefits he has given you make you yearn and make your heart restless with desire to possess him, then you will ask for nothing else than himself. Seek nothing apart from him; he will be enough for you.

The explanation is followed by a fine illustration.

Think of marriage and try to understand what it means to have a heart that is chaste toward God. Marriage is certainly a human thing. A man does not love his wife if he loves her for the dowry, nor does a wife love her husband chastely if she loves him for the things, big or small, that she has received from him. If a wife's love is chaste, he is her husband when he is rich and he is still her husband if he becomes poor. Think of the many outlawed men whose chaste wives have loved them all the more. Many a chaste wife has been tested by the misfortunes of her husband; far from thinking of loving anything but him, she has not only not deserted him but has shown him all the greater devotion. Now, if an earthly husband is loved freely and chastely . . . then how should we love God, the true and faithful spouse of the soul?[40]

Pure and disinterested love

Augustine the shepherd wants to lead the faithful to a pure and disinterested love that asks of God only himself. He does so in a surprisingly effective way. He describes the joys of heaven and then an earthly life full of all blessings and lacking any and every evil; then he has God make this extraordinary proposal: If you wish, you may live forever amid all these good things, but you shall not see my face. If one were to respond: "I have abundant possessions, I am well off, I seek nothing further," such words would show that this person had not yet even begun to love

God. The reaction of true lovers of God would be quite different; they would immediately say: "Away with these seductive goods, away with these deceitful enticements, away with everything that daily says to us, 'Where is your God?' . . . Anything we have that is not our God is not pleasing to us, for of what good is all that he gives to us if he does not give himself, the giver of all else?"[41]

In fact, such was the reaction of some of Augustine's flock. Under the guidance of this great teacher they had learned what it means to love God and seek him alone. The pastor himself tells us so. Speaking again of chaste love on another occasion and showing the faithful how to determine whether or not they possessed it, he repeats the same hypothetical divine offer. From the congregation comes a sighing, a tremor; he has his answer. He continues: "Brothers and sisters, why do you sigh, unless the chaste fear that remains forever has already been born in you? Why has your heart been pierced [by my words]?" The faithful tremble because they truly love God and regard it as the supreme evil not to see him face to face. That is precisely the attitude proper to chaste fear. At such a proposal the heart groans and exclaims: "Let everything else vanish provided I see the face of God!"[42]

To reach these heights, however, love must travel a long road and overcome many obstacles; that is the third factor that determines progress. "You must love justice. But in this love there are steps that you must mount to make progress. First, then, your love of justice must be greater than your love of the things that give you pleasure. This is the first step." This first step is not enough, however; we must climb to a second. "It is not enough to scorn what used to delight you; you must also scorn what used to instill fear in you. Scorn prison and chains, scorn the rack and other tortures, scorn death." We show our love for justice in both of these ways, as the martyrs did.

The example of the martyrs reminds Augustine of the highest and fullest expression of love, and with this his eloquence, already so powerful and persuasive, soars to mystical heights. He continues: the martyr "loves, burns, is on fire; treads underfoot all that delights, and passes on; comes to what is bitter, terrible, ferocious, and threatening; treads it underfoot, scorns it, and pas-

ses on. Oh, to love, to journey, to die to self and come to God!"
After this flight the speaker falls back to peaceful exhortation and
concludes: "Such is the armor in which the lover of justice, the
lover of invisible beauty, must be clad."[43]

He armed himself in this fashion and taught others to do the
same.

37

"Higher still we climbed"

AUGUSTINE outlined a complete program for the interior ascent while he was staying in Rome after the mystical experience at Ostia and the death of his mother. Perhaps this was the context for his writing of the dialogue on *The Greatness of the Soul,* in which he discusses the various activities of the spirit, ranging from the animation of the body to the contemplation of truth. As a result of personal experience, the theme of contemplation, which had always been dear to him for many reasons, had now become even more credible, important, and attractive. His careful and subtle discussion of it in this early dialogue brings out its depth and value.[1]

The soul has seven activities proper to it: it gives life to the body, perceives by means of the senses, reasons and thereby creates science and art, struggles against the vices, entrenches itself in the good, enters into light, and abides in the realm of light. The first three of these activities belong to human beings by nature and are found in the good and the wicked alike. The fourth activity marks the beginning of the journey of virtue, which ends on the heights of perfection.

The first of these final four activities is *virtus* (literally, "manliness") or courageous struggle, that is, the existence of temperance and justice. These two virtues are especially needed if human beings are to break the spell of vice and turn in a decisive way to the good. Therefore this initial moral activity calls for "an effort, an intense and painful struggle against the trials and seductions of the world."[2]

The next activity is named *tranquillitas* ("calm") from the effects it produces, for it strengthens the soul in virtue by rendering it strong and free of the fear of losing the goods it naturally loves. These goods are: pleasure, honor, freedom, friendship, and life. "On this step the soul reaches a full cognizance of its own value; as a result, it turns with immense and even unbelievable confidence to God, that is, to contemplation of the truth, which is the lofty and hidden reward for which it has toiled so greatly."[3]

The soul then passes from the second to the third step, on which it "turns its gaze, now serene and rectified, to the object to be contemplated," namely, "what is in a true and absolute sense." The soul is here entering into the light. But human beings cannot do this unless their interior eye has been purified and long trained.

> Those who seek [to contemplate] before being purified and healed are dazzled and thrown back by the light of truth; they are led to think that there is no good but a great deal of evil in that light. They even deny it the name of truth, and, driven by a kind of evil desire and a wretched quest of pleasure, they take refuge in their own darkness, which is the only thing their illness enables them to endure.[4]

After this step comes the fourth and last, which deserves to be called a dwelling rather than a step. At this point Augustine, who is the chief speaker in the dialogue, exclaims: "How can I put into words the soul's delights, its enjoyment of the supreme and true Good, the air of everlasting serenity that fills this dwelling? Some incomparably great human beings—whom I believe saw and now see these things—have expressed them in the measure they judged good."

Among these great human beings we must undoubtedly place Augustine himself, and not as the least among them. He spoke much of these things, and in an incomparably rich way; he spoke of them because he had "seen" them.

Requirements for contemplation

Because of its wealth of detail, Augustine's teaching on contemplation is not easily summarized. We find him describing the long and laborious ascent to the goal; the swift and dazzling attainment of the goal; the return, full of nostalgia and regret, to ordinary life; the precious and lasting fruits of the contemplation. The ascent requires an asceticism, recollection, and silence. Moreover, the road leads not only through the various activities of the soul, as we have seen, but also through the evangelical beatitudes and the gifts of the Holy Spirit.

The beatitudes trace out an ascending journey that leads from poverty of spirit (which for Augustine means humility) to peace, which implies an ordering of the whole person and a reconciliation with the self and with God. The gifts of the Holy Spirit, which support us on this journey, likewise follow a road from fear of God, which is the beginning of wisdom, to wisdom itself, which is identical with the contemplation in question and manifests the same characteristics.[5] "Finally, the seventh step is wisdom, that is, contemplation of the truth that pacifies the entire person and brings to perfection our likeness to God. Such is the end of the journey: 'Blessed are the peaceful, for they shall be called the children of God.' "[6]

By "contemplation" is meant "the knowledge and love of that which abides eternal and unchanging, namely, God."[7] The knowledge is experimental, a knowledge shot through with love and full of light, even though it is attained in darkness. In this knowledge we "know things divine," "touch them" and "reach them," and in them we "concentrate" all our faculties and our entire being.

> When we seek after wisdom, what else do we do but zealously concentrate our entire soul in that which we touch with the mind? We place our soul therein and fix it firmly there so that it may no longer rejoice in its own ego, which is enthralled by transitory things, but instead, being stripped of all affections for time and place, may lay hold of the Being that is one and always the same.[8]

While the ascent to contemplation is long and laborious, the mystical union at the end of the ascent is dazzling and momentary. "And so, in the twinkle of a trembling glance, my mind reached that Which Is."[9] "We just touched it a little with one whole beat of our heart, and we sighed."[10] "We enjoyed a certain interior sweetness and saw with the mind's eye something changeless, even if only for a fleeting instant,"[11] "a vision in ecstasy but one that could not long endure."[12]

After this swift instant of direct vision with its momentary taste of something not belonging to our present world there comes the return to the occupations of everyday life, a kind of descent or falling back among things that are no longer loved and are tolerated only for the sake of that vision. "I could not fix my gaze upon [God]; and my weakness being beaten back and returning to my habits, I carried nothing away with me but a loving memory and a longing after that, the scent of which I had, as it were, perceived, but was not yet able to feed upon."[13] "We returned to the sound of our mouth, where the word has its beginning and its ending."[14] "As by a spiritual touch he [the psalmist] reached that changeless light, but because his sight was weak, he could not tolerate its radiance and fell back as it were into his sickness and languor; he compared his power with the vision and realized that the eye of his mind was not adapted to the light of divine wisdom."[15]

Explanation of contemplation of God

Not only does Augustine expound this lofty and by no means easy teaching in his books; he also speaks of it to the people. In addition to the passage just cited, which is from a sermon, many others might be adduced. I shall, however, give but one lengthy example from the commentary on Psalm 42 (41 in the Vulgate). It is indeed a magnificent passage, as readers may judge for themselves:

> When I heard the words "Where is your God?" I too went seeking my God in order that if possible I might not simply believe but also see to some extent. For I see in fact the things my God has made but I do not see my God who made them. But . . . what shall I do to find my God? I shall consider the earth: the earth was created. It possesses extraordinary beauty, but it has a maker. . . . I return into myself and examine who I am that observes these things. . . . But perhaps God is something like the soul? Certainly he cannot be seen except by means of the soul, but he cannot be seen as the soul can be seen. . . .
>
> I seek my God in visible and corporeal things, but I do not find him. I seek his substance within myself, as though he were something like me, but neither do I find him there. I realize, therefore, that God is a being higher than my soul. In order, then, that I might touch him, "I have meditated on these things and poured out my soul above me." How can my soul reach what I seek above my soul unless it is poured out above itself? If it were to remain within itself

it would see only itself; but seeing itself it would certainly not see its God.

Let my attackers say, "Where is your God?" Let them say it: for my part, as long as I do not see him, as long as the vision is deferred, I eat the bread of tears day and night. Let them go on saying, "Where is your God?" I seek my God in every corporeal being on earth and in heaven, but I do not find him. I seek his substance in my own soul, and I do not find it. Still have I meditated on how to find my God and, desiring to see with my intellect the invisible attributes of God through created things, I "have poured out my soul above myself," but there is nothing left to know (*tangere*, touch) except my God himself.

There, above my soul, is the house of my God; there he dwells, from there he gazes upon me, from there he created me and governs me and takes thought for me, from there he rouses me and calls me and directs me and guides me and leads me to the goal.

But he who possesses this high and hidden dwelling also has a tent on earth. His tent on earth, which is the Church, is still on pilgrimage. Yet it is here that we must seek him, for in the tent the way will be found that leads to the house. . . . "I will enter the place of the marvelous tent so that I may reach the house of God. . . ." God's tent on earth is the faithful; in them I admire their mastery of their members. . . . I admire the virtues of their souls, but I am still walking in the tent. I pass beyond these virtues and the tent itself, wonderful though it is, and I marvel when I reach the house of God. . . .

By going up to the tent [the psalmist] reached the house of God. While wondering at the parts of the tent he was led on to the house of God, as though drawn by a mysterious sweetness, an indescribable interior and hidden pleasure, as though some instrument were sending its melody from the house of God. And as he walked in the tent he heard this interior sound and, drawn by the melody whose sound he traced, and withdrawing himself from all the noise of flesh and blood, he reached the house of God. He tells himself of his journey and how he was led. It is as though he had said to him, "You admired the tent here on earth; how did you come to the sanctuary of God's house?" He answers: "In the sounds of jubilation and praise, the sounds of a celebrating throng." . . .

In the house of God there is unending festivity. The feast celebrated there is never over, and the choirs of angels keep everlasting holiday, for the face of God there present bestows a joy that never grows less. That festal day has no beginning and no end. From that everlasting and ceaseless festivity a sweet and melodious music reaches the ears of the heart, but only if the world's noise does not disturb it. The sound of that feast soothes the ears of those who walk in the tent and see the miracles God works in the redemption of the faithful; it draws the hart to the springs of water.

But . . . the corruptible body drags down the soul. . . . Therefore, even though the clouds have sometimes moved aside for me as I walk filled with desire, and I have heard this sound and strained to perceive something from the house of God, yet because of the weight of my weakness I fall back into my customary ways and sink down into my ordinary self. And just as I found there a reason to rejoice, so here there is every reason to lament.

For this hart that feeds day and night upon its tears, and is filled by a desire that drives it to the springs of water, that is, the interior sweetness of God, and pours out its soul above itself in order to touch what is superior to its soul, and walks in the wonderful tent as far as the house of God, and is drawn by the delight of the interior sound that the mind hears, and therefore despises everything external and is swept up by what is within—this hart is nonetheless still a human being, still groans, still has flesh that is weak, still meets perils amid the stumblingblocks of this world.

It looks at itself in the light of where it has just been and compares present sorrows with what it had entered in to see and, after seeing, had left. It then says to itself: " 'Why are you sad, my soul, and why do you disquiet me?' I have already enjoyed a certain interior sweetness and have seen with the mind's eye something changeless, even if only for a fleeting moment. Why then do you still disquiet me, and why are you still sad? You have no doubts about your God, and you now have an answer for those who say to you 'Where is your God?' I have glimpsed something changeless; why then do you still disquiet me? 'Hope in God!' "

Then its soul, as though silently answering, says: "Why do I disquiet you? Because I do not yet dwell where the sweetness is that ravished me for a moment. Do I as yet drink of that fountain and have nothing to fear? Do I no longer fear any stumblingblock? Am I safe from my desires as though they had all been subjected and tamed? Does my enemy the devil no longer keep watch against me? Does he no longer lay his deceitful snares for me each day? Do you want me to stop disquieting you while I am still in the world and exiled from the house of my God?" But the hart answers its disquieted soul: "Hope in God."[16]

Mystical experience

The man who spoke to his people in this way had a history of mystical experiences behind him.[17] The most celebrated of these experiences, though not the only one, occurred at Ostia. The pages that tell of it in the *Confessions* have a philosophical and even a Plotinian cast, but the spirit that pervades them is religious, and the goal reached in the experience is the direct "perception" of the presence of God, a rapture of the soul's powers, a foretaste of heavenly bliss, or, in short, an extraordinary manifestation of grace. Sure proof of the specifically Christian character of the experience is the presence of Monica who, though she certainly had a sharp mind, was not an intellectual and neither knew philosophy nor had any great esteem for philosophers.

We two alone discoursed together very sweetly, and forgetting what is behind, and straining forward to what is before, we were inquiring between ourselves in the presence of Truth, which you are, what the eternal life of the saints was to be, which eye has not seen nor ear heard nor has it entered into the human heart. Yet, we panted with the mouth of our heart after the heavenly streams of your fountain, the fountain of life that is with you, that being sprinkled from thence, according to our present capacity, we might, in some small measure, conceive so great a thing.

When our conversation had come thus far as to conclude that the greatest delights of the bodily senses, in however great a corporeal light, were not to be compared, or even mentioned, in respect to the pleasures of that life to come, rising yet higher, with a more ardent affection in pursuit of the self-same, we ascended by several steps through all corporeal things, and through that sky itself, from whence the sun, moon, and stars shine upon earth. Higher still we climbed interiorly, thinking and speaking of you and admiring your works.

At last we came to our own minds, and passed beyond, that so we might reach that country of never-failing plenty where you feed Israel forever with the food of truth, and where the life is that Wisdom, by which all these things are made, and the things that have been and shall be; but itself is not made, but so is, as it was, and so always will be. For, neither "to have been" nor "to be in the future" is in that Wisdom, but only "to be," because it is eternal; for anything that "has been" or "is to be hereafter" is not eternal. And while we were speaking and gasping after it, behold we just touched it a little with one whole beat of the heart; and we sighed, and there we left fastened the firstfruits of the spirit; and we returned to the sound of our mouth, where the word has its beginning and its ending. . . .

Therefore, we said to one another: If any soul were silent from all tumult of the flesh and from all impressions or images of the earth, water, or air; if the heavens also were silent, and the soul were silent to itself, and should pass beyond itself, by not thinking of itself; and if dreams and all imaginary revelations were silent, and every tongue, and every sign, and whatever has its being by passing away, were absolutely silent (because if anyone could hear them, they all would say: "We did not make ourselves, but he made us who abides forever"); if, I say, after having said this, they should all be silent, having directed our ears to him who made them, and so he should speak alone, not by them, but by himself, that we might hear his word, not by the tongue of the flesh, nor by the voice of an angel, nor by the sound of a cloud, nor by the obscurity of a similitude, but that we should hear his own self without any of these things, his own self, whom we love in all these things (as just now for a start, we two had strained ourselves, and, with a swift thought, had touched upon that eternal wisdom, which abides above all things); if such a thing, I say, were to be continued and all other sights, of a far inferior kind, were to be withdrawn; and this one were totally to ravish, and swallow up, and engulf the beholder into its interior joys, so that our life forever should be such as that one moment of understanding, for which we had sighed—would not this be what is written, "Enter into the joy of your master!"[18]

Contemplation and action

It is from these heights of mysticism that we ought to view and judge Augustine's asceticism, which was austere and vigorous, but also moderate, serene, and prudent. It included celibacy chosen for the sake of the kingdom of heaven; poverty to the point of identification with the lowliest in the ecclesial community; courage in bearing his many infirmities; control of the passions; a constant attentiveness to do the will of God; generosity in forgiving the offenses done him by others; humility in asking forgiveness for his own offenses against others.

Of this last quality we have a typical example in connection with the question whether after the resurrection our bodily eyes will be able to see God. In a letter to a lady named Italica, Augustine had rejected this view in a strong statement.[19] A bishop who had maintained the opinion resented Augustine's words. Even though Augustine was sure he was right, he wrote to his colleague Fortunantius and asked him to intercede with the offended bishop, "that he may forgive me if he took as meant for himself any strong and excessively harsh words I used in that letter."[20]

It is from the same high vantage point that we should evaluate Augustine's unconditional readiness to meet the needs of the Church and his tireless application to work, no less than his zealous meditation on the Scriptures, his voracious appetite for truth, and his converse with God.[21] At an early stage he had sketched out the relations between contemplation and action[22]; he summed up the matter for himself and others in *The City of God.*

> Love of truth makes us seek the quiet of contemplation (*otium sanctum*), while charity makes us accept the functions of the apostolate (*negotium iustum*). If no one imposes this burden on us, we ought to apply ourselves to study and contemplation of truth; if it is imposed on us, we must accept it as an obligation of charity. But even in this second case we ought not entirely renounce the joys of truth, lest if we lack this pleasure, the necessity imposed on us may become oppressive.[23]

If Augustine himself was not crushed by the burden of so much apostolic work, it was only because his love of the truth filled him with delight and restored his powers.

Finally, it is from the same lofty vantage point that we should appreciate his theological discernment, which was extraordinarily profound and sure. Even in this area his mystical experience exerted a controlling influence. Among the fruits of contemplation as described in his early work, *The Greatness of the Soul,* the spiritual fruits admittedly come first. These include, for example, a clear realization of the emptiness of earthly things, which, "when considered in themselves, are wonderful and beautiful" but "when compared with eternal blessings, are as though they were not." But there are also fruits of an intellectual kind, which give greater keenness to the eye of the mind and greater depth to theological understanding. "We will recognize then how true are the things that we are commanded to believe and in what an excellent and salutary way we have been fed at the bosom of Mother Church" with the milk of faith.

> We will also see the many great changes and alterations in corporeal nature as it obeys the laws of God, and in consequence we will be as certain about the resurrection of the flesh—which some believe with a weak faith, others not at all—as we are that the setting sun will rise again. We will pay no heed to those who ridicule the incarnation of the . . . Son of God . . . and his birth from a virgin and the other miracles in the history of salvation, any more than we pay heed to children who, after seeing a painter copying another painting, are convinced that no one can make a picture that is not a copy of a picture.

> The delight that comes from contemplation of truth is so great, so pure, so heartfelt, and gives such certainty about the truth, that those who experience it are convinced they never really knew the things they thought they knew. Moreover, as the soul is increasingly less hindered from clinging wholly to the truth in its entirety, it comes to desire as a supreme reward the death . . . it had previously feared.[24]

Such were the fruits Augustine himself reaped from mystical experience. The intellectual fruits would find their concrete expression in the great doctrinal synthesis that he constructed, the spiritual fruits in the lofty ideal of perfection that he achieved. Henceforth he was to be counted not among those who "tolerate death" but among those—the more perfect—who "tolerate life."[25]

Part IV
The Last Years

38

The End Approaches

AUGUSTINE'S last years were marked by much toil and suffering. As we saw earlier, on September 26, 426, he chose a successor and entrusted to him the administration of the diocese.[1] On that occasion he told the people:

> In this present life all of us will die, but the last day of life is always uncertain for the individual. Nevertheless in childhood we hope to reach adolescence, and then in succession young manhood, adulthood, maturity, and finally old age. We are not sure we will reach these successive stages but we hope we will. In old age, however, there is no further period of life to hope for; even the duration of old age is uncertain. The only thing certain is that there will be no further period of life. By God's will I came to this city as a vigorous grown man, but now I am old.[2]

He was old, but he did not feel his powers to be exhausted; he handed over the administration of the diocese to Eraclius, but not so that he himself might rest. "Finally, if God grants me a few more years of life I shall not spend them in idleness or laziness but will dedicate them to the study of Sacred Scripture, insofar as God permits and grants it."[3]

After his appointment Eraclius spoke to the people in the bishop's presence. One thing he said was: "The cricket buzzes, the swan falls silent."[4] But in fact the swan did not yet fall silent. He had only four years of life remaining, but they were years of astonishing activity. The *otium* (leisure) he had asked for truly became, as he had foreseen and pledged, a *magnum negotium* (filled with intense work). During these years he finished *The City of God*, continued the *Revisions*, replied to the monks of Gaul, held a debate with Maximinus, an Arian bishop, responded to Maximinus' false version of the proceedings, began his work *Heresy*, undertook the refutation of Julian's second reply to him, and wrote letters to counts Boniface and Darius on the occasion of the former's falling out with the imperial court, and other letters to comfort and advise the victims of the Vandal invasion. I have already spoken of one of these many activities: the reply to Julian.[5]

On September 24, 427, a council, perhaps of all the African Churches, was held at Hippo in the Leontine Basilica; it was the last in which Augustine took part. It is natural to think that Hippo was chosen as the site of the meeting because the African bishops were mindful of the age and health of their brother in Hippo and did not want to deprive themselves of his authoritative presence.

Meeting with Aurelius

For us of a later time the choice was symbolic, for this council evokes the memory of an earlier one, that of 393, and marks the close of a glorious period for the African Church. It was a period in which the Catholic episcopate, under the leadership of two providential figures, Aurelius and Augustine (the one a skillful organizer, the other a profound theologian and tireless writer), had given proof of an immense vitality. In these years the bishops had in fact overcome the Donatist schism and restored Christian unity; they had firmly defended the Catholic faith against Pelagianism; they had promoted Christian life and had organized and spread monasticism.

At the council of 427, the two close friends, Augustine and Aurelius, met once more, perhaps for the last time. They had taken part together in many councils for the sole purpose of revitalizing the African Church; together they had promoted the great conference of 411; they had suffered together at the treacherous murder of Marcellinus the Tribune. But even if this meeting at Hippo was their last, it did not signal the end of their collaboration. I like to think that the two men worked together in suggesting a peaceful resolution to the serious dispute between Count Boniface and the imperial court and in resisting the Arian infiltrations that resulted from the dispute. Certainly Augustine played a part in these affairs.

From these final years we have a letter to Boniface, the correspondence with Count Darius, the acts of the debate with Maximinus, and a work in two books against him.

Some years earlier, Augustine, accompanied by Alypius, had met Boniface near Tubune.[6] On that occasion he had advised the Count not to leave military service for a monastic life, as the man, now a widower, wanted to do. The advice may seem surprising when we recall how in 391 Augustine left Tagaste for Hippo in order to found a monastery and how zealously he promoted the spread of monasticism.[7] He gave the advice because of the benefits the entire region would derive from the military activity of Boniface, on whom the defense of the area against barbarian incursions from the Sahara depended, and for the sake, too, of the earthly peace of which he speaks so much in *The City of God*.[8]

Now the situation had changed. Boniface had remarried; before the wedding his new wife, a rich Arian heiress, had abjured her heresy, but in practice she continued to follow it; her daughter had been baptized by the Arians, and rumor had it that they had rebaptized other holy virgins.

This state of affairs was a painful one for Augustine, both because of Boniface's failure to practice continence as he had proposed and because of the danger that Arianism would spread. In addition, the falling out with the court of Ravenna had led to incalculable evils, since it had removed the barrier against the inroads of the Moors.

> What can I say of the devastation inflicted on Africa by native barbarians with no one to oppose them, since you are so preoccupied with your own critical situation that you issue no orders to prevent the disaster? Who would ever have believed or feared that after Boniface, General of the Household Guard, had come to Africa as governor with a mighty army and great power, the barbarians would have shown themselves so bold, have advanced so far, caused so much destruction, and rendered desolate regions that were hitherto well populated, whereas when Boniface was simply Tribune he had with a few provincial troops defeated and subjugated all those tribes and made them afraid of him?[9]

In this letter Augustine has no intention of entering into the merits of the dispute between Boniface and the court, or of playing judge in the matter. He addresses himself to Boniface the Christian and urges him, whatever the merits of his case, not to return evil for evil.

> If you have received benefits from the Roman Empire . . . you certainly should not repay good with evil. But even if evils have been done you, do not repay evil with evil. I do not know, nor am I capable of deciding, which of the two alternatives represents your situation. I speak to you as one who is a Christian: do not repay good with evil nor evil with evil.[10]

At this same time (so we are told by recent studies of the chronology of some letters of Augustine[11]), the Saint wrote a note to Count Darius, who had been sent to Africa in order to settle the dispute between Boniface and the court. Augustine would have liked to meet the man but "bodily weakness and the cold of both winter and age" made this impossible. He wrote instead, praising Darius' mission of peace, which is the most glorious of all possible missions since it has for its aim to secure peace through peace, not through war.

> Outstanding indeed, and possessing a glory peculiar to them, are military men who not only have great courage but are also inspired by great faith, which is a legitimate claim to glory. It is by the hardships they endure and the risks they run that with God's help they protect us and come to our aid, subdue ruthless enemies, secure peace for the state and its provinces, and restore order and tranquillity.

> But even greater glory belongs to those who slay war itself with their words rather than slaying human beings with the sword, and who restore or maintain peace through peace and not through war. There is indeed no doubt that fighters, if they be good persons, are looking for peace, but they establish it at the cost of bloodshed. You, on the contrary, have been sent precisely to prevent any bloodshed. . . . Your mission is an enviable one.[12]

Darius answered with a letter of praise for Augustine; he asked for a copy of the *Confessions* and sent medicine for his ills and money to buy or replace books for the library.[13] In his reply Augustine offered some fine, friendly reflections on the praise given him and sent the *Confessions* with some words of touching humility[14]; he also dispatched five additional books that Darius had not requested, and, with his usual kindness, asked Darius for his opinion of them. "If you read them all while you are here in Africa, please let me know your opinion of them. You can send it to me directly or leave it there for Aurelius, my brother and lord, to forward to me."[15]

The coming of Count Darius, a Catholic, on a mission of peace filled him with joy, but he must have felt an equally great sadness at the preceding arrival of Segisvultus as governor in place of Boniface. His dismay would have been due not only to the threats issuing from the contending parties but also to the fact that in the train of the new governor came the Arians, among them Bishop Maximinus, whom Segisvultus sent to Hippo, probably in 427, on "a mission of peace" (*contemplatione pacis*).[16]

Debate with Maximinus

On this occasion many people asked Augustine to debate the Trinitarian faith with Maximinus. Augustine agreed. "At the desire and request of eminent persons he also held a debate at Hippo with an Arian bishop [surely Maximinus] who had come to Africa with the Goths."[17] But Maximinus played a cunning game: he dragged out his final speech as long as possible so that Augustine would have no time to answer, then he returned speedily to Carthage and claimed he had won the debate. When he was asked to continue the discussion the next day he answered that he was compelled to leave for Carthage. The two men therefore promised, Augustine to give his response to Maximinus in writing, the other to answer in turn. Augustine kept his promise, Maximinus did not. The result was Augustine's work *Against Maximinus*, the purpose of which the author explains in the preface to the first book. "First, I shall show that you did not refute what I said; then, to the extent necessary, I shall refute what you said."[18]

The correspondence between Augustine and Quodvultdeus can be assigned to this same period (427-28). This latter, a deacon at Carthage, asked Augustine to compile a short handbook on heresies. Augustine referred him instead to the works of Philastrius, bishop of Brescia, "whom I myself saw at Milan in the company of blessed Ambrose,"[19] and Epiphanius, bishop of Cyprus. The deacon was not satisfied and repeated his request. Augustine agreed and promised to begin the work as soon as he should have finished replying to the fifth book of Julian—unless Books 6-8 of Julian's work arrived from Rome in the meantime. Augustine felt obliged to give priority to the reply to Julian and to his *Revisions*.

The awaited three books did not come and, in keeping with his promise, Augustine began his work *Heresies,* continuing meanwhile to reread his letters and sermons with a view to the *Revisions.* Then the last three books of Julian finally came, and, as planned, Augustine laid aside the work on heresy to continue with the reply to Julian. Death overtook him, however, and all three works remained unfinished. How unfortunate for us!

The second book on heresies, which was never written, would have discussed a basic question: in what does heresy consist and when can and must a Christian be called a heretic?[20] The answer would have called for a summa, or comprehensive treatise, on ecclesiology, such as was still lacking at this time and in fact never made its appearance in the patristic period, to the serious disadvantage of theology generally.

The two books of *Revisions* that did not get written would have dealt with the letters and sermons kept in the library at Hippo; they would have provided valuable historical and theological information and would have told us the number of these letters and sermons.

Finally, the completion of the second reply to Julian (two books were still to be written) would not have been without its usefulness. Above all, it would have transmitted to us the complete work of the bishop of Eclanum. It would perhaps have also clarified some points of doctrine that are stated but not explained in the earlier books.

Another factor that helped prevent the completion of these three works was the arrival of some letters from Gaul. On the other hand, these letters elicited a reply in two books that crowns the entire Augustinian teaching on grace.

Prosper and Hilary told Augustine of the strong reaction of the monks of Marseilles to his teaching.[21] In order to explain his thinking Augustine wrote *The Predestination of the Saints* and *The Gift of Perseverance.* He set forth his thought with humility but also with conviction, admitting that his views on such a profound and difficult question might be wrong, but also reminding his opponents that they should reflect carefully whether the error might not be on their side.[22]

While Augustine was carrying on these theological discussions and worrying about the internal situation in the African provinces, a decisive event occurred that would eventually lead to the collapse of the *Pax romana* on that continent: in May of 429 the Vandals crossed the Strait of Gibraltar. They began their conquest in Mauretania and then moved quickly toward the richer provinces to the east. In May and June of 430 these "destroyers of the Roman Empire"[23] surrounded Hippo and set siege to it. Count Boniface, who had settled his quarrel with the court, had gathered his forces here and was endeavoring in vain to prevent the barbarians from passing.

Suffering caused by barbarian invasion

Augustine's first biographer tries to describe his suffering at this painful time. He is unable and therefore refers us to the words of Scripture: "They who increase their knowledge increase their suffering," and we can appreciate the truth of the statement. Possidius tells us, however, that "tears were more than ever his food night and day, and now that he had reached the end of his life, he was destined, beyond the common lot, to pass his old age in bitter struggle." The biographer then gives some concrete details:

> And in fact the man of God saw cities ravaged and destroyed; dwellings in the countryside razed and their inhabitants slain by their enemies or put to flight and scattered; churches deprived of priests and ministers; consecrated virgins and religious men scattered to all quarters; some of these swooning under torture, others put to the sword, others imprisoned, having lost the integrity of body and soul, as well as their faith, and being reduced to long and painful enslavement by their enemies. No longer were hymns and the praises of God heard in the churches, while in many places the churches themselves were burned. No longer were solemn sacrifices offered to God in their former places; the sacraments of God were abandoned or, if someone asked for them, it was not easy to find a minister.[24]

The entire fruit of forty years' pastoral toil, Augustine's own and that of his colleagues, was suddenly and heartrendingly lost.

But Augustine was not a man to spend his time in peevish laments, for the past. Although he was old and infirm, he felt that his place was still in the breach, and there he remained. First of all, he supported himself and his followers by meditating on the mysterious plans of providence; what he had said many years earlier to console the refugees from Italy he repeated now for the besieged of Africa. He spoke of the world as having entered its old age. In old age misfortunes increase: coughs, catarrh, bleary eyes, anxiety, exhaustion. But even though the world grows old, Christ remains forever young: Cling to Christ and your youth will be renewed like the eagle's.[25] This was the substance of *The City of God*, which he had completed some ten years earlier and had sent, in twelve large fascicles, to Firmus who was to see to its diffusion at Carthage.[26]

For himself Augustine also found strength in the sayings of the pagan sages, as in this one of Plotinus: "They are not great who regard it as a disaster that trees and rocks should fall and mortals should die."[27] In addition, he himself had written so many fine pages on the transiency of earthly life that in this time of crisis some of them must surely have come to his mind and his lips as he conversed with his friends and spoke to the people. Perhaps the passage in which he compared the human race to a mighty torrent caused by the rains: the torrent swells, rumbles, speeds along, and rushes down an abyss; then there is silence once again.[28]

But this was not a time solely for comforting and being comforted; it was also a time for action and for helping to clarify people's notions. Augustine did both of these things. We may recall what Possidius says in general about his charity to the needy, which he carried to the extent of melting down the sacred vessels, as Ambrose had.[29] He showed this kind of charity not only to the Italian refugees from the Gothic invasions or to the prisoners taken in Moorish raids, but also to the victims of Vandal devastation.

We know, moreover, that the clergy were quite confused about the proper attitude to be taken in face of the barbarian advance. Some thought that in this situation bishops and priests should apply to themselves the Gospel saying, "When they persecute you in one town, flee to another" (Mt 10:23).

Words of counsel in times of crisis

Once again they had recourse to Augustine. His colleague Quodvultdeus, for example, appealed to him and received a brief answer, but one that was clear, prudent, and balanced. In substance Augustine said that no one should be forbidden to move to a safer place, but that on the other hand "we ought not to break the ties created by the ministry to which the love of Christ binds us, or to abandon the Churches we are obliged to serve." "Our ministry is so necessary that no one should be deprived of it. Therefore, if even a remnant of the people of God remains in the place in which we find ourselves, we can only say to the Lord: 'O our God, be our protector and our fortress.' "[30]

Another colleague who appealed to Augustine was Honoratus, Bishop of Thiave, a small town not far from Tagaste. He was sent a copy of the letter to Quodvultdeus.[31] This did not satisfy him, however; he gave his reasons and looked for a more detailed answer. Augustine wrote one; it was his last letter.[32] Possidius included it in his portrait of the Saint as being "very useful and even necessary for ordering the conduct of priests and other ministers of God."[33] He was right. The letter was a declaration from a great thinker and man of action who, after more than forty years in the service of the Church, traced in it a valuable program for the conduct of all priests in a period when profound changes and difficult times lay ahead.

> When danger threatens all, that is, bishops, clerics, and laity, those who need others should not be abandoned by those whom they need. In this case, all should move to a secure place. If, however, some must remain, they must not be abandoned by those whose duty it is to help them with the sacred ministry; let them all either be saved together or together endure the affliction that the Father of the family wills that they suffer. . . . Then it will become clear who among them suffers for the others; it will evidently be those who, though they could have fled and avoided the scourge, preferred to remain and not abandon the rest in a critical time. This is the supreme proof of love. . . .[34]

This is the message of heroism that so many priests down the centuries have heard and accepted. It marked the end of Augustine's mission as pastor and teacher.

39

Death

ANUMBER of Augustine's episcopal colleagues had taken refuge in Hippo, which was fortified; among these was Possidius, who tells us of these details. One day at table Augustine said to them: "I would have you know that during this terrible time I pray God either to liberate this city from the enemies around it or, if he decides otherwise, to grant his servants the strength they need to do his will; as for myself, I ask him to take me from this world and bring me into his presence."[1] This final part of his prayer was heard.

"In the third month of the siege Augustine took to his bed with a fever; it was his final illness."[2] We do not know how long the illness lasted; presumably not very long. Short or long, he devoted his time, now free at last, to prayer. In conversations with friends he had often said that no one, lay person or bishop, however blameless in conduct, should face the narrow passage through death without due and sufficient repentance. Even though he was aware of having spent his entire life since baptism for Christ and the Church, he did not think he should be an exception to his own rule. Therefore he had the penitential psalms written on large sheets of paper and attached to the wall opposite his bed; lying there, he recited them and, as he recited them, "he wept continuous, passionate tears."[3]

He had often recited these psalms with the people and had commented on them at great length so that they might form and feed the Christian devotion of all. Now that he was alone in the presence of death, he found them to be still an expression of his sentiments. We would be sure from his writings what these sentiments were, even if the first biographer had not told us. We would know them even from his theological writings, since no one has, to the same extent as Augustine, been so much the autobiographer in all his discourses and writings.

He was not troubled by the thought of death; in fact, it even intensified his love. As a lover who had been purified by a life of sacrifice, he rejoiced now that he was drawing close to God his source, and his love burned with a more intense and purer flame. He had meditated a great deal on death; he had written extensively on its mystery; he had shown the passage from fear of death to longing for it to be a sure path for the ascent to God. Now that death was at hand, he awaited it with serene confidence.

Perhaps he thought back now to words of Ambrose that he had so often recalled with approval. When Ambrose was asked to pray that the Lord might prolong his life, he had said: "My life is such that I need not be ashamed to live on among you; but neither do I fear death, for our Lord is a kindly Lord." Possidius comments: "Our Augustine, now an old man, admired and praised this circumspect reply and its carefully weighed expression."[4] Or perhaps he thought back to another saying, likewise often quoted, of an episcopal friend; this man, not highly educated, but a good person, being asked if he was sorry to die, replied: "If I never had to die, that would be fine; but if I must some day die, why not now?"[5]

Prayerful preparation

The more ill Augustine became, the more he felt a need to be alone in order to prepare himself by prayer for the face-to-face meeting with God to which he had looked forward, "day and night,"[6] for so many years. "In order that he might remain recollected, he asked us, about ten days before his death, not to admit anyone to his room outside the hours when the doctors came to see him or when his meals were brought to him. We carried out his wishes to the letter, and during all that time he gave himself to prayer."[7]

His great heart ceased to beat on August 28, 430. Prosper writes in his *Chronicle* for this year: "Bishop Augustine, a man distinguished in every way, died on August 28."[8] He was seventy-six.

"We took part in the sacrifice offered to God at his funeral, and then he was buried."[9] Presumably he was buried in the Basilica of Peace; from here, at a date that is uncertain, the remains were transferred to Sardinia and then, about 725, to the

Basilica of St. Peter in Ciel d'Oro in Pavia, where they now rest. Venerable Bede, in whose lifetime the second translation occurred, writes in his martyrology for August 28: "In Africa, the deposition . . . of St. Augustine, bishop, whose remains were first transferred from his own city because of the barbarians and were recently brought to Pavia by Liutprand, King of the Lombards, and buried there with honors."[10]

Three great treasures

The dying Augustine "made no will, because this poor man of God had nothing to leave."[11] He did, however, leave the Church three great treasures: his books, his clergy, and his monasteries. One of these, the first, was indeed a vast trove that thieves could not steal nor the Vandals destroy.

> He left the Church a numerous clergy, as well as monasteries full of men and women vowed to continence and living under obedience to superiors. He also left a library of books and sermons, both his own and those of other saints. From these we can gauge the merits that were his by the grace of God, and the great place he has in the Church. In them, too, the faithful have him ever alive before them.[12]

To this assessment, which posterity has confirmed, Possidius adds another regarding a privilege that posterity to its regret has not shared. "I believe, however, that he profited even more those who saw him alive in the Church and could hear his very words, and especially those who were witnesses to his life among us."[13]

40

Survival and Relevance

AUGUSTINE'S writings survived the destruction of Hippo, for the flames that ravaged the city after a three months' siege spared the library. Possidius, writing after the disaster, tells those desirous of obtaining the most accurate copies of Augustine's works that they should appeal to the library in Hippo.[1] From Hippo, therefore, and Carthage, and other scribal centers that had sprung up or would later spring up on the continent of Europe copies of Augustine's works would continue to make their way everywhere.

The heritage of the Bishop of Hippo, despite its extent and variety, has been preserved almost in its entirety. Of the extended works—over 100 in about 250 "books"—only a few have been lost, and these were of lesser importance.[2] We do not know how many letters time has swallowed up; we do know that various ones were lost, but it is reasonable to think that the more than 200 that we do have represent the bulk of his correspondence.

On the other hand, many sermons have been lost; this was inevitable. The great mass that has survived falls into several categories. There were sermons delivered or written on a single subject: 134 on the Gospel and first letter of John, and about 200 on the psalms. Of the sermons on various subjects we know about 500; we do not know, however, how many there were altogether in the library at Hippo and how many of these in turn were revised and published. In his invaluable list of Augustine's works Possidius counts 1,030 books, letters, and sermons, but he adds: "I omit those that I could not list because they had not been assigned a number."[3] We have no idea how many uncataloged works there were. Because of the tragic situation in which he found himself, Possidius had neither the time nor the heart to carry on as a good librarian, that is, to organize the notebooks and parchment scrolls, number them, and indicate their subject matter.

Apart from these unavoidable gaps, the works of Augustine were not only carefully preserved but also diligently copied and eagerly read. A careful student of these manuscripts can say of *The City of God:* "Next to the Sacred Scriptures no book has been more read and copied, with perhaps the one exception of St. Gregory's *Moralia* [a lengthy commentary on the Book of Job dealing with moral and ascetical questions].[4] To the transcription of whole works we must add anthologies, extracts, and catenae, which were widely read.[5] In addition there were works that were not from Augustine's pen but were nonetheless largely compiled from his works and passed under his name.[6]

The invention of printing brought several complete editions; the most recent and best is that of the Maurists,[7] which was often reprinted and eventually found a place in the *Patrologia Latina* [Latin Patrology] of Migne.[8] When the need arose of making the works available to larger circles of readers, numerous translations in many languages, whether of individual works or of the complete works,[9] were made and are still being made. Meanwhile scholarly studies of the works go on multiplying beyond counting.

Influence on the Church

"Few persons have exercised as profound and continuous an influence as Augustine has on the thinking of later generations."[10] He has always been a living, present figure in the Catholic Church and throughout the entire Christian West, of which he can legitimately be called the "Common Father."[11] In his lifetime Innocent I praised "the faith and vigorous Catholic religion" of Augustine and his brother bishops,[12] while a year after Augustine's death Celestine I defended his memory and counted him among "the Church's best teachers" and one who was loved and esteemed by all."[13] Ever since that time Augustine has had an uninterrupted teaching ministry.

Down the centuries many popes have praised his wisdom and defended his teaching, especially his teaching on grace, which has sometimes been interpreted in a one-sided and therefore distorted way. Let me mention only the popes closer to our time.

Leo XIII called him the greatest of the Fathers.[14] Pius XII spoke of him as "undeniably the greatest Doctor of the Church"[15] and as a man "to whom none or, at most, a very few since the beginning of history can be compared."[16] And when Paul VI was opening the Patristic Institute in Rome that bears Augustine's name, he said: "Not only do the characteristic virtues of the Fathers shine in him to an eminent degree. It can also be asserted that the entire thought of Christian antiquity finds a place in his works and that from these in turn flow currents of thought that permeate the entire tradition of later centuries."[17]

The Councils, too, have drawn extensively on the teaching of Augustine and on his often striking way of expressing it; they have thus shown that his teaching is not simply that of a local bishop but that of the Church as a whole. The Council of Orange adopted his teaching on grace, the Council of Trent his teaching on original sin and justification, and Vatican I his teaching on the relations between reason and faith. In our own day Vatican II has made its own his teaching on the mystery of the Church and the mystery of the human person and, in presenting this teaching, has drawn upon themes, problems, and solutions that are frequently emphasized in Augustine's writings.[18]

It is also a fact that, as in the case of Gottschalk of Orbais, the Reformers, and the Jansenists, thinkers have appealed to Augustine's authority in support of theological views at odds with Catholic teaching. The writer of the present book is convinced, however, that such interpretations do not take adequate account of Augustine's teaching in its totality. His is a doctrine that has for one of its principal merits a multiplicity of facets combined with great synthetic power.

The history of Augustinianism is coexistensive with the history of Western thought. I refer not only to the theological thought of the West but also to its philosophy, its spirituality, and its political thought.

In the early Middle Ages, early Scholasticism, and classical Scholasticism the most varied writers turned to Augustine as the highest possible authority. Thus nine-tenths of Peter Lombard's *Books of Judgments* (*Sententiae*) consists of statements from Augustine, which thus became the standard heritage of students of theology. Lombard's famous work was in fact for centuries the textbook for theological studies, and voluminous commentaries were written on it.

After the discovery and rapid assimilation of Aristotle in the West, Augustine continued to be the unchallenged authority in theology, while in philosophy he shared first place with "the Philosopher." The result was two currents of thought—Augustinianism and Aristotelianism—which coexisted amid agreements and disagreements and culminated in the great syntheses of Bonaventure and Thomas. Even Thomas, however, is a disciple of Augustine; in certain basic ways he is even the greatest of his disciples, and this not only in theology. He is, of course, a disciple as only one can be who is in turn a great teacher. The two teachers are closer to one another than is commonly thought; they are certainly closer than some historical forms of Thomism and Augustinianism would have us believe. The two men show the doctrinal continuity and complementarity between patristic thought and Scholasticism, both of which are glories of the Christian mind.

After Thomas, Augustine continued to be a great Christian teacher, whether by reason of the extent to which his thinking had become part of the Thomist synthesis or by reason of certain theses specific to—or regarded as specific to—Augustinianism. These theses are in the areas of theology, philosophy, spirituality, and political thought.

In theology I may mention the Augustinian school whose great light was Giles of Rome (Aegidius Romanus) and whose other major representatives were Gregory of Rimini, Girolamo Seripando, and Enrico Noris.

Influence on philosophy

In philosophy the names of Descartes, Pascal, Vico, Rosmini, Bergson, Blondel, and Sciacca come to mind. The presence of Augustinian motifs and the influence of Augustinian thought are also undeniable in idealism, existentialism, and spiritualism. The same presence and influence are even more evident in spirituality, from the *Devotio moderna* ("Modern devotion") movement to St. Teresa of Avila, St. Francis de Sales, and Cardinal Berulle.

As everyone knows, and as I mentioned earlier, medieval political thought was largely inspired by the views expressed in *The City of God.*

Of course, not everything in these various forms of Augustinianism is in fact Augustinian, and it is still necessary to look for the "real" Augustine through a careful study of his complete works. But the emphatic and constant appeal to his authority by thinkers of such varied temperament and from such diverse quarters does show the presence and perennial fruitfulness of his teaching.

This extraordinary phenomenon was due both to the course taken by the development of Western civilization and to the personality of Augustine himself. The Saint effected a vast synthesis of Christian thought, of which *The City of God* is the most profound expression. Not until the thirteenth century did the West see another synthesis worthy of being compared with *The City of God.* Nine centuries provided more than enough time for an author to become a classic and to show the depth and power of his genius.

Augustine was, then, philosopher, theologian, mystic, and poet in one, and this in an eminent degree. His lofty powers complemented each other and made the man fascinating in a way difficult to resist. He is a philosopher, but not a cold thinker; he is a theologian, but also a master of the spiritual life; he is a mystic, but also a pastor; he is a poet, but also a controversialist. Every reader thus finds something attractive and even overwhelming: depth of metaphysical intuition, rich abundance of theological proofs, synthetic power and energy, psychological depth shown in spiritual ascents, and a wealth of imagination, sensibility, and mystical fervor.

Augustine, like every human being, doubtless had his limits. These can be seen, for example, in his learning, for though he had this in an uncommon degree, he did not move freely in the world of Greek literature; in his polemical ardor, which did not always permit him to polish his language; in the different ways in which he moved in the world of ideas, on the one hand, and in the world of facts, on the other; in the relentless power of his dialectic, which tended to shed light on one truth at the seeming cost of forgetting another. These limitations were due to the personality of the man, who knew the torments of conversion and had the radical outlook of the convert, to his philosophical and theological formation, and, perhaps most of all, to the times in which it was his destiny to live.

These limitations did not, however, prevent his being in the past the common teacher of Western Christendom. And in fact he has been a source far more of light than of shadow. Guitton writes: "Take away Augustine from the patristic age, Paul from the early Church, and the course of Western history would have been quite different."[19] Nor do the limitations keep him from being a teacher even today, and to the benefit of all.

He is a humble and unobtrusive teacher. He does not give himself airs; he does not feel superior to others, because he regards truth as a good common to all; he limits himself to a simple statement of his own painful experiences and exhorts all to become disciples of the one Teacher so that they will not need other teachers.[20] On the other hand, the "real" Augustine—the Augustine of history and of the writings—is a far richer and more harmonious personality than he appears when seen through the disintegrating prism of certain currents of thought that have little justification for claiming his authority.

Relevance of Augustine

This, the "real" Augustine, is the one who is perennially relevant. The Augustine of "Christian" philosophy: of the "interior and eternal" that summons us to the interior life and supplies a basis for transcendence; of the human person as "a deep abyss" and image of God, who receives from God gifts of being, knowledge, and love that can be preserved only in God; of human beings as weak sinners who long for a freedom and salvation that Christ alone can give them; of the relationship between time and eternity, reason and faith, nature and grace, all seen in a synthesizing vision that unites opposites without confusing them; of the City of God, which being based on "social" love is by its nature universal and recruits its citizens from every nation, its members from every language, caring nothing about diversities in custom, law, and institution . . . neither suppressing nor destroying, but rather accepting and preserving everything that, despite being different in different nations, tends to one and the same goal of earthly peace, provided only that these diverse ways do not hinder the religion that teaches us to worship the one true and sovereign God.[21]

The perennial Augustine is also Augustine the great theologian: theologian of the Trinity, of redemption, of the "whole Christ," and of history. He is Augustine the developer of scholarly theological method, who combines an ardent desire for understanding with a firm adherence to the authority of the faith, a keen sense of mystery with a constant subordination of knowledge to love.[22] He is the Augustine of profound religious experience, who teaches us to pray, communicates a passionate love, and speaks words of hope.

Not the least reason for Augustine's relevance is his ecumenical importance. In an age when we are keenly aware of the sad and painful division of Western Christendom, there is a great deal of debate over the proper interpretation of Augustine's thought, and he is appealed to from quarters sometimes far removed from one another. That thought, when studied in its authentic sources, can provide a common meeting ground and serve as an effective starting point for a synthesis at once new and old. Such a synthesis will acknowledge the doctrinal points that unite all Christians and, in truth and love, will work through those that still divide, thus preparing the way for that restoration of unity that was the great ideal of Augustine as thinker and pastor. The City of God recognizes but one victory, the victory of truth—*ubi victoria, veritas*[23]; it is a victory that humiliates no one and does honor to all.

Biographical Note

354 (Nov. 13)	Birth of Augustine at Tagaste
361-366	First studies in his homeland
367	Sent to Madauros to pursue further studies
370	Return to Tagaste after secondary studies
371	At Carthage for superior studies
372	Birth of Adeodatus
373	Reading of the *Hortensius* and adherence to the Manicheaens
374	Returns to Tagaste to teach grammar
375	Opens a school of eloquence at Carthage
383	Transfers to Rome
384 (fall)	Invited to Milan as Professor of Rhetoric
385	Joined by his mother at Milan
386	Return to the Catholic faith
387 (Apr. 24-25)	(On the night of Holy Saturday) baptized by Ambrose.
387 (summer)	Leaves Milan to go back home; at Ostia on the Tiber his mother dies
388 (Aug.)	Departure from Rome and return to Tagaste
391	Priestly ordination; founding of a monastery for lay people
395-396	Episcopal ordination; beginning of the lengthy pastoral activity at Hippo
411	The great conference between Catholics and Donatists at Carthage in which Augustine played a leading role
426 (Sept. 26)	Calls the people together and designates his successor in the person of the priest Eraclius
430 (Aug. 28)	Dies while Hippo is under siege by the Vandals
725 (approx.)	His bones are taken from Sardinia—where they had been transferred from Hippo because of the devastation of the barbarians (Ven. Bede)—to Pavia, in the Basilica of St. Peter in Ciel d'Oro

Abbreviations for Notes

1. The works of Augustine

Ad Don. post. col.	*Ad Donatistas post collationem* (To the Donatists after the Conference)
Brev. col. cum Don.	*Breviculus collationis cum Donatistis* (Summary of the Conference with the Donatists)
C. Acad.	*Contra Academicos* (Against the Academics)
C. duas ep. Pel.	*Contra duas epistolas Pelagianorum* (Against Two Letters of the Pelagians)
C. ep. Man.	*Contra epistolam Manichaei* (Against the Letter of Mani)
C. Faust.	*Contra Faustum* (Against Faustus)
C. Jul.	*Contra Julianum* (Against Julian)
C. litt. Petil.	*Contra litteras Petiliani* (Against the Letters of Petilian)
C. Max.	*Contra Maximinum* (Against Maximinus)
C. Secund.	*Contra Secundinum* (Against Secundinus)
Coll. cum Max.	*Collatio cum Maximino* (Debate with Maximinus)
Conf.	*Confessiones* (Confessions)
De act. cum Fel. man.	*De actis cum Felice manichaeo* (Proceedings with Felix the Manichaean)
De bapt.	*De baptismo* (Baptism)
De beata vita	*De beata vita* (The Happy Life)
De bono conjug.	*De bono conjugali* (The Blessing of Marriage)
De cat. rud.	*De catechizandis rudibus* (The Instruction of Beginners)
De civ. Dei	*De civitate Dei* (The City of God)
De conjug. adult.	*De conjugiis adulterinis* (Adulterous Marriage)
De cons. evang.	*De consensu evangelistarum* (Agreement among the Evangelists)
De corrept. et grat.	*De correptione et gratia* (Correction and Grace)
De cur. ger. pro mort.	*De cura gerenda pro mortuis* (The Care to be Taken of the Dead)

De div. qq. 83	*De diversis quaestionibus LXXXIII* (Miscellany of Eighty-Three Questions)
De div. qq. ad Simplic.	*De diversis quaestionibus ad Simplicianum* (Miscellany of Questions, in Response to Simplician)
De doct. christ.	*De doctrina christiana* (Christian Instruction)
De duabus anim.	*De duabus animabus* (The Two Souls)
De dono persev.	*De dono perseverantiae* (The Gift of Perseverance)
De excid. urb. Rom.	*De excidio urbis Romae* (The Destruction of the City of Rome)
De fide et symb.	*De fide et symbolo* (Faith and Creed)
De Gen. ad litt.	*De Genesi ad litteram* (The Literal Meaning of Genesis)
De gest. Pel.	*De gestis Pelagii* (The Acts of Pelagius)
De gest. com Emer.	*De gestis cum Emerito* (Proceedings with Emeritus)
De grat. Christi et de pecc. orig.	*De gratia Christi et de peccato originali* (The Grace of Christ and Original Sin)
De grat. et lib. arb.	*De gratia et libero arbitrio* (Grace and Free Will)
De her.	*De heresibus* (Heresies)
De lib. arb.	*De libero arbitrio* (Free Will)
De mor. Eccl. cath. et de mor. man.	*De moribus Ecclesiae catholicae et de moribus manichaeorum* (The Morals of the Catholic Church and the Morals of the Manichaeans)
De mus.	*De musica* (Music)
De nupt. et concup.	*De nuptiis et concupiscentia* (Marriage and Desire)
De op. mon.	*De opere monachorum* (The Work of Monks)
De ord.	*De ordine* (On Order)
De pecc. mer et rem.	*De peccatorum meritis et remissione* (The Merits and Forgiveness of Sins)
De praed. sanct.	*De praedestinatione sanctorum* (The Predestination of the Saints)

De quant. anim.	*De quantitate animae* (The Greatness of the Soul)
De serm. Dom. in monte	*De sermone Domini in monte* (The Lord's Sermon on the Mount)
De sanct. virg.	*De sancta virginitate* (Holy Virginity)
De Trin.	*De Trinitate* (The Trinity)
De util. cred.	*De utilitate credendi* (The Value of Belief)
De vera rel.	*De vera religione* (True Religion)
Enarr. in ps.	*Enarrationes in psalmos* (Sermons on the Psalms)
Ench.	*Enchiridion* (Handbook)
Ep.	*Epistolae* (Letters)
Ep. ad Rom. inchoata	*Epistolae ad Romanos inchoata expositio* (Unfinished Commentary on the Letter to the Romans)
Ep. Sec. ad Aug.	*Epistola Secundini ad Augustinum* (Letter of Secundinus to Augustine)
In ep. Jo. tr.	*In epistolas Joannis tractatus* (Sermons on the Letters of John)
In Jo. ev. tr.	*In Joannis evangelium tractatus* (Sermons on the Gospel of John)
Op. imp. c. Jul.	*Opus imperfectum contra Julianum* (Unfinished Work against Julian)
Psalmus c. part. Don.	*Psalmus contra partem Donati* (Psalm against the Donatist Party)
Retract.	*Retractationes* (Revisions)
Serm.	*Sermones* (Sermons)
Serm. ad Caes. eccl. plebem	*Sermo ad Caesariensis ecclesiae plebem* (Sermon to the People of the Church of Caesarea)
Solil.	*Soliloquia* (Soliloquies)

2. Other References

Aug. Mag.   *Augustinus Magister.* International Augusti-
                     nian Congress, Paris, September 21-24,
                     1954 (3 vols. Paris: Etudes Augustiniennes,
                     1954-55)

Enc. Catt.   *Enciclopedia Cattolica*
Enc. Ital.   *Enciclopedia Italiana*
ETL   *Ephemerides Theologicae Lovanienses*
Misc. Agost.   *Miscellanea Agostiniana* (2 vols. Rome, 1930-
                     31). The first volume is *Sermones post
                     Maurinos reperti,* ed. by G. Morin

NBA   *Nuova Biblioteca Agostiniana*
REA   *Revue des Etudes Augustiniennes*
Rech. Aug.   *Recherches Augustiniennes. Homage à R. P.
                     Fulbert Cayré* (2 vols. Paris: Etudes Augus-
                     tiniennes, 1962)

Notes

Notes for Chapter 1

1. Augustine calls himself an African. He does so when speaking of Apuleius "who being an African is better known to us Africans" (*Ep.* 138, 19), Ponticianus, "a fellow-countryman of ours from Africa" (*Conf.* VIII, 6, 14), and Maximus of Madauros, "an African writing to Africans, both of us being settled in Africa" (*Ep.* 17, 2). He calls Cyprian of Carthage an African: "Cyprian an African, Hilary a Gaul, Ambrose an Italian, Gregory a Greek" (*Op. imp. c. Jul.* 2, 33) and says that Faustus of Milevi is "African by race" (*C. Faust.* 1, 1). When Julian contemptuously calls him "Punic," he does not reject the description but mentions Cyprian, also Punic, and reminds his adversary that it is reason and not race (Julian was an Italian from Apulia) that wins the victory.

2. G. Charles-Pichard, *La civilisation de l'Afrique romaine* (Paris, 1959).

3. *Vita Melaniae,* ed. by Rampolla (Rome, 1905), 4

4. O. Perler, *Les voyages de saint Augustin* (Paris, 1969), 120.

5. *Conf.* IV, 7, 12.

6. *De quant. anim.* 21, 36.

7. *Conf.* II, 4, 9.

8. In Africa, unlike Italy, lamps burned through the night in the houses of the well-to-do. See H. Comps-Falaer, *L'olivier et l'huile dans l'Afrique romaine* (Algiers, 1953).

9. The fruits did not include strawberries or cherries, which Augustine knew only in Italy: see *Ep.* 7, 3, 6.

10. *Ep.* 220, 7.

11. See R. Cagnat, *Carthage, Timgad, Tébesse et les villes antiques de l'Afrique du nord* (Paris, 1912). See also the extensive bibliography in Ch. A. Julien, *Histoire de l'Afrique du Nord,* 2nd ed. revised and updated by Ch. Courtois (Paris, 1951).

12. *Conf.* I, 19, 30; II, 3, 6.

13. *De beata vita.* 6.

14. Prosper, *Chronicon,* an. 430 (PL 51:595): "Bishop Augustine died on August 28"; Possidius, *Vita* 31, 1: ". . . he was 76 years old."

15. *Serm.* 345, 1: "They alone truly live!"

16. F. Vattioni, "S. Agostino e la civiltà punica," *Augustinianum* 8 (1968) 434-67.

17. *Conf.* VI, 7, 11.

18. *Ibid.,* VI, 14, 24.

19. *Ibid.,* II, 3, 5.

20. *Serm.* 356, 13.

21. *Conf.* IX, 9, 20.

22. Possidius, *Vita* 3, 1.

23. *Ep.* 27, 5.

24. C. Acad. 2, 2, 3.
25. *Conf.* II, 3, 5.
26. *Ep.* 126, 7.
27. Possidius, *Vita* 31, 7.
28. *De beata Vita* 6.
29. Possidius, *Vita* 1, 1.
30. *Conf.* IX, 9, 19-22; see St. Augustine, *Mia Madre*, ed. by A. Trapè (Milan, 1975).
31. *Conf.* I, 16, 25.
32. *Serm.* 167, 4.
33. *Ep.* 84, 2; 209, 3.
34. *Conf.* I, 14, 23.
35. On the survival of Punic see Vattioni, *op. cit.*
36. *Serm.* 111, 6; 167, 4; *C. litt. Petil.* 2, 104, 239; *Ep. ad. Rom. inchoata* 13.
37. *Ep.* 66, 2.
38. *Ep.* 108, 14.
39. *Ep.* 17, 2.
40. *De civ. Dei* XXI, 14. On the threats and punishments used in school see also *Conf.* I, 14, 23; *Op. imp. c. Jul.* 3, 154.
41. *Ep.* 261, 5. See D. De Bruyne, "St. Augustin reviseur de la Bible," in *Misc. Agost.* II, 521-606.
42. *Ep.* 71, 6.
43. *C. Jul.* 1, 5, 18; 1, 6, 21.
44. *De civ. Dei* IX, 17; X, 14, 16 and 23 (a translation *directly* from Plotinus).
45. *Ep.* 222, 2, on St. Epiphanius' book on heresies (not translated into Latin), which is therefore one of the sources of Augustine's *De heresibus* (published in 428). See G. Bardy, "Le *De heresibus* et ses sources," in *Misc. Agost.* II, 397-416.
46. For this reason he asks Jerome to translate the Greek Fathers: *Ep.* 28, 2. On his knowledge of Greek see H. Marrou, *St. Augustin et la fin de la culture antique*, Part 2: *Retractatio* (Paris, 1949), 631-37.
47. Who are paid back in the same coin by the Africans; see *De ord.* II, 17, 45.
48. See C. Mohrmann, "St. Augustin écrivain," in *Rech. Aug.* I, 43-66.
49. *Conf.* IV, 4, 7; Possidius, *Vita* 1, 1; *C. acad.* II, 2, 3.
50. *Conf.* IV, 3, 5.
51. *Ibid.* V, 13, 23.
52. *C. litt. Petil.* III, 25, 30; see P. Courcelle, *Recherches sur les Confessions de saint Augustin* (Paris, 1968²), 79-87.
53. *Conf.* IV, 16, 20.
54. *De quant. anim.* 33, 70.
55. *Retract.* 1, 6; see Marrou, *op. cit.,* 1-158.

56. *Conf.* I, 13, 21.
57. *Ibid.* III, 4, 7.
58. *De cons. evang.* I, 22, 30.
59. Ep. 164, 4; see below, ch. 29, p. 235.

Notes for Chapter 2

1. *Ep.* 232, 1.
2. *Ep.* 17, 4.
3. *Ep.* 16 (among the letters of Augustine).
4. *Enarr. in ps.* 34, serm. 2, 8.
5. *De civ. Dei* II, 26.
6. P. de Labriolle, in *Storia della Chiesa* III, 181-207.
7. *Conf.* I, 11, 17.
8. *Ibid.* II, 3, 6; II, 9, 19.
9. *Ibid.* IV, 13, 37.
10. *Ep.* 16, 4 (Maximus); 103, 2 (Nectarius) (among the letters of Augustine).
11. On the closing of the temples in Africa and the dates of some antipagan legislation see O. Perler, *Les voyages de saint Augustin* (Paris, 1969), 391-95.
12. *Ep.* 17, 1.
13. Cicero, *Disputationes Tusculanae* I, 26, 65.
14. *Conf.* I, 16, 25.
15. *Ibid.* I, 16, 26.
16. *Serm.* 198, 3.
17. *Conf.* IX, 11, 28: "When she was fifty-six . . . her religious and devout soul was released from the body." The year was 387.
18. *Ibid.* IX, 8, 17.
19. *Ibid.* IX, 8, 18.
20. *Ibid.* IX, 11, 28: When his mother died Augustine was thirty-three.
21. *Ibid.* IX, 9, 19 and 22.
22. *Ibid.* IX, 9, 20.
23. *Ibid.* I, 11, 17.
24. *Ibid.* V, 17.
25. The custom arose from the desire to honor the martyrs by eating at their tombs and distributing part of the food to the poor; in the final analysis, however, it was an imitation of the pagan festival of Parentalia and lent itself to numerous abuses.
26. *Conf.* III, 11, 20—12, 21; V, 8, 15.
27. *Ep.* 36, 14 and 32.
28. *Conf.* VI, 2, 2.
29 *Ibid.* I, 11, 18.

30. Even Alypius had not been baptized as a child; see *Ibid.* IX, 6, 14.

31. *Ibid.* II, 3, 8.

32. *Ep.* 24, 6 (among the letters of Augustine).

33. Gerontius, *Vita Mel.* 21 (SC 90: 170ff).

34. *Ep.* 93, 5, 17.

35. Mansi 4:122.

36. *Vita S. Augustini* 1, 1, 1 (PL 32).

37. *Conf.* I, 9, 14.

38. *Ibid.* VI, 5, 8.

39. *Ibid.* VI, 16, 26.

40. *Ibid.* III, 4, 8.

41. *Ibid.*

42. *Ibid.* III, 6, 10; *C. ep. Man.* 8, 9.

43. *Ibid.* V, 3, 3.

44. *Ibid.* V, 14, 25.

45. *Ibid.* VII, 21, 27.

46. *C. Acad.* II, 2, 5.

47. *Ibid.* III, 30, 43.

48. Same judgment in R. Guardini, *The Conversion of Augustine*, trans. E. Briefs (Westminster, Md., 1960).

Notes for Chapter 3

1. G. Wilpert, "Il piu antico ritratto di S. Agostino," in *Misc. Agost.* II, 1-3.

2. *Conf.* I, 10, 17.

3. *Ibid.* V, 9, 16.

4. *Ibid.* IX, 2, 4.

5. *Ibid.* IX, 4, 12.

6. *Ep.* 118, 34.

7. *Ep.* 220, 2.

8. *Ep.* 10, 1.

9. *Serm.* 355, 7.

10. *Ep.* 122, 1.

11. *Ep.* 124, 1; 269.

12. *Ep.* 38, 1.

13. *Serm. Mai* 126 (= *Misc. Agost.* I, 356); *Enarr. in ps.* 50, 1.

14. See *Serm.* 42, 1; 94; 320; 348, 4; 350, 2; *In Jo. ev. tr.* 19, 20.

15. Possidius, *Vita* 31. See B. Legewie, "Die korperliche Konstitution und die Krankheiten Augustins," in *Misc. Agost.* II, 5-21.

16. *Conf.* I, 20, 31.

17. *Ibid.* I, 13, 21.

18. *Ibid.* I, 17, 27.

19. *Ibid.* III, 3, 6.
20. *Ibid.* IV, 16, 28.
21. *Ibid.* IV, 16. 30.
22. *Ibid.* I, 12, 19.
23. *Ibid.* I, 9, 15.
24. *Ibid.* II, 4, 9.
25. *Ibid.* I, 19, 30.
26. *De quant. anim.* 21, 36.
27. *Conf.* IX, 12, 30.
28. *Ibid.* III, 11, 19.
29. *Ibid.* V, 8, 15.
30. *Ibid.* III, 3, 6.
31. *Ibid.* V, 8, 14.
32. *Ep.* 93, 13, 51.
33. *Codex Theodosianus* XIV, 9, 1.
34. *Conf.* V, 8, 14.
35. *Ibid.* III, 1, 1.
36. *Ep.* 130, 2, 4.
37. *Conf.* II, 9, 17.
38. *Ibid.* IV, 4. 7.
39. *Ibid.* IV, 4, 9 and 6, 11—7, 12.
40. *Ibid.* IV, 4, 7; see *Ep.* 258.
41. *De civ. Dei* XIX, 8.
42. *Conf.* IX, 4, 7; see VI 7, 11.
43. *Ibid.* IX, 3, 6.
44. *Ep.* 84, 1.
45. *Ep.* 38, 1.
46. M. A. McNamara, *Friends and Friendship for Saint Augustine* (Staten Island, N.Y.: Alba House, 1964).

Notes for Chapter 4

1. I refer the reader to my Introduction in *Le Confessioni* (NBA 1; Rome: Editrice Città Nuova, 1975³) 9-121.
2. *Conf.* I, 19, 30.
3. *Ibid.* I, 12, 19.
4. On the innocence of children, which Augustine defends as far as personal sin is concerned, see *De pecc. mer. et remiss.* I, 34, 62—35, 65.
5. *Conf.* I, 19, 30.
6. This is the context in which Catiline is recalled: *Conf.* II, 5, 11.
7. *Ibid.* II, 4, 9—9, 17.
8. *Ibid.* II, 3, 6.

9. *Ibid.* II, 3, 7.
10.. *Ibid.* III, 1, 1.
11. *Ibid.* III, 2, 2.
12. *Ibid.* III, 3, 5.
13. O. Tescari, "Verità e fantasia nella vita di S. Agostino anteriormente alla sua conversione," in *Augustiniana* (Naples, 1955), 73-78.
14. *Solil.* I, 11, 19.
15. *Conf.* IV, 2, 2.
16. *De gubernatione Dei* VII, 16-17.
17. *Serm.* 9, 9, 11.
18. See above, ch. 2, p. 24.
19. See below, ch. 16, p. 104.
20. See Legewie 9.
21. See P. Brown, *Augustine of Hippo. A Biography* (Berkeley and Los Angeles: University of California Press, 1967), 390.
22. See below, ch. 24, p. 179.

Notes for Chapter 5

1. *De beata vita,* 4.
2. *Conf.* III, 4, 7-8.
3. Cicero, *Opera,* ed. Müller (Bibliotheca Teubneriana IV/3; Leipzig, 1890), 312-27.
4. *Conf.* III, 4, 8.
5. *De Trin.* XIII, 4, 7; fr. 36 in Müller's ed.
6. *Ibid.* XIII, 5, 8, and *De beata vita* 10; fr. 39.
7. *De Trin.* XIV, 19, 26; fr. 97.
8. *Ibid.* 9, 12. Just before this passage Augustine cites the *Hortensius,* fr. 50.
9. *C. Jul.* IV, 14, 72; fr. 81.
10. *De beata vita* 10.
11. *Ibid.* 2, 16.
12. *De Trin* XIV, 19, 26.
13. *Solil.* I, 10, 17.
14. *Conf.* III, 4, 7.
15. See M. Testard, *St. Augustin et Cicéron* I (Paris, 1959) 142-49.
16. *Conf.* VI, 11, 18.
17. *De beata vita* 4.

Notes for Chapter 6

1. *De beata vita,* 4. Courcelle *(Recherches* 65) maintains that the "puerile scruple" of which Augustine speaks was acquired from the Catholic circles in which he was living. But a simpler explanation may be Augustine's own psychological state and a false approach to the problem.

2. *Conf.* III, 5, 9.
3. *Ibid.* V, 11, 21.
4. *Serm.* 51, 5, 6.
5. *De duabus anim.* 1, 1.
6. *Conf.* III, 6, 10.
7. *Ibid.*
8. *De util. cred.* 1, 2.
9. *Ibid.*

Notes for Chapter 7

1. *De beata vita,* 4.
2. *De util. cred.* 1, 2.
3. *Ibid.*
4. *Conf.* VIII, 7, 1.
5. *Ibid.* V, 10, 19 and 13, 23.
6. *De util. cred.* 1, 2.
7. *Conf.* III, 6, 10—10, 18.
8. *De util. cred.* 1, 2.
9. *Conf.* III, 7, 12.
10. *Ibid.* V, 10, 20.
11. *Ibid.*
12. *Ibid.*
13. *Ibid.* III, 7, 12.
14. *Ep. Sec. ad Aug.* 3; see below, ch. 23, p. 157.
15. *Conf.* III, 7, 12.

Notes for Chapter 8

1. *C. ep. Man.* 3, 3.
2. *Conf.* IV, 1.
3. Many fragments of Manichaean writers were discovered at Turfan in Chinese Turkestan at the end of the last century, and in 1930 some Manichaean books, in copies dating from between 350 and 400 (therefore barely a hundred years after the death of Mani), were found near Medinet Mahdi in the Faiyum (Egypt). See H. C. Puech, in *Histoire générale des religions* 5 (Paris, 1945) 446-47.
4. H. C. Puech, *"Le manichéisme. Son fondateur, sa doctrine* (Paris, 1949), with extensive bibliography. J. Ries, "Introduction aux études manichéennes. Quatre siècles de recherches," *ETL* 33 (1957) 453-82.
5. F. Decret, *Aspects du manichéisme dans l'Afrique romaine* (Paris, 1971) 31.
6. *Kephaleia* CLIV; see C. Schmidt, *Neue Originalquellen des Manichäismus aus Aegypten* (Stuttgart, 1933) 16-20.

7. Schmidt 25.
8. *De her.* 46; translation from The De Haeresibus of Saint Augustine, trans. with introduction and commentary by Liguori G. Muller (Catholic University of America Patristic Studies 90; Washington, D.C.: Catholic University of America Press, 1956) 85-89, 95-97.
9. *Conf.* V, 10, 19.
10. *Ibid.* IV, 16, 31.
11. *De lib. arb.* I, 2, 4.
12. *Conf.* V, 10, 18.
13. *De mor. Eccl. cath. et de mor. Man.* I, 1, 2.
14. *C. Faust.* V, 1.
15. *De duabus anim.* 9, 11.
16. *Conf.* IV, 1, 1.
17. *Ibid.* III, 10, 18.
18. *Ibid.*

Notes for Chapter 9

1. *Conf.* IV, 4, 7; 7, 12; *De util. cred.* 1, 2.
2. *Conf.* III, 11, 20.
3. *Ibid.* IV, 4, 7; Possidius, *Vita* 1, 1.
4. *Ibid.* IV, 7, 12.
5. *C. Acad.* II, 2, 3.
6. *Conf.* IV, 16, 30.
7. *De civ. Dei* XIX, 22; *De cons. evang.* I, 22, 30. See my article, "Varro et Augustinus praecipui humanitatis cultores," *Latinitas* (1975) 248ff.
8. *Conf.* IV, 3, 4-6.
9. *Ibid.* V, 3, 3.
10. *C. Acad.* II, 2, 5; see P. Courcelle, *Les lettres grecques en Occident de Macrobe à Cassiodore* (Paris, 1948) 179-81.
11. *De her.* Preface (Muller 59).
12. *De civ. Dei* IX, 4, 2.
13. See the important study of A. Solignac, "Doxographies et manuels dans la formation philosophique de saint Augustin," in *Rech. Aug.* I, 113-48.
14. *De civ. Dei* VI, 10-11; *Conf.* V, 6, 11, where it is said that Faustus, who of all the liberal arts had only a smattering of grammar, had read some books of Seneca. Augustine had an education far superior to that of Faustus, and it is impossible to believe that he had not read Seneca.
15. H. Diels, *Doxographi graeci*, ed. Reimer (Berlin, 1879) 174.
16. *Conf.* V, 3, 6.
17. *Ibid.* V, 5, 8.
18. *Ibid.* V, 6, 10; *De util. cred.* 8, 20.
19. *Conf.* V, 11, 21.
20. *De act. cum Fel. man.* 2, 14-20.

21. *Conf.* VII, 2, 3.
22. *Ibid.* V, 14, 25.
23. *Ibid.* V, 10, 19.
24. *Ibid.* V, 10, 20.
25. *Ibid.* IV, 14, 21-23.
26. *Ibid.* V, 7, 13.
27. *Ibid.* V, 8, 14.
28. *Ibid.* IV, 14, 23.
29. *Ibid.* V, 8, 15.
30. *Ep.* 258, 5.
31. *Ep.* 138, 17; *De civ. Dei* II, 29.
32. *Conf.* V, 9, 16.
33. *Ibid.* V, 12, 22.
34. *Ibid.* V, 10, 19; *De mor. Eccl. cath. et de mor. Man.* II, 19-69.
35. *Codex Theodosianus* XVI, 5, 3 and 9 (ed. Mommsen 857-59).
36. *Conf.* V, 10, 18.
37. *C. Faust.* V, 5.
38. *De mor. Eccl. cath.* II, 20, 74.
39. *Ibid.* II, 19, 68.

Notes for Chapter 10

1. *Conf.* V, 10, 19.
2. *Ibid.* V, 13, 23.
3. *Ibid.* V, 14, 24.
4. See above, ch. 9, p. 62.
5. *Conf.* V, 14, 25.
6. *Ibid.* VI, 16, 26.
7. *C. Acad.* III, 17, 28.
8. *Conf.* VII, 1, 2.
9. *C. Acad.* III, 19, 37.
10. *Ibid.* III, 19, 42.
11. *De beata vita* 4.
12. *Conf.* V, 10, 19.
13. *C. Acad.* II, 5, 11.
14. *Ibid.* III, 17, 37—18, 41; *Ep.* 1; 118, 5, 33.
15. *Conf.* V, 14, 24.
16. *Ibid.* VI, 1, 1.
17. *Ibid.* VI, 2, 2.
18. *Ibid.* VI, 1, 1.
19. *Ibid.*

Notes for Chapter 11

1. *Conf.* IV, 14, 21.
2. Symmachus, *Relationes* 3, 10.
3. *Ep.* 18.
4. *Conf.* V, 13, 23.
5. *Ibid.* VI, 11, 19. That is how the passage is understood by P. de Labriolle, *Confessions* I (Paris, 1961⁸), 137. Courcelle, *Recherches*, 83, understands the governorship of a province..
6. Courcelle, *Recherches*, 78f.
7. O. Perler, *Les voyages de saint Augustin* (Paris, 1969) 136.
8. *C. litt. Petil.* III, 25, 30.
9. On Marcella and her world see Bianca M. Margarucci Italiani, *L'Aventino. Le sue dee, le sue donne e le sue sante* (Rome, 1965) 41-65.
10. *Conf.* V, 13, 23.
11. *Ibid.* VI, 3, 3.
12. *Ibid.* V, 13, 23.
13. *Solil.* II, 14, 26.
14. See O. Faller, *Enc. Catt.* 1:985; J.-R. Palanque, *Saint Ambroise* (Paris 1933); A. Paredi, *Saint Ambrose: His Life and Times,* trans. M. J. Costelloe (Notre Dame, 1964)..
15. Especially Basil and Didymus.
16. Courcelle *(Recherches* 93-138) has shown the presence of Neoplatonism in the sermons of Ambrose.
17. See the *De officiis ministrorum,* which depends on the *De officiis* of Cicero.
18. *Conf.* VIII, 1, 1.
19. *Ibid.* VIII, 2, 3.
20. *Ibid.* VIII, 2, 3—4, 9.
21. *Ibid.* VIII, 2, 3.
22. Courcelle, *Les lettres grecques en Occident de Macrobe à Cassiodore* (Paris, 1948) 119-29, has shown the existence of this group.
23. *De beata vita* 1, 1-5.
24. *De ord.* I, 1-4; *Ep.* 2.
25. *Ep.* 1.
26. Courcelle, *Les lettres grecques* 126-28.
27. Ambrose, *De virginibus* I, 10, 57.
28. *Conf.* VIII, 6, 15.
29. *Ibid.* VIII, 1, 2.
30. Ambrose, *Ep.* 20, 10; O Faller, *Enc. Catt.* 1:991.
31. *Conf.* IX, 7, 15; see *EP.* 44, 4 and 7.
32. *Ibid.* IX, 7, 16.

33. *Ibid.* Augustine often mentions this incident. See *Serm.* 268, 5, 4; *De civ. Dei* XXII, 8, 2; *De cur. ger. pro mort.* 17, 21. See Courcelle, *Recherches* 139-55. Ambrose tells the story of the finding of the relics at greater length (*Ep.* 22, 17); he gives the name of the blind man and tells us he had been a butcher before going blind.

34. *De beata vita* 1, 1.

Notes for Chapter 12

1. *Conf.* VIII, 2, 3.
2. *Ibid.* V, 13, 23.
3. *Ep.* 36, 14, 32; 54, 2, 3.
4. *Conf.* VI, 2, 2.
5. *Ibid.* VI, 3, 3.
6. *Ibid.* IX, 5, 13.
7. *De util. cred.* 8, 20.
8. *Conf.* VI, 3, 4.
9. See above, ch. 11, p. 75.
10. *Conf.* V, 14, 24.
11. *Ibid.;* see *De util. cred.* 8, 20.
12. *De beata vita* 4.
13. See Ambrose, *Exaemeron* VI, 7, 40—8, 46.
14. *Conf.* VI, 3, 4.
15. Ambrose emphasized this truth in his lost work *De philosophia;* see Augustine, *C. Jul.* II, 7.
16. *Conf.* VII, 3, 5.
17. *Ibid.* VI, 3, 4.
18. *Ibid.* VI, 4, 6.
19. *Ibid.* V, 14, 24.
20. *Ibid.* VI, 4, 6.
21. *Ibid.* V, 14, 25.
22. *De util. cred.* 8, 20.

Notes for Chapter 13

1. *De util. cred.* 8, 20.
2. See above, ch. 6, p. 46.
3. *Conf.* VI, 5, 7.
4. *Ibid.* .
5. *C. Acad.* III, 20, 43.
6. *De ord.* II, 9, 26.
7. *De mor. Eccl. cath.* I, 2, 3 and 7, 11.
8. *De util. cred.* 1, 2.

9. *Conf.* VI, 4, 6.
10. *Ep.* 118, 32.
11. *Serm.* 51, 5, 6.
12. *Conf.* 102, 38; *De cons. evang.* I, 35, 53.
13. *De mor. Eccl. cath.* I, 2, 3 and 7, 11.
14. *Conf.* VI, 5, 7.
15. See above, ch. 2, p. 27.
16. *Conf.* VI, 5, 8.
17. See above, ch. 12, p. 82.
18. See *Ep.* 137, 5, 18.
19. *Conf.* VI, 5, 8.
20. See my introduction to: St. Augustine, *La Trinità* (NBA 4; Rome: Editrice Città Nuova, 1973), 11-13.
21. *Conf.* VI, 5, 8.
22. *Ibid.* VII, 7, 11.
23. *Ibid.* VI, 11, 19.
24. See Augustine's reflections on this point in *Ep.* 118, 5, 33.
25. See above, ch. 2, pp. 27-29.
26. See *util, cred.* 14, 32—17, 35; *C. ep. Man.* 4, 5.
27. *C. ep. Man.* 5, 6.
28. See my introduction to: St. Augustine, *Le Confessioni* (NBA 1; Rome: Editrice Città Nuova, 1975³), 25-40.
29. *De beata vita* 4.
30. *Conf.* VII, 5, 7.
31. See above, ch. 12, p. 82.
32. *Conf.* VII, 1, 1.
33. See above, ch. 8, pp. 58-59.
34. See above, ch. 12, p. 83.
35. *Conf.* VII, 19, 25.
36. *De her.* 44.
37. *Ibid.* 55.
38. *Conf.* VII, 19, 25.
39. See my Introduction in *Le Confessioni,* ibid.
40. *Conf.* VII, 7, 11.

Notes for Chapter 14

1. *Conf.* IV, 3, 4-6.
2. *Ibid.* VII, 6, 8-10.
3. *Ibid.* VII, 7, 11.
4. *Ibid.* VII, 9, 13.

5. *Ibid.* VII, 10, 16.

6. Courcelle, *Lettres grecques en Occident* 126-28, and *Recherches* 153-56, identifies the individual with Manlius Theodore, but this seems rather improbable.

7. P. Henry, *Plotin et l'Occident* (Louvain, 1934), 20, opts for the *Enneads* of Plotinus, and especially the treatise *On Beauty* (I, 6); W. Theiler, *Porphyrios und Augustin* (Halle, 1933), 1-74, for Porphyry alone; Courcelles, *Lettres grecques en Occident*, 159-76, and *Recherches*, 157, and J. J. O'Meara, *The Young Augustine* (London, 1954), 149, for both. O'Meara focuses in particular on Porphyry's *Return of the Soul*, which he identifies with the *Philosophy from Oracles*; see O'Meara, *Porphyry's Philosophy from Oracles in Augustine* (Paris, 1959). J. Hadot, "Citations de Porphyre," *REA* 6 (1960) 244, makes Plotinus, not Porphyry, the main philosopher read by Augustine.

8. It is commonly held, and for sound reasons, that he had read Plotinus' treatises *Beauty* (*Enneads* I, 6), *Three Hypostases* (I, 8), and *The Origin of the Soul* (V, 1), as well as the above-mentioned *Return of the Soul* of Porphyry. See A. Solignac, *Les Confessions* (Bibliothèque Augustinienne 13), 682-89.

9. See my introduction to *Le Confessioni*, 35-38.

10. *C. Acad.* III, 18, 41.

11. *Ep.* 118, 5, 33.

12. *De civ. Dei* IX, 10 = *Enneads* IV, 3, 12); IX, 17 (= I, 6, 8; I, 2, 3); X, 14 (= III, 2, 13); X, 16 (= I, 6, 7); X, 23 (= V, 1, 6); X, 30 (= III, 4, 2); XI, 9 (= III, 2, 5); etc.

13. Possidius, *Vita* 28, 11, ed. and trans. M. Pellegrino (Milan: Ed. Paoline, 1955), 155.

14. *Ep.* 118, 5, 33.

15. *De civ. Dei* X.

16. Plotinus, *Enneads* VI, 9, 7.

17. *Ibid.* I, 6.

18. *Conf.* VII, 17, 23.

19. See above, ch. 8, p. 58.

20. *Conf.* VII, 10, 16.

21. *Ibid.* VII, 11, 17.

22. *De civ. Dei* VIII, 9.

23. *Conf.* VII, 12, 18.

24. Plato supposedly met Jeremiah on a Journey to Egypt. This is Ambrose's explanation in his book *Philosophy*; Augustine first accepted it but later rejected it: *De doct. christ.* II, 28, 43; *De civ. Dei* VIII, 11; *Retract.* II, 4, 2.

25. *Ep.* 31, 8; see *C. Jul.* II, 7, 19.

26. P. Alfaric, *L'évolution intellectuelle de St. Augustin* (Paris, 1918), 385.

27. *De civ. Dei* X, 29.

28. *Conf.* VII, 9, 13.

29. *Ibid.* VII, 9, 14.
30. *Enneads* II, 9.
31. J. Lebreton, "The Pagan Opposition," in J. Lebreton and J. Zeiller, *The History of the Primitive Church*, trans. E. C. Messenger (New York: MacMillan, 1949), 2:875-89.
32. *De civ. Dei* X, passim.
33. *Conf.* VII, 9, 15.
34. Following Plato, Plotinus accepted the transmigration of souls even into the bodies of animals *(Enneads* III, 4, 2); Porphyry accepted it only between human bodies. See *De civ. Dei* X, 30.
35. *De civ. Dei* X, 29 and passim; *Retract.* I, 4, 3.
36. *De Gen. ad litt.* VII, 27, 28; XII, 35, 68.
37. *De doct. christ.* II, 40, 60—42, 63.
38. *Conf.* VII, 9, 15.

Notes for Chapter 15

1. *De natura deorum* III, 36.
2. *Ep.* I, 18, 112.
3. Porphyry, *Vita Plotini* 2.
4. *C. Acad.* II, 2, 5-6.
5. See above. ch. 5, p. 41.
6. Porphyry, *Vita Plotini* 23.
7. *Conf.* VII, 17, 23.
8. C. Boyer, *Christianisme et néoplatonisme dans la formation de saint Augustin* (Paris, 1920), 111.
9. *Conf.* VII, 20, 26.
10. *Ibid.* VII, 18, 24.
11. *Ibid.* VII, 21, 27.
12. See above, ch. 6, p. 47.
13. See above, ch. 6, pp. 47-48.
14. See above, ch. 13, p. 91.
15. *Conf.* VII, 18, 24.
16. *Ibid.* VII, 21, 27.
17. *Ibid.* VII, 18, 24; see VII, 20, 26.
18. *De civ. Dei* X, 29, 2.
19. *Enarr. in ps.* 31, 6.

Notes for Chapter 16

1. *Conf.* III, 4, 7-8; VI, 11, 18; VIII, 7, 17; see above, ch. 5, p. 45.
2. *Ibid.* III, 5, 9; see above, ch. 6, p. 47.
3. See above, ch. 7, pp. 50-51.

4. See above, ch. 15, p. 99.
5. *Conf.* VIII 5, 11.
6. *Ibid.* IX, 3, 5-6.
7. *Ibid.* VI, 6, 9.
8. *Solil.* I, 10, 17.
9. *Conf.* VIII, 5, 10.
10. *Ibid.* VI, 12, 21.
11. *Ibid.* VI, 14, 21.
12. *Ibid.* VI, 13, 23.
13. *Solil.* I, 10, 17.
14. *Conf.* VI, 15, 25. On Adeodatus see *Ibid.* IX, 6, 14, and *De beata vita* 6, 12.
15. *Solil.* I, 10, 17.
16. *Conf.* VIII, 1, 2.
17. *Ibid.* VIII, 7, 17.
18. *Ibid.* VIII, 5, 12.
19. *Ibid.* VIII, 6, 15.
20. *Ibid.* VIII, 8, 19 and 12, 28.
21. *Ibid.* VIII, 12, 29.
22. *Ibid.* VIII, 12, 30; see my Introduction to *Le Confessioni*, 59-60.

Notes for Chapter 17

1. *De beata vita* 5. In *Retract.* I, 2, he qualifies the praise contained in the last sentence.
2. *De ord.* II, 20, 52.
3. *Conf.* IX, 10, 26.
4. *C. Acad.* III, 20, 43.
5. *Solil.* I, 6, 12.
6. *Ep.* 1, 1 (written to Hermogenianus, probably from Cassiciacum; end of 386).
7. On the identification of Cassiciacum see F. Meda, "La controversia sul Rus Cassiciacum," in *Misc. Agost.* II, 49-59; O. Perler, *Les voyages de saint Augustin* (Paris, 1969) 179-96.
8. See my introduction to *Le Confessioni*, 35.
9. *C. Acad.* III, 11, 26.
10. *Ibid.* III, 17, 37—19, 41.
11. *Retract.* I, 2.
12. *Ibid.* I, 3, 1.
13. *Solil.* II, 13, 24.
14. *De ord.* I, 8, 25.
15. *Ep.* 3, 4.
16. *De ord.* I, 3, 6.

17. *Ibid.* I, 8, 22.
18. *C. Acad.* II, 6, 14.
19. *Ibid.* III, 4, 7.
20. *De ord.* I, 10, 29.
21. *Solil.* I, 14, 26.
22. *Ibid.* I, 1, 3 and 5.
23. *Conf.* IX, 4, 7 and 12.
24. *Conf.* IX, 6, 14.
25. *De mor. Eccl. cath.* I, 33, 70.
26. *Retract.* I, 6.
27. *Ibid.*
28. *De mus.* VI, 1, 1.
29. This is the term Augustine uses in referring to the renunciation of marriage and the consecration to complete chastity.
30. *Conf.* IX, 8, 17.
31. *Ep.* 10, 1.
32. Possidius, *Vita* 2, 1 (Pellegrino 48).
33. On September 8, Maximus the usurper was at Milan; we must suppose that Augustine had already departed. See Perler 145.
34. *Conf.* IX, 8, 17.
35. See *C. litt. Petil.* III, 25, 30.
36 Appealing to Augustinian sources, Perler, 197-203, opts for July 28.
37. *Conf.* IX, 11, 28: "In the fifty-sixth year of her life and the thirty-third of mine, her religious and devout soul was released from the body."
38. *De mor. Eccl. cath.* I, 33, 70.
39. *De quant. animae* 33, 73-76.
40. *Retract.* I, 9, 1.
41. *Ibid.* I, 7, 1.
42. *De mor. Eccl. cath.* I, 1, 1; II, 12, 26.
43. *Serm.* 81, 9.
44. A fragment of this marble slab with part of the epitaph was discovered in 1945 by A. Casamassa, who gave an account of it to the Roman Academy of Archeology; see the *Atti,* sec. III, *Rendiconti* 27 (1952-54) 271-73, and idem *Scritti patristici* I (Rome: Lateran University, 1955), 217-18.
45. *De civ. Dei* XXII, 8, 3, where Augustine says of himself and Alypius that they were "not yet clerics but already servants of God."
46. Possidius, *Vita* 3, 1-2 (Pellegrino 49).
47. *Ep.* 10, 2.
48. *De vera rel.* 8, 12; *C. Acad.* II, 3, 8; *Ep,* 15, 1.
49. *Retract* I, 13, 1.
50. *De vera rel.* 55, 107-10.

52. Possidius, *Vita* 5, 1 (Pellegrino 52).
53. *Ep.* 5 (among the letters of Augustine).

Notes for Chapter 18

1. *Serm.* 355, 2.
2. Possidius, *Vita* 4, 2.
3. *Ep.* 24, 4 (among the letters of Augustine).
4. St. Jerome, *Ep.* 51, 1, and 60, 10.
5. Possidius, *Vita* 15, 7.
6. The details can be pieced together from *Ep.* 126, which provides a very interesting insight into the not always peaceful ecclesial life of the Hippo community. For the pressure exercised by the faithful in the episcopal consecration of some great Fathers of the Church see my little book, *Il sacerdote uomo di Dio e servo della Chiesa* (Milan, 1968).
7. *Ep.* 21, 1.
8. *Ep.* 21, 3.
9. Possidius, *Vita* 5, 2.
10. *Ep.* 21, 4.
11. *Ep.* 10, 2.
12. For Augustine's dependence on the Neoplatonists on this point see G. Folliet, *"Deificari in otio. Augustin, Ep.* 10, 2," in *Rech. Aug.* II, 225-36.
13. *Ep.* 6, 1 (among the letters of Augustine).
14. *De op. mon.* 29, 37; *Conf.* X, 43, 70.
15. *Ep.* 48, 2.
16. *De civ. Dei* XIX, 19.

Notes for Chapter 19

1. *Serm.* 355, 2.
2. See L. Verheijen, *La Règle de saint Augustin* (2 vols.; Paris, 1963); St. Augustine, *La Regola,* introd. by A. Trapè (Milan, 1971).
3. Possidius, *Vita* 5, 1 (Pellegrino 53).
4. See A. Manrique, *La vida monastica en San Agustín* (El Escorial, 1969), 89-152.
5. *Conf.* IX, 6, 14.
6. *Ep.* 24, 6 (among the letters of Augustine).
7. See Manrique, *ibid.,* and U. Moricca, "Spunti polemici di S. Agostino e falsi interpreti del suo ideale monastico," in *Misc. Agost.* II, 931-75.
8. Possidius, *Vita* 11, 2-5 (Pellegrino 73-75).
9. *Serm* 355, 2.
10. See the two well-known sermons, 355 and 356, which had a major influence on the formation of the clergy in the Middle Ages.

1. Possidius, *Vita* 22, 1—27, 5 (Pellegrino 118-41).
2. *Serm.* 356, 13.
3. Possidius, *Vita* 22, 2 (Pellegrino 121).
4. *Ibid.*, 22, 7 (123).
5. *Ibid.*, 23, 1 (125).
6. *Serm.* 113, 1.

Notes for Chapter 20

1. *De util. cred.* 6, 13.
2. See my introduction to *La Trinità*, XI-XIV; *C. Jul.* I-II.
3.. *De fide et symb.* 9, 18-19.
4. See my introduction to *La Trinità*, XLI.
5. *De serm. Dom. in monte* I, 1, 1.
6. *Retract,* I, 19, 8.
7. *Ibid.* I, 18.
8. *Ibid.* I, 23.
9. *Ibid.* I, 24.
10. *Ibid.* I, 25.
11. *Ibid.* I, 26.
12. *De div. qq. 83,* qq. 68-68.
13. *De div, qq. ad Simplic.* Praef.
14. *Retract.* II, 1, 1.
15. *De praed. sanct.,* 3, 7—4, 8.
16. *C. Jul.* VI, 12, 39.
17. *Retract.,* II, 1, 1.
18. *Ibid.* I, 23, 1.
19. *Ibid.* II, 1, 1.
20. For Jerome see *Ep.* 28.
21. *De doct. christ.* III, 30, 42—37, 56. On this subject see A. Casamassa, *Il pensiero di Sant'Agostino nel 396-397* (Rome, 1919); A. Pincherle, *La formazione teologica de S. Agostino* (Rome: Edizioni Italiane, n.d.).
22. *De Trin.* I, 4, 7.
23. *C. Jul.* II, 10, 33.
24. *Retract.* II, 4, 1.
25. *De doct. christ.* II, 40, 60.
26. *Ibid.* III, 30, 43.

Notes for Chapter 21

1. Possidius, *Vita* 8, 3 (Pellegrino 65).
2. *Ep.* 213, 2-3.
3. *Ep.* 31, 4; 213, 4.

4. *C. Cresc.* III, 80, 92; IV, 64, 79; *C. litt. Petil.* III, 16, 19.

5. See A. Casamassa, in *Enc. Ital* 2:915; *Studi patristici* 2 (Rome: Lateran University, 1956), 285-86.

6. *Retract.* II, 1; *De praed. sanct.* 4, 8; *De dono persev.* 20, 52.

7. O. Perler, *Les voyages de Saint Augustin* (Paris, 1969), 164-78.

8. *De op. mon.* 29, 37.

9. *Ep.* 217.

10. *De civ. Dei* XIX, 19.

11. *Ep.* 134, 1.

12. *Ep.* 124, 2.

13. *Ep.* 122, 1.

14. *Serm. Guelferb.* 22, in *Misc. Agost.* I, 563-73.

15. *Serm.* 340, 1.

16. Possidius, *Vita* 19, 2-5 (Pellegrino 113).

17. *Ep.* 48, 1.

18. *In Jo. ev. tr.* 123, 5.

19. *Serm.* 137, 4.

20. *Serm.* 78, 6.

21. *De civ. Dei* XIX, 19.

22. *Serm.* 340, 1.

23. *Serm. Cas.* 1, 133, in *Misc. Agost.* I, 404.

Notes for Chapter 22

1. Possidius, *Vita* 31, 4 (Pellegrino 191). On this point see F. Van der Meer, *Augustine the Bishop,* trans. B. Battershaw and G. R. Lamb (New York: Sheed & Ward, 1961), 412-52; F. Pontet, *L'éxegèse de saint Augustin, prédicateur* (Paris: Aubier, 1944).

2. *Retract.* Praef. 2.

3. See above, ch. 3, p. 30.

4. *Serm* 339, 4, in *Misc. Agost.* I, 193.

5. *De cat. rud.* 2, 3.

6. *De doct. christ.* IV, 4, 6.

7. *Ibid.* IV, 5, 7.

8. *Serm.* 179, 1.

7. *Enarr. in ps.* 126, 3.

10. *Serm.* 339, 4, in *Misc. Agost.* 1, 193.

11. See my introduction to *La Trinità,* LXVI.

12. *Conf.* IX, 4, 8-11.

13. *In Jo. ev. tr.* 1, 8-17; 29, 3-5; 38, 8-10.

14. *De doct. christ.* IV, 15, 32.

15. *Enarr, in ps.* 138, 1.

16. *Serm.* 352, 1.
17. *Enarr. in ps.* 36, serm. 3, 6; 50, 19; 123, 8; *In Jo. ev. tr. 2, 14. [The active form fenerat,* "lend," *instead of the deponent form feneratur, because the former was in the Latin text of the Bible that Augustine was using. Ossum,* "bone," *as the singular of ossa, because os, the classical form, could mean either* "mouth" *or* "bone." *Sanguinibus* (plural of "blood") *instead of sanguine* (singular) *in Jn 1:13, because the Latin text of the New Testament has it* (representing the plural form in the Greek text).— Tr.].
18. *Serm.* 311, 4.
19. *Serm.* 339, 1, in *Misc. Agost.* I, 190.
20. *Serm.* 52.
21. *Serm.* 339, 1, in *Misc. Agost.* I, 190; see *Conf.* X, 37, 60-62.
22. *Ep.* 29.
23. *De doct. christ.* IV, 24, 54.
24. *Serm.* 17, 3.
26. Possidium, *Vita* 31, 8-11 (Pellegrino 193-97).

Notes for Chapter 23

1. *Conf.* IX, 4, 8.
2. See above, ch. 17, p. 117.
3. See above, ch. 17, p. 119.
4. *Retract,* I, 15, 1.
5. *Ibid.* I, 16, 1.
6. Possidius, *Vita* 6, 1-8 (Pellegrino 57-59).
7. *Retract.* I, 22, 1.
8. *Ibid.* II, 2.
9. *C. Faust,* I, 1, 1.
10. *Conf.* V, 13, 23.
11. *C. Faust.* I, 1, 1; *Retract,* II, 7, 1.
12. *Retract.* II, 9.
13. *Ibid.* II, 10.
14. *C. Secund.* 11.
15. *Ep.* 79, which must have been addressed to Felix.
16. For this date see my introduction to *Le Confessioni,* 23.
17. *C. Fel. man.* 2, 22; Possidius, *Vita* 16, 4 (Pellegrino 95-97).
18. See above, ch. 17, p. 117.
19. See above, ch. 13, pp. 85-86.
20. See *Serm.* 43, 4; *In Jo. ev. tr.* 26, 9; *De lib. arb.* II, 2, 6.
21. *Serm.* 43, 9.
22. *De vera rel.* 24, 45.
23. *De praed. sanct.* 2, 5.

24. *Ep.* 120, 2, 8.
25. *De lib. arb.* III, 21, 60.
26. *De util. cred.* 13, 29.
27. *De Trin.* XIV, 1, 3.
28. *Ep.* 118, 5, 32.
29. *Ibid.*
30. *C. ep. Man,* 4, 5; see above, ch. 13, p. 88.
31. See above, ch. 17, p. 117.
32. *C. Faust.* XI, 2.
33. *Ibid.* XXXIII, 9.
34. *Retract.* I, 4, 4; I, 8, 2; *De Trin.* XII, 15, 24.
35. *De beata vita* 7; *Solil.* II, 1, 1.
36. *De Trin.* X, 10, 14.
37. *De civ. Dei* XI, 26.
38. *De vera rel.* 39, 72.
39. *In ep. Jo. tr.* 8, 6.
40. *Serm.* 6, 4.
41. *Enarr. in ps.* 101, serm. 2, 10.
42. *De mor. Eccl. cath.* II, 1. 1.
43. *De civ. Dei* XII, 2.
44. *De Gen. ad litt. I ,* 14, 28.
45. *De vera rel.* 18, 35.
46. *C. Fel. man.* II, 18.
47. *De vera rel.* 18, 35.
48. See above, ch. 14, pp. 95-96.
49. *C. Jul.* I, 8, 36-37.
50. See above, ch. 16, pp. 105-106.
51. *Conf.* VIII, 10, 22.
52. *Enarr. in ps.* 31, serm. 2, 16.
53. *Serm.* 50, 7.
54. *De civ. Dei* XII, 8.
55. *Ibid.* XII, 7.
56. See above, ch. 8, p. 59.
57. *Conf.* VII, 3, 5.
58. *Ibid.*
59. *C. Fortun. man.* 25 and 37.
60. *Retract.* I, 9, 1.
61. *Op. imp. c. Jul.* 1, 39.
62. See Vatican Council II, Pastoral Constitution *Gaudium et spes* on the Church in the Modern World, 13.

63. *De civ. Dei* XXII, 24.
64. Vatican II, *Gaudium et spes*, 12-22.

Notes for Chapter 24

1. B. Häring, *Marriage in the Modern World*, trans. G. Stevens (Westminster, Md.: Newman, 1966); *idem*, in G. Grasso, B. Häring, and L. Picco, *Dove va la famiglia* (Rome, 1966).
2. *De bono conjug.* 1, 1.
3. *De Gen. c. Man.* I, 19, 30; see *Retract.* I, 10, 2.
4. *De bono conjug.* 2, 2.
5. *De Gen. ad litt.* IX, 5, 3—11, 19 (the ninth book of this work was written a little after *De bono conjugali* and therefore a little after 401; see *ibid.* IX, 7, 12).
6. *De civ. Dei* XIV, 22.
7. *De nupt. et concup.* II, 31, 53.
8. Eph 4:13; Matt 22:30 (Jerome held this opinion, appealing to Origen for support).
9. *De vic. Dei* XXII, 17.
10. *De sancta virg.* 12, 12.
11. *Retract.* II, 22.
12. *De sancta virg.* 18, 18.
13. *Serm.* 9, 11-12; 132, 2.
14. *De conjug. adult.* II, 8, 7.
15. *Serm.* 153, 6; 392, 2; *De conjug. adult.* II, 8, 7; see *Serm.* 355, 5.
16. *De more. Eccl. cath.* II, 10, 19—18, 65; *C. Secund.* 21-22; *De her.* 46.
17. *De bono conjug*, 1, 1.
18. *Ibid.* 3, 3.
19. *C. Jul.* V, 3, 8; V, 5, 22; *Op. imp. c. Jul.* 4, 41; 4, 58; 4, 69.
20. *Op. imp. c. Jul.* 4, 29; 4, 69.
21. *De nupt. et concup.* I, 7, 8.
22.. *Ibid.* I, 1, 1.
23. *Ibid.* I, 1, 1; II, 8, 20; II, 35, 58; *De civ. Dei* XIV, 23-24, 2.
24. *De civ. Dei* XIV, 26, 1.
25. *De Trin.* XII, 7, 12.
26. *De civ. Dei* XIII, 16, 1.
27. See above, ch. 5, pp. 42-43.
28. *C. Jul.* IV, 14, 72.
29. *De nupt. et concup.* I, 14, 16.
30. *De bono conjug.* 6, 6.
31. See my Introduction in St. Augustine, *Matrimonio e verginità* (Rome: Editrice Città Nuova) IX-CIV.

Notes for Chapter 25

1. The basic work on the subject is P. Monceaux, *Histoire littéraire de l'Afrique chrétiènne*, vols. 4-7 (Paris, 1912-23).

2. See Y. Congar, "Instruction générale" to Saint Augustin, *Traités antidonatistes* (Bibliothèque augustinienne 28; Paris: Desclée De Brouwer, 1963), 7-133.

3. Possidius, *Vita* 7, 3 (Pellegrino 61).

4. *Retract.* I, 20.

5. *Ep.* 23.

6. *Retract.* II, 19.

7. *Ep.* 33.

8. *Ep.* 51.

9. *Ep.* 49.

10. *Serm.* 358.

11. *Ep.* 128.

12. See *Brev. coll. cum Don.*

13. *Retract.* II, 39.

14. *Ibid.* II, 40.

15. *Ibid.* II, 46.

16. *Ep.* 185; *Retract.* II, 48.

17. *Retract.* II, 59.

18. *Histoire littéraire* 4:76.

19. *C. Cresc.* I, 28, 33.

20. See above, p. 184.

21. *Ep.* 23, 2.

22. *De bapt.* IV, 17, 24; VI, 1, 1.

23. *C. Cresc.* IV, 16, 19.

24. *In Jo. ev. tr.* 6, 7. The whole of this and the preceding sermon should be read.

25. *In ep. Jo. tr.* 7, 11; *In Jo. ev. tr* 6, 15-16.

26. *Enarr, in ps.* 25, serm. 2, 5.

27. See below, ch. 30, pp. 240ff.

28. *C. litt. Petil.* III, 9, 10.

29. *Ep.* 105, 16.

30. *In Jo. ev. tr.* 119, 4.

31. *Serm.* 295, 2.

32. *Serm.* 46, 13, 30.

33. *C, litt. Petil.* III, 9, 10.

34. *De bapt.* III, 16, 21.

35. *Serm.* 267, 4.

36. *Ep.* 185, 11, 50.

37. *In Jo. ev. tr.* 26, 13.
38. *Ibid.* 32, 8.
39. *Ibid.* 6.
40. *Psalm. c. part. Don.* lines 272-73, 287-91.
41. P. Batiffol, *Le catholicisme de St. Augustin* (Paris, 1920, 1929⁴).
42. *De bapt.* IV, 17, 24.
43. *Serm. ad Caes. eccl. plebem* 6.
44. *Ep.* 43, 1.
45. *De bapt.* IV, 16, 23.
46. See *De bapt.* V, 26, 38. There is an extensive bibliography on this difficult question. See S. J. Grabowski, *The Church. An Introduction to the Theology of St. Augustine* (St. Louis: B. Herder, 1957).
47. See above, ch. 12, pp. 83-84.
48. E.g., *Ep.* 93, 6, 20—9, 28; 129, 2-3.
49. *Enarr. in ps.* 86, 2.
50. *Ep.* 53, 2-3.
51. *Enarr. in ps.* 88, serm. 2, 14.

Notes for Chapter 26

1. *De gest. Pel.* 11, 23.
2. *Retract.* II, 33.
3. *Serm.* 294, 21, 20.
4. *Retract.* II, 37.
5. *Ibid.* II, 42.
6. *Ibid.* II, 47.
7. *Ep.* 182 (among the letters of Augustine).
8. *Serm.* 131, 10.
9. *C. duas ep. Pel.* II, 3, 5; see A. Trapè, "La *Sedes Petri* in San Agostino," in *Miscellanea A. Piolanti* (Rome, 1964) 2:1-20.
10. *De grat. Christi et de pecc. orig.* II, 8, 9.
11. *Retract.* II, 50.
12. *Ibid.* II, 61.
13. *Ibid.* II, 53.
14. *Ibid.* II, 62.
15. See *Ep.* 224, 2.
16. *Ep.* 194.
17. *Ep.* 214; 215; see 215A.
18. *Retract.* II, 66.
19. *Ibid.* II, 67.
20. *Ep.* 225-26 (among the letters of Augustine).
21. *De dono persev.* 6, 12.

22. *Ep.* 177, 6.
23. *De nat. et grat.* 1, 1.
24. Horace, *Sermones* I, 2, 25.
25. The words that follow are: "but is earthly, unspiritual, and devilish."
26. *De nat. et grat.* 6, 7.
27. *C. duas ep. Pel.* III, 8, 24.
28. *Ibid.* IV, 4, 4.
29. *Ibid.* II, 1—2, 4; *De nupt. et concup.* II, 3, 9; *Op. imp. c. Jul.* 5, 25; etc.
30. *De nupt. et concup.* II, 23, 38.
31. *De pecc. mer. et remiss.* I, 26, 39.
32. *De nat. et grat.* 9. 10.
33. *Enarr. in ps.* 68, serm. 2, 11.
34. See my article, "A proposito di predestinazione: S. Agostino e i suoi critici moderni," *Divinitas* 2 (1963) 243-84.
35. *De Trin.* IV, 13, 16—14, 19.
36. *Op. imp. c. Jul.* II, 146. 190. 192.
37. *De pecc. mer. et remiss.* II, 7, 3.
38. See my article, "S. Agostino e le correnti teologiche eterodosse," in *S. Agostino e le grandi correnti della filosofia contemporanea* (Tolentino, 1954) 221-60.
39. *C. duas ep. Pel.* IV, 5, 11.
40. *De spir. et litt.* 3, 5.
41. *Ibid.* 30, 52.
42. *de corrept. et grat.* 12, 33.
43. *In Jo. ev. tr.* 41, 9. 10. 13.
44. *De pecc. mer. et remiss.* II, 18, 28; *De grat. Christi* 47, 52; *De grat. et lib. arb.* 1, 1; *Ep. 212,* 2; *214,* 2.
45. *Serm.* 169, 11, 13.
46. *Ep.* 157, 2, 10.
47. *Conf.* IV, 9, 14; *De nat. et grat.* 26, 29; *De corrept. et grat.* 11, 31; 13, 42; *Op. imp. c. Jul.* 3, 116.
48. *De dono persev.* 6, 12.
49. See my article, "A proposito di predestinazione" (n. 34), 146 and 183.
50. *C. Jul.* III, 18, 35.
51. *De civ. Dei* XII, 28, 2.
52. *Serm.* 27, 7.
53. For these interpretations see my article, "Verso la riabilitazione del pelagianesimo?" *Augustinianum* 3 (1963) 482-516, and G. Bonner, *Augustine and Modern Research on Pelagianism* (The St. Augustine Lecture 1970; Villanova, 1972). On the new and radical interpretation of G. Greshake in his *Gnade als knokrete Freiheit. Eine Untersuchung zur Gnadenlehre des Pelagius* (Mainz, 1972), see A. Zumkeller in *Augusti-*

nian Studies 5 (1974) 209-26. On the interpretation given by Peter Brown in his Augustine of Hippo, A Biography (Berkeley and Los Angeles: University of California Press, 1967), see A. Trapè, "Un S. Agostino della storia?" Augustinianum 12 (1972) 342-49.

Notes for Chapter 27

1. C. ep. Man. 2-3.
2. See C. Fortun. 1; C. ep. Man. 3, 4.
3. De dono persev. 24, 68.
4. De bapt. II, 3, 4.
5. Enarr. in ps.32, 29.
6. Ibid. 36, serm. 3, 13.
7. Ep. 33, 1.
8. Ep. 128, 3 (among the letters of Augustine).
9. De gest. cum Emer.7.
10. See above, ch. 21, pp. 144-145.
11. Possidius, Vita 9, 4 (Pellegrino 69).
12. Ibid. 12, 1-2; Ench. 17.
13. Enarr. in ps 36, serm. 3, 10.
14. Retract. II, 62.
15. Op. imp. c. Jul. III, 70; III, 212; VI, 14; etc.
16. Ibid. IV, 56.
17. Ibid. I, 42.
18. Ibid. I, 88.
19. Ibid. II, 102; see II, 106; II, 197; etc.
20. Ibid. I, 68.
21. Ep. 140, 37, 83; De pecc. mer. et rem. II, 16, 25.
22. Ep. 188, 18.
23. De nat. et grat. 6, 6.
24. Retract. II, 23; De gest. cum Emer. 22, 46—23, 47.
25. De pecc. mer. et rem. III, 1, 1.
26. Ep. 146.
27. Ep. 101, 4.
28. C. Jul. III, 1, 1.
29. Ep. 224, 2.
30. See my article, "Un celebre testo di S. Agostino sull' 'ignoranza e la difficoltá,' " in Aug. Mag. II, 795-803.

Notes for Chapter 28

1. See Peter Brown, Augustine of Hippo. A Biography (Berkeley and Los Angeles: University of California Press, 1967), 234ff and 336ff, and my article, "Un Agostino della storia?" Augustinianum 12 (1972) 341-49.

2. *Enarr in ps.* 132, 6.
3. *Ep.* 111, 1.
4. *Ep.* 88, 8.
5. *Ep.* 105, 2, 4.
6. *Ep.* 23, 6-7.
7. *Ench.* 17; Possidius, *Vita* 12, 1, 3 (Pellegrino 77).
8. *Ep.* 105, 4; Possidius, *Vita* 12, 1, 3 (Pellegrino 79).
9. *Ep.* 185, 7, 26-27.
10. *Ep.* 185, 7, 26.
11. *Ep.* 93, 5, 17; 185, 7, 25.
12. *Ep.* 93, 5, 16.
13. *Ep.* 185, 8, 32; 93, 5, 18.
14. *Retract.* II, 5.
15. *Ep.* 93, 5, 16.
16. *Ep.* 185, 7, 29; see *Ep.* 83, 1, 2.
17. *Ep.* 185, 6, 21-24.
18. *Ep.* 93, 1, 3; 100, 2.
19. *Serm.* 296, in *Misc Agost.* I, 412.
20. *Ad Don. post coll.* 35, 58.
21. *Ep.* 133, 2.
22. *Ep.* 139, 2.
23. *Ep.* 134, 2-4.
24. *In Jo. ev. tr.* 6, 15.

Notes for Chapter 29

1. P. Courcelle, "Propos antichrétiens rapportés par St. Augustin," in *Rech. Aug.* I, 149-86.
2. *Retract.* II, 43, 1.
3. *Ibid.*
4. *Serm.* 296. in *Misc. Agost.* I, 449.
5. *De excid. urb. Rom.;* critical ed. by M. V. O'Reilly (Patristic Studies 89; Washington, D.C.: Catholic University of America, 1955).
6. *Serm.* 105, 12.
7. *De excid. urb. Rom* 6.
8. See above, ch. 17, p. 118.
9. *Ep.* 137; 138.
10. *Ep.* 136, 3 (among the letters of Augustine).
11. *De civ. Dei* I, 35-36.
12. *Ibid.* VI, 1; X, 32; XI, 1; XVIII, 1.
13. *Retract.* II, 43; *Ep.* 212A (NBA 33, 533-35); *Ep.* 184A, 5 (NBA 32, 937).
14. *De civ. Dei* I, Praef.

15. See above, ch. 1, pp. 20-21.
16. *De civ. Dei* V, 12, 1-6.
17. *Ibid.* V, 1.
18. *Ibid.* V, 11.
19. *Ep.* 138, 7.
20. *De civ. Dei* II, 29, 1-2.
21. *Ep.* 138, 15.
22. *De civ. Dei* IV, 4.
23. *Ibid.* VIII, 9.
24. *Ibid.* XII, 17, 1-2.
25. *Ibid.* X, 9.
26. *Ibid.* VIII, 5.
27. *Ibid.* IX, 15.
28. *Ibid.* X, 32, 2.

Notes for Chapter 30

1. See *De doct. christ.* I, where the teaching of the faith is summed up in terms of *uti* and *frui* ("use" and "enjoy"), and the *Enchiridion,* which uses faith, hope, and charity as synthesizing themes and gives an explanation of the Creed and Our Father.
2. *De vera rel.* 37, 50.
3. *De cat. rud.* 20, 31.
4. *De civ. Dei* XIV, 28.
5. *In Jo. ev. tr.* 123, 5.
6. *De Gen. ad litt.* XI, 15, 20.
7. *De lib. arb.* II, 19, 53; *Conf.* XII, 23, 35; De civ. Dei XII, 1, 2.
8. *De civ. dei* XIX, 13, 1.
9. See above, ch. 29, p. 237.
10. *De civ. Dei* XI, 21.
11. *Ibid.* XI, 24.
12. *Ibid.* XII, 8, 2.
13. *Ibid.* XII, 1, 2.
14. See above, ch. 7, p. 51, and ch. 12, pp. 82-83.
15. *De civ. Dei* XVIII, 51, 2.
16. *Ibid.* I, 8, 2.
17. *Ibid.* XIX, 20.
18. *C. Jul.* IV, 3, 14-32.
19. *Ep.* 138, 3, 17.
20. *De spir. et litt.* 28, 48.
21. *De civ. Dei* XIX, 25.
22. See above, ch. 29, p. 237.
23. *De civ. Dei* XIX, 24.

24. *Ibid.* II, 21, 4.
25. *Ibid.* XIX, 19 and 21-25; see II, 21, 4.
26. *Ibid.* XIX, 14.
27. *Ibid.* XIX, 15.
28. *Ibid.* XV, 4; see XIX, 12, 1.
29. *Ibid.* XIX, 13.
30. *Ibid.* XI, 24.
31. *Ibid.* XXII, 30, 5.
32. *Ibid.* XV, 1, 1.
33. See above, p. 241.
34. See above, ch. 24, p. 175.
35. *De civ. Dei* XII, 21.
36. *Ibid.* XIX, 14.
37. *Ibid.* XV, 4.
38. *Ibid.* XIX, 26.
39. See H. X. arquillière, *L'augustinisme politique. Essai sur la formation des théories politiques du moyen âge* (2d rev. and enl. ed.; Paris: Vrin, 1955).
40. For this topic in the first five books see above, ch. 29, pp. 232ff.

Notes for Chapter 31

1. *De civ. Dei* VI, 2.
2. See above, ch. 21, pp. 147-148.
3. *Ep.* 213, 5-6.
4. See above, ch. 3, p. 31.
5. On the travels of Augustine see the richly informative book of O. Perler, *Les voyages de saint Augustin* (Paris, 1969).
6. Possidius, *Vita* 18, 9 (Pellegrino 109).
7. PL 83:1109.
8. *Ep.* 110, 5.
9. *Conf.* XI, 2, 2.
10. *Ep.* 213, 6.
11. *C. Acad.* III, 4, 7; *Conf.* X, 31, 43-47; Possidius, *Vita* 22, 2 (Pellegrino 121).
12. *De ord.* I, 3, 6.
13. *Ep.* 224, 2.
14. Possidius, *Vita* 24, 11 (Pellegrino 129).
15. *De Trin.* I, 3, 5.
16. *Retract.* II, 13.
17. *Ibid.* II, 2.
18. *Ep.* 118, 5, 34.
19. *Retract.* I, 6.

20. *Ibid.* I, 5, 1.
21. *Ibid.* I, 26, 1; see above, ch. 17, p. 120, and ch. 20, p. 139.
22. *Retract,* I, 23, 1; see above, ch. 20, p. 139.
23. On the catalogue or *indiculus* of the library at Hippo see *Retract.* II, 41.

Notes for Chapter 32

1. Possidius, *Vita* 24, 12 (Pellegrino 171).
2. See the lengthy survey of the controversy in M. A. Mandouze, "Où en est la question de la mystique augustinienne?" in *Aug. Mag.* III, 103-68. A recent negative response: J. A. Mourant, "Ostia Reexamined. A study in the Concept of Mystical Experience," *Philosophy of Religion* 1 (1970) 34-45.
3 C. Butler, *Western Mysticism* (London: Constable, 1922, 1926²); Harper Torchbooks ed., 1966), 20.
4. *Conf.* IV, 13, 20.
5. *Ibid.* X, 33, 50.
6. *Ep.* 101, 3.
7. *Conf.* X, 6, 9.
8. *Ibid.* XI, 4, 6.
9. *Ibid.* X, 27, 38.
10. *Solil.* I, 1, 2.
11. *Conf.* III, 6, 10.
12. *Solil.* I, 1, 3.
13. *Ep.* 3, 4.
14. *Conf.* X, 8, 15.
15. *Conf.* X, 34, 53.
16. *Ep.* 120, 4, 20.
17. *Ep.* 138, 1, 5.
18. See *Serm.* 125, 5; *De civ. Dei* XI, 23.
19. *Conf.* XI, 2 3.
20. *Ibid.* XIII, 9, 10.
21. See *Enarr. in ps.* 109, 20.
22. *Serm. Frang.* 3, in *Misc. Agost.* I, 115.
23. *Enarr. in ps.* 101, serm. 2, 10.
24. *Serm.* 51, 5, 6.
25. *In ep. Io. tr.* 2, 10.
26. *Serm. Denis* 20, in *Misc. Agost.* I, 115.
27. *Conf.* X, 6, 8.
28. *Ibid.* X, 27, 38.
29. *Solil.* I, 1, 2-4.

Notes for Chapter 33

1. For the many questions that arise concerning the composition of the *Confessions* see my Introduction in *Le Confessioni* (NBA 1; Rome, Editrice Città Nuova, 1975³).

2. E.g., *Serm.* 29, 2; 67, 1.

3. *Ep.* 231, 6.

4. *Retract.* II, 6, 1.

5. *De dono persev.* 20, 53.

6. See above, ch. 27, p. 217.

7. *Conf.* II, 7, 15; IV, 1, 1; ix, 12, 33.

8. *Ibid.* I, 6, 10; XI, 31, 41; XII, 29, 40; XIII, 10, 11.

9. *Ibid.* XII, 16, 23; XII, 25, 34.

10. *Ibid.* IX, 8, 17.

11. See above, ch. 3, pp. 33-34.

12. *Conf.* II, 8, 16.

13. *Ibid.* II, 4, 9.

14. *Ibid.* II, 5, 10—9, 17; see above, ch. 4, pp. 37-38.

15. *Ibid.* VII, 10, 16.

16. *Ibid.* VII, 11, 17.

17. *Ibid.* XIII, 31, 46.

18. On the much discussed question of the unity of the *Confessions* see my Introduction, 19-24.

19. *Conf.* I, 4, 4; VI, 3, 4; IX, 4, 10; III, 6, 11.

20. *Ibid.* III, 11, 19.

21. *Ibid.* I, 10, 16.

22. *Ibid.* X, 42, 67; 43, 68.

23. *Ibid.* X, 43, 68.

24. *Enarr. in ps.* 101, serm. 2, 10.

25. *Conf.* X, 43, 69.

26. *Ibid.* I, 5, 5.

27. *Ibid.* IV, 10, 15.

28. *Ibid.* X, 30, 41.

29. *Ibid.* X, 34, 53.

30. *Ibid.* X, 35, 57.

31. *Ep.* 231, 2.

32. *Conf.* X, 37, 60-62.

33. *Ibid.* XI, 29, 39.

34. *Ibid.* X, 40, 65.

Notes for Chapter 34

1. *Ep.* 174.
2. *Ep.* 169, 1, 1.
3. *De Trin.* I, 3, 5.
4. *Ep.* 143, 4.
5. *Ep.* 174.
6. *Conf.* XIII, 11, 12.
7. *De Trin* I, 5, 8.
8. For a fuller explanation I refer the reader to my Introduction to St. Augustine, *La Trinità* (NBA 4; Rome: Ed. Città Nuova, 1973), 7-65.
9. *De Trin.* I, 8, 17.
10. *Ibid.* XV, 20, 39.
11. *Ibid.* I, 5, 8.
12. *Ibid.* XV, 28, 51.
13. *Ibid.* I, 8, 17.
14. *Ibid.* IV, 1, 2.
15. See my Introduction to *La Trinità*, 46.
16. *De Trin.* I, 8, 17.
17. *Ibid.* XII, 15, 25.
18. *Ibid.* XIV, 17, 23.
19. *Ibid.* VIII, 2, 3.
20. *Ibid.* VIII, 3, 4.
21. *Ibid.* VIII, 8, 12.
22. *Ibid.* XV, 6, 10.
23. *Ibid.*
24. *Ibid.* XV, 28, 51.

Notes for Chapter 35

1. *Retract.*, Prol. 3.
2. *Ibid.* Prol. 1.
3. *Ibid.* Prol. 2.
4. *Ep.* 224, 1.
5. *Retract.* Prol. 1.
6. *Ep.* 143, 2.
7. *Ep.* 143, 3.
8. *Retract.* II, 11.
9. *Ibid.* II, 15.
10. *Ibid.* II, 21.
11. *Ibid.* II, 23.
12. *Ibid.* II, 34.

13. *Ibid.* II, 58.
14. *Ibid.* II, 13.
15. *Ibid.* I, 20.
16. *Ibid.* II, 3.
17. *Ibid.* II, 29.
18. *Ibid.* I, 18; see above, ch. 20, pp. 137-138.
19. *Ibid.* I, 27.
20. *Ibid.* I, 9, 2-6.
21. *Ibid.* I, 15, 4.
22. *Serm.* 69, 2.
23. *De sanct. virg.* 51, 52.
24. *Ep.* 118, 22.
25. *Serm.* 160, 4.
26. *Ep.* 82, 5, 36.
27. *Ep.* 155, 1, 1.

Notes for Chapter 36

1. *In ep. Jo. tr.* 9, 11.
2. See above, ch. 30, p. 241.
3. *De Trin.* IX, 10, 15.
4. *Conf.* XIII, 9, 10; *De civ. Dei* 28; *Ep.* 155, 10, 18; 157, 9.
5. *Conf.* XIII, 9, 10.
6. *De civ. Dei* XIV, 6.
7. *Ep.* 155, 4, 13.
8. *Ep.* 167, 15.
9. *De civ. Dei* XV, 22.
10. *Ep.* 155, 4, 13.
11. *De Gen ad litt.* I, 5, 11.
12. *Conf.* XIII, 38, 53: "We see the things that you have created because they are. But they are because you see them."
13. *De doct. christ.* III, 10, 15.
14. *Serm.* 350, 1-3.
15. *In Jo. ev. tr.* 87, 1.
16. *Ibid.* 26, 4-5.
17. *Expos. ep. ad Gal.* 57. In this passage the aphorism differs slightly: "Love, and say what you will."
18. *In ep. Jo. tr.* 7. 8.
19. *Ibid.*
20. For some unexplained reason P. Brown adopts this last explanation in his *Augustine of Hippo. A Biography* (Berkeley and Los Angeles: University of California Press, 1967). We need only recall here that Augus-

tine first uttered the dictum at a time when he was utterly opposed to any type of suppression. See above, ch. 28, pp. 221ff.

21. *De Trin.* VIII, 7, 10.
22. *De fide et symb.* 9, 19.
23. *In Jo. ev. tr.* 96, 4.
24. *De div. qq. 83,* qu. 35, 2.
25. *In ep. Jo. tr.* 2, 14.
26. See above, ch. 26, p. 206.
27. *In Jo. ev. tr.* 19, 11.
28. *Enarr. in ps.* 49, 2.
29. *De div. qq. 83,* qu. 35, 2.
30. *In Jo. ev. tr.* 32, 8.
31. *In ep. Jo. tr* 7, 8.
32. *Ibid.* 8, 9.
33. *De nat. et grat.* 70, 84.
34. *Serm.* 169, 15, 18.
35. *Serm.* 34, 4, 7: "Totum exigit te qui fecit te."
36. *Ep.* 109 (among the letters of Augustine).
37. *Conf.* XIII, 8, 9.
38. *Solil.* I, 13, 22.
39. *In Jo. ev. tr.* 43, 7.
40. *Enarr. in ps.* 55, 17.
41. *Ibid.* 85, 11.
42. *Ibid.* 127, 9.
43. *Serm.* 159, 2-8.

Notes for Chapter 37

1. *Retract.* I, 8, 1. Among the many studies of the subject see C. Butler, *Western Mysticism* (London: Constable, 1922, 1926²; Harper Torchbooks ed., 1966); F. Cayré, *La contemplation augustinienne. Principes de spiritualité et de théologie* (Burges-Paris: Desclée De Brouwer, 1954²).

2. *De quant. anim.* 33, 73.
3. *Ibid.* 33, 74.
4. *Ibid.* 33, 75.
5. *De serm. Dom. in monte* I, 1, 3—4, 12; *De doct. christ.* II, 7, 9-11; *Serm.* 347.
6. *De serm. Dom. in monte* I, 3, 10.
7. *Enarr. in ps.* 135, 8.
8. *De lib. arb.* II, 16, 41.
9. *Conf.* VII, 17, 23.
10. *Ibid.* IX, 10, 24.

11. *Enarr. in ps.* 41, 10.
12. *Serm.* 52, 16.
13. *Conf.* VII, 17, 23.
14. *Ibid.* IX, 24.
15. *Serm.* 52, 16.
16. *Enarr. in ps.* 41, 7-10.
17. See above, ch. 33, p. 279, and *Enarr. in ps.* 134, 4-6.
18. *Conf.* IX, 10, 23-25.
19. *Ep.* 92.
20. *Ep.* 148, 1.
21. See above, ch. 33, pp. 268, and 273.
22. See above, ch. 18, pp. 128-129
23. *De civ. Dei* XIX, 19.
24. *De quant. anim.* 33, 76.
25. *In Jo. ev. tr.* 9, 2.

Notes for Chapter 38

1. See above, ch. 31, p. 252.
2. *Ep.* 213, 1.
3. *Ibid.* 6.
4. Pl 37:1717.
5. See above, ch. 27, p. 216.
6. See above, ch. 31, p. 253.
7. See above, ch. 20, p. 141, and ch. 19, p. 131.
8. *Ep.* 230, 3: see above, ch. 30, pp. 248ff.
9. *Ep.* 220, 7.
10. *Ibid.* 8.
11. V. Paronetto, "Nota sulla datazione dell'epistolario agostiniano," *Augustinianum* 14 (1974) 363-67.
12. *Ep.* 229, 2.
13. *Ep.* 230 (among the letters of Augustine).
14. See above, ch. 33, p. 269.
15. *Ep.* 231, 7.
16. *Coll. cum Max.* 1.
17. Possidius, *Vita* 17, 7 (Pellegrino 101).
18. *C. Max.* 1, Praef. On the famous text regarding the distinction between generation and procession see my article, "Nota sulla processione dello Spirito Sancto nella teologia di S. Agostino e di S. Tommaso," in *Studi tomistici* I (Rome: Editrice Città Nuova, 1974), 119-25.
19. *Ep.* 222, 2.
20. *De her.* Prol.

21. *Ep.* 225 and 226 (among the letters of Augustine).
22. *De dono persev.* 24, 68.
23. Possidius, *Vita* 30, 1 (Pellegrino 159).
24. *Ibid.* 28, 6-8 (151-53).
25. See *Serm.* 81, 8.
26. *Ep.* 212A (NBA 23, 353-55).
27. Possidius, *Vita* 28, 11 (Pellegrino 155); see Plotinus, *Enneads* I, 4, 7.
28. *Ennar. in ps.* 109, 20.
29. Possidius, *Vita* 24, 15 (Pellegrino 131).
30. *Ibid.* 30, 4-5 (161).
31. This letter has not been preserved.
32. *Ep.* 228.
33. Possidius, *Vita* 30, 1-51.
34. *Ep.* 228, 2-3.

Notes for Chapter 39

1. Possidius, *Vita* 29, 1 (Pellegrino 151).
2. *Ibid.* 29, 3 (157).
3. *Ibid.* 31, 2 (191).
4. *Ibid.* 27, 7-8 (143-45).
5. *Ibid.* 27, 9 (145).
6. *Conf.* VII, 10, 16.
7. Possidius, *Vita* 31, 3 (Pellegrino 191).
8. *Ibid.* 31, 1 (189).
9. *Ibid.* 31, 5 (191).
10. PL 94:1023; H. Quentin, *Les martyrologes historiques du moyen âge* (Paris, 1908), 109. See also Bede's *Chronicon* (ed. Mommsen, III, 321). On the double translation of the remains see A. C. De Romanis, *San Agostino*, 393-419, and A. Trapè in *Bibliotheca Sanctorum* I (entry "San Agostino").
11. Possidius, *Vita* 31, 6 (Pellegrino 193).
12. *Ibid.* 31, 8 (193).
13. *Ibid.* 31, 9 (195).

Notes for Chapter 40

1. Possidius, *Vita* 18, 10 (Pellegrino 109, and see his note 11 on this chapter, p. 216).
2. See *Tract.* II, 5; II, 11; II, 19; II, 27; II, 32; II, 35; II, 46.
3. *Operum S. Augustini elenchus*, ed. A. Wilmart in *Misc. Agost.* II, 208.
4. A Wilmart, "La tradition de grands ouvrages de Saint Augustin," in *Misc. Agost.* II, 261.
5. It will be enough to mention Prosper of Aquitaine, Eugippius, Florus, Venerable Bede, and, later on, Bartolomeo da Urbino.

6. Many spurious works claimed Augustine for their author. On the other hand, many of these, for example the various "Meditations," contained many passages from Augustine that were collected and stitched together (not always in a felicitous way) by people who had some familiarity with the Saint's works.

7. The Maurist edition was compiled from 1679 to 1700. There had been earlier editions by Amerbach, Erasmus, and the theologians of Louvain.

8. PL 32—46. New critical editions have been appearing for many years in the Corpus Scriptorum Ecclesiasticorum Latinorum (CSEL) and the Corpus Christianorum, Series Latina (CCL)

9. There are also a number of bilingual editions, either completed or now appearing: Spanish (Biblioteca de autores cristianos, Madrid), French (Bibliothèque Augustinienne, Paris), Italian (Nuova Biblioteca Agostiniana, Rome), and German for the antipelagian works (Aurelius Augustinus, Würzburg).

10. C. Boyer, *Essais anciens et nouveaux de St. Augustin* (Milan, 1970), 15.

11. A. De Giovanni, *Mortalità ed essere in San Agostino* (Palermo, 1975), 113-36.

12. *Ep.* 183, 1 (among the letters of Augustine; NBA 22, 923).

13. *Ep.* 21, 2, 3, written in May 431 (PL 45:1756).

14. *Acta Leonis XIII* I, 270.

15. *AAS* 22 (1930) 270.

16. *Ibid.* 233.

17. *Ibid.* 62 (1970) 426.

18. J. Morán, "La presenza di S. Agostino nel Concilio Vaticano II," *Augustinianum* 6 (1966) 460-88.

19. J. Guitton, *The Modernity of St. Augustine*, tr. A. V. Littledale (Baltimore: Helicon, 1959), 7.

20. See my article, "L'azione educativa di S. Agostino," in *San Agostino educatore* (Pavia, 1970), 19-39.

21. *De civ. Dei* XIX, 17.

22. See my "San Agostino," in *Bibliotheca Sanctorum* I, 428-596.

23. *De civ. Dei* II, 29, 2: "Incomparably more glorious is the city on high, in which victory belongs to truth, holiness is the only dignity...."

INDEX